Principle & Practice in Applied Linguistics

Studies in honour of H.G. WIDDOWSON

Editors
GUY COOK
BARBARA SEIDLHOFER

Principle & Practice in Applied Linguistics

Studies in honour of
H. G. WIDDOWSON

OXFORD UNIVERSITY PRESS

Oxford University Press
Walton Street, OXFORD OX2 6DP

Oxford New York
Athens Auckland Bangkok Bombay
Calcutta Cape Town Dar es Salaam Delhi
Florence Hong Kong Istanbul Karachi
Kuala Lumpur Madras Madrid Melbourne
Mexico City Nairobi Paris Singapore
Taipei Tokyo Toronto

and associated companies in
Berlin Ibadan

OXFORD and OXFORD ENGLISH
are trade marks of Oxford University Press

ISBN 0 19 442147 3 Hardback
ISBN 0 19 442148 1 Paperback

© Oxford University Press 1995

First published 1995
Second impression 1996

Set by Wyvern Typesetting Ltd, Bristol
Printed in England by St. Edmundsbury Press,
Bury St. Edmunds, Suffolk.

OXFORD UNIVERSITY PRESS is privileged to publish this volume in recognition of the invaluable contribution made by Henry Widdowson over the years, both as Applied Linguistics adviser to the ELT Division at the Press, and as a scholar and author whose work has promoted the development of professionalism in English Language Teaching in so many ways.

THE PUBLISHERS would like to express their gratitude to the editors and authors for all their work in making this book possible. Their goodwill and readiness to participate is a reflection of the respect, admiration, and affection in which Henry Widdowson is held throughout the profession.

Contents

CONTENTS

CONTENTS

Acknowledgements

WE ARE GRATEFUL to the following for permission to reprint extracts from copyright material:

Faber & Faber Ltd. for extract from 'In Memory of W. B. Yeats' from *Collected Poems* by W. H. Auden edited by Edward Mendelson (1976); extracts from 'The Backward Look' from *Wintering Out* by Seamus Heaney (1972), and from 'Act of Union' and 'Bog Queen' from *North* by Seamus Heaney (1975); extracts from 'Getting There' and 'Nick and the Candlestick' from *Collected Poems* by Sylvia Plath edited by Ted Hughes (1981); and 'In a Station of the Metro' from *Collected Shorter Poems* by Ezra Pound (1952).

Farrar, Straus & Giroux Inc. for extracts from 'The Backward Look', 'Act of Union' and 'Bog Queen' from *Poems 1965–1975* by Seamus Heaney. Copyright © 1980 by Seamus Heaney.

HarperCollins Publishers Inc. for extracts from 'Getting There' by Sylvia Plath, Copyright © 1963 by Ted Hughes, Copyright Renewed; and from 'Nick and the Candlestick' by Sylvia Plath from *The Collected Poems of Sylvia Plath*, Copyright © 1966 by Ted Hughes, Copyright Renewed.

Braj B. Kachru for his translation of 'The moon rose like a *tsoţ*' from *Kashmiri Literature* by Braj B. Kachru (Otto Harrassowitz, 1981).

New Directions Publishing Corporation for 'In a Station of the Metro' by Ezra Pound.

Random House Inc. for extract from 'In Memory of W. B. Yeats'

ACKNOWLEDGEMENTS

from *Collected Poems* by W. H. Auden, edited by Edward Mendelson. Copyright © 1940 and renewed 1968 by W. H. Auden.

Reed Consumer Books for extracts from 'In Memory of Segun Awolowo' and from 'Death in the Dawn' by Wole Soyinka from *Idanre and Other Poems* (Methuen, London, 1967).

Solo Syndication Ltd. for extract from article by Richard Kay in the *Daily Mail*, 3.8.89.

Although we have tried to obtain permission where necessary before publication this has not been possible in the cases indicated below. If contacted, the publisher will be pleased to rectify any errors or omissions at the earliest opportunity.

English translation of a *masnavī* by Lachman Rainā from J. Kaul: *Kashmiri Lyrics* (Srinigar: Rinemisary, 1945).

Extract from the poem 'The Snowflakes Sail Gently Down' by Gabriel Okara, from *The Fisherman's Invocation* (African Writers Series, No. 183, Heinemann Educational, 1978).

'Ibadan' by John Pepper Clark Bekerderemo, from *A Reed in the Tide* (Longman, 1965).

1

An applied linguist in principle and practice

GUY COOK & BARBARA SEIDLHOFER

If we claim that our activities have any professional status, then we have to accept the need for a careful appraisal of the principles upon which they are based. And this must require the exercise of intellectual analysis and critical evaluation not as specialist or élite activities, but ones which are intrinsic to the whole pedagogic enterprise. Naturally, there are risks involved: ideas can be inconsistent or ill-conceived; they may be misunderstood or misapplied; they may induce doubt. Some of us believe that such risks are worth taking.
[WIDDOWSON 1985a]

Enquiry, theory, and practice

IN ANY DISCIPLINE there are easy options. One is separatism. It may be inter-disciplinary separatism which ignores other areas of enquiry, or intra-disciplinary separatism which creates manageable sub-disciplines. In both cases researchers and teachers proclaim themselves unable to comment on a particular problem because it is 'not their area'. A second easy option is to establish, and then kowtow to, an all-encompassing theory, either for the discipline as a whole, or for each sub-discipline within it. Such theories are often associated with an individual name; they make little reference to rivals; and debates with their adherents are terminated not by rational argument, but by quoting from the founder's seminal works. A third safe option (also a kind of separatism) is the divorce of theory from practice. This too is easily recognized. Theorists are heard to say that—although of course their ideas are significant for practitioners—it is not for them to interfere directly; while practitioners refer disparagingly to theory as something disconnected from their own concerns. Together these three easy options bring stability. The discipline becomes a federation of academic principalities with a common defence policy and tough immigration laws. Its local and central governments are moribund and autocratic. It is a dull place, but a safe one to live and develop a career.

There are powerful human reasons why disciplines tend towards this splendid isolation. Academic enquiry is not only an intellectual matter, but inevitably intertwined with personal careers and lives. Maintaining academic fluidity is at odds with the individual need for stability, especially when the age of academic leadership often coincides not with mercurial youth or wild old age, but with the personal responsibilities of middle age. In the 1990s, moreover, we are living at a time of widespread cuts in education budgets throughout the world, and there is an almost universal pressure on academics to give accounts of themselves in terms of immediate economic return and technological application. This too is an incentive to be content with neat compartments. Life is less stressful when the outsider's question 'What do you do?' and its dreaded sequel 'What use is that?' can both be answered with equanimity. Philistine governments and other purse holders are unlikely to place their confidence in disciplines and individuals that they perceive as always changing identity, always courting change and confusion, always coming up with new theories only immediately to reveal their weaknesses.

Yet certain objects of enquiry—perhaps even all of them—hardly lend themselves to stability and isolationism. Language is the epitome of such an object. It encompasses, of its nature, almost every aspect of human life. It is inextricably linked to our biology and neurology, to our individual personalities and mental states, to our relationships and social structures. Through language we perceive both the internal and external world. Without it, thought, identity, interaction, education, and society could be only rudimentary.

Language

Even if no one knows quite how, language is an outcome of evolution, and our understanding of it, and of appropriate principles for its study, may be helped by considering it in this perspective. There is a sentimental view of evolution, popular in natural history broadcasting, which presents the current state of nature as perfection. In this view, dubbed 'Panglossia' by the biologist Stephen Jay Gould (1990: 51)[1], modern species and their attributes are viewed as 'improvements' on their ancestors, the culmination of long processes of refinement, neat and efficient in every feature of 'design'. But the outcomes of evolution, including the human ones, are not—as Gould observes—quite like that. They are 'not made by an ideal engineer [but] jury-rigged from a limited set of available components' (Gould 1990: 20). In illustration of this, Gould describes the 'thumb' which allows the herbivorous Giant Panda skilfully to manipulate and strip the leaves from bamboo shoots. From a functional and synchronic viewpoint, this 'thumb' seems to be a perfectly adapted 'design'[2]. Its history and underlying structure, however, turn out to be much messier. It is not a thumb at all, but an evolved outgrowth of bone from the side of the wrist. The real fifth digit, which might have become a thumb, had in the Panda's carnivorous ancestors already become rigid, and is thus redundant, an evolutionary dead end. This is not directed development but an ad hoc adaptation: one of Nature's 'odd arrangements and funny solutions' (ibid.)[3].

Language, for all its obvious wonders, is in many ways like the Panda's paw: partly straightforwardly functional, partly dysfunctional, and partly functional in unpredictable ways (Lass 1990). Though efficient for its purposes, it does not have the kind of efficiency which a designer would impose if starting from scratch. The evolution of language has left it with quirks and oddities, while the subsequent branching and splitting of individual languages has also left anomalies, so that the inheritance of every natural language is a hotchpotch of exceptions and contradictions quite alien to the nature of a Newspeak or an Esperanto. Language and languages are, like Pandas, complex adaptive systems. 'They cannot, in general, be successfully analyzed by determining in advance a set of properties or aspects that are studied separately and then combining those partial approaches in an attempt to form a picture of the whole' (Gell-Mann 1992: 14).

Complex systems, whether biological or linguistic, can often seem disordered and anarchic (in a pejorative sense), and there is always a temptation for theorists to neglect the irregular aspects of the system

[3]

and to try to reduce everything to a few simple rules. There is plenty of sentimental Panglossia in theories of language, seeking to impose too much elegance and parsimony, as though language were indeed the outcome of rational design[4]. Humans (quite justifiably) are impressed by their own abilities to communicate; for this reason their theories of language reflect their beliefs about what makes a good system. As there is a widespread belief that order, symmetry, and rational design are systemic virtues, so these features appear prominently. Yet on the contrary it may be the very complexity of language—and the degree of disorder and irreducibility which that entails—which makes it so strong and resilient. The very appearance of *disorder* derives from an accumulation of complementary strategies for multiple uses. Workable anarchy often outlives imposed order.

Recognition of complexity implies that many of the current theoretical attempts to impose too much unity and order by seeing language as determined by a few forces cannot *on their own* be a source of principles for its study. Language is viewed in various theories as a genetic inheritance, a mathematical system, a social fact, the expression of individual identity, the expression of cultural identity, the outcome of dialogic interaction, a social semiotic, the intuitions of native speakers, the sum of attested data, a collection of memorized chunks, a rule-governed discrete combinatory system, or electrical activation in a distributed network. But to do justice to language, we do not have to express allegiance to one or some of these competing—and aspiringly hegemonic—views. We do not have to choose. Language can be all of these things at once. Recognition of complexity implies that the object of enquiry is not reducible to description by any one of these theories, but needs to invoke several at once (even contradictory ones). Principles are needed which can accommodate complexity and relate theory to experience (Widdowson 1984a: 7–27; 1990a: 1–6). In this sense the formation of principles may be seen as both deriving from theory but also subjecting theory to assessment and evaluation. Theory becomes the servant and not the master of principle.

Linguistics

Given the all-pervasiveness of language in human life, and its complexity, multiplicity, and internal contradictions, it seems strange at first glance that the study of language—linguistics—should have sought both to simplify it, and to isolate it from its social and psychological context. From its inception modern linguistics—at least in its most influential branches—has operated by establishing dichotomies and exhorting its practitioners to focus their attention upon one half of them, with the effect of detaching the study of language from neighbouring disciplines. The underlying principles of this detachment derive from de Saussure ([1915] 1974)[5]. The concerns for signifiers not signifieds, for *langue* not *parole*, for synchronic rather than diachronic study serve to divorce language, respectively, from meaning and cognition, from interaction and context, and from both its prehistoric and its historical background (Widdowson 1986a). Language is detached both from people (their thoughts and meanings, relationships and societies) and from peoples (their conflicts, invasions, migrations, and subjugations). In a similar way, the Chomskian dichotomy of competence and performance, seeking to concern linguistics only with the former, isolates the object of study and its acquisition from 'grammatically irrelevant conditions as memory limitations, distractions, shifts of attention and interest, and errors (random or characteristic) (Chomsky 1965: 3) deviations from rules (ibid.: 4) semantic reference . . . and situational context (ibid.: 33)', thus in effect excluding from linguistics the study of pragmatics and discourse. While acknowledging—indeed defining—linguistics as a branch of cognitive psychology, Chomsky (1979: 46) has at the same time sought to keep language separate from other cognitive faculties through the notion that language is modular, both externally, in the sense that it is separate from other mental faculties, and internally, in the sense that it is composed of phonology, syntax, and semantics. (Significantly, as Widdowson observes, the word 'components', which implies parts only operational within a whole, has gradually been ousted by the word 'module', which suggests insularity, a change which 'reflects the failure to find coherent relationships between components' (1990b: 42).) There is some ambivalence among followers of Chomsky as to whether the justification for isolating language as an object of study derives primarily from its ontological nature (i.e. it is actually separate from other mental faculties) or is merely a heuristic (i.e. separation makes it easier to study) or both. But whatever the justification, the modularity of the subject matter, language, goes well with the modularity of the discipline, linguistics

(Widdowson 1990b). It is a metaphor of the separatism, both inter-disciplinary and intra-disciplinary, referred to above. The Saussurean and Chomskian dichotomies define an area of study (one half of each dichotomy) for linguists, and banish the study of the remaining halves elsewhere (Beaugrande 1994).

But the reinstatement of the banished half of a dichotomy need not entail taking vengeance on the favoured half. It would be foolish, if uncomplicated, for applied linguists to disparage the insights of main-stream linguistics, as easily as—for example—some formal linguists dismiss the insights of sociolinguistics[6]. To do so would be to take the easy option of dogmatic theorizing referred to above, dethroning one dynasty, as in *Animal Farm*, to replace it with another. The ontological modularity of language is not without evidence, and cannot be lightly dismissed. It captures an aspect of language. It also makes sense in an account of the human condition and evolution, for the insulation of the language faculty from environmental interference ensures that humans have the capacity to adapt to new contexts but not to be overwhelmed by them (Pinker 1994: 417). But modular or not in its mental representation, language cannot remain disconnected, whether in actual minds (where if it did it would be useless and would presumably never have evolved) or in the theories which seek to understand it. Although there are undoubtedly arguments in favour of isolating language as a tempo-rary heuristic, the objective must be, in each individual mind as in lin-guistics, to establish the links between the components of language, and then between this composite system and its use, acquisition, and context. This was the maxim of Firth when he talked of the 'renewal of connection' (1968: 176–177). There is, though, a danger of simplifica-tion here too. The reconnection of the form of language with its con-text and practical applications is not the same as merely replacing one side of the dichotomy with the other so that language becomes *only* social interaction and *only* practice (with form seen rather vaguely as somehow entirely determined by them and inseparable from them). Where formal linguistics has erred on the side of seeing language as an entirely insular system, divorced from either meaning or use, func-tional linguistics lives with the danger of the opposite and complemen-tary simplification.

[6]

Applied linguistics

The rationale for applied linguistics is exactly the reconnection of language not only (as Firth wished) to the contexts of situation in which it occurs, but also, more generally, to the many social practices involving an understanding of language. This process, as many have observed, should not be a one-way imposition, but a dynamic interaction in which theories of language will also be illuminated by insights from practical activities (Widdowson 1984a: 7–20; Wilkins 1994[7]). Given such an ideal, it would seem impossible for the subject to fragment. The very name 'applied linguistics' should guarantee eclecticism and openness, and guard against the separation of theory and practice. Yet the subject seems always on the verge of fragmentation, and always susceptible to dogma (Widdowson 1990a: 7–29). Its very dynamism and openness entail an associated drive towards simplification, as though the complexity of language is too much to bear. The human emotions and desire for stability and order which lead to separatism in 'purer' disciplines are not suspended simply because the subject is 'applied'.

Defining 'applied linguistics' has always been difficult. The relevant entry in the *International Encyclopedia of Linguistics* defines applied linguistics as follows:

> Whenever knowledge about language is used to solve a basic language-related problem, one may say that A[pplied] L[inguistics] is being practised. AL is a technology which makes abstract ideas and research findings accessible and relevant to the real world; it mediates between theory and practice.
> (Kaplan and Widdowson 1992: 76)

Among the areas listed in the same entry as of frequent concern to the subject are: speech therapy, communicative interactions, language planning and policy, language in education, and language teaching and learning[8]. Many other areas of enquiry, such as, for example, translation and lexicography, while sometimes by convention considered separate, might equally well be encompassed by the definition.

Yet despite this potentially wide scope of the field, it is with language teaching and learning, and particularly *English* language teaching and learning, that many works on applied linguistics (and the present volume is no exception) are primarily concerned[9]. Such a specific focus need not narrow the scope of the issues however. For the study of language teaching and learning, like the study of all the other areas listed above, necessarily foregrounds the general principles which underlie the endeavour to link 'knowledge about language' to 'the real world'. Applied linguistics may validly make reference to specifically educational contexts:

> Its scope delimited in this way, applied linguistics is in my view an activity which seeks to identify, within the disciplines concerned with language and learning, those insights and procedures of enquiry which are relevant for the formulation of pedagogic principles and their effective actualization in practice.
> (Widdowson 1990a: 6)

Language teaching

To consider what language is for the successful language learner must involve consideration of both theory and practice and guarantee connection between the two. Except as a temporary pedagogic measure, the acquisition of a language cannot be modularized, for successful language use must involve the operation of different aspects of language knowledge, both in concert and in context. In addition language teaching, being (like the other areas of applied linguistics) a social and often institutional activity, brings theories of language and of language learning into contact with practical constraints: the whims of governments, the availability of resources, the social conditions of those involved, and the ideological climate in which they live. For these reasons language teaching is a rich source of understanding of the relation of knowledge about language to activities involving language. It is an area in need of principles to mediate between linguistic theory and pedagogic (or other) practices, and it must look to applied linguistics to provide them. The relationship of applied linguistics and language teaching is symbiotic.

This is the ideal. There are of course other reasons for the mutual attraction apart from reciprocal intellectual enlightenment. One is that language teaching—and especially English language teaching—is big business: successful theories, methodologies, and textbooks make money. Another reason—and here there is an obvious overlap with language planning—is that the spread of languages through teaching raises urgent political issues of immediate concern to both individuals and societies about the connection between *which* languages are taught and learned, *where* and *by whom*, and their own empowerment or disempowerment—economic, military, and cultural. Yet another reason is that learning a language, because it demands both emotional and mental involvement, and because individuals often depend upon it for their economic status and welfare, is a matter of personal importance. Similarly, for teachers, a feeling of direction and control may be crucial to self-esteem and job satisfaction, as well as instrumental in obtaining employment or promotion. All these forces—commercial pressures, political urgency, and student/teacher anxieties—have combined to create a constant demand for new methodologies and pedagogic panaceas.

The fashion changes in ELT, often justified by appeals to applied linguistics theory, are both famous, and—understandably—the cause of considerable scepticism (Maley 1983). Since the term 'applied linguistics' was first used to name a university programme in 1956 (Grabe and Kaplan 1991: 14), there has been a series of dominant language teaching paradigms, short-lived enough for some teachers to have been through every one of them. In rapid succession, language learning has been conceived as habit formation, as the internalization of rules, as gaining an ability to mean and do things with language. Now, in some quarters, there is a return to emphasis on form. This is sometimes justified by observation of the positive role of conscious language awareness, but is sometimes not theoretically justified at all and is merely fashion change for its own sake (Widdowson 1990a: 40). Many theoretical ideas have led to pedagogic excess, and the notion that the problems inherent in language teaching are amenable to solution (Widdowson ibid.: 7–27)[10]. With such distortions, teachers are pulled in all directions: to focus on the code, on its use, on grammar, on lexis, on meaning, on the book, on the task, on the learner, on the teacher, on society. But as with the competing theories of language, so with theories of language teaching and learning: we do not have to express allegiance to one or other. Language teaching, if it is to promote language learning, must go in all of these directions.

Fortunately, teachers are not a gullible audience. Their enterprise demands education, reflection, and sensitivity. They tend to be cautious about theories of language teaching which shun submission to the test of falsifiability. Though there may be no such thing as 'methods that work' (Oller 1993), there may well be methods that do not help. Nor can teachers ignore the practical circumstances of what they do: the size of classes, the expectations of learners, the availability of technology. To view matters optimistically, a reason for the rapid turnover of language teaching methodologies may be that the simplification of complex issues cannot hold the beliefs of a sophisticated audience for very long. Teachers like to have a sound theoretical underpinning for what they do: one which does justice to the complexity of language, language learners, language learning, and the social context in which these exist.

The reconnection of linguistic theory and the practical activity of language teaching is a complex and often thankless area. This is especially true in an academic climate where 'careers are made by specialization and it is taken for granted that serious work can be done only by looking at one or a few aspects of a complex system' (Gell-Mann 1992: 14). There are a number of possible ways in which individuals can react to this situation. One is to ignore the interaction of theory and practice, to be concerned only with teaching or only with theory. A second is to have a hegemonic theory which explains everything. A third (often a useful and realistic way) is to maintain the connection of theory and practice but delimit an area within this interaction. But a fourth and more difficult option is to be open to insights from an array of theories, while also remaining aware of how they contribute to, and are altered in, their encounter with practice, to be constantly surveying and assessing and evaluating, to be constantly formulating principles. This last, and rare, reaction demands a particular kind of intellectual commitment, and a particular kind of individual: an individual who can tolerate complexity.

An applied linguist

H. G. Widdowson has often been accused—affectionately, appreciatively, or critically—of a fondness for dichotomies. In this, it might seem, he has inherited the tendency of mainstream linguistics (in which he is well versed) to label and divide with the aim of making *his* subject—*applied* linguistics—more manageable. Dichotomies seem of their nature simplifications, turning complex dynamic interactions into stark alternatives. So by accepting such divisions, applied linguistics may create not only a basis for subdivision of the subject ('you study this, I'll study that') but also an overarching and rigid categorization by which all evidence is interpreted. If one dichotomy is that of theory and practice, then all the easy options for a discipline referred to at the beginning of this paper would seem to have been fulfilled, and the peculiar complexity of language in use to be betrayed.

At first glance some of Widdowson's favourite dichotomies may seem of this kind: language/communication; usage/use; code/context; text/discourse; product/process; systemic/schematic; reference/representation; training/education; special purpose/general purpose. But considered carefully, these Widdowsonian dichotomies are not simplifying at all. Rather, they take a potentially narrowing term, and without denying entirely its validity, re-situate it in a more intricate environment which does justice both to the scientific principle of isolation for analysis, and to the complexity of human language and learning. Thus the first term refers often to a theoretical construct, while the second contextualizes this first notion, including rather than excluding it, reconnecting it to practice, and refusing it modularity. Thus *language*—the stripped-down, decontextualized object of linguistics—is not disowned by Widdowson; it is incorporated into a broader view of language as—and for—*communication*. Language *usage* is a factor in language *use*. The ability to en*code* and de*code* the relatively fixed denotative meanings of linguistic signs is acknowledged as an aspect of language processing (and therefore also an aspect of language teaching), but needs *context* for interpretation. *Text*[11] is re-conceived as the starting point or alternatively the trace of *discourse*. The textual *product* enters into the *process* of its interpretation, demanding both *systemic* knowledge of the language and *schematic* knowledge of the world. In literature, systemic code and textual product not only allow the achievement of *reference* to the non-linguistic world as in any discourse, but also—and it is in this that their literariness resides—become part of their own context in a process of *representation*. These are the kind of 'dichotomies' which characterize Widdowson's discussions of language use: the second term extending and encompassing the first. A similar relationship of terms is present in the more specifically pedagogic dichotomies: *training* is a part of *education*, and *special purpose* a part of *general purpose*. In Widdowson's writing on education, however, there is a more urgent and didactic note which *does* exalt the including over the included term. This reflects the fact that wherever there is conflict between intellectual interests favouring a broader outlook and interests of economic gain and administrative convenience advocating a narrower approach, he consistently and fervently champions the former.

What this pattern of thought reveals is an unusual ability to engage two ways of seeing simultaneously, to hold a contradiction, not to surrender to the easier intellectual option of seeing different perspectives as exclusive alternatives and then professing allegiance only to one. It is an intellectual habit particularly suited to the study of language, which is itself an array of contradictory but complementary strategies allowing users to shift in and out of various perspectives to achieve their ends, so that, for example, what cannot be understood by guesswork based on context or memory may be teased out by syntactic and semantic analysis. In the most urgent current debates of applied linguistics, this cast of mind is especially valuable, both on the psycholinguistic front—as in the debate on the balance between holistic and analytic processing—and in sociolinguistic (and more political) debates such as those concerning the rival claims of cultural relativity and cultural universalism, and which varieties of English should be models or standards.

What all these apparently various debates have in common is an opposition of two very different tendencies: the one towards a rule-less anarchy which, while it may do justice to the complexity of language, allows no principled basis for overview and evaluation; the other an over-regimentation which arranges and separates our observations and intuitions about language use in ways which blatantly do *not* do justice to its nature. They echo conflicting directions within both individuals and societies—one towards fluidity and openness (with a concomitant danger of insecurity), the other towards order and certainty (with a concomitant danger of rigidity)—and disciplines, as mini-societies composed of individuals, also display conflicting tendencies towards disintegration on the one hand, or towards stagnation on the other.

These polarizing tendencies are ubiquitous in language study, and in recent years there has been a tendency for rule-bound approaches to be challenged. Thus in psycholinguistics the notion of rule-less connectionism has replaced the metaphor of mind as a serial algorithmic computer. Both in theories of competence and in descriptions of use, the notion that language involves 'tens of thousands' of memorized conventional collocations and sentence stems (Pawley and Syder 1983) has encroached upon the vision of a parsimonious competence in which grammar generates an infinity of original utterances. In the cultural component of language teaching the notion of total relativity—in which anything goes—is more fashionable than that of cultural universalism—in which everything goes. In the debate on standards and models, a strong critique of British and American chauvinism about standards and of the desirability of the native speaker as a model has replaced the older traditional certainties (Widdowson 1986a; 1994a).

Such debates are images of tensions endemic in the study of language: between language as a social and language as a biological phenomenon; between contextualized applied linguistics and decontextualized linguistics; between the emphasis on reconnection versus the desire to regard language, and study it, as modular. What we see is a subject—and the individuals within it—pulled in opposite directions: towards authority and towards anarchy. Both tendencies have manifest advantages and disadvantages, but the tension between them is hard to endure, and perhaps most thinkers or groups of thinkers, though they may live with this tension for a while, eventually go in one direction or another.

What is remarkable in Widdowson's thinking is the ability to exploit this tension as a source of insight, rather than to be overwhelmed by the competing claims of these two directions. He does not reduce academic debate to a polarization in which one must be on one side or the other, but preserves both the scientist's ability to categorize and objectify, and a practitioner's sensitivity to the pragmatic uncertainty of social concerns and human values. By moving between the two perspectives he uses one to enlighten the other, in much the same way as—in a process he has often described—the mind itself shifts from one strategy to another (top-down/bottom-up; pragmatic/semantic; collocational/ grammatical) in the negotiation of meaning in discourse. This energetic engagement can be disconcerting, and it has not drawn the following of insecure and obedient disciples which gathers around the leaders of more dogmatic approaches, but it gives his voice a distinctive authority which is simultaneously democratic, and never authoritarian. Significantly, the word 'Widdowsonian' is used to describe not disciples, but an elegance of style and a rigorous mode of argument.

Widdowson's breadth of vision makes it difficult to identify him either with any particular area of the subject, or with any particular ideology within it. He is in many ways a troubleshooter, a master of all trades, both fox (who knows many things) and hedgehog (who knows one big thing) (Berlin 1957). What marks out his work is the consistent—and persistent—ability, within applied linguistics, wherever an area seems to be walling itself off with dogma and terminology, not to take the easy option of either joining or ignoring the movement (itself a dichotomy). Rather, he has engaged with each incipient movement, critically but constructively, so that the issues are debated not on—or in—the insiders' terms, but for the whole discipline (both teachers and academics). What is remarkable is that very often his criticisms—though sharp and effective—have in their turn not been rejected out of hand by their recipients, but had an impact both within the emerging area itself, and within the subject as a whole.

In part this effectiveness—both in person and in print—derives from the style and charm of its delivery, but it also reflects the intellectual calibre of the critiques, and the fact that he can build upon people's strengths. He rarely argues by destroying an argument entirely, but rather by making its supporters see its weak points, thus strengthening—if also changing—their case, with the result that potential adversaries feel, not that they have been dismissed or defeated, but that they have themselves generated new insights. And while critical of what is weak in the arguments of others, he simultaneously assimilates into his own views their strengths. Many colleagues, students, and authors can testify to these abilities in one-to-one encounters as well as in the public arena.

He is not, however, only a catalyst or a critic, promoting rigour and guarding against easy options in the work of others. The sum of his work in applied linguistics is a distinctive and original contribution which amounts to much more than the addition of one or more new theories associated with his name. What he has created is meta-theory, a mode of enquiry providing guidance through the claims and counter-claims of competing theories and the demands of practice. His mode of thought is so closely woven into the practice of applied linguistics that it is, for many people, not so much a *contribution to* the discipline as *the foundation of* it, providing principles which enable the separate components to come together into a meaningful and valuable whole.

This has been going on now for a considerable period of time. He has been on the academic scene, like the term 'applied linguistics' itself, for nearly forty years[12]. The range of applied linguistic concerns to which he has made a substantial and influential contribution during this period are legion. Among the topics he has written on are literature and literature teaching, discourse analysis, grammar, lexis, second language acquisition, culture and language, translation, corpus linguistics, language planning and international English, communicative language teaching, teacher education, the teaching of writing and reading, curriculum and syllabus design, methodology, ESP, learner and teacher roles, simplification and accessibility[13]. But it is not only in his own writings that Widdowson maintains the breadth of applied linguistics. As a founding editor of the discipline's main journal *Applied Linguistics*[14], as Applied Linguistics adviser to the Oxford University Press, and as one of two editors for the series *Language Teaching: A Scheme for Teacher Education* (Candlin and Widdowson 1987–1996)[15], he facilitates the expression of the views of others, on occasion even views which run quite contrary to his own. He is a disseminator of ideas with an apparently inexhaustible energy to speak at both academic and teachers' conferences throughout the world. He is a popularizer in the best sense, striving to make ideas clear and accessible without simplification, able to engage at any level of debate with a manifestly anti-élitist belief in the ability of all his audiences to respond to intellectual and philosophical challenge. To his students—language teachers following postgraduate courses—he has given inspiration and confidence, and a sense of purpose, dignity, and professionalism.

In his own practice as an applied linguist he exemplifies the principles which applied linguistics should follow.

The present volume

The contributors to this volume have in a variety of ways been associated professionally, and share areas of professional interest, with H. G. Widdowson. The wide range of his interests is thus reflected in the topics covered here. The result, however, is not only of personal significance for those involved. It is a collection which provides the student and researcher with an overview of current directions in a subject where it is often difficult to gain a broad perspective.

[15]

The volume brings together papers on a wide range of crucial areas in contemporary applied linguistics—but broad coverage is not achieved simply by the sum of the parts. What unifies the papers in this book—despite their diverse subject matter—is the determination of the authors to consider the implications of their own specialized areas in the context of the discipline as a whole. This characteristic is striking and thematic. There is no academic modularity here. These are papers seeking connections between areas which are often kept separate, and they accept the complexities inherent in the study of language in the context of its applications. This makes them sometimes hard to classify, for they seem often to be about several areas at once. In this respect they share the spirit as well as merely the subject matter of Widdowsonian applied linguistics.

The volume treats the principles which derive from theory and connect it to practice. In keeping with the complexity of such an approach, there are no sections as such, though shared themes create (often overlapping) groups of papers.

The first four papers are all directly concerned with the relation of theory, research, and teaching. They each, in their different ways, express concern with dangers to dynamism and intellectual creativity. CHRISTOPHER BRUMFIT stresses the dangers of relativity in educational value systems and argues the case for more extensive and systematic research as a basis for teacher professionalism. CLAIRE KRAMSCH, considering the different discourses of language teacher and applied linguist, deconstructs the limiting effects of some current metaphors of language and language learning. N. S. PRABHU proposes four components—the ideational, the operational, the ideological, and the managerial—which, he argues, must all be taken into account and remain integrated in a principled approach to language pedagogy. ROD ELLIS discusses the validity of second language acquisition theories, criteria for their assessment, and the nature of their application to pedagogy in a paper which, though it deals with one specific area of research, formulates principles for relating any academic theory to any field of practice.

There follow three further papers on second language acquisition (SLA). To many, this area of study has at times seemed insular and dogmatic, concerned almost entirely with the acquisition of grammar, and neglecting not only discourse but even pronunciation and lexis

(Widdowson 1990b). Acquisition has been depicted as a universal process invariable in different types of learners, different contexts of use, and different language backgrounds. Some applications of such SLA theory to pedagogy have been correspondingly narrow and dogmatic, and threatened to create a serious rift between SLA and other branches of applied linguistics (Widdowson 1990a: 7–29).

The four papers on second language acquisition here are testimony to an opposite tendency, and markedly at odds with these isolationist trends. All are concerned with the reconnection of SLA theory to pedagogy and to the contexts of language use which it has often neglected. They combat, respectively, four different common assumptions of SLA study: the pre-eminence of theory; the centrality of grammar; the fixed route of acquisition; the primacy of input and the unimportance of conscious awareness.

Ellis, as already discussed, does not take theory for granted, but proposes principles for its assessment. PETER SKEHAN steps beyond the traditional SLA concern with grammar and confronts the interaction of holistic chunk learning with grammatical analysis. Taking his cue from Widdowson (1989c), he relates both processes, not only to an abstract detached competence, but to the deployment of that competence as 'ability for use'. ELAINE TARONE and GUO-QIANG LIU, by demonstrating the effect of interpersonal context upon the order of acquisition, cast doubt upon the notion of a fixed route in SLA, thus extending the notion of variability to include the route of its acquisition. MERRILL SWAIN, in a similarly well-documented argument, demonstrates the role of output and of conscious attention to linguistic form in learner progress.

A principled study of language learning must consider not only the route but also the destination of the process, and propose criteria for assessment and evaluation as well as theory and description. ALAN DAVIES addresses the controversial issue of whether approximation to the native speaker, or some other measure of proficiency, should be the criterion of language-learning success. The concept of the native speaker, while it has been axiomatic and unquestioned in many theories of linguistics, has recently been effectively challenged both for its theoretical validity and for its pedagogic relevance (Davies 1991; Widdowson 1994a). As a notion at the heart of mainstream linguistic theory, yet also deeply intertwined with the sociology of language

[17]

teaching and its politics, its reconsideration necessarily entails a complex connection of theory and practice.

Assessment of the characteristics of the successful learner, and of the validity of the notion of native speaker, involves (as we have already seen in Skehan's paper) the definition of both competence(s) and abilities for use, and discussion of the relationship between them. HEIKKI NYYSSÖNEN considers the relationship between knowledge of grammar and knowledge of lexis, and the role of both in communicative competence. This is a theme at the centre of current applied linguistics debate and it is taken up in several other papers (see especially Skehan, Batstone, Stubbs, Aston).

Highly appropriate to this *festschrift*, the next five papers are all concerned in different ways with discourse analysis: an area of applied linguistics to which Widdowson has made a profound and seminal contribution. His doctoral thesis 'An applied linguistic approach to discourse analysis' (Widdowson 1973)—sadly never published— exerts both a direct influence (for the researchers who read it in the original) and an indirect influence (in that it informed his later publications on the subject). Though the origins of discourse analysis can be traced back to theoretical and descriptive work of the 1950s (Harris 1952; Mitchell 1957), Widdowson was the first to develop the relevance of this field to language teaching (Widdowson 1973, 1978b, 1979a) and to literary stylistics (Widdowson 1975). His work on discourse analysis in these two areas both pre-dated and inspired the later flowering of interest from the 1980s onwards, and he continues at the forefront of this field today.

Discourse analysis, by definition, must be concerned with language operating in context. It is not surprising therefore that the papers in this section maintain the spirit of reconnection, whether of language and context, or of discourse and learning. YAMUNA KACHRU surveys current views on the contrastive rhetoric hypothesis[16] and assesses their relevance to language pedagogy, arguing that while contrastive rhetoric is a legitimate descriptive activity, it should not be used to direct or condition students to conform to a cultural norm. GEORGE YULE, drawing upon attested data, examines the reporting and dramatization of speech in conversational story-telling, thus demonstrating a discrepancy between conventional pedagogic representations of reported speech and its authentic realization. ROB BATSTONE, taking up the theme of grammar and lexis in discourse, shows how discourse considerations affect choices among what are apparently the most formal aspects of the language system such as tense. JOHN SWALES demonstrates the role of knowledge of genre structure in top-down discourse processing and illustrates how this can be used in ESP classes to facilitate linguistic processing. So far all the papers on discourse analysis have at least touched upon language teaching. MALCOLM COULTHARD, however, takes us out of the classroom and into the courtroom, another arena in which language and its interpretation is self-evidently and pre-eminently important. Drawing upon his own appearances in court as an expert witness, he describes and illustrates an increasingly active branch of applied linguistics: forensic linguistics, the use of language analysis as evidence in legal proceedings.

Corpus linguistics has in recent years been one of the most stimulating and productive areas of linguistic research. The discovery of the extent to which actual language use is composed of conventional habitually performed collocations (while many grammatically possible combinations do not actually occur) has given rise to new theories of the relation between grammar and lexis (Sinclair 1991a), and generated considerable interest in the degree to which language acquisition, processing, and use may be memory-driven rather than analytic. It has also (because it suggests that earlier accounts of language are inadequate) raised urgent doubts about the validity of intuition in language theory and description, and about the merit of invented as opposed to authentic data. (In Yule's paper we have already seen a corpus used to show how a particular discourse function is realized in ways which differ radically from popular belief.) Clearly these developments have potentially profound implications for language teaching, suggesting as they do that we should reconsider the relative emphases given to the development of grammatical and collocational knowledge, and also the kind of materials students are given. The principles governing the relationship between corpus linguistics and language teaching, however, are by no means straightforward (Widdowson 1991b). Corpus linguistics provides both theories and descriptions, but principles are needed to connect this theory and description to practice.

The two papers on this area are complementary in their approach. MICHAEL STUBBS, by considering a number of words in their most frequent collocations, gives a detailed account of the kind of insights

[19]

which corpus linguistics can provide, but takes care to make no assumptions about the applications of such knowledge in language teaching. GUY ASTON, on the other hand, surveys and assesses the relevance of corpus linguistics to language pedagogy, adducing important principles for application, and stressing that—while corpus linguistics undoubtedly does offer revolutionary insights into both the learning, processing, and use of language—the interaction of these insights with the practice of pedagogy may lead to unexpected outcomes.

The forte of corpus linguistics is to uncover regularities and recurrent patterns: the unoriginal use of language. The corollary (Stubbs 1994) is that it has implications for the study of a discourse often marked by the most original uses of language: literature. It can uncover what is 'counter, original, spare, strange'[17] as well as what is 'coated with the glass armour of the familiar' (Shklovsky 1974: 68). The next three papers deal with literature.

BRAJ KACHRU challenges the widespread myth that—with very few exceptions—it is only the native speaker of a language who has the necessary sensitivity to produce this most original of discourses. He traces this dogma to Romantic European nationalism, and shows, using the example of the Kashmiri poetic tradition, that in a wider historical and cultural perspective, it is far from unusual for the literary artist to write successfully in another tongue. Though not directly concerned with teaching—either of language or literature—this paper has clear implications for the debate on the authority of the native speaker (see Davies above) and also exposes the degree to which contemporary applied linguistics is distorted and impoverished when it discusses language from a monolingual rather than a polylingual perspective. JOSEPH BISONG considers the teaching of poetry in Nigeria, and from this specific context derives principles of general relevance. He reflects in particular upon the alienation students often feel from written poetry, and suggests ways in which the early use of accessible spoken verse may initiate students into a later appreciation of more problematic, but more rewarding, writing. RONALD CARTER and MICHAEL MCCARTHY consider literature teaching more generally and propose ways in which students may be encouraged to appreciate literary uses of language through consideration of non-literary uses.

One recurrent theme of this volume is the exposure of myths: the ascendancy of the native speaker, the fixed route of SLA, the primacy of input, the mechanisms of reported speech, the meaning of tense, the direct applicability of corpus linguistics. Myths simplify, and Widdowson, as we have remarked, has often been concerned to combat simplification. One easy strategy for avoiding complex problems in language teaching is to make saints or demons out of movements and methods from the past. (The use of translation, for example, has been fashionable as a demon.) BERNARD SPOLSKY presents a detailed examination of one canonized methodology: The Army Specialized Training Program, widely believed to have effected miraculous results. By showing that it was neither as innovative nor as successful as popularly supposed, he reopens a closed debate about this method in particular, and by implication about the importance of methodology in general.

A last group of papers concerns the most rigorous test of principles derived from theories and description of language: their use in classroom teaching. CATHERINE WALLACE describes and assesses a course in critical reading which she has devised and implemented. LUIZ PAULO DA MOITA LOPES demonstrates how teachers, while appearing to allow students to choose topics, are in fact often following their own agenda. Finally, MARIANNE CELCE-MURCIA discusses the neglected area of listening in discourse teaching, giving examples of how contextualization can develop student discrimination.

Principle and practice

There is a popular dichotomy which distinguishes the practitioner from the theorist in a way detrimental to the latter. Those who theorize, it is held, cannot also do: the educationalist cannot actually teach, the literary theorist cannot actually write. In this anti-intellectual view, theorizing is seen as cold and self-regarding, hopelessly removed from experience and reality. Grand overviews of formal structures seem unable to capture the processes by which efficient communicators move forward with an eye for local detail and the way in which one word leads on to another. The dry formulae of the analyst cannot explain the inspiration of the expert user.

These irreconcilable perspectives, this disillusion with the analytic, may be hard to shrug off in a world where principle seems increasingly elusive. Knowledge can no longer be laid out under the dome of a single reading room, but comes at us as a succession of flickering screens.

[21]

Amid such fragmentation it is essential both to assert the significance of theorizing, and to guard against its losing touch with actuality.

Widdowson's distinction between analyst and user (1984a: 9ff.) presents them, not as types of people, and not in terms of superiority and inferiority, but as equally valuable modes of thought. The landscape of his extensive publications, seen from the air, might suggest someone exclusively in the tradition of the grand analyst, primarily concerned with two areas: language teaching and literature. Those who know him for his writing on the one may be surprised how much he has written on the other. But his readers and students, navigating on the ground among his words, know how appropriate to him are these two areas of intellectual enquiry—for both demand facility with words. His analyses of language teaching and literature are never far from each other or from educational and literary practice. His teaching is inspired, and his writing displays the care and precision of literature. He has an ability to be carried away by language as well as to analyse, a dual perspective which yields a rich and distinctive synthesis. In his work, theory and practice are equally valued, and mutually informative.

The editors, contributors, and publishers hope that in this book H. G. Widdowson may find both an echo of this achievement, and a tribute to it.

Note of thanks

The editors would like to thank a number of people for their help during the preparation of this volume. First and foremost, we are grateful to Jennifer Bassett, who carried out the editing process with sharp perception, creativity, and professional expertise, and whose sparkle, energy, and unassailable tranquillity withstood the toughest 'ordeals by computer'. We should also like to thank Rob Batstone, Robert de Beaugrande, Christopher Brumfit, Elena Cook, Alison Crutchley, Braj Kachru, Christine Klein, Arthur Mettinger, Harald Mittermann, Nikolaus Ritt, Karen Ross, Herbert Schendl, Peter Skehan, Ute Smit, and Catherine Wallace for their help, support, and advice. At Oxford University Press Cristina Whitecross conducted the project with sound judgement, great enthusiasm, and unfailing determination. Many thanks to her and to Anne Conybeare, Jeff Borer, Mark Tilley-Watts, and Sarah Ashton for making the impossible possible.

Notes

1 Invoking the name of Dr Pangloss, a character in Voltaire's novel *Candide ou l'optimisme*, whose conviction is that the world is as good as it can possibly be, and everything that happens will lead to the best possible outcome. 'Our noses were made to carry spectacles and we wear them. Legs were clearly intended for breeches, and we wear them.' The name Pangloss, a coinage from the Greek for 'all' and 'language', suggests that Pangloss' language is capable of explaining everything.

2 Superficially it resembles the human opposed thumb: the feature which together with language is traditionally supposed to give us the edge over other species.

3 For drawing our attention to this passage we are grateful to Michael Foster (see Foster 1994).

4 In these approaches nothing must be superfluous. Take for example the accounts of one of the universal 'design features' of language, redundancy (Hockett 1958: 87–91; Lyons 1977: 256). This is rationalized as protection against loss through interference, or a way of allowing more time for processing. Though both explanations may be partly true, redundancy may also have an element of pure inefficiency.

5 No narrowness should be imputed to de Saussure himself who recognized (and indeed practised) both the diachronic study of language and the study of other semiotic systems.

6 Chomsky describes Labov's work, 'on the linguistic level', as 'evident and banal' (Chomsky 1979: 55) and warns that 'such work must not be confounded with research' (ibid.: 57).

7 Taking his cue from Widdowson 1980a, Wilkins (1994: 166) suggests that 'there are sound reasons for arguing that the concerns of applied linguistics are in some ways more comprehensive than those of theoretical linguistics'.

8 Derived from a survey of articles in *Applied Linguistics, The Annual Review of Applied Linguistics,* and of the scientific commissions of AILA.

[23]

9 Applied linguistics and language teaching overlap 'to the extent in some quarters of virtual synonymy' (Widdowson 1984a: 7).

10 Most notably, the observation—partly true like most harmful generalizations—that second language learners maintain some of the child's ability to absorb form unconsciously, led to the notion that *all* that is needed is to expose L2 learners—like L1 infants—to meaningful interaction (Krashen 1982; Krashen and Terrell 1983).

11 The notion of textual meaning is not rejected completely, as it is for example in some versions of reader-response literary theory (Fish 1980).

12 He was not quite in at the beginning. When the term 'applied linguistics' was first used in an official capacity in 1956 he was (literally) at sea as (ironically) a coder in the Royal Navy. In 1965 he went on to do a diploma at Edinburgh University in the first Applied Linguistics department in Britain, and completed his Ph.D., 'An applied linguistic approach to discourse analysis', in the same university in 1973 (Widdowson 1973).

13 This list is by no means exhaustive. Many articles and books range across a variety of topics, establishing connections between them. The following references, however, give some guidance as to where Widdowson has written on the topics listed here:

- literature and literature teaching (Widdowson 1972a, 1972b, 1974a, 1974b, 1975, 1978a, 1979a chapter 11, 1982a, 1982b, 1983a, 1984a section 4, 1986b, 1987a, 1987b, 1988a, 1989a, 1989b, 1992a, 1993a, 1994b)
- discourse analysis (Widdowson 1973, 1979a section 4, 1984a sections 2 and 3, 1990b)
- grammar (Allen and Widdowson 1975; Widdowson 1986c, 1990a chapter 6)
- lexis (Widdowson 1990a chapter 6, 1993b)
- second language acquisition (Widdowson 1984a chapter 18, 1984b, 1990a chapter 2, 1990b, 1993c, 1994c)
- culture and language (Criper and Widdowson 1975; Widdowson 1992b, 1993d)

- translation (Widdowson 1991a)
- corpus linguistics (Widdowson 1991b)
- language planning and international English (Quirk and Widdowson 1985; Widdowson 1982c, 1988b, 1994a)
- communicative language teaching (Allen and Widdowson 1974; Widdowson 1978b, 1979a chapter 20, 1984a chapter 16, 1993e)
- teacher education (Widdowson 1979b, 1984c, 1990a chapter 4, 1992c, 1993f, 1994d)
- the teaching of writing and reading (Davies and Widdowson 1974; Widdowson 1972c, 1979a section 5, 1980b)
- curriculum and syllabus design (Brumfit and Widdowson 1981; Widdowson 1979a section 8, 1984d, 1987c, 1990a chapter 9, 1993e)
- methodology (Widdowson 1990a chapter 10, 1993e)
- ESP (Widdowson 1974a, 1979a sections 1–3, 1983b, 1984a section 5)
- learner and teacher roles (Widdowson 1983c, 1990a chapter 11)
- simplification and accessibility (Widdowson 1979a section 6).

14 The other founding editors were J. P. B. Allen and Bernard Spolsky.

15 This list of editorial work is by no means exhaustive. He has also been a series editor of the *English in Focus* series (Allen and Widdowson 1973–1980), and consultant editor of *Reading and Thinking in English* (1981–1983) and *Communicative Grammar* (1981–1985). He is currently launching, as series editor and contributor, a new series of books entitled *The Oxford Guides to Language Study* (Widdowson 1996).

16 The idea that 'different speech communities have different ways of organizing ideas in writing which reflect "their cultural thought patterns"' (Y. Kachru in this volume).

17 From the poem *Pied Beauty* by Gerard Manley Hopkins.

2

Teacher professionalism and research

CHRISTOPHER BRUMFIT

Introduction

THE PURPOSE OF this paper is to explore two currently unfashionable views of education. As they are both compatible with the rigour, scholarship, and respect for research that Henry Widdowson has consistently advocated, they seem appropriate topics for a volume in his honour. In the first main section of the paper I shall outline a set of beliefs on which attitudes to education may be based, incorporating the unfashionable universalist views on which much pre-modernist educational discussion has been predicated. I shall concentrate particularly on a liberal-humanist approach to historical and political processes, reflected in (for example) sensitive response to literature, using recent British experience to illustrate some of the tensions affecting education throughout the world as governments become suspicious of inherited optimism about its value. In the second section I shall turn, with a more practical intention, to the issue of empirical research and one major area, language teaching classroom studies, where understanding is crucial, but opportunity limited for researchers.

The paper is thus concerned with questions in applied linguistics as a problem-centred discipline. The definition of the discipline I prefer is

The theoretical and empirical investigation of real-world problems in which language is a central issue.

This definition enables 'application' to centre on problems that require resolution, but does not limit studies to either language or linguistics (because problems of language in social life are never solely about language and such a limitation means that studies will always be defective, because partial, in their effort to address the particular application). Thus in applied linguistics, the problems will always be defined in the first instance by external needs, and the tasks of the applied linguist will be threefold: (1) to conceptualize the problem so that rational argument and empirical research can be brought to bear on it; (2) to clarify the precise research questions (which will necessarily draw upon interdisciplinary research traditions as no one tradition can explain the psycho/sociolinguistic interface in which all language-based problems are played out); (3) to design and carry out relevant research and analysis.

This paper addresses the relationship between teacher professionalism and research, and is engaged in the first task, and the beginnings of the second.

Belief
Education in culture

In Britain, this is a time of substantial change in public attitudes to teacher education. In the pace of change, first principles are liable to disappear as the short-term manoeuvres necessary for survival occupy practitioners' time and effort. Let us therefore start by asserting a fundamental belief in the continuity of civilized values, and the inherent similarity of human cultures. For if we do not accept some version of this position, the educational enterprise, as it has developed in the post-industrial world, becomes either trivial (being merely a matter of technical skills), or incoherent (advocating communication between incommunicable cultures), or evil (being merely a means for the rich to control the poor).

The push towards triviality is accelerated by strong political pressures to see education as essentially about technical skills (in language teaching exemplified by the more extreme needs analysis models). Incoherence is sometimes welcomed (or at least seen as inevitable) by post-modernist arguments about the impossibility of cross-cultural communication (exemplified in language teaching by the advocates of local models and local content). As for evil, anti-imperial arguments have pointed to the repressive effects of English in various parts of the world and the role of language teaching in supporting these. It is possible, of course, for language teaching simultaneously to accept each of these positions as contributing to a critique of complacent acceptance of tradition. In any education there are indeed technical issues; education is indeed about encountering cultural diversity; and it is indeed closely bound up with power relations so that it may well become an instrument of repression. But the history of educational thinking from Plato onwards is a record of arguments about values more than skills, and there is no evidence to suggest that we shall ever produce a society in which cultures do not resist others' values, assimilate with others, adapt to others, or conquer them—in every cultural contact there will be evidence at any one time of all of these responses simultaneously. This is because societies are never monolithic; however we define a society, there are always many within it who have much, even more, in common with others outside than with most of their companions inside it. As human beings we are multi-valenced, which is to say that we all belong simultaneously to an enormous range of cultures, most of which we share with only a small number of our fellow citizens. Thus, apart from the major allegiances of religion, educational group, nation, or profession, we all have roles as potters and poets, bird-watchers and baseball-players, cooks and cricket-statisticians, lovers of Pushkin and lovers of Pugin, workers against torture and workers for selfhood, not to mention the social choices surrounding apparently biological classifications of gender and ethnicity. All of these, however fundamental or however trivial to others, will for some be a major defining allegiance, a base for a cultural grouping that transcends nation, politics, gender, religion, or class. And even the most rigidly attached to religious, ethnic, or class loyalties will in parts of their lives belong to the other cultural groupings, as they read or sing, make or mar, adore or argue. In a post-industrial world, most of us belong to minorities most of the time.

So is this not a description of the break-up of western tradition? Is not the fragmented and provisional world of post-modernism implicit in such a scenario? If we see this diversity as a consequence of education, and of increased freedom of choice, we do not need to see it as a decisive break with previous views of human history. One characteristic of this change is that it is possible for many, rather than the élite few, to read a book like *The Odyssey*, which is over 2000 years old, or to talk to colleagues from distant cultures, or to communicate across barriers of religion and belief, with people from all times and all places. Literature, history, and philosophy form our dialogues with the past, but out of them we make our conversations in the present. Technology (the CD-ROM, e-mail, let alone the paperback book) makes this dialogue accessible to all cultures in principle, but education is the most systematic means of influencing whether it is used for good or ill. Of course this capacity to communicate is always partial—even two people who have been brought up together in the same household achieve only partial communication—but what is shared in achieving this sense of human connection may be much more important than what separates us. Working within the range of rich and varied frameworks which people use, it is possible for individuals with goodwill to co-operate in the development of our understanding of the world, in the creation of useful and beautiful artefacts, and in the elimination of evil and poverty and hunger. Education, however relative its success, has in the last century brought that capacity to many, not just to the few of a ruling class.

It is important to state this as a context, because there has been considerable emphasis in recent times on the separateness and individuality of cultures. While remaining cool-headed about the features that separate, we need to emphasize also, particularly if we are concerned with language teaching, our capacities to communicate successfully, to co-operate, and to overcome disabilities. History is a record of the difficulties of improving the human condition, but it is not a record of the impossibility of doing so. Furthermore, once we believe that improvement is impossible, we leave ourselves no defence against bullying and the worship of power and success; if we are forbidden to live in hope, we are condemned to live in fear.

The current climate in popular discussion of education

The kinds of attacks on education that are current in Britain surprise outsiders, though they reflect views that are public in discussion throughout at least the English-speaking world. In *The Independent* newspaper of Wednesday 31 October 1990 there was an article 'Who loves the Education Establishment?' in which it became clear that the Education Establishment was considered to include academics in teacher education, academics concerned with the funding of research, head teachers and people who had worked as officials in the then Department for Education and Science, leaders of teachers' Trades Unions, and other similar bodies. All of these were people who were held to be contributing towards the decline in British education. The local authorities, the school inspectorate, and similar bodies were also attacked. It is clear from columnists varying from Melanie Philips in the liberal *Guardian* to Janet Daley in the conservative *Times* that teaching, broadly conceived as a professional activity, has very few friends in the press, let alone among politicians. The general tendency of British government policy since January 1992 to remove initial teacher education as much as possible from higher education and to locate it in the schools is an approach seen as suitable in the UK only for teachers, for there are simultaneous government calls for training for nurses and social workers to move in the opposite direction. Furthermore, Britain is out of step with other countries in Europe, where the tendency is for teacher education to be more fully integrated with higher education.

The press comments reflect a number of disparate and unsophisticated positions. But behind these, this discussion can be related to a more serious change in attitudes to knowledge. Influenced (though no doubt indirectly) by challenges in the work of philosophers like Foucault, Bourdieu, and Derrida, public discussion reflects an increasing disbelief in any privileged state of objectivity in knowledge. It is clear for example that many people would regard privileged knowledge essentially as a manifestation of a power struggle within society. In Britain, views of this kind, with an emphasis on the relativity of any particular mode of understanding, have shown themselves in as diverse phenomena as the inaugural lecture of Terry Eagleton, Professor of English at Oxford University, and in discussions of the kind of knowledge that ought to form part of a National Curriculum.

This academic dispute links with a stereotyping process, in which people attack many aspects of teacher education and many alleged beliefs underlying the training of teachers (including language teachers), for the following reasons:

[31]

a) Teacher training is held to be arid and irrelevant;

b) It is held to be 'leftist' and dangerous in reflecting outmoded, and undesirable, belief systems;

c) It is held to be ineffective.

We should note that these are inconsistent with each other. If in fact teacher education is arid and irrelevant it is unlikely to be influential; if it is a dangerous influence on teachers then it must be perceived as in some sense relevant or it would have no effect on them. None the less, consistency is not the prime concern of this particular argument.

Language education in the UK

Within British education there has been substantial discussion of a fairly amateur kind about the nature of language curricula in order to provide a foundation for the development of English and Foreign Language work in the National Curriculum. However, there is little contact with the very substantial body of international theory/ research, of considerable distinction, which may be found in the applied linguistics and ELT literature. Admittedly, in the late 1980s Henry Widdowson did serve on the Kingman Committee which the British Government established to inquire into the teaching of English language, while another applied linguist, Michael Stubbs, contributed to the discussions on the National Curriculum English component, but neither had any influence on the design of the curriculum. There was no comparable input into the foreign languages curriculum, and the impact of all serious, research-based advice was reduced as the recommendations were put through the legislative process. The notable 1960s-1970s British tradition in applied linguistic work has not been drawn upon in discussions underlying the new curriculum.

It is also true to say that there has been less empirical research than is desirable in these areas. This has been substantially because of a lack of funding compared with what is available in the United States, coupled with a lack of urgency about the need for foreign language research of the kind that is found in other European countries and in some places outside Europe. For example, there are no substantial longitudinal studies of second or foreign language learning within Britain for researchers and curriculum developers to draw upon.

Essentially the externally imposed arguments are couched in terms that may be described by the following distinctions:

Competences   v Thought
Skill   v Knowledge
Accountability v Authority.

There are a number of problems with the kinds of distinctions which are being put forward. First of all, whatever the arguments for specifying competences very clearly and precisely, we have to recognize that the process of teaching, and particularly the process of teaching language, is an enriching rather than an impoverishing activity. Competences imply that you can specify in advance what people are going to do. But a true language teaching model, compatible with the view of human history outlined above, must enable people to do anything with the language they are learning that they have any wish to do. Specifying in advance exactly what they want may be helpful as a means towards getting to the richer environment that they require, but the role is limited because precise specifications cannot become goals in themselves without imposing restrictions, limiting rather than increasing options. Someone has to lay down appropriate language behaviour separated from questions of motivation, identity, and aspiration. If that person sees language learning as a simple instrumental matter, they will fail to connect with learners' perceptions at all. At worst, the effect will be the opposite of liberating.

Secondly, there is a concern about the means by which we learn languages. Is it the case that we can separate individual competences for teaching purposes without extracting from the totality of the language situation elements which will in fact be dysfunctional if treated separately from everything else in the system? This whole debate, which is one about the nature of language acquisition, and the relationship between second language learning and mother tongue acquisition, is extremely complex. It would be unfortunate, indeed educationally disastrous, if decisions made for administrative convenience conflicted with the ways in which people actually do learn languages. Similarly, the emphasis on skills and on accountability reflects a pull away from an integrated, humane, and trusting view of knowledge and from those who claim to have it. Such correctives are often necessary to prevent professions from themselves becoming exploitative—but to see either knowledge or authority as simple concepts, easily described and assessed, is to risk destroying understandings that have been painfully built up over the past century of educational study and practice. Knowledge may be closely bound up with power, but it cannot be *merely* power.

None the less, we have to admit that for one major area of applied linguistics, language teaching theory and practice, the lack of a really strong empirical research base is striking, in spite of decades of discussion and development. Socially contextualized language learning, in which learners move from mother tongue to second and foreign language use, is by no means clearly understood. In some areas, notably second language acquisition work and discourse analysis, there have been considerable advances in the past twenty years—but in the areas most within teachers' control and in which they can influence learning, there is far too little that is systematic. The work of the Centre for Language in Education at Southampton University has attempted to cross the boundaries between mother tongue, second language, and foreign language work, in order to clarify some of the areas in which we are still vague. For example, it has had large research projects on the role of explicit knowledge about language in both foreign language and mother tongue classes, and on the longitudinal development of competence in French. There are similar projects in various other places, but generally there are too few to provide a secure knowledge base for the profession, with the kind of reinterpretation of each other's data, and constant generation of new and reliable information which can be found in other areas of empirical science.

How can we respond?

So where can teachers and teacher educators stand in relation to this not entirely sympathetic environment?

First we have to acknowledge that there is some force in the claim that professionals are liable to protect themselves against the opinions of outsiders. There have been occasions in which parents have been excluded from expressing views on matters relating to language education. There have been occasions in which teachers have preferred to cope rather than move towards the most effective change necessary, even when the arguments for change have been very well supported and rigorously argued. Even if we acknowledge this, though, we have to acknowledge also the essential professionalism of people who spend the whole of their lives working in classrooms with learners. Nobody else is in a position to speak from direct close experience of large numbers of learners. Whatever teachers are able to learn from research, from theory, and from interested outsiders, will be valuable to them but will require reinterpretation in the light of their personal professional experience. To take that away from them is to insist that teaching is simply a technology, in which people carry out somebody else's agenda and are merely cogs in the system. You will not get teachers of any calibre being willing to come and work in those circumstances.

The only solution to this position, as I see it, is to ensure that there are multiple opportunities for teachers to move to and fro between situations in which they can contemplate, reflect, read, and carry out empirical research if they wish to, in relation to their professional practice, and situations where they can carry on teaching as effectively as possible. The constant iteration between research (which is a form of contemplation) and practice (which is a form of action) is essential. However, it is not my belief that the two can be carried out simultaneously all the time. Action in teaching requires decision making which is instantaneous, automatized, and not necessarily capable of being analysed in detail, from moment to moment. It is no criticism of teachers to say that this is what they are supposed to be doing, but it *would* be a criticism if they refused to allow such automatization to be subject to careful investigation. Yet the process of careful investigation is not something which can be carried out for most people simultaneously with the action itself. There are limits too to practical activity as a basis for development. Something which teachers must necessarily have is an awareness of what is going on in other contexts and in other parts of the world, because it is only from other parts of the world that we get an awareness of the *limitations* of the particular institution in which we operate intensively. Creating the conditions within which such international cross-breeding of ideas can operate is the basic requirement for any organization, or any individual, who is concerned with true professionalism.

It will be apparent from the earlier discussion that there is currently an alien atmosphere for professionalism of this kind to operate in. Yet without such professionalism, it is very difficult to see how people can regard themselves as serious practitioners. The one thing they must not do is opt out of the system altogether. However strong and tempting the alternatives are, teaching, and particularly language teaching, is too important to be left to people who do not fully understand it by close relationship with classrooms. Even if it is uncomfortable to stay within an overworked and under-appreciated profession, it is necessary for a civilized, humane, and practical-principled view of language teaching to be exemplified by the teaching profession at large. Discouragingly but necessarily, we have to maintain the view that the more powerful the critique, the more ferocious the attack, the more determinedly practitioners have to stay within the profession, constantly asserting humane and undogmatic values based on close experience of learners' problems.

At the same time, professionals need to address their own perceived weaknesses as well as those emphasized by outsiders. Particularly, in language teaching, we need to promote research that is both classroom-based, and systematic. How can we do that?

Research needs

What is needed is research for people whose prime concerns are practical. The major argument for educational research, carried out by people who are closely involved with teaching, is that teaching is a complex activity, and no one else will produce the kind of research needed. When psychologists, linguists, or other scholars approach classrooms they have agendas that derive from their own disciplines. Teachers, however, have to understand something that is much richer and more complicated than 'how people learn', or 'what is the difference between classroom questioning and real-world questioning'. They have to *act* effectively to help learners learn, drawing on their understanding of their cultures and personalities, their previous experiences and their future hopes, their needs and their limitations. They operate with the untidiness of groups of people whose interests conflict, who are often in their classes rather unwillingly, and whose motivation fluctuates. Their experience of this gives them insight into classrooms, but also makes them resistant to solutions that try to make them tidy, or to interpret them in the light of only one type of explanation. In practice, they act by professionally informed intuition. The best of them are creative, have a flair for good practices and a sensitivity to students' needs that is a matter more of art than science. Yet within this there is still a need for understanding.

And this understanding will inform the kind of research that is most useful. Research needs to be interdisciplinary, because our reactions to the people with whom we work cannot be constrained by single disciplinary perspectives; it needs to recognize the inevitable subjective element in human relationships; it needs to be concerned with quality and with value, not simply with what is accessible to external measurement.

What kind of research?

How, within this general approach, could classroom-oriented research be useful? Let me offer a general proposal, preceded by a brief rationale.

Foreign language classroom research is fragmented. English for Speakers of Other Languages benefits from considerable US and European investment in research, but that is substantially geared to Second Language Acquisition work, and takes little notice of general educational research, or of work in teaching other languages. Other language traditions are either limited in geographical range, or fragmented into disconnected small-scale work by lack of major funding. Work crossing the boundaries of different language teaching traditions is exceptional.

In Britain, there have been book-length research-based studies of particular aspects of language teaching, but they do not between them constitute even the beginnings of a research programme. The effect of such fragmentation is to imply that understanding second language pedagogy is not appropriate for sustained research work, because researchers do not build substantially on others' work, but concentrate on locally important specific research questions without providing the data base for generalization or well-informed policy-making.

There is a major need for a *programme*, rather than just *projects*. The situation just described could generate a number of different programmes. What follows is simply one suggestion. However, for a research programme to be effective, it must persuade enough researchers that their work is complementary, and capable of mutual

[37]

interconnection. We have to build on each other's work in a way that is recognizable to outsiders if we are to attract research funding and have our judgements recognized as useful by policy-makers.

There are two major reasons for wanting to be ambitious in this way. One is that we need empirical support for the many inevitable generalizations that we make about language teaching. Whether we teach, educate teachers at pre- or in-service levels, write textbooks, or organize teaching programmes, we are always involved in a process of drawing on past, and different, experience, and taking what was generalizable from it to apply productively to our next task. This is a truism, but needs to be asserted in the face of strong support for action research which is defended for being local and specific. Interpreting such local accounts still requires us to resort to generalization if we are to make any sense of the *significance* of what we have observed, and local projects without interconnecting knowledge bases have no defence against whim and fashion.

Secondly, there is a political reason for being ambitious. The notion that research is possible or appropriate for 'soft' or 'common sense' issues like educational practice is under attack. If we are to preserve a systematic knowledge base at all, we have to ensure that funding remains available, and that the kinds of projects proposed can convince sceptical outsiders of their potential usefulness to a broad-based profession and to society at large. Higher education research has increasingly to be bid for in competition with technical disciplines which have a commitment to expensive plant and to major generalization as a goal. To avoid being squeezed out altogether, foreign language research cannot afford to take too parochial a view of its own ambitions. Funding is unlikely to be obtained for locally significant projects, but may be available for those which offer the hope of a genuine advance in scientific understanding that will be useful internationally as well as locally.

I suggest that we need a programme which maps what we need to know to make sense of language teaching, noting the areas in which we shall overlap with other educational or linguistic research concerns, and define within this the sort of programme that could link a body of classroom researchers most fruitfully in a network of specific projects.

There appear to be three broad areas of interest, which are mutually interdependent, but which have been investigated to varying degrees.

1 First is the issue of description of classroom practice. This takes the classroom and its behaviour as a given, and documents, in so far as it can, how things are, without any motivation to change practice. Such studies will concern themselves with descriptions of classroom events, with teachers' and learners' attitudes and beliefs, home attitudes, managerial policies, and so on. To interpret the present in one situation, some degree of historical and comparative understanding will be necessary (what were practices in previous periods? what are they in other countries, with other languages, in other subjects?).

This kind of study shades gradually into explanation, of course, but its importance should not be underestimated. We are astonishingly ignorant of the extent to which practices that we advocate are typical of current practice, or radical and threatening; and we do not have a sound empirical base on which to build many of the assertions about good practice that are widely made (which is not to invalidate the assertions, of course, for the judgement of experienced teachers and teacher educators may be crucial—but it *is* to question the value of a profession which is not trying constantly to *test* its assertions against a knowledge of typical practice).

2 Second, then, is explanation. This does not take the classroom as a given, but views it as problematic. At this point studies of language become important (descriptions of the language being learnt, contrastive studies, sociolinguistic studies), as do analyses of learners' practices (SLA work, L1 acquisition work, longitudinal classroom studies, error analyses, etc.), policy studies of curriculum theory, and social psychological studies of interaction.

There is more research available to appeal to in this area, but it derives substantially from people whose interests are outside teaching. Without the data base provided by work in description, assertions about educational practices from these sources cannot be tested against the accumulated professional wisdom (as well as the accumulated survival strategies) of regular practitioners. Indeed, there is a substantial risk that explanatory research will constantly have as its main reference research paradigms and current theoretical models outside (and possibly irrelevant to) education, unless the descriptive base in education is strong.

[39]

3 Third, but only third, come pedagogical studies, to which many scholars have devoted much time and energy. Because the profession, and thus the market, demands constant thought about how to teach best, this has been the subject of much serious and original work. However, I suspect I am not alone in feeling that we have had to work philosophically, so to speak, in a pre-scientific period. Pedagogical studies view classrooms (correctly) as *directed* communities, in which teachers try to influence learning behaviour. Hence, the descriptive concerns of our first area above are all mirrored in pedagogical studies, but with a concern not for what *does* happen but for what *ought* to happen. Since education is necessarily about improving performance, this is of course the payoff—but without the first two sets of studies, assertions of desired practice in this area risk losing touch with any form of principle.

My proposal, then, is that we desperately need to link researchers together, initially, for the modest purpose of filling in the first-stage descriptive map, but in the context of a wider intention—to develop through explanatory studies a better grounded series of pedagogical understandings, and better understanding of learning and interactional processes.

The project I propose, therefore, is the first stage of the more ambitious programme outlined above. Its initial purpose would be to document the major variables in language classrooms, and the differences in behaviour by teachers and learners in different contexts. The key variables might be: class size, level of learner proficiency, age of learner, native or non-native speaking teacher, internal or external assessment/ examination goal, single or multi-language learners, technology-rich or technology-poor classroom, and possibly mother tongue, second, or foreign language teaching. These categories are all difficult to define, and we should not underestimate the problems of definition; none the less, they all potentially reflect categories which are used in basic classification by teachers who move around the world into different classroom contexts.

It should be possible to devise a scheme for classroom observation that would not be too hard to administer, and which could give us much more information, across a wider area, than we currently have of practices and processes in different countries and different types of classroom.

We may feel that such a study should be augmented by others, for example, interview studies of teacher and learner attitudes, and the other areas referred to in the first section above. This is clearly feasible. But unless such studies are put into a framework such as the one I have outlined, I believe language-education researchers will always be seen as marginal dabblers in research rather than contributors to a substantial body of systematic knowledge.

Finally, in case anyone feels that grandiose claims accompany a fairly low-level initial proposal, could I repeat my claim that without a descriptive base that looks for what is common across language teaching, the *significance* of local practices that we have traditionally studied in depth cannot be assessed. To aim high we have to be more willing to start low.

3

The applied linguist and the foreign language teacher: can they talk to each other?

CLAIRE KRAMSCH

WHILE THE FIELD of applied linguistics has become a highly multidisciplinary one, operating as a bridge between several academic disciplines, for example, linguistics, psychology, sociology, anthropology, education (Pennycook 1994), foreign language education has also expanded its domain of inquiry to include such fields as second language acquisition research, methodology, curriculum development, institutional policy, testing (Kramsch 1993a). The number of fields and disciplines that can further our understanding of language learning and teaching has grown, and so has the number of metaphors, that each try to domesticate and render familiar the eminently unfamiliar process of acquiring a language other than one's own.

The possibilities of mutual enrichment between applied linguists and language teachers have thereby increased dramatically, but so have the buzzwords and shorthand verbal practices, which constitute as many opportunities for misunderstanding. It is urgent, as Patsy Lightbown stated eloquently in 1994, that applied linguists and language teachers see themselves as being in the same boat, 'both oars in the water' (Lightbown 1994). But the question is: do they have a common discourse?

If applied linguistics is, according to Stern, 'the mediating discipline between theoretical developments in the language sciences and the practice of language teaching' (1983: 35), it has been widely assumed up to now that, provided the language sciences have the theory, its application, i.e. the mediation itself, will be unproblematic. However, there has been some concern among educational linguists that this might not be the case (see, for example, Lightbown 1985 and Widdowson, cited in Phillipson 1992: 259).

In this paper[1] I will first review briefly the reasons for the emergence of a discourse problem in language study; I will then examine the nature of this problem and suggest ways in which applied linguists and foreign language teachers can engage in intellectual dialogue, putting indeed both oars in the same water.[2]

Why we have a discourse problem

Two developments in the modern history of foreign language study are making the relationship between applied linguists and language teachers into a discourse issue.

The first relates to developments in foreign language education. Due to demographic and social changes, the educated élite of industrialized countries has changed. The concept of a stable, consensual discourse community composed of belletristically inclined students has given way to the recognition of a diverse population of learners with changing needs who not only know little about the world beyond their national borders, but also very often cannot agree on any one definition of their national identity. Learning a foreign language, then, is no longer presented as a way of celebrating a recognized cultural canon, composed of the great works of Shakespeare, Goethe, or Voltaire, but as a way of discovering another people's multifaceted living culture. No longer limited to a corpus of literary texts, the current model of foreign language study now includes the ethnographic variability of language as it is used by native speakers in the variable practice of everyday life.

Language educators have ceased therefore to look to their colleagues in literature for pedagogic guidance; they have turned instead to applied linguists like Henry Widdowson (1975, 1984a, 1992a), to ESL and FL methodologists, syllabus designers, and curriculum developers. The discourse of these fields is usually foreign to literature scholars. It gives foreign language teachers professional credibility but not always intellectual respectability in the eyes of the literature professoriate. And

[44]

yet, language teachers need to talk to their colleagues in their own foreign language and literature departments. The double allegiance of language teachers to their national target culture and to applied linguistics forces them to mediate between several, often incommensurable, discourses.

The second development occurred with the growth of the field of applied linguistics. The programmatic chart proposed by Michael Halliday in 1978 expanded the object of language study to four distinct but overlapping entities: (1) language as system, i.e. phonic and graphic system, grammar and vocabulary; (2) language as knowledge and thought; (3) language as behavior enacted in a social context; (4) language as art, or as a particular way of representing and constructing reality (Halliday 1978: 11). These four aspects of language, which are interdependent, correspond to the way in which at least four different discourse communities—language teachers, psycholinguists, sociolinguists, literary scholars—talk about language study. For example, the notion of *context* in the work of sociolinguists (as in, for example, Duranti and Goodwin 1992) is quite different from that used by psycholinguists (as in, for example, Ellis 1987a) or language methodologists (as in, for example, Omaggio 1986).

The problem is not just that foreign language educators and applied linguists give different meanings to identical words, but that they are themselves positioned at the confluence of several discourse communities or audiences. For example, in 1990, a teacher trainer I had invited to give a workshop on communicative competence spent the day teaching the students how to negotiate meaning the way one would negotiate a turn in the road with one's automobile. He was using *negotiating meaning* as a synonym for *problem-solving*, a pretty much goal-oriented, controlled procedure, that had little to do with the vagaries and unpredictabilities of the communicative process that applied linguists like Breen and Candlin had tried to capture with this phrase in their early theory of communicative competence (1980), and that Widdowson expounded upon in much of his own work (for example, 1984a: chapter 8). However, this new meaning of the term, allowed by the English lexicon, resonated better with foreign language instructors in institutional settings in the 1990s, because it matched their current focus on cognitive, problem-solving processes in language learning. Thus the audience accepted without difficulty the new meaning given to the phrase, and probably was not even aware of the discourse switch.

This brief anecdote should make us pause and examine what has happened since Widdowson defined the scope of applied linguistics and its relevance to language learning and teaching in the early eighties (Widdowson 1984a). Widdowson called then for a model of language in applied linguistics that would be 'congruent with the knowledge and attitudes of language users' (1984a: 26). Language, he insisted, should be viewed as 'the rightful property of language users, not as the special preserve of the linguist' (ibid.: 27). Teachers should 'devise problems which will require learners to engage procedures for discourse processing' (ibid.: 123), rather than teach items as products. Widdowson was, as Seidlhofer (1994) remarks, 'making ideas accessible, and pointing to their (potential) relevance for learners' and, I would add, to teachers. That's what educational linguistics, after all, is about.

Since 1984, other applied linguists have made Widdowson's concepts—'language use', 'procedures', 'processes vs. products'—widely *accessible* to language educators, through the mediation of textbooks, monographs, workshops, public lectures, and discussions. In turn, educators have made these concepts *relevant* to other educators through the mediation of school guidelines, national standards descriptors, and global educational statements. But the mediation itself between people who are differently situated in the power structure, in historical memory and in social loyalties, is never unproblematic, as Seidlhofer and Widdowson themselves have shown (1994). Each mediation attempts to bring together discourse worlds separated by divergent interests and spheres of influence.

In sum: because each discourse domain has its own metaphors, its own categorizations, its own way of relating the parts to the whole, the broadened intellectual agenda now available to language teachers and applied linguists has made it more difficult to communicate across historically and socially created discourses. As Hayden White puts it: 'Discourse itself mediates between our apprehension of those aspects of experience still "strange" to us and those aspects of it which we "understand" because we have found an order of words adequate to its domestication' (1978: 21).

CLAIRE KRAMSCH

The surface structure of the discourse problem

This domestication presents two major difficulties for researchers and teachers. First they have to find the specific words to apprehend and understand their specific object of inquiry. Then they have to use these words to communicate with various audiences.

A problem of discourse specificity

As an example, let us first look at the ways in which various groups talk about the goals of language education.

Researchers in second language acquisition and psycholinguistics talk about learners 'developing an *interlanguage*', 'processing *input*', 'making input *comprehensible*', 'using good *learning strategies*'. This way of talking about language learning is the discourse of linguistic observation and experimentation. It shows evidence of scientific objectivity and stresses the importance of empirical research to understand how human beings actually learn foreign languages (see, for example, Selinker 1972; Long 1983; O'Malley and Chamot 1989; Van Patten 1992).

By contrast, scholars in the social sciences or in the humanities talk about learners 'exercising *critical reflection*', 'demystifying *ideologies*', 'becoming *empowered*', 'developing an *awareness of self and other*'. This is the discourse of critical pedagogy, cultural criticism, and postmodern thought. It shows evidence of social and political consciousness and stresses the importance of theory to understand concrete realities (see, for example, Fairclough 1989: Aronowitz and Giroux 1991; Kramsch and von Hoene 1994).

Foreign language educators, who are close to taxpayers, parents, communities, local employers, local politicians, talk about teachers 'establishing *goals and objectives*', 'setting *priorities*', 'setting up *procedures*', 'evaluating *progress*', 'determining *outcomes*'. This is the discourse of organizational management, the idiom of business, industry, and politics. It shows evidence of efficiency, rentability, utility, and measurable evidence of success (see, for example, ACTFL National Standards 1994).

We can contrast the scientific, the critical, and the corporate discourses with that of methodologists and teacher trainers. They are likely to talk about ways of 'integrating *skills*', 'contextualizing *activities*', 'sequencing *tasks*', and 'designing *tests*'. Theirs is the discourse of schooled learning in institutional settings. It focuses on professional expertise, instructional management and control (for example, Omaggio 1986). You will note that the discourse of the first two groups tends to focus on the learner, that of the last two on the teacher.

These different ways of talking about goals have found their counterpart in the discourse of various methods and approaches in language teaching. The current approaches that purport to go 'beyond proficiency' are reactions to general trends in education that themselves respond to international competition. Consider, for example, the following three approaches: content-based instruction, task-based instruction, and strategy-based instruction.

'Content-based instruction' (CBI) claims to put content back into the (mere) language skills curriculum. In the United States, CBI is a direct response to the criticism from funding agencies like the National Endowment for the Humanities that language classes lack intellectual content. It is also a response to the current national and international interest in the cultural component of language teaching (Krueger and Ryan 1993). Languages-across-the-curriculum initiatives are but one variant of CBI. Although the term 'content-based instruction' has generated innovative thinking in the teaching of foreign languages, it runs the risk of reinforcing the skill vs. content distinction in language teaching and of upholding the illusion of the transparency of language.

'Task-based instruction' claims to replace methods and approaches by learner-centered tasks. It is characterized by its local treatment of local problems through local solutions (for example, Nunan 1989). In its educational philosophy it is as different from, say, German educational philosophy as American engineering is different from German engineering.

'Strategy-based instruction' activates procedural knowledge. It too focuses on local problem-solving, not on contemplation or reflection (for example, Oxford 1990). It can be contrasted with the emphasis on declarative knowledge in foreign language education in France, and the emphasis on hermeneutic understanding in some foreign language instructional approaches in Germany (for example, Krusche 1985; Hunfeld 1990).

Inasmuch as content-based, task-based, and strategy-based

approaches separate skill and informational content, and stress tactics and strategies for information retrieval and processing, they bear the mark of the growing influence on education of the discourse of the cognitive and computer sciences. Inasmuch as they stress professionalism, i.e. procedure, they reflect the influence of ELT on the teaching of all foreign languages. As Phillipson remarks, 'anglocentricity and professionalism . . . disconnect culture from structure by limiting the focus in language pedagogy to technical matters, that is, language and education in a narrow sense, to the exclusion of social, economic, and political matters' (Phillipson 1992: 48).

A problem of mediation

The domain-specific discourses about goals and approaches in foreign language education represent as many different domains of knowledge, each with their own mode of representation, their own power structures, and claims to legitimacy. As long as researchers and teachers talk only to members of their own discourse community, breakdowns in communication are minimized. But more often than not, they have to mediate between multiple audiences. Applied linguists have to mediate between the everyday language users whom they observe and record, the community of scholars for whom they analyze and interpret these observations, and the language teachers together with whom they want to influence instructional practice. Language teachers, in turn, have to act as mediators between the researchers, the politicians, and the language learners. The problem is then not only a problem of discourse specificity, but a problem of mediation between different discourse communities. This mediatory process is at its most visible where the discourse of applied linguistics intersects with the dominant discourse of political, professional, and commercial ideology.

Applied linguistics and political ideology

In their efforts to 'domesticate the strange', applied linguists like any other researchers use the metaphors of politically dominant discourse communities. Gregg, for example, has noted how Krashen's *affective filter* and *acquisition* metaphors echo and reinforce a certain anti-intellectualism prevalent among US American language teachers, thus accounting for much of Krashen's impact on foreign language education in the US (Gregg 1984). Similarly, one cannot but notice that other phrases from second language acquisition research, like *learners' needs, individual differences, individual variability, natural order,* echoed later by the discourse of methodologists (*natural* approach, *learner-centered* instruction), happen to fit nicely into a certain dominant democratic discourse that values learner autonomy and self-reliance, and views with distrust any artificial manipulation of a learner's interlanguage by social or political forces. This distrust of political manipulation can be interpreted as evidence of the pluralistic belief that everyone should be taught according to his or her particular needs and be expected to perform according to his or her ability. One could argue that this is the old nature vs. nurture debate or the free market ideology at work in language education.

Lest these associations of applied linguistics with political ideology be considered outrageously far-fetched, let me just mention the virulent debates that took place in Germany in the mid-eighties between the educationalists and the naturalists in second language acquisition. Between the applied linguists in language teaching and learning research or 'Sprachlehr-und lernforschung' represented by Bausch and Koenigs (1983) and those in second language acquisition research or 'Zweitspracherwerbsforschung' represented by Felix (1978), and Clahsen, Meisel, and Pienemann (1983), the battle raged over who had what to say about language instruction in schools. What was at stake was not so much which theory of language learning, one more interactionist, one more innatist, was the better one, but rather, what political discourses they were implicitly serving, and what professional implications these discourses had for practitioners in the field.

Applied linguistics and professionalism

Phillipson (1992) describes the encroachment of ELT professional talk into all areas of language teaching. Indeed, in order to be listened to and be viewed as academically legitimate, foreign language educators often borrow the metaphors of psycho- and sociolinguistics and re-index them to fit their own discourse community. For example, the term 'communicative competence', originally coined by Hymes (1972) in contradistinction to Chomsky's notion of 'competence', was defined by Gumperz in sociological terms as 'the ability to select, from the totality of grammatically correct expressions available to [the speaker], forms which appropriately reflect the social norms governing behavior in specific encounters' (Gumperz 1972: 205). The concept was redefined in social interactional terms by applied linguist Savignon as 'the expression, interpretation, and negotiation of meaning involving interaction between two or more persons belonging to the same (or different) speech community (communities)' (Savignon 1983: 303). In contrast, the linguist and foreign language educator Terrell defined 'communicative competence' in individual, albeit interlocutor-directed, terms to mean 'that a student can understand the essential points of what a native speaker says to him in a real communication situation and can respond in such a way that the native speaker interprets the response with little or no effort and without errors that are so distracting that they interfere drastically with communication' (Terrell 1977: 326). Finally, with methodologist Omaggio, the term has come to denote an individual's linguistic ability to 'handle everyday social encounters . . . with some degree of appropriateness' and to 'hold up [one's] own end of the conversation by making inquiries and offering more elaborate responses' (Omaggio 1986: 16). Within a competitive educational system that has to assess and reward individual performance, communicative competence has been re-indexed to become synonymous with 'proficiency'. Thus, different political and professional agendas, born from different historical conditions, make communication between researchers and practitioners treacherous. We observe the same phenomenon happening at the boundary between foreign language education and political/commercial discourse.

Foreign language education and political/commercial discourse

In the United States, because foreign languages have traditionally had low priority on the national educational agenda, competition for visibility and funds is more acute than in other fields. Because foreign language education has had to stay close to the sources of economic power for support and funding, it has often had to adopt the discourse of the funding source; and this, in turn, has affected the educational

[51]

discourse about goals and approaches in the field. For example, as the term *proficiency-based instruction* fell into disfavor in the early nineties because it was perceived by taxpayers as serving the monopolistic special interests of the American Council on the Teaching of Foreign Languages (ACTFL), applications for grants from Washington now have to use other hyphenated adjectives like *competency-based*, or *performance-based*, to get funded.

The co-opting by textbook authors and publishers of the discourse of scientific investigation further muddles the mediation by applied linguists of the results of their research. For example, the notion of learning strategy first observed as a cognitive *process* by psycholinguists (Færch and Kasper 1980) quickly became the latest instructional *product* to be *delivered* by teachers and textbooks (Oxford 1990).

In sum: cross-disciplinary excursions on the part of both applied linguists and language teachers have opened to them domain-specific discourse forms that expand their thinking about their respective fields and enable them to reach larger audiences. But at the same time, reaching larger audiences entails a mediation through language that creates its own discourse problems. For language not only reflects the interests and biases of the discourse community which generated it, but creates and perpetuates them as well.

The deep structure of the discourse problem

I would like to examine, on the example of one particular metaphor, how language came to shape the consciousness of applied linguists and language teachers and the way they talk with or past one another.

In the early sixties, when applied linguists abandoned the stimulus–response metaphor of experimental psychology to describe the language learning process, the one they chose instead was taken from electrical engineering, and from its later incarnation, electronic information-processing: input – black box – output. The term *input*, which served to name originally the electric wire that went into the black bakelite fuse box, and later by metonymy the current itself, became a metaphor for the language to be learned.

Note that, seen in retrospect, other metaphors might have been chosen to describe the process of language learning: electromagnetism, for example, where the introduction of one foreign body reconfigures the whole electromagnetic field; biology, where organic growth shapes physical contexts; sociology, where verbal rituals reframe interactional contexts. But these were not the metaphors that were to dominate the fields of applied linguistics and language teaching for forty years. The choice of the *input* metaphor at a time when electrical engineering was the upcoming prestigious field in the physical sciences ensured applied linguistic research respectability and funding. It was going to have a substantial impact on the teaching and learning of foreign languages, because it matched the traditional discourse of education as the *delivery* of knowledge.

Once the language to be learned had been identified as *input*, the notion of input itself became an object of research in need of further refinement through words. This refinement was made possible through what Hayden White calls 'tropological restructuration' (1978: 6).

When applied linguistics adopted the input metaphor for language learning, it used heavily the tropes of metonymy and synecdoche to construct its object of research. First, by metonymic reduction, it moved from an abstract entity called language or information flow to a tangible, concrete reality called input, which it could then endow with causal attributes (for example, 'input as condition for language learning') and with agency ('teacher input', 'native speaker input'). This metonymic shift allowed applied linguists to ask researchable questions such as: What is the *nature* of the input? How does it contrast with *intake*? Does it need *output* to be effective? What is the role of input vs. *interaction* in acquisition? How can teachers and learners *adjust, modify, simplify, reduce, clarify* this input to make it *comprehensible* and ultimately make it fit to be *acquired*?

But because the input metaphor had metonymically reduced the field of research to that aspect of language that supposedly *went in*, it was only a matter of time before researchers would ask the question: What *counts as* input? This question has spawned a fruitful area of inquiry, and the proliferation of other metaphors, taken from psychology, sociology, or education: *saliency, attention, awareness, consciousness.*

The question 'what counts as input?' was justified because, at the same time as metonymy played its role in anchoring the input metaphor into the concrete realities of research projects and experimental designs, the other trope of discourse, synecdoche, ensured that it expanded well beyond its original confines. In this discourse

[53]

movement from the part to the whole, from the particular to the general, input came to be viewed as anything in the teaching and learning environment that might affect the acquisition of a foreign language: bystanders and eavesdroppers, turns-at-talk, routines and speech act realizations, mental representations and cultural assumptions were all co-opted into an input–output model of language acquisition. This model in turn inevitably affected the questions asked and the answers provided by research.

All happened as if the input metaphor had had to restrict the vast context of *language* to make it apprehensible, but now the metaphor had acquired a life of its own and was creating a new context of which researchers had great difficulty freeing themselves. Thus, for example, the acquisition of cultural competence or of foreign discourse competence never did fit into an input–output model of language acquisition and so has not really been tackled yet by second language acquisition research.

The input metaphor is by now all the more difficult to shed as it has long since found a fertile ground in foreign language education circles, which have their own metonymic reductions and synecdochic expansion practices. For the notion of input at educational institutions gets mingled with questions of academic legitimation and institutional entitlement, intellectual power and the politics of knowledge. As the applied linguistic notion of input entered the schools, it was made to reinforce the mode of consciousness through which administrators and language teachers ask the questions relevant to their own discourse community.

For example: in the academic discourse community, the question is not 'what kind of language input is most effective?', but 'what kind of input is academically legitimate?'. Vernacular orality is still viewed as inferior to, because much less controllable than, academic literacy. Similarly, the question is not 'who is best qualified to deliver this input?', but 'who is entitled to do so?'—native speakers? non-native speakers? Moreover, schools have always reluctantly given academic credit for knowledge that could as well be acquired on the street, such as the non-schooled, or 'authentic', uses of language. Hence, the acquisition vs. learning dichotomy advocated by Stephen Krashen cuts at the heart of academic legitimation. Finally, the input metaphor reinforces the traditional dichotomy in academia between those who explore the nature of the input (researchers and scholars), and those who mediate it (teachers). As we know, delivery and mediation have never been as highly valued in academia as discovery and exegesis. Mediation is viewed with suspicion because it is more difficult to evaluate, assess, and control.

In sum: by passing from the physical sciences to the language sciences and from the language sciences to the science of education, the *input* metaphor has shaped discourse realities for people who, although they might use the same words, end up meaning different things by these words. What has been missing in each of these transmutations is the fourth trope of discourse, the one that Hayden White identifies, besides metaphor, metonymy, and synecdoche, as the only guarantee of social change. That is *irony*, by which he means the rhetorical movement where language itself becomes an object of reflection and where 'the sensed inadequacy of language to the full representation of its object becomes perceived as a problem' (1978: 207). Through irony, one comes to understand that the notion of input is itself determined by larger social and political forces of which it is in fact the output. Irony can help applied linguists and language teachers to situate themselves and the discourses they use within their respective historic and social contexts and to start questioning these contexts. In fact, current challenges to the input metaphor in language learning all use some form of irony (see, for example, Fairclough 1989; Pennycook 1990).

Irony is, of course, a 'third place' which enables one to see both subject positions, one's own and that of the other, from the inside and the outside in a dialectical relationship (Kramsch 1993b). It is a view from the margins: for example, it is the perspective of a L3 speaker teaching a L2 to speakers of L1; or it is a cultural studies vantage point on both applied linguistics and foreign language teaching; or an educator's stance with respect to both the theory and the practice of language teaching. Such off-center subject positions are to be sought and cherished, for they alone can provide the distance and the freedom necessary to look at and through the various discourses used by various audiences. These are not, to be sure, comfortable positions. On the contrary, as Edward Said wrote recently (1994), they entail 'constantly being unsettled, and unsettling others'. But such is, Said argues, the inevitable condition of the intellectual.

[55]

Conclusion

Applied linguists and language teachers are more interested than ever in talking to one another as they both have to mediate between different discourse constituencies. The current proliferation of metaphors related to language learning and teaching, caused by the growth in the multidisciplinary interests of researchers and practitioners alike, is a source of unprecedented intellectual stimulation. However, this expansion urgently calls for increased irony and ethical judgement in discourse, as the currently prevalent metaphors might not be the only ones we wish to live by.

In Foucault's terms (1970), applied linguists invent their domain of inquiry as much as they investigate it. So do language teachers with the way they (re)present the field of language learning to their students and to the public at large. As we have seen, several factors make true intellectual dialogue between them difficult: the necessities of overspecialization, the cult of the expert, the current passion for professionalism, the pressures of commercial and political ideologies. Applied linguists and language teachers can understand one another not so much by informing one another of the results of their expert research, or of their professional teaching practices, but by engaging together in an intellectual exploration of the historical and social forces that have shaped their respective discourses. Ultimately, what is important for each to understand is not the different answers they give but the different questions they ask.

Notes

1 This is a revised version of a keynote address delivered at the XIX Annual Congress of the Applied Linguistics Association of Australia, Melbourne, 15 July 1994.

2 I will refer throughout to 'foreign language teachers'. I have in mind mostly teachers who teach foreign languages as part of a general education curriculum, rather than adult education or foreign language instruction for special purposes.

4

Concept and conduct in language pedagogy

N. S. PRABHU

THIS PAPER IS an attempt to identify the different kinds of thought and action that play a role in language teaching theory and practice. It may be regarded as yet another discussion of theory–practice relationships in the field but my aim here is not to propose or argue for one kind of relationship in preference to another, but rather to try to understand what may be called the composition of the theory–practice enterprise—to divide it into its component parts and to see how the parts are interrelated. I identify four main components, two in the general area of concepts or theory and two in the area of pedagogic conduct or practice.

The ideational component

I would like to refer to the first component as 'ideational'. It consists essentially of ideas or concepts about what constitutes knowledge of a language and what the process of learning a language consists of. It involves, that is to say, a conceptualization of what it is that enables a person to use a language and how it is that a person develops that ability—a mental picture, or ideation, of language competence and language learning. The ideation may, of course, include a division of language competence into different parts or aspects, or a perception of incomplete levels of competence; and it may include perceptions of different factors or conditions that play a role in the process of learning. Equally, the ideation of second language competence and second language learning may be similar to or distinct from that of first language competence and learning, in varying degrees. The point being made here is simply that such ideation, in whatever specific form, constitutes a major component of language pedagogy. It is, as I see it, the essential content of the term 'understanding': we can be said to have an understanding of some phenomenon when we have a sufficiently well-formed, and sufficiently satisfying, mental image of its content or process. Consequently, language teaching without an ideational component would be a purely mechanical activity, unrelated to any understanding.

Let me give a few examples of what I mean by ideation. It is possible to think of a language as a large set of words and variously sized expressions, more or less rigidly constructed. It is also possible to think of a learner's mind as receiving, perhaps repeatedly, a steadily increasing number of these words and expressions, and storing them such that they are generally available for recall at will, given an appropriate stimulus. This is how we are likely to think of people's knowledge of the names of the persons and places they know, and it would only be an extension of that concept to something much larger in size but perceived to be similar in nature to think of the knowledge and learning of a language in that way. One would think of names being stored and recalled in association with the faces or features of the persons and places concerned and, indeed, of such association being a contributory or causative factor in the process; and one can similarly think of the meanings or contexts of words and expressions playing a contributory or causative role. One can also think of different people achieving different degrees of accuracy or efficiency in the storing and recalling of names or language forms, or of the same person achieving successively higher levels of accuracy, thus accounting for learners' errors and learning progress.

A related, but different, picture would be that language competence is a form of patterned behaviour—not knowledge as stored material, but knowledge as ingrained habit, a kind of neuro-muscular inscription, developed through a procedure of imitation and repeated rehearsal. This would be an extension of the way we think of various kinds of socio-cultural behaviour, such as table manners or routines at a place of worship; or the way we think of such skills as driving, horse-riding, or playing tennis. Learning consists essentially of replicating the knower's behaviour—of acting as if one knows—and achieving different degrees of accuracy or approximation at different times.

An alternative conception of language use is that it is rule-governed construction; not a reproduction of stored expressions or habitual actions, but the creation of expressions in accordance with a set of rules. Knowing a language is having the relevant set of rules represented in the mind, and learning a language is forming that mental representation. The actual expressions of the language, or patterns of language behaviour, have at best the role of facilitating the mental rule formation, in the case of a learner, and of manifesting the rule system formed, in the case of a user.

This concept can lead to two different ideations of language learning. In the first, one sees the rules represented in the user's mind (hence, the rules to be formed in the learner's mind) as having essentially the same form as the rules formulated by linguists, in terms of the relevant units, relations, constraints, etc. Seeing such isomorphism between the two involves crediting the linguist's rules with a substantial degree of psychological reality (as distinct from logical validity), but if one does see such isomorphism, one can then perceive the process of rule formation in the learner's mind as a matter of receiving the formulated rules (from a teacher or a book), retaining them in the mind (as some form of cognitive representation) and bringing them into operation at will, given the relevant stimulus. This is perhaps the way we would think of arithmetical ability or knowledge, where the rules learnt or used are more obviously of the same form as the rules formulated in the development or explication of arithmetic.

In the second possible ideation, one does not assume any isomorphism between the linguist's rules and the rules in the mind. The linguist's rules are only logical constructs, testable in terms of whether their consequences (namely, the well-formedness of the expressions they yield) match those of the mental rules. There is no psychological modelling involved, and the linguist's rules can only provide a rational understanding of what the mental rules have to do, not of what the rules themselves are like and how they do what they do. There is therefore no perception of the learner's mind receiving the rules formulated by the linguist; instead, the learner's mind is seen to formulate or create whatever rules are involved for itself from the language forms it encounters—or rather, to re-create them, since different users of a language are perceived to possess the same (or almost the same) set of mental rules, and different learners therefore to be creating the same set of rules. The only things the learner's mind receives are the actual expressions of the language, from which it re-creates or abstracts the rules, along with the meanings, contexts, etc., of those forms which can facilitate the rule abstraction.

There can of course be other forms of ideation arising from the concept of rule formation in the learner's mind, partially overlapping with the two just outlined. One can, for instance, assume an isomorphism between mental rules and the linguist's rules but nevertheless think of the learner's mind abstracting/re-creating the rules directly from language forms. This rules out the learner's mind receiving the linguist's rules but perceives facilitative value to language forms being pre-arranged in accordance with the linguist's rules for the learner's mind to abstract rules from. Or, perhaps, one can see non-isomorphism between mental rules and the linguist's rules and yet perceive value to the learner's mind receiving the linguist's rules, as some form of facilitative support to the process of abstracting (perhaps quite different) rules.

As these examples show, ideation is essentially the formation of a mental image, a conceptual model or a theory, about some phenomenon. The image one forms is typically a metaphorical or analogical extension of some other image arising from one's experience of some other phenomenon, or a sympathetic response to someone else's image of the same phenomenon. The latter is what is often thought of as receiving or adopting theories from 'feeder' disciplines, such as linguistics, psychology, or sociology, in the case of language pedagogy. However, although I think it entirely legitimate, and potentially beneficial, for language pedagogy to receive or adopt theories from such feeder disciplines, just as it is for any discipline to receive or adopt concepts from any other, I do not think the ideational component of language pedagogy is merely a site for theories developed in linguistics, psychology, or sociology. It is at most what I am referring to as a 'sympathetic response' to theories in those disciplines, and I believe the basis of the sympathetic response lies in pedagogic experience and reflection, not in the forms of argument employed in the feeder disciplines themselves, as will be seen below.

[60]

N. S. PRABHU

The operational component

The second component, which I will refer to as 'operational', has to do with pedagogic action or practice. It does not, however, embrace all the practical decisions and actions called for in teaching, but only those that relate to, and interact with, the ideational component. There is, as I see it, a two-way relationship between ideation and operation. On the one hand, teaching is an operationalization of some concept of the learning process and learning outcome: one is asking what form of classroom activity might be most consistent with, contributory to, or essential for, the learning process and outcome envisaged. On the other hand, teaching is also a source of experiential knowledge in pedagogy, knowledge which can stimulate or influence particular ideations of the learning process and learning outcome: one can be asking what conceptualization of the learning process or outcome is most consistent with or explanatory of the evidence arising from classroom activity. Teaching is thus not only a matter of translating learning theory into teaching action; it is also a matter of using teaching action as a source of knowledge with which to confirm, disconfirm, or help develop learning theory.

It is common to think of the translation of learning theory into teaching action as a rational, or commonsensical, procedure, based on what looks like a reasonable match between particular concepts of learning and particular types of classroom activity. It is also common to think of learning theory being supported or validated by some form of objective evidence of learning, resulting from relevant teaching action. Both these notions, however, run into problems. It is, on the one hand, difficult to establish any one-to-one correspondence, on rational or commonsensical grounds, between specific types of classroom activity and specific concepts of what learning they promote. Thus, the type of activity called 'practice', involving a planned encounter for the learner with a large set of language expressions all similar in form, can be variously thought of as enlarging the store of language expressions in the learner's mind, or establishing the shared form of the expressions concerned as a behavioural habit, or facilitating a process of rule abstraction by the learner. Explicit attention to grammatical rules, which is another type of classroom activity, can be seen to be leading directly to a mental representation of those rules as competence, or building up a store of such rules in memory for exclusive use in self-correction, or to be creating a general condition of rule awareness which facilitates the learner's perception/re-creation of other, unspecified, rules. The learner's engagement in meaning-exchange with an incidental encounter with language expressions, which is yet another type of classroom activity, can be viewed as providing a favourable condition for rule creation by the learner or the reception and storage of the expressions themselves in memory. The employment of both meaning-exchange activity and explicit grammar activity, alternately, in the classroom is consistent with both the concept of the learner developing two different forms of knowledge, for two different uses, and the concept of two different mind-sets of the learner together promoting the same form of knowledge. It is even more difficult, on the other hand, to capture evidence of learning in some objective way, and to establish cause–effect relationships between specific teaching activities and specific learning outcomes. When a learning outcome does emerge, it can still be viewed either as having been caused directly by the teaching activity concerned, or as having been only stimulated or facilitated by it, or as having emerged entirely from other factors, in spite of, rather than because of, the teaching activity in question.

Such difficulties arise because of a fundamental difference between teaching and learning: teaching is a physical activity which can be planned, observed, and controlled, as it takes place, in some explicit, objective way; learning is a mental process which cannot be observed, controlled, or even detected, as it takes place, in any objective way. It is therefore quite unreasonable to expect to establish explicit, objective correspondences, either between concepts of the learning process and types of teaching activity, or between types of teaching activity and the actual process of learning. Attempts to establish such objective correspondences can be said to represent an adoption of the modes of enquiry followed in the 'feeder' disciplines, just as learning theories themselves are often seen to be adopted from those disciplines. If, however, such modes of enquiry are unfeasible in pedagogy, as I have argued, because of the essential nature of learning, we need to ask what other modes might be available in pedagogy for interrelating concepts of learning and types of classroom activity. I believe that the answer lies in the nature of the teacher's classroom experience and the personal, subjective perceptions arising from it.

Teachers in classrooms are not only carrying out the activities they have planned but are interacting with learners in the process, in both overt and covert ways, by both verbal and non-verbal means. They perceive, interpret, and respond to a variety of signals from different learners, indicative of attitudes, states of mind, intentions, judgements, etc. At least some of these signals are likely to be indicative of (or interpretable in terms of) success, failure, or difficulty in learning, at particular moments. All such perceptions are necessarily subjective, since only the overt and verbal signals are open to external observation and even they are multiply interpretable. Nevertheless, the learning that takes place in the classroom takes place in the presence of the teacher, in the course of the teacher's complex interaction with learners, repeatedly, over a long stretch of time. The teacher is in this sense continually present where the mental process of learning is taking place, continually involved in activities in the course of which it is taking place, and continually receiving and responding to indications from learners in whom it is taking place. The teacher can thus be said to be in contact with the ongoing process of learning, in a way that no one else can be or at least far more than anyone else can be. If the actual process of learning can be noticed, or sensed, to any extent by anyone at all, it is the teacher who is likely to be able to do so, and even the teacher is likely to develop the ability only gradually over time, with many errors along the way, without much conscious awareness of it, and with a continuing tentativeness and uncertainty about it. This gradual development of a teacher's feel for learning is an important part of what is commonly called classroom experience, and the part most relevant to what I am calling the operational component. It is subjective, inexplicit, perhaps unavailable for explicit formulation, less than certain at any given point and generally in an indeterminate state. But that does not mean that it does not exist or operate. It is a form of practitioner's knowledge, as distinct from specialist's knowledge, comparable to what one finds in medical practice. A medical practitioner is, at one level, applying the specialist knowledge received in his or her training, doing the diagnosis and treatment as suggested by it. At another level, however, a medical practitioner develops, as a result of recurrent treatment of patients over a length of time, something of an intuitive sense for different ailments and conditions of ill-health, which goes beyond or diverges from specialist knowledge but is real enough in its operation and of value in the treatment of patients. That intuitive sense, too, is subjective, inexplicit, and indeterminate.

I am not of course suggesting that all teachers develop the feel for learning I have described, much less that all teachers who have taught over a stretch of time possess it in equal measure. There are no doubt many teachers who carry out their work in the way expected of them, without an engagement of their own intuitive sense for learning—work which, for that reason, can be called mechanical. There is, however, the possibility in all cases of an intuitive sense developing in the course of practice, as a result of being in continual contact with the actual phenomenon of learning. More importantly, when an intuitive sense has arisen and is operative, it can be expected to interact continually with the ideational component of pedagogy, influencing it in various ways, attaching different values to alternative conceptualizations or to different parts of a given conceptualization, thus selecting, rejecting, or reshaping the concepts concerned. Further, such interaction is likely to be an ongoing process, rather than a one-time event, with each reshaped ideation interacting with the further feel for learning arising from further teaching, and being further reshaped as a result. A teacher's ideation about the learning process and his or her feel for learning are neither determinate nor permanent; indeed, their value lies, I think, in their continued openness to change, since they can be engaged in the daily act of teaching only to the extent they are active or 'alive', and what is active or alive is necessarily open to change or growth. We can refer to a given teacher's ideation of the learning process, resulting from an interaction with his or her feel for learning, at a given time, as that teacher's sense of plausibility about teaching and learning, representing what he or she 'believes', or most identifies with, at that time. If one thinks, as I do, that pedagogy cannot be a matter of discovering and conducting in the classroom a set of physical procedures carrying a guarantee, or assurance, of learning outcomes—if, that is to say, one sees little value in mechanical teaching—it seems to me to follow that teaching can be of value only when the teacher's sense of plausibility is active and engaged. One can also say that a teacher is likely to be able to enhance learning to the extent he or she has developed a feel for learning and has a way of keeping that feel alive through its interaction with ideation—to the extent, that is to say, he or she is operating with a sense of plausibility. It is then possible to suggest that learning outcomes depend on an active engagement of the teacher's sense of plausibility, rather than on the actual content of the ideation involved—that is to say, that it does not really matter which particular ideation or theory of learning guides the teaching, as long as that particular theory is in fact what constitutes the teacher's sense of plausibility at that time. The value of an ideation does not lie in its intrinsic truth, whatever that may mean, but in its ability to interact productively with a given teacher's classroom experience and to help develop and keep alive his or her sense of plausibility.

The ideological component

I am calling the third component 'ideological'. It has to do with concepts, like the ideational component, but is different from it in that it centrally involves the pursuit of an ideal—a desire to change, maintain, or resist the order of the world, in some way, through the practice of pedagogy. The ideational component is concerned centrally with ideas which help to make sense of the phenomenon of learning and the experience of teaching; what ideal it has, in the form of a wish to promote learning in learners, is integral to the effort to make sense, as both its motive and its result. The ideological component, in contrast, involves ideals which, while being pursued through pedagogic activity, go beyond, or fall outside, the direct pedagogic aim of understanding and facilitating learning.

Language pedagogy necessarily includes an ideological component because language is not just a mental system, store, or capacity but a means of exchanging meaning and messages about the world outside, and language teaching necessarily involves such exchange of meanings and messages in the classroom. Language teaching, that is to say, has to employ subject content of some kind, and subject content typically consists of views of the world or of world orders, hence ideology of some kind. Further, language also tends to carry traces, in its internal system, of the views of the world it has been employed to express in the past, thus reflecting or perpetuating elements of past ideologies. Besides, views of the world include views of particular languages as well, with various positive or negative values (that is to say, manifestations of ideology) attached to them. Ideology thus becomes a part of language pedagogy simply because language is bound up with ideology.

[65]

Ideology also becomes a part of language pedagogy because teachers and learners are not just teaching and learning organisms, but individuals who function within a social system and are therefore a part of the ideologies expressed by that social system. They can also, of course, have their own views of existing or desirable world orders, influencing their pedagogic practice in some way. Indeed, teachers can be said to constitute a social class by themselves as teachers, and learners a social class by themselves as learners, so that the power relation between the two can be viewed as an expression of ideology. Beyond this, there are ideologies expressed by the institutional goals and internal structures of the schools in which teachers and learners engage in their work, as well as the ideologies being pursued by larger educational systems and the state (in forms such as language planning or workforce planning), together with different counter-ideologies provoked by them.

There is, in addition, a strong commercial ideology operating in language pedagogy, thanks to the scale of the language teaching enterprise in the modern world, in particular the scale of English language teaching. There is a vast market for books and other forms of teaching material, opportunities of employment as teachers and teaching experts, and possibilities of selling language instruction at a profit. This inevitably brings into play the familiar forces of commercialism and consumerism, sometimes overriding considerations in other components of language pedagogy.

A very different form of ideology arises from the widely prevalent perception that theories about the nature of language and language learning are provided for language pedagogy by other, 'feeder' disciplines such as linguistics or psychology. This perception leads to periodical attempts to bring language pedagogy in line with this or that theory in linguistics, psychology, or sociology, either as a way of gaining theoretical status (or respectability) for pedagogic practice or as a means of enhancing the claims of the theories concerned within those feeder disciplines. The theories themselves can no doubt be viewed as being ideational in nature, rather than ideological, within their respective disciplines, being attempts to make sense of phenomena according to their own modes of enquiry; but their use of language pedagogy to propagate themselves or to gain dominance, sometimes by giving themselves attributes like truth, authenticity, or a knowledge of 'real'

language for the purpose, makes them a matter of ideology in pedagogy, not unlike commercial ideology.

The point I am making about these different forms of ideology is not
that they are irrelevant to the language teaching enterprise or that they
are necessarily harmful. On the contrary, I think that they are necessarily a part of the enterprise, given that language is, among other
things, a social entity, that teachers and learners are constituents of
social orders, that teaching needs to be carried out in institutions, that
classroom activities need the support of books, and that language
pedagogy would only be impoverishing itself by shutting out ideas and
theories developed in other disciplines. Besides, even an attempt to
counter the influence of some of the ideologies (or what are seen to be
their excesses) will constitute a form of counter-ideology, thus constituting a part of the ideological component. I do wish to make the point,
however, that the ideological component is distinct from the ideational
one, and that it is important to bear the distinction in mind.

The managerial component

I am calling the fourth and final component 'managerial', referring
thereby to the making of practical decisions of various kinds in the
planning and conduct of teaching, both at the individual teacher's level
and at the institutional level. Individual teachers have to cope with
multiple demands on the teaching they do, such as those of their own
current sense of plausibility, those of their learners' expectations, those
of the school's expectations, etc., as well as those related to their sense
of security, their self-image, their career aspirations, etc., making and
remaking decisions that reconcile these demands as well as possible. In
addition, they need to reconcile their teaching preferences with the
time available, the resources available, the classroom logistics possible, and contingencies of various kinds. At the institutional level,
there are decisions to be made about the goals of teaching at different stages, choice of the methods or procedures to recommend or
require, forms of material to be provided, expectations of learners'
progress, modes of assessment, etc., all of them being at best accom-
modations or reconciliations of conflicting demands—attempts at
a measure of uniformity despite differences, displays of certainty
through a suppression of uncertainty, and various measures of risk

reduction. There are also balances to be struck, or compromises to be made, between what is seen to be desirable and what is likely to be feasible, between estimated costs and probable benefits, between educational value and institutional acceptability, all in the hope of arriving at optimal overall results. While the ideational and operational components are concerned with mental activity which is by nature in an uncertain, changing state, and the ideological component is marked by relative certainties about different goals, the managerial component is concerned with deciding on action despite those uncertainties, conflicting over-certainties, and many kinds of limit on possible action.

General comments on the frame

I have now stated what I regard as the four components of language pedagogy. Although two of them have to do with concepts, or theories, I consider it important to distinguish between the two, rather than to see them as the same general area of theory. The ideational component consists of pedagogic perceptions of language ability and language learning, by which I mean perceptions shaped and supported by pedagogic experience, not perceptions recommended for use in pedagogy. The ideological component, in contrast, consists of a variety of non-pedagogic perceptions (in the sense of 'pedagogic' just indicated) which nevertheless play a role in the practice of pedagogy, influencing it in various ways. I have also divided what is often regarded as the general area of practical decisions in pedagogy into two distinct components. The operational component is related directly to the engagement and emergence of pedagogic perceptions, that is to say, to the teacher's classroom decisions and reflections acting as a source of knowledge, thought, and professional growth. The managerial component, on the other hand, consists of decision-making of various other kinds, not motivated by pedagogic perceptions or their operation in the act of teaching, but very necessary in other ways for the act of teaching to take place, especially in institutional settings.

We can also look at the distinction between the ideational and operational components, on the one hand, and the ideological and managerial components on the other. It will be noticed that the ideational and operational components have as their focus the individual teacher engaged in the act of teaching and, further, that they focus on the act of teaching and the teacher's mind only in so far as they relate to an understanding and promotion of learning. The ideological and managerial components, in contrast, have teaching as an institutional activity as their focus, including those aspects of an individual teacher's teaching which result from or reflect the fact that the teaching is part of an institutional activity. Ideology becomes relevant because the individual teacher's teaching is apt to be influenced by or have an influence on institutional, social, political, or disciplinary goals and their complex workings; and managerial decisions become relevant because teaching simply cannot be carried out as an institutional activity without them.

This distinction between teaching as an individual activity and teaching as an institutional activity points to some interesting features of the language teaching enterprise. Notice, first, that specialist-level discussion of language pedagogy (in professional conferences and journals, for example) is largely preoccupied with theories about language and learning, and their consequences or applications in classroom teaching, that is to say, with the ideational and operational components (though not quite in the sense I have outlined them above). Teachers, schools, and educational administrators, on the other hand, are preoccupied much of the time with practical decision-making of various kinds and with furthering their institutional goals, that is to say, with ideological and managerial components. This may well be one reason why specialist-level professionals and the actual people involved in the profession frequently find it difficult to communicate or interact with each other, or even find each other incomprehensible or irrelevant.

Secondly, the term 'method' can be taken to refer either to the individual teacher's teaching activity (as envisaged in the operational component) or to teaching as an institutional activity (as resulting from the managerial component). It seems to me that, when attempts are made to assess, rigorously, the effectiveness of particular methods, what one sets out to assess (and believes one is assessing) is a method in the sense of the operational component (the translation of a theory of learning into pedagogic activity) but what one actually assesses is a method in the sense of the managerial component (the result of varied practical decisions in an institutional setting). It is also very likely that

[69]

what are clearly distinct methods in the operational component (distinct forms of teaching relatable to distinct ideations of learning) tend to converge and become less distinct from each other when influenced by the managerial component, since they all have to meet the same demands of the institutional setting concerned. This may well be a major reason (apart from the problem of objectivity noted earlier) why method-assessment and method-comparison studies seldom yield clear results and why one can seldom find a method being implemented in classrooms in its 'pure' (ideational-operational) form.

Thirdly, although the four components are all parts of the language teaching enterprise, it is possible to give different priorities to teaching as an individual activity and teaching as an institutional activity, depending on how much value one attaches to each. If one gives a higher priority to teaching as an institutional activity, perhaps regarding it as a minimal requirement for teaching to take place at all on the scale needed, one is then likely to accommodate the perception of teaching as an individual activity only to the extent possible without unsettling the institutional process. If, on the other hand, one gives a higher priority to teaching as an individual activity, regarding it as the main source of learning outcomes and teachers' professional growth, one is likely to try to see in what ways the demands of institutional teaching can be met with a minimum of sacrifice on the value of individual teaching. The two approaches can lead to different forms of teaching, each (claiming to be) workable in classrooms but each attempting to move in a direction opposite to the other's.

It may also be of some value to see particular proposals in language pedagogy as arising from (or located in) one or another of these four components, or from a source outside of the four. Pedagogic proposals can arise from classroom experience and reflection on it, from a wish to pursue some social/institutional ideal through the practice of pedagogy, from experience in making managerial decisions and a wish to ease the difficulty of such decisions, or from the espousal of a theory in some other discipline. Similarly, professional discussion of pedagogy can be seen to be dominated, at different times or in different places, by concerns having to do with one or another of the different components. Indeed, different specialists in the field can be regarded as being occupied primarily with different components, thus talking at cross-purposes at times in professional debate. Although seeing specialists and their arguments in terms of these different components will not by itself result in any resolution of conflicts in the debate, it can at least help to clarify the conflicts and provide a greater understanding of their nature.

5

Appraising second language acquisition theory in relation to language pedagogy

ROD ELLIS

Introduction

SINCE THE INCEPTION of second language acquisition (SLA) as an identifiable area of enquiry in the late 1960s, there has been no shortage of theories to explain how people acquire a second language (L2). In the eyes of some, there have been too many theories. As early as 1979 Schouten complained that 'in second language learning, too many models have been built and taken for granted too soon, and this has stifled relevant research' (1979: 4). Since then theories have continued to be spawned, for, as Spolsky (1990: 609) notes, 'new theories do not generally succeed in replacing their predecessors, but continue to coexist with them uncomfortably.' For some, like Schouten, the multiplicity of theories is problematic, indicative of the immaturity of the field. Long (1993) has suggested that in cases where theories are in clear opposition, 'culling' needs to take place. He points out that the history of science shows that successful sciences are those that are guided by a 'dominant theory'.

However, although it is probably true that no single theory currently dominates in SLA, some theories have clearly attracted greater followings than others. In Ellis (1985) I considered seven theories, McLaughlin (1987) examined five, and Larsen-Freeman and Long (1991) also examined five, although not the same as McLaughlin's. Only three theories are common to these three reviews: Krashen's Monitor Model, Schumann's Acculturation Theory, and Universal

Grammar. It is pertinent to ask, therefore, whether there is any real need for 'culling', as these theories address somewhat different aspects of L2 acquisition and do not appear to be in obvious opposition. A more useful question, however, is to ask why these three theories have been so prominent. This calls for their appraisal.

Appraisal, following Widdowson (1990a), entails two principal activities: interpretation and conceptual evaluation. Widdowson defines interpretation as the elucidation and critical examination of ideas 'within the context of their own theoretical provenance' (1990a: 31). Conceptual evaluation concerns a consideration of the validity/ relevance of the ideas to some other domain of enquiry—in Widdowson's case, language pedagogy. It entails, therefore, a consideration of the practical purposes that a theory might serve. Widdowson's scheme is helpful because it distinguishes two aspects of theory appraisal which are often confusingly conflated. It does not follow that a theory which is highly thought of within its own theoretical provenance and which serves practical purposes within it will automatically be of value in some other domain (such as language pedagogy).

The focus of this paper will be one of the three theories mentioned above—Universal Grammar. I shall begin with an interpretation of the theory, providing a summary of its main tenets and a critical examination. I will then embark on a conceptual evaluation of the theory of the kind Widdowson has in mind by considering the theory in relation to language pedagogy. I shall argue that the main factor involved in determining the uptake of a theory is less its internal qualities than the extent to which it is perceived as 'purposeful' by consumers of the theory. A theory achieves prominence because it meets the needs of a particular group of consumers. It does not follow, however, that this theory has any value to other groups of consumers. In other words, the value of theories is necessarily relative and any attempt to evaluate them in absolute terms is doomed to failure.

Universal Grammar—an appraisal
Interpretation: an overview

The Theory of Universal Grammar has been expounded in Lightbown and White (1987), White (1989), Gregg (1989), and Ellis (1994), among others. It derives from Chomsky's conceptualization of the nature of the linguistic universals that comprise a child's innate linguistic knowledge. According to Chomsky (1976), there is a 'system of principles, conditions, and rules that are elements or properties of all human languages'. These take the form of highly abstract principles, some of which are absolute and some parameterized (i.e. afford a number of options which define the variation possible among languages).

Generative linguists argue that first language acquisition would be impossible unless the young child was endowed with an innate knowledge of these principles and their parameters. This is because the input seriously underdetermines the final grammar that the child constructs. The child is only exposed to a subset of the total sentences possible in the target language and has no way of knowing whether a given property of the grammar has simply not been experienced in the available input or is not present in the language at all. Furthermore, the input does not provide an adequate basis for determining the restrictions that apply to a grammatical property, given that negative evidence (in the form of corrections) is not commonly available in first language acquisition. If input alone cannot explain L1 acquisition, what can? This constitutes what has been called 'the logical problem of language acquisition'. The answer given is that the child must be equipped with an innate knowledge of grammar that guides him or her in the acquisition of the grammar of a particular language. This innate knowledge, it is claimed, takes the form of Universal Grammar.

The theory specifies narrowly what it is that has to be explained. It aims to account only for the child's 'knowledge' of grammar, not for his or her ability to use this grammar in communication. In other words, the domain of the theory is *grammatical competence*, not the variable use of grammatical knowledge in actual performance. Chomsky (1981a) acknowledges that other types of knowledge, in particular 'pragmatic knowledge' (i.e. the knowledge of how language is used to construct discourse and to behave in socially appropriate ways), are also needed to explain language. However, he claims that 'grammatical knowledge' can be considered separately from 'pragmatic knowledge'. Furthermore, the theory limits itself to an account of how the child acquires *formal* knowledge of grammatical properties on the grounds that these exist independently of the meanings they realize in communication. Thus, the theory does not seek to account for how the child learns form–function mappings. The theory is also restricted to an account of those 'core' grammatical properties that are governed by UG; 'peripheral' properties of grammar, such as those that originate in the historical development of a language, are excluded from consideration.

UG Theory, therefore, assumes the autonomy of grammar. It claims that grammar constitutes an autonomous body of knowledge which is independent of other cognitive systems such as perception, memory, or problem-solving. This contrasts with holistic positions, which view language as part of communication. According to such positions, it is impossible to consider grammatical form independently of function because form is determined by function. Chomsky and his followers claim otherwise. Gregg (1989: 26) argues that 'one *can* understand form independent of function; however, function is not enough to explain form.' He suggests that phenomena like grammatical gender, third-person singular –s, and vowel harmony have no identifiable function. Of course, there is more to language than grammar—this is not disputed—but the point is that grammar exists as a significant and autonomous phenomenon which must be studied in its own right.

The application of UG Theory to SLA has centred on whether 'the logical problem of language acquisition' is the same as for L1 acquisition or needs to be restated. According to some, such as Cook (1988), the goal of a theory of L2 acquisition is the same as that of L1 acquisition—to account for how acquisition is possible given the 'poverty of the stimulus' (i.e. the inadequacies of input described above). According to others, however, the problem is somewhat different. Bley-Vroman (1989) points out that whereas all children acquire the grammar of their mother tongue, there is considerable variation in L2 acquisition, with most learners failing to achieve full competence. He argues that the logical problem of foreign language acquisition is to explain 'the quite high level of competence that is clearly possible in some cases, while permitting the wide range of variation that is possible' (1989: 50). In essence, this debate concerns whether UG is or is not available to the L2 learner. A number of positions have been advanced—a complete access position (Flynn 1987); a no-access view (for example, Clahsen and Muysken 1986); a partial-access position (for example, Schachter (1988) suggests that learners may have access to principles but not to the full range of parameters, while White (1989) has suggested that learners have access to those universals and parameters evident in their L1); and a dual-access position (for example, Felix (1985) argues that learners have continued access to UG but also use 'a general problem-solving module', which competes with the language-specific system).

UG Theory has been closely tied to generative grammars, such as Chomsky's (1981b) Government/Binding model. A major goal of these grammars is to identify and describe the principles and parameters that comprise UG. They provide a rich source of highly specific hypotheses that can be tested through language acquisition studies. For example, it has been suggested that a range of grammatical phenomena are implicated in specific universals. 'Pro-drop' (that is, whether a language permits subject pronouns to be deleted) is linked to such phenomena as variable word order, expletives (dummy 'it' and 'there' in English), 'that' trace in pro-drop languages (as in the example that Gass (1989) gives from Italian: *Chi hai detto che è venuto?*—Who have you said that is come?), and modal verbs. It is possible, therefore, to conduct studies to investigate whether the emergence of one grammatical property has some kind of triggering effect on the emergence of other, implicated properties. There have been a number of studies of 'pro-drop' in L2 acquisition which have followed this line (see Ellis 1994 for a review).

Interpretation: a critical examination

But how good a theory is UG? As Beretta (1991) has pointed out, there are no clear criteria for choosing between competing theories. This is because there is no consensus regarding criteria for evaluating any specific theory. Nor is there agreement about the relative weight to be assigned to different criteria in reaching an overall evaluation. Theory evaluation is perhaps more an art than a science, affording impressionistic overviews of the strengths and weaknesses of this and that theory. It is none the less valuable, as McLaughlin's (1987) excellent book on theories of second language learning demonstrates, although it is doubtful whether theory evaluation can provide a basis for the 'culling' that some commentators, like Beretta and Long, seem to see as desirable.

The evaluation of the UG Theory of L2 acquisition that follows is—like all other evaluations of theories in SLA I have read—impressionistic. I have identified a list of criteria by inspecting recent literature on

[77]

theory evaluation in SLA (see McLaughlin 1987, Beretta 1991, Crookes 1992, and the articles in *TESOL Quarterly* 24/4 and in *Applied Linguistics* 14/4). They suggest that a theory of SLA should aim for:

- limited scope
- completeness
- accountability
- simplicity
- operational constructs
- falsifiability
- power of prediction
- aesthetic appeal
- fruitfulness

1 Limited scope

Not surprisingly, this criterion is particularly controversial. On the one hand, the dangers of attempting to explain everything about a complex phenomenon are clearly recognized but, on the other hand, so too are the dangers of focusing narrowly on individual modules. As Hatch, Shirai, and Fantuzzi (1990: 702) note, modules 'leak' with the result that explanations that seem satisfactory when a module is considered in isolation are seen to be incomplete or plain wrong when the wider picture is examined.

As we have seen, UG Theory is explicitly modular. It focuses narrowly on competence as opposed to performance, on grammatical competence as opposed to pragmatic competence, on the formal as opposed to the functional properties of grammar, and on 'core' rather than 'peripheral' properties. It is argued that this is not only desirable on procedural grounds but is theoretically necessary, given that 'functional theories cannot explain the acquisition of competence' (Gregg 1989: 28). This claim is, of course, highly contentious and one subject to an ongoing debate between the protagonists of competence-based grammar and functional grammar. I shall argue in the following section that this controversy can only be resolved by reference to the *use* to which a theory is put—that there is no absolute virtue in narrowly restricting the scope of a theory.

2 Completeness

A theory that is restricted in what it tries to explain cannot be complete, so the criterion of completeness may appear to be in opposition to the criterion of limited scope. However, completeness may be considered in another way. According to Long (1990a), a theory of language acquisition must propose one or more 'mechanisms' to account for change. Mechanisms are 'devices that specify how cognitive functions operate on input to move a grammar at Time 1 to its new representation at Time 2' (1990a: 654). In this respect, UG Theory is clearly inadequate. As Gregg (1993) acknowledges, theories of generative grammar constitute 'property theories' in that they provide an explanation of the 'language acquisition device' that guides acquisition. They are not 'transition theories' because they offer no account of how the process of acquisition takes place. There is no 'mechanism' to explain why learners appear to acquire some grammatical structures before others.[1]

3 Accountability

The criterion of accountability requires that a theory is able to explain the relevant known facts. In the case of UG, the 'relevant known facts' consist of the linguistic universals which linguists in the generative school have uncovered—the principles and parameters that comprise the 'core' of language. UG Theory is, in essence, an explanation of the role these play in L2 acquisition. The problem is that the grammatical models that underpin the theory twist and turn. For example, differences exist with regard to which grammatical properties are believed to be implicated in 'pro-drop', making it difficult to test the claim that the acquisition of one feature can trigger the acquisition of related features. This uncertainty is perhaps inevitable, given the relative infancy of generative grammar, but it does raise an awkward question: 'when linguistics coughs, should second language acquisition catch pneumonia?' (Van Buren and Sharwood Smith 1985: 21).

4 Simplicity

The criterion of simplicity requires that the unnecessary multiplication of variables is avoided. In this respect UG scores highly. In contrast to many cognitive theories of L2 acquisition, in which constructs seem to proliferate endlessly, UG Theory is elegant in its simplicity. It has few principal tenets and these can be expressed straightforwardly (for example, 'input underdetermines the final grammar'). The tenets form a recognizable logical sequence, rather than just a list. However, the theory achieves considerable depth because it is related to 'a rich, well-developed linguistic theory' (Gregg 1993: 285) from which specific hypotheses, based on the main tenets of the theory, can be formed. It should be noted, however, that, as the theory is tested in empirical research, there is a tendency for simplicity to give way to complexity. For example, there has been a notable increase in the number of different positions regarding the availability of UG to the adult L2 learner.

5 Operational constructs

A theory can be said to employ operational constructs if it is possible to devise empirical means of measuring them. Tarone's (1988) belief in the importance of this criterion led her to argue that theories should only propose causes that are directly observable. Gregg (1993), however, distinguishes what he calls 'shallow theories', which stick to what is observable as much as possible, and 'deep theories', which acknowledge the importance of the unobservable aspects of nature. He points out that observation is not the only way of obtaining data, reflecting, no doubt, the reliance of UG-based research on grammaticality judgement tests as a way of eliciting learners' intuitions about the L2 grammar.

UG Theory has been operationalized by investigating whether L2 learners manifest behaviour that is compatible with their access to specific linguistic principles. The main problem lies in interpreting the behaviour that has been measured. What constitutes confirming or disconfirming behaviour? Do learners demonstrate access to UG if they perform judgements or produce sentences correctly above the level of chance? This question is usually answered with the help of qualitative statistics, but in the case of UG Theory it is not clear if this is appropriate. As Bley-Vroman, Felix, and Ioup have noted:

> The consequences of UG are not merely statistical. Violations . . . are not just ungrammatical 'more often than not'. They are ungrammatical—period.
> (1988: 27)

In effect, Bley-Vroman *et al.* are suggesting that even a single instance of a UG principle being violated cannot be overlooked. The standard response to such an argument is that occasional violations reflect 'performance' rather than 'competence'. But this leads to doubts as to whether the constructs of UG are, in fact, operational, for, we can ask, on what grounds are we to decide whether a violation is a performance lapse or a gap in competence? This question has rarely been addressed, let alone resolved.

6 Falsifiability

A theory is falsifiable if the hypotheses it affords can be framed in such a way that they can be disconfirmed. Conversely, a theory is unfalsifiable if its hypotheses are so constructed that it is impossible to disconfirm them. A good example of an unfalsifiable hypothesis in the field of SLA is Krashen's 'Input Hypothesis'. This claims that learners can move from 'i+1' to the next level in the order of acquisition as a result of understanding input containing 'i+1'.[2] It is unfalsifiable because it is impossible to operationalize 'i+1' and, also, because the conditions under which understanding input will or will not bring about acquisition are not specified.

UG Theory also runs the danger of being unfalsifiable. What happens when a linguistic hypothesis based on the theory is disconfirmed? This might be taken as evidence that the theory itself is wrong. Alternatively, it might be argued that the problem lies not in the theory but in the linguistic model that spawned the particular hypothesis. In this case, it is possible to protect the theory by revising the linguistic hypothesis. This is not a hypothetical argument, as the research which has addressed 'pro-drop' in L2 acquisition demonstrates (see Ellis 1994). As a number of researchers have pointed out (for example, Gass 1989), SLA research serves as a means of testing linguistic models. The problem is that this testing can be undertaken only if it is assumed that the underlying theory is correct, in which case, of course, the theory itself runs the risk of becoming unfalsifiable.

The value of the falsifiability criterion, however, has been queried. Schumann (1993: 296) argues that 'falsification is . . . extremely difficult, if not impossible to achieve' for the very reason discussed above—the impossibility of knowing whether the flaw rests in a specific hypothesis or the underlying assumption. His solution is that instead of trying to falsify hypotheses we should try to 'explore' a theoretical idea more fully in the sense of revising, altering, understanding, and assessing the validity of a construct. Arguably, this is, in fact, what has taken place.

7 Power of prediction

A strong theory not only explains the available facts but is also capable of predicting what will occur if certain conditions are met. In this respect, UG Theory can claim to be a strong theory. The notion of 'clustering' (as in the case of 'pro-drop') allows researchers to predict that once a particular parameter has been set a whole range of linguistic properties will become available to the L2 learner. Again, though, the theory's powers of prediction are diminished by lack of agreement as to which features cluster around a parameter.

8 Aesthetic appeal

Schumann (1983) has advanced a radically different approach to theory evaluation based on the idea that all enquiry, including SLA, is less of a 'science' than an 'art'. He argues that this calls for a very different set of criteria to those usually applied and suggests 'innovation', 'tone of voice', and 'metaphor' are more appropriate. It is not clear to me how such criteria can be applied to the UG Theory. Indeed, the whole notion of aesthetic appeal seems to be a highly subjective one. Gregg (1993), for example, unsurprisingly, considers UG Theory to provide a 'lovely explanation', which he considers superior to the 'likely explanation' afforded by variabilist theories such as my own (Ellis 1985) and Tarone (1983). He suggests that UG Theory is 'lovely' because it connects with 'a rich, well-developed linguistic theory'. For many, however, UG Theory, while interesting, is far from 'lovely' because of its failure to connect with the issues they count as important.

9 Fruitfulness

UG Theory has proved very fruitful, as evidenced by the growing number of empirical studies based on it. It is a theory that commands allegiance and, as Beretta (1991) has pointed out, there are merits in 'tribal models' that are aggressively advocated and that stimulate a strong research following. However, as I will try to show in the next section, the tribe that shows allegiance to UG Theory is a very particular one, with its own special customs, rites, and beliefs. There are, however, other tribes, with different ways of looking at the world, for whom UG Theory is of little value and who, therefore, show it no allegiance.

How, then, does UG Theory fare as a theory of L2 acquisition? This critical examination suggests that, at best, it only passes muster and, at worst, is seriously deficient. It fails conspicuously with regard to the completeness criterion and arguably also where operational constructs and falsifiability are concerned. It is also in danger of overcomplexifying. This is not to say, of course, that UG Theory is weaker than any other theory of L2 acquisition. Indeed, other theories might fare worse in a similar evaluation. The real point is that this kind of evaluation is, in the final analysis, not what counts. What matters is *utility*—the extent to which a theory is perceived as useful to a particular group of consumers. As Long (1993: 229) has pointed out, the 'structural qualities of social networks which make up intellectual communities will always function to preserve more than one theory.' UG Theory is attractive to that particular group of SLA researchers who have an interest in theoretical linguistics. Specific hypotheses derived from grammatical models such as Government/Binding can be tested out on L2 learners within the framework of the theory. The fact that this research has done little to either support or refute the central tenets of the theory does not matter and can be easily dismissed as the fledgling attempts to apply 'developing theories . . . to a particular domain' (White 1989: 137). What is important is that the theory affords a close link between mainstream linguistics and SLA. It is this, quite understandably, that ensures the relative popularity of UG Theory in SLA and makes it possible to overlook any shortcomings in the theory itself. Gregg (1989: 34) observes that a commitment to UG offers 'a sense of direction'.

A conceptual evaluation in relation to language pedagogy

The acceptance of a theory within its own contextual domain cannot serve as a basis for the application of that theory to an entirely different domain, such as language pedagogy. As Widdowson (1990a: 37) states, 'the recognition of validity . . . in its own terms does not commit us to acknowledge its pedagogic relevance in principle.' Unfortunately, this is not always recognized. The history of applied linguistics is full of examples of the uncritical advocacy of some theoretical or descriptive apparatus that was initially developed for an entirely different domain. In a previous era, this was most evident in linguistic description, where the view was widely held that teachers should use the 'best' linguistic description available. In the current era, it is most evident in attempts to apply SLA theory to language pedagogy, most obviously illustrated by Krashen's forceful advocacy of his Monitor Model.

In fact, there have been relatively few attempts to apply UG Theory to language pedagogy and in this respect UG contrasts with other theories of L2 acquisition. One reason for this is clear; members of the community of SLA researchers who show allegiance to UG have little or no interest in pedagogic issues. A second reason is that the theory is very difficult to apply. That is, it is difficult to demonstrate the relevancy of its central claims to teachers. I will begin this appraisal by considering one attempt to apply UG Theory to language pedagogy (V. Cook 1989) and then go on to show why the theory is of little utility to teachers.

Cook's article is entitled 'Universal Grammar Theory and the classroom'. In it he advances a number of proposals concerning the possible application of the theory to classroom learning and to language teaching. He begins by wisely acknowledging that 'UG Theory is neutral about many of the issues that arise in the classroom' (1989: 174).

The first set of proposals concerns what is *not* important for the classroom rather than what is—a rather odd way to approach the issue. It is not important to engage in 'teacher-talk' (shorter utterances, less subordination, etc.) since this is not a crucial property of input in the UG model. It is not important to engage learners in interaction nor to encourage them to develop effective learning strategies as the learner's grammar will automatically and inevitably conform to the principles of UG. It is not important to ensure plentiful productive practice, audiolingual or communicative, as all that is needed is a 'handful of sentences' containing the appropriate information to set parameters. In short, Cook suggests that UG Theory provides a justification for *laissez-faire*. Teachers do not have to bother themselves with how learners learn 'core' rules of grammar because acquisition is easy and automatic. These are radical ideas; they fly in the face of mainstream pedagogic practice. To use Widdowson's (1990a) terms, it is unlikely that such ideas can be easily *assimilated* into current theories of pedagogy. Rather they call for a major *accommodation*. But is such an accommodation justified? I will argue below that it is not, on the grounds that the goals of UG Theory and language pedagogy are incompatible.

[84]

Cook also makes a number of positive suggestions. One is that given that grammar is acquired simply and easily, teachers might spend less time teaching it and more time on other aspects of language, such as vocabulary. In particular, he notes, learners need to be taught how words behave in sentences—their syntactical properties. This proposal accords with similar ideas derived from entirely different theoretical frameworks and as such is worthy of serious consideration. It should be noted, however, that because UG Theory does not directly address how vocabulary learning takes place, Cook does not advance any specific proposals as to how language pedagogy should tackle vocabulary. Another positive suggestion is that grammatical syllabuses should be reorganized around principles, with structures that relate to the same underlying principle grouped together. Such a suggestion runs into a number of objections. One is, as we have seen, there is not always agreement about the constellations of structures governed by a particular principle. A more fundamental problem is that UG Theory only addresses 'knowledge', whereas most teachers view grammar learning in terms of their students' abilities to use grammar in comprehension and production. Grouping structures according to underlying principles may not be the best way to ensure actual use of the structures. We have come now to the essential problem of applying UG Theory to language pedagogy.

The domain of UG is a highly restricted one—competence rather than performance, linguistic competence rather than pragmatic competence, grammar rather than language, 'core' grammar rather than 'periphery', formal rather than functional properties. This delimiting of what needs to be explained is seen by UG supporters as a strength of the theory and, as we have seen, is justifiable from the perspective of linguistic enquiry. However, teachers do not have the luxury of such a narrowly defined target. They must concern themselves with the whole of language, not just 'core' grammar. Also, many teachers probably see their primary goal as that of teaching the 'ability' to use the language in communication rather than 'knowledge' of rules. As Widdowson (1990a: 95) puts it:

> . . . for language learners to learn only the intricacies of the device without knowing how to put it to use is rather like learning about the delicate mechanisms of a clock without knowing how to tell the time.

Clearly, then, there are major differences between what UG Theory seeks to explain and what teachers need to do.

It is not surprising, therefore, that applied linguists, who play a mediating role between 'pure' and 'pedagogic' theory, have looked elsewhere than UG Theory for ideas of potential value to teachers. What is needed is a functional theory of grammar that explains how grammatical properties are put to use in communication and a theory of acquisition that explains how learners learn the indexical values of grammatical properties.

Widdowson (1990a: 79–98) offers such a theory of grammar. He sees grammar as a set of tools that frees speakers from a dependency on context. The properties of grammar are devices for 'enhancing the indexical precision of lexical items'. Thus, whereas context and world knowledge suffice to arrive at an understanding of utterances like 'Scalpel!' or 'farmer kill duckling' (or even 'farmer duckling kill'), they do not suffice for utterances like 'hunter kill lion' or 'lion kill hunter'. In utterances such as the last two, word order serves as a grammatical signal of the semantic roles (agent and patient) of the verb. Other grammatical devices, such as tense and aspect markers, work similarly. Articles and other determiners help to increase the specificity of the lexical meaning of nouns. For Widdowson, language always works in relation to context. Lexis and grammar are means of narrowing down the range of inference, but some degree of inference is always required. Languages vary in what they leave to pragmatic inference and what can be encoded linguistically (i.e. lexically or grammatically). Widdowson's view of language and of language learning, then, differs widely from that which underlies UG Theory. For Widdowson 'language learning is essentially learning how grammar functions in the achievement of meaning and it is a mistake to suppose otherwise' (ibid.: 97).

Widdowson's views accord closely with those of a group of linguists and SLA researchers concerned with *grammaticalization*. Hopper and Traugott (1993: xv) define this as 'the process whereby lexical items and constructions come in certain linguistic contexts to serve grammatical functions, and, once grammaticalized, continue to develop new grammatical functions'. Grammaticality is seen as a cline, with a lexical element at one pole and a morphological element at the other. Klein (1986) views language learning as the mastery of a number of fundamental functions of language—spatial and temporal reference, for

[86]

example. Whereas the L1 learner has to learn both the functions and the means for performing them, the L2 learner already knows the functions. According to Klein (1991), L2 learners start with these and search the input for the linguistic devices which encode them. L2 acquisition is, thus, functionally driven and is characterized by a gradual process of grammaticalization, as learners substitute grammatical for lexical means to encode specific functions.

This view of language and language learning accords much more closely with the goals of language pedagogy. Its conceptualization of the domain of enquiry matches the teachers' own conceptualization of what they are about. It provides, therefore, a clear basis for application. Of course, the applications that derive from such a view are not to be seen as prescriptions or proscriptions but rather as proposals in need of 'empirical evaluation' by teachers in the classroom.

It would be possible, of course, to submit functional theories of SLA such as that proposed by Klein to the same kind of critical analysis as was undertaken for UG Theory. Doubtless, such an analysis would highlight a number of problems with functional theories, some, perhaps, more serious than those identified in UG Theory. The point is that such an exercise can never serve as a basis for determining which theory to apply to language pedagogy. The whole question of application cannot be addressed from the perspective of the theory to be applied; it must take as its starting point the needs of language teachers. If there is a gross mismatch between the theory and the teacher's needs, application becomes difficult and perhaps impossible, no matter how 'good' the theory is considered to be. Such, I suggest, is the case where UG Theory is concerned.

Conclusion

A theory is constructed to meet the needs of a particular group of consumers. SLA researchers wishing to establish firm links with mainstream linguistics have adapted Chomsky's views about Universal Grammar to the context of L2 learning. The theory serves them well. Applied linguists with an interest in language pedagogy, however, are unlikely to find much in UG Theory for the simple reason that it does not address their paramount concerns. They will need to look elsewhere and, indeed, have done so.

[87]

There are two general lessons to be learnt from this. The first is that it is unwise and probably impossible to attempt to evaluate theories without reference to the context in which they were developed (in particular, the purposes they were intended to serve). Thus, in deciding whether theories are complementary or oppositional—the initial step in the 'culling' process—it is necessary to consider what it is the theories are trying to do. No theory of SLA is concerned just with explaining L2 acquisition; it is directed at offering a particular kind of explanation which has a particular purpose and is appropriate for a specific group of researchers. Gregg's attacks on Krashen's Monitor Model and the Variabilist theories of Tarone and myself (see Gregg 1984; 1990) seem to me essentially mistaken because they treat these theories in absolute terms and seek to brand them as 'bad' theories without any consideration of what motivated them in the first place. I would argue that once it is recognized that theories must be considered in relation to their intended purpose some degree of relativism in theory evaluation is inevitable. This is one reason why theories in SLA have been able to resist closure despite the attacks mounted on them.

The second point is related to the first. A necessary condition for applying a theory of SLA to a domain other than that for which it was devised is the demonstration of relevancy. This cannot be achieved solely by pointing out the strengths of the theory. It requires also proof that the goals of the theory are, in part at least, compatible with those of language teachers. As Brumfit (1994: 270) puts it, 'second language acquisition theory needs to be compatible with the practice of teaching, as much as teaching needs to be compatible with second language acquisition theory.' It is not the second language acquisition theorist who determines whether a particular theory is of use to pedagogy but the applied linguist who, in Widdowson's terms, provides an 'appraisal' and, of course, teachers, who provide the ultimate empirical test of any proposal in their own teaching.

Notes

1 Not all theorists agree that it is necessary to specify a 'mechanism' to account for acquisitional sequence. Cook (1985) suggests that acquisition sequences reflect 'development' (i.e. the child's

increasing channel capacity) rather than 'acquisition' and, as such, lie outside the purview of a theory of UG.

2 'i+1' refers to the idea that learners acquire the grammar of an L2 in a natural order. Thus 'i' is the current stage of a learner's interlanguage development and '+1' the next grammatical feature or features to be acquired. According to Krashen, learners need to be exposed to input that contains these features in order to progress.

6

Analysability, accessibility, and ability for use

PETER SKEHAN

Concepts of competence: linguistic and communicative

THE ORIGINAL VERSION of the competence–performance relationship (Chomsky 1965) proposed an underlying linguistic knowledge-base which is implicated in actual language performance. This underlying knowledge base was seen as abstract, rule-governed, organized, and pervasive in its effects, since it would underlie creative, generative language use. The bridge to performance then drew in psychological processing factors which, in some unspecified way, constrain the direct operation of competence during the rough-and-tumble of actual language use.

Hymes (1972) criticized this (limited) Chomskyan account of competence and performance (and their relationship). Centrally, he proposed that there are competences which go beyond the linguistic domain discussed by Chomsky (1965), and that we also have to take into account *appropriateness* of language use. But Hymes (1972) retained the idea of underlying competence, extending its scope to include contextual relevance, and so implying that appropriateness has an abstract element, is organized, rule-governed, and pervasive. Consequently there was still need to consider a competence–performance relationship (Murata 1994). Problems in this area, though, would not only involve grammatical lapses, but also those of appropriateness, as when, for example, nervousness leads to a social gaffe which is instantly recognized as such by the perpetrator.

[91]

Drawing on these insights, Canale and Swain (1980) proposed a three-component framework for communicative competence. Canale (1983) later extended this to four component competences: linguistic, sociolinguistic, discourse, and strategic. The first three of these are proposed as underlying knowledge systems, akin to that proposed in the linguistic domain by Chomsky (1965), with the first of the components substantially based on Chomsky's formulation. Sociolinguistic knowledge will include the individual's understanding of social relations and the potential impact such understanding has for communication, and for choosing what to say that is appropriate. It also, under some formulations, includes knowledge which helps the language user relate language to context, and to interpret and encode meanings. Similarly, discourse competence concerns the language user's knowledge of rules of discourse, of how spoken and written texts are organized, and what might influence whether they are considered to be well formed. (In passing, it is interesting to note that it is much easier to define a native speaker norm for linguistic competence than for the other two underlying competences. It is possible, that is, to be a native speaker of a language and not to have extensive sociolinguistic or discourse competence.)

Canale and Swain (1980) then use strategic competence to cover the way in which the language user, when faced with a communicative problem, improvises his or her way to a solution. In other words, strategic competence is compensatory in nature, coming into play when the other competences are lacking, either because, in the case of the foreign language user, there is an area of deficiency, or in the case of a native language user (perhaps dealing with incipient senility), maybe a word is lacking, producing a problem which needs to be circumvented. Importantly, we are dealing here with strategic *competence*, i.e. an underlying knowledge system. The implication is that we are concerned with knowledge about how to solve communicative problems in general, which may then be exploited when actual problems occur and performance is required.

This presents a rudimentary model which may underlie performance. The first three competences combine in some manner to achieve communication, and when there is some sort of problem which obstructs this smooth operation, strategic competence comes into play to extricate the language user, one hopes, from the difficulty.

Performance, that is, draws upon the component competences *in some way* to enable actual communication to occur. We will return later to the issue of what 'in some way' may mean.

The Canale and Swain approach has been further developed by Bachman (1990) and Bachman and Palmer (forthcoming). Bachman has proposed a model which is more complex than its predecessor in a number of ways. First, the structure of the components of communicative competence has become more complex. Bachman (1990) discusses a tree-structure for these components, dividing language competence into an organizational competence and a pragmatic competence. The former is then subdivided into linguistic competence (Canale and Swain 1980), and textual competence. Thus Canale and Swain's discourse competence has been moved (and renamed) to come closer to linguistic competence. Pragmatic competence (i.e. the relationship between language and context) is then concerned with areas such as illocutionary competence, sociolinguistic competence, and lexical competence. These developments constitute a more organized and differentiated account of the underlying and basic competences concerned. It is similar to the earlier formulation by Canale and Swain in general nature, but not in detail.

More radical is the change that Bachman proposes for the role of strategic competence. It is no longer seen as compensatory, only coming into play when other competences are lacking. Instead, it is central to all communication. It achieves this role by discharging a mediating role between meaning intentions (the message which is to be conveyed), underlying competences (i.e. those that have just been briefly examined), background knowledge, and context of situation. It carries out this role by determining communicative goals, assessing communicative resources, planning communication, and then executing the plan. Bachman considers these capacities to constitute metacognitive skills. They are cognitive because of the nature of the operations that they involve, and *meta* since there can be a self-awareness built in to their operation. This level of detail of the structure of strategic competence goes some way to justify why we are dealing here with something underlying, organized, and wide-ranging in its effects—a component of competence, in other words.

Even so, the nature of the relationship between competence and performance is being redefined, since Bachman is proposing a dynamic for

[93]

communication. He sees this relationship as being mediated through the operation of a pervasive strategic competence. One issue which arises is to decide whether the operations which are carried out in this area relate more to an underlying knowledge system (i.e. competence), or are concerned with the real-time processes which influence what is actually said (performance). A second issue is whether consciousness of one's own strategic competence in operation, and the possible modification of its workings which result, also lead us to performance or competence issues. Thirdly, there is the problem of what the different operations within strategic competence—assessment, goal-setting, planning, and execution—actually mean, and further, what processes serve them. Currently they seem to have programmatic, rather than precise, status, and what actually happens is not clear.

Analysability and accessibility: users and learners

One way of addressing this issue of how strategic competence actually operates is to consider how linguistic competence may be represented psychologically, and what processes are implicated in its use. In this respect, two distinctions made by Henry Widdowson are extremely helpful. This section will present the distinctions, and the next will review relevant evidence which has emerged in recent years.

Widdowson (1989c) makes an important (and characteristically two-way) distinction between analysability and accessibility. The former is concerned with differentiated and organized knowledge systems, and is clearly connected with Chomsky's notion of competence. It concerns the underlying, rule-governed system which has been internalized through the operation of a Language Acquisition Device (LAD), and which is the basis for language. The system will conform to the constraints of a Universal Grammar, and will be parsimoniously organized, with rules of language connecting with lexical elements, with language being produced which satisfies the rule requirements and also the combinatorial constraints of the lexical elements. There is a sense, with the emphasis on analysability, of rules being primary in importance, and the lexical elements merely fitting into such rules. What are paramount are system-design, elegance, and compactness.

Accessibility, in contrast, is concerned with operational requirements, and the way in which language is used in real time. The central criterion, that is, is ease of use, where ease is mainly determined by speed of access. The focus is not on the elegance of the system concerned, but on how a system can handle communicating under pressure, and where extensive planning and the use of an analysed system which requires excessive 'on-line' computation may be luxuries that the user has no time to afford.

The analysability–accessibility contrast leads in turn to the need to make a (not so typically Widdowsonian) *three*-way distinction between analyst's, user's, and learner's models. The first type of model is concerned with linguistic structure, viewed as a self-contained system. The focus is on the power of abstract rules to generate, to account for linguistic facts, and on the parsimony with which an elegant set of rules accounts for the well-formed sentences in a language. A user's model, in contrast, is concerned with how real people achieve the task of communication, in context, and in real time. From a processing perspective we need to consider how language is represented, and how it is accessed and deployed. Clearly, these processes are likely to have some connection with an analyst's model, but the fit is unlikely to be exact, since there is no requirement for the user to observe rules, however parsimonious and elegant, but simply to operate a system which is functional.

The analyst–user contrast deals with a static situation, and does not account for how such a situation came about, either for first or for second language acquisition. This deficiency leads us to consider the learner's model separately. Learners need to both develop underlying language systems *and* cope with ongoing and immediate communication. To the extent that there is competition between a concern for system development, and a concern for language use, there may be a conflict here, a conflict which goes to the heart of the distinction between analyst's and user's models, since its resolution requires us to clarify how these two models interrelate, and play themselves out when faced with language users who are learners needing to engage in language system development.

Before returning to this conflict, it is necessary to review some of the evidence relevant to these distinctions.

[95]

The role of memory in language use

An analytically oriented system is likely to make a clear distinction between syntactic and lexical elements, and the way in which rules govern their functioning. In contrast, if we emphasize accessibility, and a user's model, we do not have to consider that the 'word' is the basic unit of organization. My discussion here follows work by linguists such as Bolinger (1975), Pawley and Syder (1983), and Peters (1985), all of whom suggest that far more of language is formulaic, and based on units beyond the level of the word. Communication, that is, uses 'multi-word' units which have functional autonomy within ongoing discourse. Bolinger (1975) argues that the way in which such language has often been portrayed (and dismissed) as idiomatic and marginal is misconceived, and that much of everyday language, *although analysable*, is not being used on an analysed basis. Pawley and Syder (1983), similarly, propose that the units of planning in speech are clause-based and that much communication is based on what they term *lexicalized sentence stems* which are an effective vehicle for the user to produce language in real time: the essential justification of this view being that the use of units larger than the word within a limited capacity system (Carr and Curren 1994) 'free up' resources and so enable the language user to keep up with the pressures of communication in real time, leaving more cognitive capacity for additional planning, and for the use of the metacognitive abilities that Bachman and Palmer (forthcoming) discuss. Peters (1985) proposes that the operation of a rule-based system generates language, which although in the first instance syntactically based, once created becomes available for retrieval as an exemplar, giving the benefits of speed of processing as well as syntactic organization.

In addition to the issue of the unit of language within a user's model, we also have to consider the problem of organization. The sort of analyst's model we have considered earlier implies that elegance and parsimony are important criteria, suggesting in turn that lexical elements are stored once each, and in a fashion which makes for efficient retrieval of each element, as needed, when it slots into a well-formed sentence. Bolinger (1975), in contrast, proposes that the human memory system stores material in multiple forms, and that it does not have the overriding aim of conserving space, but instead is able to access the 'same' lexical element, stored multiply, as it forms a part of a range of formulaic phrases. In this way, *assuming a fast retrieval system to access these multiple representations*, considerable processing savings are made, and ongoing real-time language use is facilitated.

This view of accessibility, which suggests a repertoire of formulaic language (Nattinger and DeCarrico 1992), also sheds light on the nature of the choices that are made during language use. Hymes (1972), for example, has spoken about the characteristic of communicative competence that it is *done*, and similarly, Pawley and Syder (1983) have spoken of the puzzle of nativelike selection. Both articles suggest that the language system enables particular meanings to be conveyed in multiple ways, and that these different paths do not all have equal value: some expressions seem to acquire some sort of valence. Widdowson's (1989c) concept of accessibility implies that the repertoire of language on which we draw when we speak may contain, simultaneously, a frequency effect of some sort for attestedness which combines with, through speed of processing, greater accessibility.

So we see that, if we take Widdowson's concepts of analysability and accessibility, and relate them to analyst's and user's models of language, there are significant implications for how competence and performance may rely on parallel processes. What seems to be the default is that accessibility has greater priority, but given that such a system, not inherently focusing on rules, may hit problems, it is possible to 'shift down' to a more rule-governed mode of processing, closer to the analyst's model, as the need arises.

So far the discussion has considered the contrast between analyst's and user's models, and has tacitly concerned native speaker language use. But it is also important to consider how language acquisition, first and second, take place. In both these cases, we need to examine the nature of learning, and of learners' models. As a preliminary to addressing this issue, it is necessary to review evidence from general psychology, and from first and second language acquisition.

A number of studies within experimental psychology have examined whether in the learning of structured material (for example, artificial languages), there is evidence that what is learned consists of abstract rules (Reber 1989), or direct exemplars (Dulany, Carlson, and Dewey 1984). The conclusion from these studies (Carr and Curren 1994) is that both sorts of learning occur, with it being difficult to claim superiority or generality for either. Interestingly, it has been claimed that *dual-mode* approaches to processing (i.e. partly abstract rule learning, and partly exemplar-based learning) present the most satisfactory accounts, and also that the two modes operate synergistically (i.e. together), allowing abstract rules and exemplars (i.e. memorized lexical 'chunks') to produce a level of performance which is more than the simple sum of the components. Schmidt (1992), in accounting for the development of second language fluency, also argues for what he calls, following Logan (1988), instance-based learning. Instances (which are similar to exemplars, and to lexical units) are linked to context and have either been learned as chunks in the first place, or were 'created' by the rule-governed system initially, but then become available as chunks for processing on subsequent occasions. (See Peters (1985) for a similar account where she discusses a process which she calls 'fusion'.) Such instance learning then enables real-time processing (and in the case of language learning, fluency) to be achieved more easily.

Skehan (1992), in discussing the process of first language development, suggests that it proceeds in three stages. An initial period of *lexical* communication is followed by a period of *syntacticization*, which in turn leads on to a phase of *relexicalization*. In other words, early attempts at language development have strong lexical dimensions (Bates, Bretherton, and Snyder 1988). Such a lexical orientation is likely to enable the child to code meanings in a more transparent manner. Then, as the LAD operates, a complex syntactic system is built, which incorporates the lexical system that has separately developed. But then, very importantly, with a syntactic system in place, the older child *relexicalizes* that which has been syntacticized (Schmidt (1992) on fluency, and Peters (1985) on exemplar-creation), precisely so that a dual processing system is available, allowing flexibility, as the main demand changes from being the need to produce complex correct language under little time pressure, to more immediate communication where time is a factor. In other words, the process of relexicalization is what enables the multiple codings of lexical elements to become available, and what enables a wide repertoire of lexical elements to be drawn on.

We now have to consider the connection between first and second language acquisition. Clearly, first language acquisition is viewed here as the consequence of the operation of an LAD, which constrains, through the operation of a Universal Grammar, the nature of language development. Such development, in other words, requires input as a trigger, but the emphasis is on the construction of the underlying syntactic system that proceeds with considerable autonomy. In contrast, if we assume a critical period for language development (Johnson and Newport 1989), the operation of such an LAD will no longer have the same role. In this respect, Skehan (1994) proposes that the nature of modularity in the cases of first and second language acquisition differs. With first language acquisition, modularity, following from the existence of an LAD, is organized in terms of syntax and semantics. With second language acquisition, in a post-critical period, there is still modularity, but now the modularity is in terms of stages of information processing. It concerns input, central processing, and output. Skehan (1994) proposes that each of these stages can be related to constructs which underlie aptitude tests, specifically in terms of auditory processing (phonemic coding ability), central processing of a cognitive nature (inductive language learning ability), and retrieval (memory). In this case, it is feasible to speak of the ways in which different learners may have strengths and weaknesses in each of these areas, and how different learners may have predispositions to process linguistic material in one of the areas to a greater extent than the others.

In effect, the consequences of this for the role of a *learner's model* of language development, in contrast to analyst's and user's models, are considerable. In the first language case, it is proposed that language has been acquired through the LAD (syntacticized), and then relexicalized to enable faster, real-time communication. In the case of second language acquisition, with an LAD now defunct, or only available through the traces it has left from first language acquisition, development will have had to proceed through *cognitive mechanisms*. In other words, syntactic second language systems will have had to develop by cognitive means, without the automatic triggering that a built-in Universal Grammar will have enabled. Further, there will not be the sequence of syntacticization–relexicalization that will have enabled the first language user to have available a dual-mode system of communication. Second language learners, that is, will have learned some things as a rule-governed system but by cognitive means, while other things will have been learned directly as lexical elements *without the preliminary syntacticization that has characterized the first language case.* To put this another way, second language learners' proneness to fossilization is the consequence of the lack of an LAD, coupled with a capacity to learn exemplars directly.

Competence and performance revisited again

These analyses enable us to view the competence–performance relationship in some new ways, and to do so differently for first and second language performance. For first language acquisition, a traditional view of the competence–performance relationship suggests that performance is based, in some sense, on competence, but that performance factors (fatigue, complexity of what is being said, drunkenness) get in the way. A dual-mode approach (with communication based on a syntactic system or a lexical/exemplar system, or some mixture of the two) implies that the underlying competence will sometimes be influential, but that when real time is a significant influence, a lexical mode of communication will predominate, in which case, performance will not be some pale reflection of competence, but will be subject to all manner of processing factors which impinge on the nature of the performance required. As a result, rather than looking at the ways in which an underlying system can come into play (for example, components of communicative competence), it may be more useful to examine the operation of these processing factors directly. So, some of the time, a traditional linguistic competence will exert an influence on performance, but on other occasions, following the dual-mode processing system, it will not.

In the case of second language performance, the situation is somewhat different. Here, we cannot so easily speak of an underlying competence in the sense of the product of the operation of an LAD. There may be a rule-governed system, but it will have developed in a radically different way—through conventional cognitive learning processes. Further, it is not so appropriate to think of language users switching down to their syntactic system as this is necessary during communication. They may not have such a system to switch down to, since they may have, during their learning of the second language, lexicalized directly. As a result, the foundation for communication may not be the consequence of anything universal, but instead the result of the situations in which the language in question has been learned, together with the predispositions (for example, syntactic orientation vs. lexical orientation) of the particular learner (Skehan 1986).

Clearly these reconceptualizations of the competence–performance relationship pose serious problems, and some sort of new analysis of the relationship involved is necessary. One such approach would be to return to the discussion presented earlier of the operation of strategic competence. It will be recalled that a major difference between the formulations offered by Canale and Swain, on the one hand, and Bachman, on the other, is in terms of the pervasiveness of the role of such a competence, with Canale and Swain restricting its operation to compensation and improvisation, and Bachman seeing such operations as simply special cases when difficulties are encountered. For him, strategic competence is implicated in all communication, since it discharges a mediating role between communicative competence, meaning intentions, context of situation, and something else. In this respect, Bachman and Palmer (forthcoming) speak of the roles of formulation of meaning, assessment of resources, planning, and execution as the processes which must be gone through to achieve such communication. They characterize such processes as metacognitive abilities which underlie the way in which competence is related to performance.

But characterizing strategic competence in this way, while helpful in providing a model of what is involved in communication, begs many questions. For example, one can ask whether the metacognitive abilities which are so involved should be located more properly within competence or within performance. One could ask similarly how, in detail, such processes of assessment, goal-setting, planning, and execution actually operate. Are they schematic labels, or do they imply actual stages which are gone through in the process of communication? And, to relate these questions to some of Widdowson's work, one could ask how such questions relate to the concept of ability for use.

To try to address these issues, I will conclude by examining how a processing perspective towards language may enable a decision to be made about the place of strategic competence. Central to this approach is a view of communication being achieved by means of an information processing system in which there are limited attentional capacities. The language user hence has to cope with the multiple demands on attention while communication is taking place, and to try to marshal their use effectively while time is passing. The demands on attention may be categorized as follows:

– *Cognitive demands*
  These concern the complexity of the message that is to be conveyed. This complexity will be greater if there are more elements which must be manipulated and kept track of during communication; if the material is abstract and not contextually supported; if the material cannot draw upon well-organized and familiar areas of knowledge which have been used as the basis for communication in the past.

– *Linguistic demands*
  These concern the complexity of the language which has to be used for effective communication.

– *Linguistic criteria*
  These concern the salience of form as a part of the communicative goal. It will be greater if the second language user is striving for greater accuracy, and will also be greater if the user wants to employ more complex syntax and linguistic elements.

– *Time, pressure, and unpredictability*
  These concern simply the passage of time, and the need to keep up communication while it passes; the existence of pressure, and the way in which a certain task may have to be completed within a certain time period; and finally, the extent to which the interaction can follow unforeseen paths, and so require adjustment mid-course.

The four influences combine to make the problems of communication more difficult, and pose problems for the limited capacity information processor. A speaker has to cope with so many things during the process of composing and comprehending language, and so has to switch attention rapidly between different areas if fluent (or even semi-fluent) communication is not to break down. Given the way in which, even for the native speaker (Bygate 1987), formulating thoughts coherently, and then expressing them through language is a very testing task, one can imagine how much more difficult this is for the non-native speaker, operating with an incomplete interlanguage system, and possibly faced with significant communicative pressure.

Not surprisingly, therefore, we need to consider some of the resources that can be used to ease the burden of communication that is implied. We will consider five such resources here:

– *Existing competences*
For the non-native speaker, fairly obviously, the greater the degree of underlying linguistic competence which is available, the easier the problems of real-time communication, since less time and attention will need to be used coping with the uncertainties and difficulties of wrestling with a still-developing system.

– *Previous experience*
A great deal of what we have to deal with in life is not completely new. Much of the time we can notice the resemblance between today's task and something we had to do in the past. To the extent that we have memory of what we did on the previous occasion, the present communication will be eased in that we will simply have to access whatever organized thought and language we used on the previous occasion.

– *Skill in using time-creating devices*
Bygate (1987: 14–21) discusses the ways in which it is normal, in native speaker communication, to rely on the use of time-creating devices such as repetition, pausing, rephrasing, reformulation, etc. All of these reduce the density of communication, and enable the language user to create time, and reduce communicative pressure. To the extent that the second language user can similarly deploy such resources, there will be attention made available to focus on other, perhaps more problematic, aspects of communication.

– *Degree of influence on the communicative encounter*
On occasions it will be unavoidable that a communicative encounter will have to be accepted on its own terms, and a second language user will not be able to modify the parameters involved. But on other occasions it may be possible to influence either the content of what is being spoken about (for example, to make it more familiar), or the manner (for example, to enable more time-creating devices to be used). In either case, exerting such influence will ease the attentional demands on the language user.

– *Planning*
The discussion of time-creating devices, and the degree of influence

exerted over the communication, imply a speaker who is simultaneously coping with a number of demands on attention, and who is exploiting a set of strategies to 'free up' attentional resources so that other operations can be performed. Included in these is the ongoing planning that occurs as discourse unfolds, and as the new developments in a conversation have to be adjusted to. But these 'on the wing' aspects of communicative resources can be matched by planning which takes place before a communicative encounter starts to unfold. Here the emphasis is on the linguistic, discoursal, and cognitive planning that can be accomplished *before* communication is under way. Research by Crookes (1989), Foster and Skehan (1994), and Ellis (1987b) has shown how important such planning processes are for second language speakers, influencing complexity, accuracy, and fluency (Skehan 1992), and demonstrating how preparation ahead of time can exert a very considerable influence on the richness of ongoing communication, and on its usefulness for longer-term development and interlanguage change.

Ability for Use

To summarize the preceding discussion, we see that on the one hand, there are demands on attentional resources during communication, while on the other, there are resources that a speaker can exploit to help these demands to be met and to maximize the effectiveness with which the limited attentional resources can be used. These involve easing the task (using time-creating devices, influencing the task itself); exploiting one's existing competences (using linguistic competence, drawing on past experience and schematic knowledge as efficiently as possible); and changing one's preparedness for the task.

One can generalize about the outcome of these activities (and return to the earlier discussion of analysability and accessibility) by saying that the net result in any particular communicative encounter will be that either a syntactic or a pragmatic/lexical mode of communication will predominate. If attentional demands are stretching, it is likely that speech will be more pragmatic, contextual, *and lexically organized*. In other words, accessibility will be the major factor, as complexity and accuracy are downgraded in importance as the communicative pressure is met. In contrast, if attentional resources are adequate, and/or if they are well managed, then a syntactic mode will be possible, complexity and accuracy will be feasible, and the emphasis will be on analysability.

This account requires us to look at the relationship between the competence and performance of the second language learner in a different way. We now have to take into account how the learner uses attention-control processes to communicate. To put this another way, if we return to the metacognitive abilities discussed by Bachman under the heading of strategic competence, we have to explore how second language speakers cope with syntactic vs. pragmatic/lexical modes of communication by using resources to cope with the pressures of real time. We have seen how important these decisions are, and how central limitations in attentional capacity are for the choice of strategies that will be employed. What this means is that it is misconceived to see competence as underlying performance in any straightforward manner. Psychological mechanisms are fundamental. If such mechanisms require a move towards lexical/pragmatic communication, then we cannot really speak of competence having a central role. Instead, formulaic language will be the norm, and the speaker will need to draw upon a repertoire of lexical units, and operate them effectively within the ongoing discourse. In contrast, if planning time is available, and it is by this means that a more syntactic mode is engaged, we have to recognize the central way in which it is cognitive planning which brings about the greater engagement with form.

We also need to discuss the second language learner's consciousness of what she or he is doing. The above aspects of managing communication, i.e. the demands on attention and the use of a variety of resources to meet these demands, represent a set of cognitive skills, which may be used automatically, but of which the user may well be conscious, in the sense that awareness of what is being done may enable more effective strategic decisions to be made. This being the case, we need to return to the question of whether strategic competence (if this is the label that we can conveniently use for all the above operations) is a component of competence at all. Presumably, clear awareness of how one copes with attentional demands during communication, and/or systematicity in the way this is achieved, would argue for a competence interpretation. In contrast, if we have to regard this behaviour as what occurs *during* communication, with different responses on different occasions, we ought to be more concerned with a performance interpretation.

Since a decision on this point is very difficult, I would propose that an effective compromise here would be to regard the operation of these processes as neither competence nor performance, but to see them as constituting *ability for use*, i.e. systematicity in the way in which various competences are mobilized in actual communication. As such, ability for use essentially has a mediating function between underlying competences, context of communication, and psychological processing. As a result, we can attempt to study such an ability, and we can even regard it as having a central organizing role, but we do not have to regard it as being on a par with the other components of linguistic, sociolinguistic, and discourse competences, where the emphasis is much more on underlying knowledge systems. Ability for use, in other words, is what goes beyond Bachman's (1990) assessment, goal-setting, planning, and execution, and is what accounts for the balance between analysability and accessibility as the processing dimension of actual communication.

7

Situational context, variation, and second language acquisition theory

ELAINE TARONE & GUO-QIANG LIU

SYSTEMATIC INTERLANGUAGE VARIATION occurs when a learner produces different variants of a particular IL form either in varying linguistic environments, or under different social conditions, for example, with different interlocutors, or in different physical locations (Tarone 1979, 1988). A learner may seem to have mastered a given target language (TL) form in one social context, yet in another social context systematically produce a quite different (and possibly inaccurate) variant of that form.

Should second language acquisition theories account for such variation in interlanguage performance? There is considerable disagreement among second language acquisition (SLA) researchers and theoreticians on this point. Those who, in Widdowson's (1978b: 2–4; 1983b: 50–52) terms, prefer to study language as idealized form, prefer to exclude the study of variation, while those who study language forms in relation to their use in context, include the study of variation.

Non-variationist theoreticians (for example, White 1989; Gregg 1990, 1993) focus upon internal mental processes and model an abstract (non-contextualized) competence, discounting the importance of variation in learner performance. Thus, they prefer to abstract away from variable data in explaining the acquisition of a second language. For such investigators, contextual variation is a performance factor, and so by definition is irrelevant to the description of the learner's idealized competence. Gregg (1990), for example, argues that interlanguage variation should not be the concern of second language acquisition theorists. SLA theorists, in this view, should concern themselves solely with idealized competence and not with performance.

In contrast, Tarone (1983, 1990) and other variationists (for example, Dickerson 1975; Ellis 1985, 1987a; Young 1991) focus upon external interactions and L2 learner performance in a variety of social contexts. They believe interlanguage variation across those contexts to be importantly related to change in learners' IL knowledge over time. The variationist position is completely consistent with Widdowson's (1978b, 1983b, 1989c) position that linguistic forms should not be studied in isolation from their communicative function in discourse, and that when a language is learned, it 'retains a trace of its situational provenance' (1983b: 39). Variation, from this perspective, is a source of information about the way in which interaction in different social contexts can influence both interlanguage use *and* overall interlanguage development. Tarone (1983, 1988, 1990) and others have argued that it is important for any second language acquisition theory to describe and explain why it is that interlanguage performance varies systematically from one social context to another, and to relate this variation in performance to the development of the learner's knowledge.

In this paper[1], we will argue that an adequate theory of second language acquisition must include an account of IL variation. We give an example of the kind of data which can be produced by an approach which studies IL in context, data which show that a learner's participation in different kinds of interactions can differentially affect the rate and route of the acquisition process.

An adequate theory of SLA needs to account for IL variation

We will begin by arguing, as has Tarone (1983, 1988) and many others (Wong Fillmore 1976; Hatch 1978; Widdowson 1978b, 1983b, 1989c; Selinker and Douglas 1985; Preston 1989; Sato 1990), that in the field of SLA research we have tended to err by divorcing the study of the internal development of an IL grammar from the study of the (external) social contexts in which the learner develops this grammar. The social context of the learner is too often viewed as unrelated to the internal cognitive process of L2 acquisition, and so, unworthy of comment. This is true particularly in studies in the UG tradition (see, for example, Rutherford 1984; White 1989; papers in Gass and Schachter 1989, and in Flynn and O'Neil 1990). As a result, our understanding of the importance of research on IL variation has been restricted. Historically too many SLA researchers have understood 'variationist' research to be focused solely upon the way in which different social variables cause patterned surface-level shifts in IL forms in performance. Such shifts have typically been viewed by many writers in SLA (for example, Gregg 1990) as temporary, ephemeral, and therefore unimportant to the diachronic change in the learner's knowledge system: merely performance factors, but not factors important to the development of competence. We have not gone on to ask or to find out whether a learner's participation in different kinds of social interactions can result in different patterns in the longitudinal development of IL grammars. Whether we posit single or multiple underlying competences is relatively unimportant; what matters is that the variation we observe is a useful guide to the understanding of the process of SLA.

Unfortunately, variationists have not always tied together several strands of research which could have been related: research on IL variation (for example, Dickerson 1975; Beebe 1980); research on the role of interaction and input in SLA (for example, Pica and Doughty 1985; Long 1985); research on the relationship between language form and discourse function (for example, Widdowson 1978b, 1983b, 1989c); research on discourse domains (for example, Selinker and Douglas 1985) and research on the longitudinal development of grammatical forms (for example, Schumann 1978; Pienemann and Johnston 1987).

In this paper we argue that work on variation is related to work on interaction and input, on the relationship between language form and discourse function, on discourse domains, and on the development of IL forms. We would like to show this by presenting as evidence data showing how synchronic variation in interlanguage performance is related to diachronic second language acquisition.

The kind of data needed to show impact of variation on SLA

The kind of data we need, we would argue, can best be produced by longitudinal case studies in which records have been kept of a learner's output in clearly different social interactions and the changes in that output in those situations over a period of some time. That is, if we are to show that synchronic variation across situations is related to diachronic change, then we must gather longitudinal data for single individuals, as each individual interacts in a constant set of situations over time.

We will describe here one such longitudinal study which supports the view that different kinds of social interactions can differentially activate internal acquisition processes. We will here attempt to describe that study in sufficient detail to demonstrate the value of the data generated in a study of this sort; an exhaustive description of the study is provided elsewhere.[2]

A study of Bob's interlanguage

Liu (1991, 1994) conducted a 26-month longitudinal study of a Chinese boy named 'Bob', beginning when Bob was almost five years old and ending when he was almost seven. Liu observed Bob speaking English in Australia in four interactional contexts: first, interacting with pre-school peers and supervisory staff, and later interacting with his teachers in his primary school classroom, interacting with primary school peers in the same classroom, and interacting with the researcher. Over the 26-month time period, 83 sessions were recorded, most of them on videotape. Sessions 23 to 83 took place during the period when Bob was in school. Each of 37 sessions recorded in the school classroom lasted about an hour; the 23 sessions with the researcher over the same time period lasted about 45 minutes. The researcher was present at all sessions, an observer in the first three contexts observed, and a participant observer in the fourth.

All the data were transcribed and analyzed according to several general criteria, including number of utterances produced by Bob, complexity of utterances produced, proportion of those utterances which were initiations as opposed to responses, functions those utterances fulfilled (Nicholas 1987), and interrogative structures produced.

First, let us examine the general nature of the three different types of social interaction observed over the period of time when Bob was in primary school, and the general effect of those interactions upon Bob's IL production during that time period. We will then report Liu's analysis of the development over time of question forms in Bob's interlanguage, and his evidence that the rate and route of Bob's acquisition of question forms was differentially affected by his participation in those different social interactions.

A general description of the social interactions and Bob's production of IL in those interactions

Liu defines the three interactional contexts in which Bob engaged after starting primary school in terms of Bob's *role relationships* with three different types of interlocutors: classroom teachers (a child-student to adult-teacher role relationship), peers in the classroom (a child to child-friend role relationship), and the researcher (a child to adult-friend role relationship). Quantitative analysis of the language produced by Bob in these three settings shows a considerable difference in the frequency (and function) of grammatical elements in these settings. The crucial thing here is the role relationships which obtain with those interlocutors. A role is a very useful construct for our purposes, in that it is simultaneously social and cognitive: it is defined both by the learner's perception of his relationship to others and by social norms which the learner has internalized. It is thus a very helpful construct for SLA researchers to use in examining the relationship between the learner's external social context and his internal cognitive processes.

Interaction with classroom teachers

In interactions with his teachers at school, Bob was very aware of the importance of doing well and getting good grades; he generally did not initiate interactions, and focused on presenting himself as a good pupil. In language use, he did not seem to take many risks. Even with T1, an extremely supportive teacher who gave very little negative feedback on his language, Bob took few risks. In the following conversation, the study had been in progress for about a year and a half. (Bob's contributions are in bold type.)

(1) Session 59 (November 30, 1987) 8185–8227

> T I: Bob what can I do for you?
> **B O B: I want to publish a book.**
> T I: You want to publish a book. OK.
> **B O B: This one. Ay. I'm now put in there.**
> T I: Now what did you do about your story, my friend?
> **B O B: Zoo.**
> T I: Do you want me to write it or you write it?
> **B O B: You write it.**
> T I: You want me to write it. Now which cover would you like? Blue one or orange one? Which colour?
> **B O B: Blue one.**
> T I: What size do you want it? Do you want it this big or that big?
> **B O B: This big.**
> T I: This big. OK. Right. So we have that size. Now do you want to write it or do you want me to write it?
> **B O B: You write it.**
> T I: Me to write it. OK. You want to put some pictures in it too?
> **B O B: Yeah.**
> T I: So we need some white paper and some paper for pictures. Have you got your stories?
> **B O B: Yeah. About zoo.**
> T I: What?
> **B O B: Zoo.**

In this conversation, as in the others with his teachers, Bob lets the teacher take the conversational initiative, and limits his responses to utterances with relatively simple syntax. Liu (1991) provides a statistical summary which documents that Bob's interactions with his teachers typically encode a small range of functions, with sentence structure which is simple relative to that in the other interactional contexts. In interactions with his teachers, Bob rarely initiates, preferring to respond. This pattern is consistent with Bob's cultural background, in which children are taught to show respect for their teachers, in part by 'only speaking when spoken to', and to learn by listening to the teacher.

Interaction with classroom peers

In interacting with peers in the classroom at desk work, Bob, as a highly competitive boy, takes a much more assertive role, initiating interactions, criticizing his classmates' work, demonstrating the superiority of his own, and speaking more fluently. This interactional context is conducive to giving commands, arguing, and insulting—functions which are not culturally appropriate in interactions with the teacher. In the following conversation, Bob and his three friends (Ben, Shayne, and Simon) are challenged on the quality of their drawing by a rival group (which includes Mark and Paul); this conversation takes place in July of 1987, four months *prior* to the conversation with the teacher recorded above.

(2) Session 43 (July 20, 1987) 5935–5976

MARK: You can't draw the same sorts as in everything you know. Like the original. (Pointing at Ben's work of wave lines)

BOB: Yeah yeah. You can draw. Look that. (To Ben)

MARK: You can't can you? So I can't either.

BOB: Look he doesn't know how to draw. (To Ben about Mark)

MARK: I can draw better than both of you.

BEN: Um can you draw peak? (Meaning mountain peak)

MARK: Yes I can.

BOB: OK you draw.

BEN: Can you draw school?

MARK: Yes I can.

BEN: Can you draw the whole world?

MARK: Yes I can.

BEN: Ah ha no one can draw the whole world.

(Paul comes to the table)

BEN: Can you draw the whole world?

MARK: He would.

BEN: You don't know because you don't know how to draw.

MARK: I don't know how to draw the whole world.

BOB: You don't know.

BEN: Do you know how to draw stars?

BOB: No he don't know.

MARK: I don't know how to draw stars. There's no one in the world knows how to draw stars.

BOB: **I know how to draw stars. It's it's very easy. You doesn't know.**
(Some time later)
PAUL: Ben I draw better than you.
BOB: **No you not. It's not. It's teacher's draw.** (To Paul) **Look look he can't.** (To Ben about Paul)
BEN: The teacher drawed that.
BOB: **Yeah.**
BEN: Bullshit.
BOB: **Bullshit.**

It would appear that there are social forces at work in Bob–peer desk work that draw Bob into the conversation; he has established a dominant role in his group from time to time, and he takes the initiative to criticize the work of rivals and to assert his and his friends' superiority. The transcript shows a great deal of linguistic modeling being provided by his peers, and evidence that Bob both notices and incorporates those models into his own utterances in the heated exchanges which are recorded. (See for example lines 22–25 above, with the modeling and repetition of 'He/you don't know . . .' and lines 27–28: 'X knows how to draw stars'.) Liu's quantitative analyses show a general pattern of increase in Bob's initiations in Bob–peer interactions, and a much wider range of 'functions'[3] expressed by Bob in interactions with his peers than with his teachers.

Interaction with the researcher

The researcher was a friend of the family, and (perhaps more importantly) an adult who (as can be seen in the interactions transcribed in the dissertation) knew how to *play* and was *interested in interacting* with Bob and drawing him out in a relaxed home environment. Bob's relationship with the researcher changed from a formal teacher–pupil relationship during the pre-school period, to a more relaxed 'adult–friend' relationship, in which Bob felt free to disobey and even (once or twice) to insult the researcher.[4] The two frequently drew pictures together and played with blocks, talking about their activities as well as about school. Bob tried hard to initiate interactions with the researcher. Bob's attempts to produce English utterances met with the researcher's approval and encouragement (though, interestingly, Liu reports that he was often more judgmental than the teachers, giving

[114]

Bob more negative feedback on his language than they did). In this third interactional context, Bob used the most multiple constituent and complex structures, and the widest variety of language functions. The following conversation with the researcher took place at roughly the same time as the conversation with the teacher recorded above.

(3) Session 61 (December 10, 1987)

BOB: Now I know what I can do.
RES: Yeah.
BOB: I'm not tell you what I'm doing now.
RES: Tell me what you're doing.
BOB: I'm not tell you. I draw all of them, so it's complete.
RES: What do you want to draw?
BOB: I'm not tell you.
RES: I know. It's nothing except colors.
BOB: No. I'm going to draw something. No. I'm not lie to you.
RES: I didn't say you were lying.
BOB: I'm just draw a ghost. Can't draw.
RES: You're drawing a ghost?
BOB: Yeah. I can draw all of them.
RES: OK. I'll see what sort of ghost you can draw.
BOB: I draw a lovely ghost.

In the conversational segment transcribed above there appears to be more initiation on Bob's part than in the previous one, with less immediate repetition of modeling. The embedded sentences represented in 'Now I know what I can do' and 'I'm not tell you what I'm doing now' seem to characterize a learner at a much higher level of proficiency than in the previous segments. The quantitative analysis provided below (and particularly in Liu, 1991) shows that there was a general pattern of increased syntactic complexity, increased initiation, and increased variety of both structure and function in the conversations between Bob and the researcher.

The three interactional contexts just described were engaged in during the same period of time, and so during that period, one might suppose that Bob had the same knowledge system of English at his disposal. However, in interaction with the teachers, he only used very simple English, which was a very small part of his knowledge system. In interacting with peers, he made more extensive use of his knowledge by producing more complex English. In interaction with the researcher, he made still more extensive use of this knowledge to the extent of attempting syntactic structures beyond his existing control.

Thus, from Liu's (1991) perspective, Bob performs his competence differentially in the three interactional contexts, contexts defined in terms of the differing role relationships the learner had with his interlocutors.

A quantitative analysis of Bob's IL performance

A number of different quantitative analyses are provided by Liu (1991) of general ways in which Bob's interlanguage production differed in the three different interactional contexts. Over the same period of time, Bob clearly produced much less language in interactions with his teachers than in the other two contexts: he produced 260 utterances in interactions with his teachers, 2449 in interactions with his peers, and 5716 in interactions with the researcher. This is not surprising, since Bob was only one among many students in the class, and had fewer opportunities to interact with his teachers. What is far more interesting is what the quantitative analyses tell us about the *quality* of Bob's participation in those three interactional contexts, a quality explainable by the different role relationships involved.

In just one of many examples (see Table 1), Bob produced complex structures[5] differentially in the context of Bob–peer and Bob–researcher interactions.

Context	Number	Percentage
With peers	40	18%
With researcher	177	82%
Total	217	

TABLE 1. *Complex structures produced by Bob in two contexts* (Liu 1991: 211, Table 8.5)

Although Bob produces roughly twice as many utterances with the researcher as he does with his peers, he produces four times as many complex structures with the researcher as he does with his peers. Other

[116]

measures show that Bob uses simpler utterances with his teachers than in the other interactions. Bob appeared to be unwilling to take risks with teachers; he seemed to be striving to be correct, and so didn't risk using utterances of which he was unsure.

Similarly (see Table 2), Bob initiates and responds to the initiations of others to different degrees in the three contexts.

Context	Initiations	Responses	Total
With teachers	74 (29%)	186 (71%)	260 (100%)
With peers	1798 (73%)	651 (27%)	2449 (100%)
With researcher	3497 (61%)	2219 (39%)	5716 (100%)

TABLE 2. *A comparison of initiations and responses in three contexts (between 3/3/87 and 10/12/88)* (Liu 1994, Table 1)

We have already seen in the excerpted transcripts we have examined that Bob appears to use his interlanguage for different purposes in the context of the three different role relationships. Specifically, he uses his language for a much wider range of speech acts in his interactions with his peers than with his teachers: acts which include criticisms, commands, arguments, insults, and even curses. Indeed, many of these speech acts would probably be inappropriate for a Chinese or Australian child to use with an adult who is in an institutional role.

In discourse, function and form are in dynamic interaction, though there is, as Widdowson (1983b) has often reminded us, no straightforward relationship between the two. For different purposes, different language forms or form–function relationships may be required. We must expect that when Bob uses his interlanguage to a large extent to (for example) make negative comments about the abilities of his interlocutors, he will have a greater need to use negative and comparative forms (for example, *You can't do X; X is better than you,* etc.) in conversations with his peers than in conversations with his teacher.

In sum, Liu shows that Bob's use of his interlanguage varies in its general shape as he moves from one situation to another: his use of his interlanguage knowledge is affected by the different interactional contexts, as defined by the different role relationships which pertain. Bob is performing his competence differently in these different interactional contexts.

But such a finding is not new; many other studies have shown that social context, identity of interlocutor, role, and task have an impact on learner performance and the language forms which are used for different purposes in different social contexts.

The crucial question for us now, is this: do the different interactional contexts simply give Bob different opportunities to show what he already knows? Or do the different interactional contexts cause Bob's competence to develop differentially?

Effect of interactional context on acquisition

Liu claims that the different interactions in which Bob engaged had an impact on his *interlanguage development*, not only in terms of the *rate* of that development, but also on the *route* of his interlanguage development. We will examine each of these claims in turn.

Rate

Liu (1991) uses Pienemann and Johnston's (1987) framework for the development of English as a second language to examine the development of various aspects of Bob's interlanguage grammar. He focuses for example upon the developmental stages in Bob's use of interrogative forms. (In the sequence which follows, the examples are from Bob's data and are marked by the session in which they occur.)

STAGE 1: Single word
STAGE 2: SVO?
  —**You like number one?** (Session 29 with researcher)
STAGE 3: Do-front without inversion
  WHX-front without inversion
  —**Why you do that?** (Session 36 with peers)
STAGE 4: Pseudo-inversion. Units can be moved from the center to the front of the string, but there can be no internal movement. ('Is' for example can be moved to the front of a string creating a Yes/No question. 'Where's' may front a question, but as an unanalyzed unit. True WH questions,

however, cannot be created as this requires the movement of a unit from one internal position to another.)

Y/N inversion

—**Where's the monkey?** (Session 24 with researcher)

STAGE 5: Aux-2nd

Suppletion

This allows the formation of true WH questions

—**What are you doing?** (Session 24 with researcher)

STAGE 6: Question tag

—**You don't like green, are you?** (Session 49 with researcher)

Liu, following Pienemann and Johnston (1987), defines Bob's acquisition of a form as occurring at the point of first use of that form. Different researchers define 'point of acquisition' differently; which definition is 'correct' is an unresolved question in our field and we will not resolve it here. What is important for our purposes is simply to note that Liu, following Pienemann and Johnston (1987), opts for first use of a form as marking the acquisition of that form.

Liu's data show a clear and consistent pattern whereby almost every new stage in this sequence (all except Stage 3, about which more below) appears first in interaction with the researcher, and only much later in other settings. For example, Stage 5 interrogative forms initially appear in Bob–researcher interactions in Session 23, but do not appear in Bob–peer interactions until Session 36, and last in Bob–teacher interactions. Stage 6 interrogative forms appear first in Bob–researcher interactions in Session 49, but do not appear in Bob–peer interactions until Session 76, nearly nine months later.

In general, new structures appear first in the interactions between Bob and the researcher, spread to the interactions with his peers, and appear last in his interactions with his teacher. Liu suggests that the context in which a form is first used is the context in which that form was acquired. His analysis suggests that different interactional contexts support different rates of development of particular interlanguage features. In other words, if the learner is deprived of the opportunity to interact in certain contexts and role relationships, then his rate of IL development will be slower. Liu states that if Bob had not had the opportunity to interact with the researcher, the overall rate of development of his interlanguage is, in fact, likely to have been much slower.

Why some interactional contexts promote faster acquisition

What is it about the Bob–researcher context which is so productive? One possible reason is that this context provides Bob with better input; the researcher may be the one who provides input which is most suited to the learner's developmental needs. The researcher is the only interlocutor in these three contexts who focuses solely upon the learner and communicating with him, and may be providing more complex input than (say) his teachers or his peers. Thus, it is possible that the researcher provides the input which is most finely attuned to Bob's needs, and that this explains why researcher–Bob interactions are so productive. But there may also be another factor at work.

Another explanation for the superiority of this context can be seen in Bob's attempts to produce comprehensible output (Swain 1985), and the resultant interplay between input and output which occurs. In this view, it is in those interactional contexts where the learner needs to produce output which the current interlanguage system cannot handle that the learner pushes the limits of that interlanguage system to *make* it handle that output, thus keeping the system 'permeable' (Adjemian 1976) and open to change. In such contexts, the learner functions in much the same way as the learner in Schmidt and Frota (1986): struggling to produce output, becoming aware of a gap or need for a structure, and *then* noticing that structure in the input. Liu's data can be argued to show that it is precisely in those contexts where Bob has to produce output which his IL cannot handle that the IL develops fastest, with the richest variety of IL structures and even possibly with structures out of developmental sequence (see *Route* below).

Liu argues that Bob pushes the limits of his competence in interaction with the researcher, thus, we might suggest, making his competence more permeable and open to change in that context. Bob takes risks with his interlanguage production differentially in the three different interactional contexts. In interacting with the researcher, as opposed to other interlocutors, Bob speaks in a wider range of styles ranging from narratives and discussions to arguments. Bob also produces a wider variety of forms in interaction with the researcher than in the other interactional contexts. Further, in speaking with this interested and supportive adult friend, Bob's interlanguage was

characterized by inaccurate syntax resulting from his exploitation of his competence in English to its limits. The consequence was that he produced much more complex structures laden with non-target forms, in this context than in any other context.
(Liu 1991: 227)

Liu's data show us first that interactional demands differ in different social contexts, and argues further that *one* context can be identified as the one in which the learner's interlanguage system is most unstable, most variable, and most open to change—and in which the first elements of more advanced developmental stages are produced. There is thus evidence that this is the context in which acquisition is most likely to have occurred. We believe that Liu's data are convincing evidence that an exploration of the causes of interlanguage variation can shed light upon the process of second language acquisition. The interactions in which Bob engages have an impact upon the interlanguage forms he is willing to use at any given time, and the degree to which he is willing to go beyond the limits of his interlanguage competence. This willingness in turn may have an impact upon the rate of his interlanguage development. His interlanguage develops differentially in different interactional contexts, as he enters into different role relationships and responds to different demands from his interlocutors.

Route

We have argued that certain types of interaction encourage faster and more complete development of certain features in the interlanguage than do others. Of course, Selinker and Douglas (1985) and others have argued this same point. But Liu's is the first study of which we are aware which examines the development of a specific grammatical form over time in several contexts and provides specific data in support of the view that different types of interaction can affect not just the rate, but the route of second language acquisition. The development of interrogative forms in Bob's interlanguage shows that interactional context affects particular sequences of development in the interlanguage. Pienemann and Johnston (1987) claim that there is a universal sequence of acquisition of interrogative forms, such that Stage 4 or 5 features should not appear before Stage 3 features. In their theory, a learner cannot progress to a higher level stage of acquisition without first going through *all* the lower level stages of acquisition of any given structure. The stages proposed in this theory are claimed to be universal. Although there may be some disagreement on some of the details of Pienemann and Johnston's theory (Hudson 1993), in fact there is general agreement among SLA researchers on the broad outlines of this sequence of acquisition of questions in English, as noted by Larsen-Freeman and Long (1991: 93). It is generally agreed that questions with non-inversion of the SVO pattern (Pienemann and Johnston's Stage 3) occur *before* questions in which inversion occurs (Stages 4 and 5).

Yet in Bob's case, Stage 4 and 5 interrogative forms did emerge in interactions with the researcher long before Stage 3 forms emerged. The data show that Stages 4 and 5 interrogative forms emerged in Bob's interaction with the researcher in Sessions 23 and 24. Stage 3 interrogative forms did not emerge until nearly three months later and were first used in Session 36 in Bob's interaction with his peers at school. Stage 3 interrogative forms started to appear in Bob's interaction with the researcher in Session 40. It would appear, then, that Bob's participation in the interactional context with the researcher altered a so-called universal sequence of acquisition of interrogatives in Bob's IL.

Liu (1991) suggests that it is the researcher's intensive use of Stage 4 and 5 forms in the input, together with an increased opportunity for Bob to produce such forms, which influenced Bob to acquire those forms first in that context. Bob's interaction with the researcher gave him a context where there were opportunities and incentive for him to acquire and use those Stage 4 and 5 forms before Stage 3 forms.

This claim implies that external social demands can be so strong that they can cause an alteration in internal psychologically motivated sequences of acquisition—even so-called universal sequences of acquisition. This is a very strong claim, one which, we believe, should be tested in further studies of the same design. If further studies provide support for this claim, then no adequate theory of second language acquisition can omit an account of this interplay between external social demands and internal sequences of acquisition.

Limitations

Clearly, this is only one study of one individual, and more data of this sort are needed. Further, Liu's (1991) analysis of Bob's sequence of acquisition is based upon Pienemann and Johnston's criterion of first use of a form as marking that form's acquisition; we need to examine Bob's acquisition process using other criteria as well. We need to examine Bob's variable use of question forms in more detail, using tools such as VARBRUL[6], in order to see how frequent these forms are in the three interactional contexts over time. Finally, we need to examine the development of other structures in Bob's interlanguage, such as negation and relative clause formation, in order to see whether interactional context affects the rate and route of development of these and other interlanguage structures in a similar way.

Conclusion

We feel we have shown that Liu's research is important, in spite of the limitations cited above, in that it points a direction for future research. The study of Bob's language development illustrates the kind of data we need to obtain in an attempt to determine the relationship between contextual variation and second language acquisition—in particular, to assess the degree to which interlanguage may develop at different rates in different social contexts, and the extent to which interactional context may be able to override or alter any claimed 'innate universal sequence of acquisition'. Such an investigation can shed light upon the delicate relationship which undoubtedly exists in SLA between internal 'innate' and external 'contextual' forces. And clearly, any adequate theory of second language acquisition must be able to account for that relationship between internal and contextual forces which occurs in the process of second language acquisition.

Notes

1 An earlier version of this paper was presented at the 22nd University of Wisconsin Milwaukee Linguistics Symposium, on Second Language Acquisition Theory and Pedagogy, October 9, 1993. An earlier version, focusing on pedagogical implications, appears in a volume containing the proceedings of that conference. We are grateful to Fred Eckman, Dennis Preston, Merrill Swain, and George Yule for comments on earlier drafts of this paper.

2 For a more detailed account of that study, we refer the reader to the dissertation (Liu 1991) and a paper based upon it (Liu 1994). At this point in time, Liu has only begun to analyze his data in any depth; we can look for a deeper and more detailed analysis of the interaction between social forces and Bob's acquisition of specific grammatical forms in future papers.

3 Liu defines functions using Nicholas' (1987) categories; see Liu (1991, 1994) for discussion.

4 The fact that Bob knew that the researcher spoke Chinese may have increased Bob's confidence in speaking with him.

5 'Complex structures' are just one category of sentence structure catalogued by Liu, and are defined as multiple constituent structures which convey multiple propositions.

6 VARBRUL is a sophisticated computerized statistical package which is designed to analyze complex relationships which obtain among language form, linguistic context, social context, and time.

8

Three functions of output in second language learning

MERRILL SWAIN

Introduction

IT SEEMS FITTING to have a paper about output in a volume for Henry Widdowson. He is, after all, the consummate 'outputter'! It may also be fitting that this paper is somewhat speculative, attempting to outline the 'output hypothesis' as I see it at this stage of its development, and provide evidence for it.

It has been argued that output is nothing more than a sign of the second language acquisition that has already taken place, and that output serves no useful role in SLA except possibly as one source of (self-) input to the learner (Krashen 1989). On the contrary, the output hypothesis claims that producing language serves second language acquisition in several ways. One function of producing the target language, in the sense of 'practising', is that it enhances fluency. This seems non-controversial, particularly if it is not confused with the adage that 'practice makes perfect'. We know that fluency and accuracy are different dimensions of language performance, and although practice may enhance fluency, it does not necessarily improve accuracy (Ellis 1988; Schmidt 1992).

Other functions of output in second language acquisition have been proposed that relate more to accuracy than fluency. I will outline those briefly now, then return to consider them in more detail. First, it is hypothesized that output promotes 'noticing'. That is to say, in producing the target language (vocally or subvocally) learners may notice a gap between what they *want* to say and what they *can* say, leading them to recognize what they do not know, or know only partially. In other words, under some circumstances, the activity of producing the target language may prompt second language learners to consciously recognize some of their linguistic problems; it may bring to their attention something they need to discover about their L2 (Swain 1993). This may trigger cognitive processes which might generate linguistic knowledge that is new for learners, or which consolidate their existing knowledge (Swain and Lapkin 1994).

A second way in which producing language may serve the language learning process is through hypothesis testing. That is, producing output is one way of testing a hypothesis about comprehensibilty or linguistic well-formedness. A considerable body of research and theorizing over the last two decades has suggested that output, particularly erroneous output, can often be an indication that a learner has formulated a hypothesis about how the language works, and is testing it out (for example, Selinker 1972; Corder 1981). Sometimes this output invokes feedback which can lead learners to modify or 'reprocess' their output.

Thirdly, as learners reflect upon their own target language use, their output serves a metalinguistic function, enabling them to control and internalize linguistic knowledge. My assumption at present is that there is theoretical justification for considering a distinct metalinguistic function of output. However, it may be that we will want to consider it as the pedagogical means by which we can ensure that the other two functions operate.

Differences between comprehension and production: implications for the roles of output

Before examining these three functions of output in more depth, I would like to make a few preliminary comments about the differences between production and comprehension. The importance to learning of output could be that output pushes learners to process language more deeply (with more mental effort) than does input. With output, the learner is in control. By focusing on output we may be focusing on ways in which learners can play more active, responsible roles in their learning.

[126]

In speaking or writing, learners can 'stretch' their interlanguage to meet communicative goals. They might work towards solving their linguistic limitations by using their own internalized knowledge, or by cueing themselves to listen for a solution in future input. Learners (as well as native speakers, of course) can fake it, so to speak, in comprehension, but they cannot do so in the same way in production. They can pass themselves off as having understood, as Hawkins (1985a) so clearly demonstrated. Hawkins showed that learners would often claim to understand their interlocutors when, in fact, they did not. However, to produce, learners need to do something; they need to create linguistic form and meaning and in so doing, discover what they can and cannot do.

To state this somewhat more elegantly, the processes involved in producing language can be quite different than those involved in comprehending language. Clark and Clark (1977: 57–79) list a set of strategies native speakers use in comprehending. The strategies represent a set of heuristics that can be used to help listeners make sense of what they hear, and fall into two general approaches: syntactic and semantic. In criticizing the assumption that listeners make heavy use of function words, prefixes, and suffixes to make guesses about the probable structure of what they are hearing, Clark and Clark point out that 'in actual speech, these are just the words and elements that are most difficult to identify' (ibid.: 72). Furthermore, in listening (and also reading), semantic and pragmatic information assist comprehension in ways that may apply differently in production in that they can circumvent the need to process syntax.

> Listeners usually know a lot about what a speaker is going to say. They can make shrewd guesses from what has been said and from the situation being described. They can also be confident that the speaker will make sense, be relevant, provide given and new information appropriately, and in general be cooperative. Listeners almost certainly use this sort of information to select among alternative parses of a sentence, to anticipate words and phrases, and sometimes even to circumvent syntactic analyses altogether.
> (Clark and Clark 1977: 72)

In concluding their research report about an ESL program in New Brunswick that was entirely comprehension-based, Lightbown and Halter (1993: 23) state:

In a sense, it is hardly surprising that students left on their own to acquire language purely from exposure to comprehensible input seem to need help with certain aspects of the language . . . [for example,] focused instruction and feedback can help to fill these gaps and enhance their performance . . . The findings of this study also lend support to the view expressed by Swain (1985, 1988), Sharwood Smith (1986) and others that the kind of processing which is necessary for comprehension is different from the kind of processing which is required for production and, ultimately, for acquisition. As Cook (1991) has expressed it, the ability to *decode* language, that is, the ability to understand the meaning conveyed by a particular sentence, is not the same as *code breaking*, that is, discovering the linguistic systems which carry that meaning.

In sum, output may stimulate learners to move from the semantic, open-ended, non-deterministic, strategic processing prevalent in comprehension to the complete grammatical processing needed for accurate production. Output, thus, would seem to have a potentially significant role in the development of syntax and morphology, a role that underlies the three functions of output with which the rest of this paper is concerned.

Three functions of output

In the rest of this paper, I intend to discuss three functions of output which I hypothesize relate to accuracy rather than fluency:

1 the 'noticing/triggering' function, or what might be referred to as its consciousness-raising role
2 the hypothesis-testing function
3 the metalinguistic function, or what might be referred to as its 'reflective' role.

In discussing these functions, I also want to raise briefly two issues which arise from the research. In particular, the research requires us to think again, among other things, about the tests we use with respect to the learning tasks we engage students in, and what we mean when we claim something is learned.

Noticing

Let me turn, then, to a discussion of the three proposed functions of output. The first to be considered is the 'noticing/triggering' role of output, or what might be referred to as its consciousness-raising function. Schmidt and Frota (1986) offer a 'notice the gap principle' which states that 'a second language learner will begin to acquire the target-like form if and only if it is present in comprehended input and "noticed" in the normal sense of the word, that is consciously' (1986: 311). Our hypothesis is that output gives rise to noticing (Swain and Lapkin 1994). That is to say, in producing the target language, learners may encounter a linguistic problem leading them to notice what they do not know, or know only partially. In other words, the activity of producing the target language may prompt second language learners to consciously recognize some of their linguistic problems; it may make them aware of something they need to find out about their L2.

To test this hypothesis, one would need to demonstrate that learners may, on occasion, notice a problem (even without external cueing) through, for example, implicit or explicit feedback provided from an interlocutor about problems in the learners' output. It seems to me that there is ample evidence from the communication strategy literature (for example, Tarone 1977; Færch and Kasper 1983; Bialystok 1990; Kellerman 1991) that learners do notice problems as they speak, and do try to do something about them. But what do they do when they notice a problem? Do they focus on morphology and syntax? Do they engage in cognitive processes related to second language learning?

In a recent study (Swain and Lapkin 1994), we attempted to examine directly the cognitive processes that are activated as a result of noticing a problem—as directly, that is, as current research methods allow. The participants in the study were grade-eight early French-immersion students (average age thirteen). The students were individually trained to use think-aloud procedures, and were then asked to think aloud while writing an article for a newspaper about an environmental problem. Students were prompted with 'what are you thinking?' if they stopped talking for very long, or if they made a change to their text without commenting on it. Students were advised that they could not have access to a dictionary or any other aid, and that the researcher would not be able to help either. These last conditions were imposed because we were interested in seeing what students would do without further input from external sources; whether they would try to work out solutions on their own.

From the think-aloud protocols, we abstracted what we have termed language-related episodes. These language-related episodes were any segment of the protocol in which a learner either spoke about a language problem he or she encountered while writing, and solved it either correctly or incorrectly; or simply solved it (again, either correctly or incorrectly) without having explicitly identified it as a problem. These episodes were categorized according to the mental processes we thought were reflected in the changes the students made to their output. Overall, in about 40% of these episodes, students paid attention to grammatical form.

The results demonstrate quite clearly that even second language learners as young as these students do indeed, as they produce their L2, notice gaps in their linguistic knowledge. Output led to noticing. Furthermore, when these learners encounter difficulties in producing the target language, they do engage in thought processes of a sort which may play a role in second language learning (see also Cumming 1990; Wood 1994). The cognitive processes identified represent processes hypothesized to be involved in second language learning: extending first language knowledge to second language contexts; extending second language knowledge to new target language contexts, and formulating and testing hypotheses about linguistic forms and functions (see, for example, Selinker 1972; Corder 1981; Kellerman and Sharwood Smith 1986; McLaughlin 1987).

It is our conclusion that this evidence supports the hypothesis that output can stimulate noticing; that it raises learners' awareness of gaps in their knowledge; in short, that it plays a consciousness-raising role. Furthermore, noticing can trigger cognitive processes that have been implicated in second language learning; cognitive processes that generate linguistic knowledge that is new for learners, or that consolidate their existing knowledge.

Hypothesis testing

The second function of output that I want to discuss is its hypothesis-testing role. It has been argued that some errors which appear in learners' written and spoken production reveal hypotheses held by them about how the target language works. To test a hypothesis, learners need to *do* something, and one way of doing this is to say or write something.

If learners were not testing hypotheses, then changes in their output would not be expected following feedback. However, recent research (for example, Pica, Holliday, Lewis, and Morgenthaler 1989; Iwashita 1993) demonstrates that during the process of negotiating meaning, learners will modify their output in response to such conversational moves as clarification requests or confirmation checks. For example, Pica and her colleagues (1989) found that in response to clarification and confirmation requests, over one-third of the learners' utterances were modified either semantically or morphosyntactically.

If output as hypothesis testing were just a matter of gaining more input, we might expect change after each instance of feedback. Why some input is taken up and not other input will, in part, have to do with comprehensibilty, learner-internal factors, etc., but that cannot be the whole story. The fact that learners modify their speech in one-third (but not in all) of their utterances suggests equally that they are only testing out some things and not others; that their output is indeed a test of a learner-generated hypothesis; that their output is the 'selector' for what will be attended to.

Although no one has yet shown directly that the modified, or reprocessed, utterances are maintained in a learner's interlanguage (though see Nobuyoshi and Ellis 1993), the assumption is that this process of modification contributes to second language acquisition. As suggested by Pica and her colleagues (1989), learners, in modifying their output, '. . . test hypotheses about the second language, experiment with new structures and forms, and expand and exploit their interlanguage resources in creative ways' (1989: 64)—in ways, I suspect, that are similar to those we found reflected in the think-alouds of the grade-eight immersion students discussed above. It might be that the modified, or reprocessed, output can be considered to represent the leading edge of a learner's interlanguage.

This is precisely one of the points made by Tarone and Liu (elsewhere in this volume) in their study of variation in the output of a Chinese boy over two years as he acquired English.

To sum up this section, we have seen that learners may use their output as a way of trying out new language forms and structures as they stretch their interlanguage to meet communicative needs; they may output just to see what works and what does not. That immediate feedback may not be facilitative or forthcoming does not negate the value of having experimented with their language resources.

Conscious reflection

I want to turn now to discuss the third function of output: its metalinguistic function. First I will explain what I mean by the metalinguistic function of output and provide an illustrative example comparing it with an example in the literature of negotiation of meaning. Following this, I will consider two studies in some depth which suggest the value for second language learning of conscious reflection about language, or, what might be referred to, in the particular dialogic conditions we have studied it, as 'negotiation about form'.

When it is argued that a function of output is to test hypotheses, it is assumed that the output itself *is* the hypothesis. That is, the output represents the learner's best guess as to how something should be said or written. We rarely ask learners what their hypotheses are, but rather infer them from the output itself. However, under certain task conditions, learners will not only reveal their hypotheses, but reflect on them, using language to do so. It is this 'level' of output that represents its metalinguistic function of using language to reflect on language, allowing learners to control and internalize it.

Thus, we can look not only at 'output-as-the-hypothesis-itself' as something learners sometimes do in order to learn, but we can also look at what explicit hypothesizing does for learners. Does it play a role in second language learning?

In order to investigate what learners make explicit and how this contributes to language development, we need tasks which encourage reflection on language form while still being oriented to getting meaning across. In most of the research tasks used in the study of interaction, this reflective process is not demanded. The focus is instead on communication where 'attention is principally focused on meaning rather than form' (Nunan 1989: 10). In fact, Ellis (1982) includes in his list of characteristics of communication tasks that 'there must be a focus on message rather than on the linguistic code' (cited in Nobuyoshi and Ellis

1993: 204). However, it is certainly feasible for a communicative task to be one in which learners communicate about language, in the context of trying to produce something they want to say in the target language. Learners negotiate meaning, but the content of that negotiation is language form, and its relation to the meaning they are trying to express; they produce language and then reflect upon it. They use language to 'negotiate about form'.

Let us consider an example. The two students in Example 1, Keith and George, are in grade eight (age thirteen) of an early French-immersion program. The task these students, and their classmates, are engaged in is a 'dictogloss' (Wajnryb 1990). The teacher had prepared a short, dense text which dealt with a topic they had been considering in class and which included grammatical features recently reviewed by her. The text has been read aloud twice, at normal speed, to the students. While it was being read, students jotted down familiar words and phrases. Following this, students worked in pairs to reconstruct the text from their shared resources. They were expected to reconstruct the text as accurately as possible, both with respect to content and grammar. They had done similar tasks several times over the last few months so were familiar with the procedures. In the example, George and Keith are reconstructing the first sentence of the dictogloss, which is: *En ce qui concerne l'environnement, il y a beaucoup de problèmes qui nous tracassent.* [As far as the environment is concerned, there are many problems which worry us.]

Example 1

058: KEITH: Attends une minute! Non, j'ai besoin du Bescherelle (verb reference book). S'il vous plaît, ouvrir le Bescherelle à la page qui, OK, à la dernière page (i.e. the index). OK, cherche *tracasse*, un page, deux pages.

059: GEORGE: *Tra, tra, tracer.*

060: KEITH: *Tracasser* page six. Cherche le s'il vous plaît.

061: GEORGE: Pas de problème.

062: KEITH: C'est sur page.

063: GEORGE: Verbe, <à la page> six. OK, c'est le même que *aimer*, (i.e. it is conjugated in the same way and *aimer* is given as the standard example for all verbs with this pattern of conjugation).

064: KEITH: Laissez-moi le voir s'il vous plaît (reading from the

[133]

page). *Le passé simple, nous tracasse; nous aime* (Keith is trying to find a first-person plural version of the verb which sounds like *tracasse*, the word he has written in his notes, but is unable to find one).

065: GEORGE: Peut-être c'est ici.

066: KEITH: Non, c'est juste *nous aime* (pause) ah, le présent. *Tracasse, aimons*, n'est-ce pas que *tracasse* (to teacher who has just arrived), ce n'est pas *nous tracasse* (what he has written down in his notes), c'est *nous tracassons*?

067: TEACHER: Ce sont des **problèmes** qui nous tracassent (deliberately not directly giving the answer).

068: KEITH: *Nous tracassons*.

069: GEORGE: Oh (beginning to realize what is happening).

070: KEITH: Oui? (so what?)

071: GEORGE: Les problèmes qui nous tracassent. Like the (pause) c'est les problèmes (pause) like, that concerns us.

072: KEITH: Oui, mais *tracasse* n'est-ce pas que c'est <o-n-s>?

073: GEORGE: *Tracasse* c'est pas un, c'est pas un, (pause), oui I dunno (unable to articulate what he has discovered).

074: KEITH: OK, ça dit, les problèmes qui nous tracassent. Donc, est-ce que *tracasse* est un verbe? Qu'on, qu'on doit conjuger?

075: TEACHER: Uh huh.

076: KEITH: Donc est-ce que c'est *tracassons*?

077: TEACHER: Ce sont les **problèmes** qui nous tracassent.

078: GEORGE: Nous, c'est, c'est pas, c'est pas, oui, c'est les problèmes, c'est pas, c'est pas nous.

079: KEITH: Ah! E-n-t (third-person plural ending), OK, OK.

The following notations have been used in this transcription:
(. . .)   indicates editorial comments added by the authors;
<. . .>   indicates text added by the transcriber to aid comprehension;
____   indicates utterances made simultaneously.
(Kowal and Swain, forthcoming)

The problem here is that Keith has written 'nous tracasse' in his notes and that does not correspond with his knowledge of French that when 'nous' is the subject of a verb, the ending of the verb is 'ons'. This example shows Keith and George jointly coming to an understanding that 'les problèmes' (represented by the relative pronoun 'qui') is the subject of the verb 'tracassent', not 'nous', and what that implies about the form of the verb, an activity entirely dependent on understanding the meaning of the sentence. After the pair has tried to find in their verb reference book (the Bescherelle) a non-existent first-person plural version of a verb which doesn't end with 'ons', Keith is able to put the problem into words in appealing to the teacher: 'ce n'est pas "nous tracasse", c'est "nous tracassons"?' *He has verbalized the problem, and now they can work on solving it.* The teacher (turn 067) deliberately does not provide the correct answer but provides strong hints which she hopes will be sufficient to help the students to work out the correct answer for themselves. At turn 069, George has a flash of understanding: he has understood how the words are related to one another. The rest of the example shows George struggling with an explanation of his understanding of why 'tracasser' should be in the third-person plural, not the first-person plural: as he says in turn 071: 'Like the . . . c'est les problèmes . . . like, that concerns us,' and in turn 078: 'Nous, c'est, c'est pas, c'est pas, oui, c'est les problèmes, c'est pas, c'est pas nous'. [Us, it's, it's not, it's not, yeah, it's the problems, it's not, it's not us.] This explanation provides Keith with the same insight that George has had, so that Keith is able to write the verb with the correct 'ent' ending.

In this example, George has made explicit the basis of his insight. He has provided, though not using metalanguage, an explanation for the form the verb must take which relates to the syntax of the sentence. This results, at minimum, I would argue, in a context-sensitive knowledge of a grammatical rule because form, function, and meaning are so intimately linked in the way this task was used.

It may be useful at this point to digress for a moment to consider Vygotsky's perspective on the importance of dialogic interaction. According to Vygotsky (1986), cognitive processes arise from the interaction that occurs between individuals. That is, cognitive development, including presumably language development, originates on the inter-psychological plane. Through a process of appropriation, what originated in the social sphere comes to be represented intra-psychologically, that is, within the individual. If one accepts this as one general process of development, from inter-mental to intra-mental, two important principles follow. First, as Donato (1994: 39) has argued: 'The focus [in SLA] should be . . . on observing the construction

[135]

of co-knowledge and how this co-construction process results in linguistic *change* among and within individuals during joint activity.' This process becomes particularly observable for language development when the task students are engaged in involves reflecting on their own language production, that is, when they are engaged in negotiating about form. Secondly, as Donato and Lantolf (1990) point out, because developmental processes are dialogically derived and constituted, they '. . . can be observed directly in the linguistic interactions that arise among speakers as they participate in problem-solving tasks' (1990: 85). In the present context, this means that what we see occurring in George's output as he struggles to explain his understanding is part of the process of second language learning. That is, through an examination of what learners do or say as they reflect on language in their attempt to produce it, we are given access to learning processes at work.

Example 1 can be contrasted with Example 2 taken from the negotiation of meaning research. It is taken from Gass and Varonis (1989: 81) as evidence that interaction drives language development. The dialogue is between two adult learners of English, where Hiroko is describing a picture while her partner, Izumi, is drawing it.

Example 2

HIROKO: A man is uh drinking c-coffee or tea uh with the saucer of the uh uh coffee set is uh in his uh knee
IZUMI: in him knee
HIROKO: uh on his knee
IZUMI: yeah
HIROKO: on his knee
IZUMI: so sorry. On his knee
(Gass and Varonis 1989: 81)

The main difference between the two examples is that in Example 1, the students talk about language form. They reflect on it, trying to make sense of it in terms of the meaning it serves. The second example is illustrative of the first two functions of output discussed in this paper: noticing and hypothesis testing. If Hiroko and Izumi were to be given a tape-recording, or transcript, of their dialogue, perhaps they might have discussed why they settled on 'on his knee' or what was wrong about 'in his knee' and 'in him knee', a process which, I am suggesting, may help learners in the appropriation of linguistic knowledge when done in the context of creating meaning. It may help learners perform their competence, or move beyond it. The output brought about through the collaborative dialogue may allow learners the necessary support to outperform their competence and in the process develop their interlanguage.

Two studies are suggestive of the value of this sort of negotiation about form for second language learning. One is a study by Donato (1994) on collective scaffolding. The second is a study conducted by LaPierre (1994) on the role of output, and of conscious reflection on output, in second language learning. Although in the Donato study the students spontaneously focused on form whereas in the LaPierre study they were taught to do so, in both studies students produced language and talked about the language they produced. The question to be considered here is whether there is evidence demonstrating some consequences for language learning as students try out language and make explicit the hypotheses that underlie their language use. I would like to consider briefly each of these studies in turn.

As part of a much larger study on collaborative planning among learners, Donato analyzed selected protocols of three students who had worked together in class over a period of ten weeks. The students involved in the study were third-semester students of French in an American university. The data consist of a one-hour session in which the students planned for an oral activity that would take place the next week. It was intended that during the planning session, the students should decide on what happens between a husband and his wife when the wife discovers her husband has purchased a fur coat for another woman. The students had been told that they could not use notes in their presentation, nor were they to memorize their scenario, but they could make notes while preparing if they wished.

Donato examined the transcript of their planning session for examples of scaffolding: a situation where, 'in social interaction a knowledgeable participant can create, by means of speech, supportive conditions in which the novice can participate in, and extend current skills and knowledge to higher levels of competence' (Donato 1994: 40). (On scaffolding, see for example, Wood, Bruner, and Ross 1976; Rogoff 1990). Example 3 shows the three learners of French mutually constructing a scaffold for each other's performance.

Example 3

A1: SPEAKER 1: ... and then I'll say ... *tu as souvenu notre anniversaire de marriage* ... or should I say *mon anniversaire?*

A2: SPEAKER 2: *Tu as ...*

A3: SPEAKER 3: *Tu as ...*

A4: SPEAKER 1: *Tu as souvenu ...* 'you remembered?'

A5: SPEAKER 3: Yeah, but isn't that reflexive? *Tu t'as ...*

A6: SPEAKER 1: Ah, *tu t'as souvenu.*

A7: SPEAKER 2: Oh, it's *tu es*

A8: SPEAKER 1: *Tu es*

A9: SPEAKER 3: *tu es, tu es, tu ...*

A10: SPEAKER 1: *t'es, tu t'es*

A11: SPEAKER 3: *tu t'es*

A12: SPEAKER 1: *Tu t'es souvenu.*

(Donato 1994: 44)

In this example, in lines A1 to A4, the students jointly produce 'tu as souvenu'. Having produced it, Speaker 3 notices that something is wrong and in line A5 questions the language they have produced expressing quite explicitly the hypothesis which underlies his shift from 'tu as' to 'tu t'as', that is, that the verb *souvenir* is a reflexive one. In line A7, Speaker 2 suggests that the auxiliary should be *être*, not *avoir*. The rest of the protocol shows the learners making use of the information they have made explicit to create the correct 'tu t'es souvenu'.

In all, thirty-two cases of scaffolded help were identified in the hour-long planning session of Donato's students. Of course, these instances of scaffolding suggest other sources of language learning than just noticing, testing hypotheses, and talking about language. However, it is significant that of the outcomes of the thirty-two cases of collective scaffolding observed in the planning session, 75% were used correctly one week later. This is, I believe, impressive evidence of language learning. Donato points out that it is not a surprising finding 'in light of Vygotskian theory which argues that individual knowledge is socially and dialogically derived, the genesis of which can be observed directly in the interactions among speakers during problem-solving tasks' (Donato 1994: 51).

The second study I would like to review has been conducted by one of our M.A. students, Donna LaPierre (1994). In this study it was hypothesized that because pair work necessitated output, there was a greater likelihood that language learning would be evidenced amongst those working in pairs than amongst those working individually on a task. Additionally it was hypothesized that when learners reflected on the language they produced, learning would result.

The study involved three grade-eight early immersion classes over a period of about a month. The task was similar to the one we saw George and Keith engaged in, in Example 1. One class of students, however, did not work in pairs to reconstruct the passage, but worked individually, while the other two classes of students reconstructed the text by working in pairs. The text was about a nightmare.

The first hypothesis, that there was greater likelihood that language learning would be evidenced amongst those working in pairs (dyads) than amongst those working individually on the task, was tested using a post-test measuring general comprehension of the passage and its vocabulary. No differences were found between those completing the task individually and those completing the task in pairs. This finding, we believe, represents a failure of the test to capture some of the learning that occurred, a point which I will return to below.

The second hypothesis, that when learners reflected on the language they produced, learning would result, was tested by means of tailor-made, dyad-specific post-tests. These dyad-specific questions are a pivotal feature of this study. They were developed from the transcripts of the students' talk as they reconstructed the passage. From these transcripts, episodes where students talked about the language they had produced were isolated. On the basis of these episodes, questions were constructed. Thus, every pair of students had a set of questions that reflected what they specifically had said in reconstructing the passage.

The expectation was that where students reflected on language form and function, and arrived at a correct solution, they would respond correctly to the relevant dyad-specific question. Similarly, when they discussed language form and function but arrived at an incorrect solution, they would respond incorrectly to the relevant dyad-specific question. That is, they would have learned, but unfortunately, what they learned was not the correct target form. Thus, each episode was classified into categories. One category involved episodes where the negotiation led to a solution, and that solution was in fact correct. The second category involved episodes where the negotiation also led to a solution, but the solution was incorrect.

What, then, are the consequences of negotiating about language form and reaching a solution? In general, the results show that when a solution is reached, it corresponds to the students' responses one week later. More specifically, of the 140 negotiated episodes where the solution was a correct one, approximately 80% were correct in the post-test. Similarly, of the 21 episodes where the negotiated solution was incorrect, approximately 70% of the answers on the post-test were wrong, although they matched the solutions the pairs had arrived at. These results suggest that talk about form in the context of a meaning-based task is output that promotes second language learning.

These results also make perfectly clear that if we are going to test the language learning that occurs in negotiated turns, we need to measure what actually goes on there. The general test of comprehension administered could not capture this learning, nor is it likely even to be captured by a general test of the linguistic feature(s) the teacher or researcher assumes has been taught. This is because, as we discovered in examining what it was that students negotiated, the researcher's goal (in this case to focus students' attention on the *passé composé* and *imparfait*) was to a considerable extent undermined in the sense that students set their own agenda as to what they discussed, according to their linguistic needs in expressing their intended meaning as accurately as they could.

The results could be strengthened through the use of other measures of language learning. Donato used as evidence of learning, actual language use in a follow-up oral activity; LaPierre used tailor-made knowledge-based questions. Both were measured about a week after the learning event. What measures will be convincing of learning having occurred and what length of time needs to pass between the learning event and the measurement of it, are highly contentious issues in our field. I am convinced by these data that highly specific language learning has taken place. Others will be less convinced.

Conclusions

By way of concluding, I would like to make four comments. The first is a disclaimer. I have suggested that output serves at least three functions in second language learning beyond that of enhancing fluency. These are the noticing function, the hypothesis-testing function and the reflective (metalinguistic) function. I want to make it clear that no claim is being made that any or all of these functions operate whenever learners produce the target language. It will be one of the tasks of future research to determine under what conditions they do operate.

My second comment relates to language pedagogy. The three functions of output that I have outlined in this paper have, I believe, the potential of promoting accuracy, an issue of concern to many second language educators. The issue has resurfaced in our field as an emerging interest on 'focus on form'. Research such as that conducted in Montreal in intensive ESL programs with a highly communicatively-oriented curriculum (for example, Lightbown and Spada 1990; Spada and Lightbown 1993) and in French immersion programs across Canada with a similar reputation for a communication-based curriculum (for example, Harley 1989; Day and Shapson 1991; Lyster 1993), has shown quite clearly that a communicatively-oriented input-rich environment does not provide all the necessary conditions for second language acquisition, and that a focus on form within these communicative settings can significantly enhance performance.

One of the pedagogic questions arising from such research is how to focus on form in a manner that still profits from the value of a focus on meaning. The output-based studies like those of Donato (1994) and LaPierre (1994) provide important evidence for the usefulness of collaborative tasks that lead learners to reflect on their own language production as they attempt to create meaning. Such tasks, I would suggest, not only stimulate output to function as a means to focus attention and to test hypotheses, but they also provide opportunities for output to function as a metalinguistic tool.

My third comment relates to the tests we use in measuring learning. My concern here is not about the nature of the test but rather about the content of the test. In the LaPierre study, one of the tests used was 'tailor-made'. That is, it was based on what individual pairs of learners said and talked about as they interacted. It was based on what learners actually did, not on what the researcher assumed instructions and task demands would lead learners to focus on. Although the task did encourage students to pay attention to accuracy and form/function links, the students established their own agenda as to what they focused on. In another classroom-based study using a similar task, but where the teacher had spent considerable prior classroom time reviewing verb tenses, an analysis of the content of the language episodes revealed that only approximately 16% of them had anything to do with verb form or function (Kowal and Swain, forthcoming; see also Coughlan and Duff 1994). Thus, it would seem crucial if we are to measure the learning which occurs as a result of task involvement, that we must consider tailor-making our tests to actual task performance. In the LaPierre study, without a dyad-specific test, the conclusion would have been that there were no differences among the experimental groups, a highly unwarranted conclusion. The preparation of learner-specific tests may seem like a daunting task for the researcher, but it may be essential if we are to capture the language learning that occurs in negotiated interaction.

My fourth comment relates to the data we use to inform ourselves of learners' cognitive processes. Introspective data have in recent years supplied us with many useful insights. I believe that another source, and perhaps a more direct source of cognitive process data, may be in the dialogues themselves that learners engage in with other learners and with their teachers. If one accepts a Vygotskian perspective that much learning is an activity that occurs in and through dialogues, that development occurs first on the inter-psychological plane through socially constructing knowledge and processes, then it must be that a close examination of dialogue as learners engage in problem-solving activity is directly revealing of mental processes. The unit of analysis of language learning and its associated processes may therefore more profitably be the dialogue, not input or output alone.

Acknowledgements

This paper is a revised version of a Plenary given at the Second Language Research Forum (SLRF) in Montreal in October 1994. I would like to thank the following people for their useful and insightful comments on earlier drafts of this paper: Hugo Baetens Beardsmore, Andrew Cohen, Alister Cumming, Kees de Bot, Rick Donato, Jean Handscombe, Birgit Harley, Eric Kellerman, Jim Lantolf, Sharon Lapkin, Helen Moore, and Elaine Tarone. I would also like to acknowledge funding from the Social Sciences and Humanities

Research Council of Canada (grant #410–93–0050) which supported in part the Swain and Lapkin (1994) and LaPierre (1994) studies.

Appendix

Translation of Example 1

058: KEITH: Wait a minute! No, I need a Bescherelle (verb reference book). Please open the Bescherelle at the page which, OK, at the last page (i.e. the index). OK, look for *tracasse*, one page, two pages.

059: GEORGE: *Tra, tra, tracer.*

060: KEITH: *Tracasser* page six. Look for it please.

061: GEORGE: No problem.

062: KEITH: It's on page

063: GEORGE: Verb, <on page> six. OK, it's the same as *aimer*, (i.e. it is conjugated in the same way and *aimer* is given as the standard example for all verbs with this pattern of conjugation).

064: KEITH: Let me see it please (reading from the page). *Le passé simple, nous tracasse; nous aime* (Keith is trying to find a first-person plural version of the verb which sounds like *tracasse*, the word he has written in his notes, but is unable to find one).

065: GEORGE: Perhaps it's here.

066: KEITH: No, it's just *nous aime* (pause) ah, the present. *Tracasse, aimons,* isn't it *tracasse* (to teacher who has just arrived), it's not *nous tracasse* (what he has written down in his notes), it's *nous tracassons*?

067: TEACHER: It's the **problems** that are worrying us (deliberately not directly giving the answer).

068: KEITH: *Nous tracassons.*

069: GEORGE: Oh (beginning to realize what is happening).

070: KEITH: Yeah? (So what?)

071: GEORGE: The problems which are worrying us. Like the (pause) it's the problems (pause) like, that concerns us.

072: KEITH: Yes, but *tracasse* isn't it <o-n-s>?

073: GEORGE: *Tracasse* it's not a, it's not a, (pause), yeah, I dunno (unable to articulate what he has discovered).

074: KEITH: OK, it says, the problems which worry us. Therefore, is *tracasse* a verb? That you, that you have to conjugate?

075: TEACHER: Uh huh.

076: KEITH: So is it *tracassons*?

077: TEACHER: It's the **problems** which are worrying us.

078: GEORGE: Us, it's, it's not, it's not, yeah, it's the problems, it's <u>not, it's not us.</u>

079: KEITH: <u>Ah! E-n-t</u> (third-person plural ending), OK, OK.

9

Proficiency or the native speaker: what are we trying to achieve in ELT?

ALAN DAVIES

Introduction

THERE ARE TWO very different views of the goal of language teaching, the goal of the native speaker and the goal of a proficiency level. This paper[1] examines both views, concluding that they are of necessity interrelated.

Attempts to define the native speaker and proficiency make very obvious the elusive nature of both concepts although proficiency appears to be more definable, for example, through oral rating scales. Proficiency is contrasted with achievement, which is shown to be a means of contextualizing proficiency. In terms of ultimate attainment the post-pubertal second language learner may, exceptionally, attain native speaker levels of proficiency and therefore be indistinguishable from a native speaker.

Two goals for language teaching

A useful starting-point is Bialystok (1994) on the cognitive foundations of second language acquisition (SLA):

The framework described in this paper is a cognitive account of how language proficiency develops. Its aim is to account for the way in which knowledge and use of the language improve over time, irrespective of the circumstances under which the language is being learned. Yet it is obvious that those circumstances are crucial to the

[145]

process. Language learned for different purposes, in different situations, starting with a different first language, under favorable or unfavorable conditions, and so on, are critical factors in determining outcomes. . . . the real mechanism for learning lies in the processes of analysis and control. Instruction is one example of an important factor in second language acquisition that determines outcomes without overriding the central mechanism of analysis and control. Language instruction is primarily a means of altering the rate of language acquisition.

(Bialystok 1994: 166–7)

As Bialystok implies, among the critical factors which determine language learning outcomes (different purposes, different situations, different first languages, favorable/unfavorable conditions), the factor over which we can exert the greatest control, the one which it is in our power as teachers to manipulate and alter is that of instruction. And central to the planning of instruction is the consideration we give to the goal of that instruction.

I shall argue that there are two very different views of the target or goal for language learning/teaching, the first is the goal of native speakerhood, the second that of a predetermined level of proficiency. I shall examine each in turn, showing the very different implications of adherence to one or the other and I shall then propose that they are in fact interdependent: that being so, it is sensible to combine the two in planning goals for instruction. But first, a word about goals.

All language learning is purposive, naturalistic SLA implicitly so, instructional SLA explicitly so. Instructional language learning is intentional and deliberate, that is to say it is predicated on learners' needs and expectations; it provides in its textbooks, syllabuses, teachers' guides, tests, and examinations operational definitions of what its purposes, its outcomes are. Whatever the quality of the instruction, therefore, descriptions of intended outcomes are always recoverable. It is therefore important to ask what it is we find when we recover these descriptions of outcomes, deoperationalize the operational. What is it that the tests mean? What is it that the textbooks and so on assume about success?

The answer appears simple: they assume that the outcome should be either the native speaker (or some copy of the native speaker) or a defined proficiency. The first, the native speaker, seems at first more obvious, less abstract. The world, after all, is full of native speakers of the language under instruction, English in our case. Proficiency, on the other hand, appears to be less easily graspable. Proficiency is an abstract construct, which, unlike the native speaker, does not occur in nature; we therefore have to invent it, define it, find something that stands for it.

The native speaker goal

First, the native speaker as goal. In Shakespeare's *The Tempest* Caliban, half monster, half man, complains to Prospero:

> You taught me language, and the profit on't
> Is I know how to curse . . .

and I pose the question about this passage (also discussed in Widdowson 1984a: 189): is Caliban a native speaker of English? I return to this question later.

What do we mean by 'native speaker'? The native speaker is often appealed to but difficult to track down. Among the few full-length treatments are Coulmas (1981), Paikeday (1985), and Davies (1991). Tay (1982) points to the problems of common criteria for defining the native speaker in situations such as Singapore. She refers to the lack of clarity of most definitions and notes that the two features usually appealed to as evidence for or against native speaker status are (1) priority of learning and (2) an unbroken oral tradition. Both, she claims, are unsafe criteria, the first because of common phenomena such as childhood bilingualism, the second because an adult may have shifted dominance from one first language to another, or because a second learned language may have had as much influence on a first learned as the other way around. Tay proposes that fluency is the necessary outcome of early acquisition and continued dominance through use, but does not of itself define a native speaker. Paikeday's (1985) suggestion that native speakerhood consists of two unconnected factors (mother tongue acquisition and proficiency) therefore seems untenable because normally *both* are necessary. Paikeday has an understandable concern about job discrimination in favour of those who can claim mother tongue (Tay's priority of learning) acquisition: by, for example, restricting jobs as English teachers to those

[147]

who claim to be mother tongue speakers of English. This suggests that the proficiency aspect of the native speaker is proficiency in the standard language, above all in its written mode.

While there appears to be a lack of clarity about the native speaker concept, it is obviously of importance, both theoretically and practically. Widdowson (1994a) argues that, as a consequence of the worldwide use of English, Britain (and the USA?) must now relinquish its claim to legislate on changes in the language. Even if we accept Widdowson's argument, the native speaker matters to us, theoretically in terms of universal grammar and sampling of data for grammatical description, and practically in terms of the content of teaching materials, of language tests and examinations, as well as in terms of implicit social norms which determine career selection and cause social stigmatizing.

Let me give a personal example of the problems related to native speaker identity that can arise in real-life encounters. Some years ago, I had a foreign visitor, an academic, whose spoken English on the telephone made him indistinguishable from a southern England native speaker of English. I was expecting him and invited him into my office, asked him to sit down, remarked on the weather, took his coat and then said: 'I'll just shut the door!' He replied: 'Why bother?' My reaction was to shut the door, thinking as I did so that in my room I decided if the door was to be open or shut and that my visitor was being aggressive and rude. On the contrary, as I realized later, he was probably trying to be polite and meant perhaps: 'Don't bother on my account!' 'Why bother?' though perfectly idiomatic was, however, quite wrong and I had reacted to his use of the idiom as if he had been a native speaker. (Which suggests, incidentally, that it is possible to perform too well in a foreign language and that a foreign accent may be a good badge to display—'don't expect me to share all your cultural assumptions!')

The implication of such an observation for language teaching seems to differ for second language teaching (for example, Singapore) and foreign language teaching (for example, Japan). For the second language situation, our sociolinguistic expectations will be higher but they will conform to a different, typically local, model with which learners are likely to identify. In the case of the foreign language situation, it makes sense for our expectations to be higher linguistically than culturally or sociolinguistically.

[148]

It is at this point in the argument that the native speaker question reduces itself to that of proficiency, whereby what matters is agreed levels of adequate performance. Foreign language learning is likely to aim towards one or other metropolitan-international standard as the ultimate goal (that is the native speaker) while recognizing that most learners will stop off on the way. But some choose not to, and as I argue later, it is not impossible for a foreign language learner to reach the ultimate proficiency of the native speaker as measured by the available objective tests.

In the meantime let us return to Caliban. In quoting his bitter words in *The Tempest* I asked the question: is Caliban a native speaker of English? Let me now try to provide a partial answer.

1 The decision is Caliban's. He is clearly a native speaker of his own code. What name he gives that code, that language, is up to him: Calibanese? Prosperian? English? The question is whom does he identify with, or, as Humpty Dumpty said—who is to be master?

2 Cursing, swearing, and telling jokes, and *doing them properly*, are evidence of high quality fluency in a language. 'I know how to curse,' says Caliban. Anyone who knows how to curse properly in a language is hard to fault as one of its native speakers. Learners do well to steer clear of these demanding tricks because it is so easy to get them wrong, to swear inappropriately, to tell a pointless, unfunny joke.

The proficiency goal

I turn now to proficiency, which has been much discussed in recent years. Valdman, referring to the so-called Proficiency Movement in the USA, writes:

There is scarcely any area of the field [of foreign language teaching] in the US that has not been affected by [the] attempt to institute a national metric based on demonstrated proficiency in the functional use of a foreign language and, more importantly, to define achievement in language instruction in terms of functional use rather than exposure to or command of a specific body of material.
(Valdman 1988: 121)

Does Valdman's discussion of the Proficiency Movement, particularly in its interest in Rating Scales[2], offer the criterion definition of proficiency that we seek? It seems clear that the Proficiency Movement represents a rejection of the native speaker type of target, which we have discussed, in favour of a proficiency defined target. Proficiency, however, proves to be no less elusive than the native speaker.

We may define proficiency in a number of ways. For example (Elder, forthcoming):

1 a general type of knowledge of or competence in the use of a language, regardless of how, where or under what conditions it has been acquired;

2 the ability to do something specific in the language, for example, proficiency in English to study in higher education in the UK, proficiency to work as a foreign language teacher of a particular language in the United States, proficiency in Japanese to act as a tour guide in Australia;

3 performance as measured by a particular testing procedure. Some procedures are so widely used that levels of performance on them (e.g. 'superior', 'intermediate', 'novice' on the FSI scales) have become common currency in particular circles as indicators of language proficiency.

(Elder, forthcoming)

In its more portmanteau sense of general language ability, proficiency was widely used in the 1970s and early 1980s under the label 'general language proficiency', or sometimes 'unitary competence'. Proficiency has since come to be regarded as multifaceted, with recent models specifying the nature of its component parts and their relationship to one another. There is now considerable overlap between the notion of language proficiency and the term communicative competence. Debates about the nature of language proficiency have influenced the design of language tests, and language testing research has been used in the validation of various models of language proficiency.

One way of clarifying the notion of proficiency is to examine what it is not. To this end, the tradition of distinguishing clearly between achievement (or attainment) and proficiency is a convenient one. Proficiency, it is suggested, is general, achievement specific and local;

proficiency is theoretical or theory-based; achievement is syllabus- or materials- or curriculum-based, parasitic, in the sense that achievement information describes the learning of a single programme; while proficiency is free-standing and describes learning in some absolute sense. From this point of view achievement is dependent through the syllabus and materials on some proficiency construct.

However, this clear-cut definition has been questioned. As Brindley (1989) and Bachman (1990), among others, have pointed out, an achievement test is often used as if it were a proficiency test, or rather it is used as a general indication of learning; equally, a proficiency test is difficult to disentangle fully from the circumstances of its use. It is not just that apparently similar performance on as robust a test as the Test of English as a Foreign Language (TOEFL), or to a lesser extent the International English Language Testing System (IELTS), can be shown to vary in terms of factors such as mother tongue, but that on a proficiency scale the criteria influencing the bands allocated to different groups (for example, groups of workplace adults, of high-school students or university postgraduates or foreign language students) will not be identical. In other words, as Bialystok (1994) concludes, 'circumstances are crucial to the process' of the development of language proficiency.

Proficiency and achievement

The increasing use of proficiency scales in language assessment (for speaking and writing) has both positive and negative aspects. On the positive side they are authentic examples of language in use; there is no gap between what Bachman calls 'the criterion of proficiency and the definition of authenticity' (1990: 409). Because such procedures are typically direct, authenticity comes free, as it were, and does not have to be appealed to or claimed elsewhere. It is therefore often argued on behalf of such techniques that they have built-in validity. On the negative side it must surely be pointed out that *all* tests (not just indirect or semi-direct ones) lack authenticity. They are all simulations of real life rather than real life itself. (Widdowson 1979a: 163–173 makes a similar point with regard to language data.) What this of course suggests is that it is the job of assessment not so much to replicate real life (because by definition that cannot be done or when done is always partial and potentially biased) but to reflect language learning abilities and to sample real-life situations rather than to collect them. The well-known example from the testing of reading makes the point forcibly: it is surely clear that when we test someone's comprehension of a text we have no serious interest in that particular text. What we are interested in is the learner's ability to read *texts*. How important it is therefore that the text used for the test, and the tasks required in the test, should be adequate samples of texts at the appropriate reading level and of the tasks required at that level.

Assessment which makes use of proficiency scales typically uses the interview as a means of sampling language data which can then be related to the scale. Interviews are said—as I have hinted above—to provide direct entry into the speaker's language ability. But they are also notoriously unreliable. Yes, there are ways of training judges and ways of pooling judgements but the extent to which they can be made less unreliable is a function of the amount of training and time and money that are available. In other words *plus* reliable means *minus* practical. Which is to say that the nearer the test approximates to real life (the longer it is, the more assessors there are, and so on) the more validity and the less reliability it will have. But the same process makes the test less test-like so that it becomes precisely what it is supposed to be predicting, which is real-life use.

There is in direct tests such as the interview the ever-present danger of routinization (as indeed there is in the analogue, communicative language teaching). But that is the danger inherent in all direct tests, that in order to be fair, to avoid subjectivity, the test becomes more and more routine as time goes on and eventually as little like real life as the most indirect test but without its special claim to be a sample of underlying language skills. Furthermore, interviews in practice depend on assessors' impressions which themselves require the combination of discrete items. True, they are supposed to allow for spontaneity, but it is doubtful if they always do so.

As far as proficiency scales (notably those designed to assess oral production) are concerned we cannot avoid the basic question of how valid they are. There is a sense in which all such scales are circular. The fact that they bring together proficiency level with assumed authenticity is taken to be itself an indication of value—but the question remains of just how valid the levels are. In the physical world we can indeed divide up nature in equal units and claim that the units are recursive, for example, in measuring height, that each unit is equivalent to the next. But just what is the status of the descriptors and of the example tasks at each level of the proficiency scales on offer? If a test's purpose is to predict a criterion, proficiency scales are a type of criterion. The interview, with all its unreliability, is a test instrument, used to predict a criterion.

There is much to be said for Brindley's position (1989: 10). What we *always* measure is achievement. Our test instruments are *always* context-sensitive. Achievement is *never* proficiency, only an attempt to iconize proficiency. Proficiency scales are simulations, subjective, approximate, and incomplete. We know only too well that tests and scores are unreliable and unstable; we know that the equal interval scale is a myth (for example, that the difference between a score of, say, 2 and 3 is the same as the difference between, say, the score of 3 and 4). If, therefore, the interval scale does not hold for test scores, it is even less applicable to band descriptors.

The paradox is that through the attempt to refine proficiency scales by removing the defects of the descriptors (the imprecise and relativistic terminology—limited range, control of some structures, many error types) their precisioning tends more and more towards a list or bank of test items. Descriptors which are usable in an objective sense are indistinguishable from test items. All the more reason for *not* making more precise, for acknowledging that a scale is not an instrument but a sort of metaphor to inform a judgement.

Proficiency scales can only tell us half the story. They are not and should not claim to be test instruments, ways of measuring. Assessment of learning needs the measure (the instrument) and the explanation (which may be in the form of a scale). Which is another way of saying that achievement and proficiency always need one another: achievement without proficiency is too local, too contingent; proficiency without achievement is unreal, unreliable, and vague.

Native speaker of a second language?

Let me now return to the native speaker by setting out my position on the second language (L2) learner and the question of whether an L2 learner can become a native speaker of the target language.

[153]

First, who is the native speaker? I want to suggest that the native speaker is commonly characterized in these six ways (Davies 1991):

1 The native speaker acquires the first language (L1) of which she or he is a native speaker in childhood.

2 The native speaker has intuitions (in terms of acceptability and productiveness) about his or her grammar.

3 The native speaker has intuitions about those features of the grammar of the common (or standard) language which are distinct from his or her idiolectal grammar.

4 The native speaker has a unique capacity to produce fluent spontaneous discourse, which is facilitated by a huge memory stock of partly or completely lexicalized units (Pawley and Syder 1983: 191–226).

5 The native speaker has a unique creative capacity which enables him or her to write or speak creatively. This includes, of course, literature at all levels from jokes to epics, metaphor to novels. Speaking creatively probably belongs here too as does linguistic creativity and inventiveness.

6 The native speaker has a unique capacity to interpret and translate into the L1 of which she or he is a native speaker.

In the terms of these characteristics, to what extent can the L2 learner become a target language (TL) native speaker? Let us again consider our six criteria:

1 (Childhood acquisition): no, the L2 learner by our own definition does not acquire the target language in early childhood. As we have noted, if she or he does, then she or he is a native speaker of both the L1 and the L2.

2 (Intuitions about the idiolect): yes, it must be possible, with sufficient contact and practice for the L2 learner to gain access to intuitions about his or her own idiolectal grammar of the TL.

3 (Intuitions about the standard language): yes, again, with sufficient contact and practice the L2 learner can gain access to the grammar of the common target language. Indeed, in many formal learning situations it is exactly through exposure to a common TL

grammar that the TL idiolectal grammar would emerge, the reverse of the L1 development.

4 (Fluent spontaneous discourse): yes, this fluent spontaneous discourse may indeed be a descriptive difference between a native speaker and a non-native speaker but it is not in any way explanatory: that is to say, it in no way argues that a second language learner cannot become a native speaker.

5 (Creativity): yes, again, with practice it must be possible for a second language learner to become an accepted creative writer in the TL. There are indeed well-known examples of such cases, for instance, Conrad, Becket, Nabokov, Narayan; but there is also the interesting problem of the acceptability to the L1 community of the second language learner's creative writing. This is an attitudinal question but so too is the question of the acceptability to the same L1 community of a creative writer writing not in the dominant Standard Language but in an alternative standard, for example, Scots.

6 (Interpret and translate): yes, again, translation and interpretation must be possible although as is well known international organizations normally require that translators and sometimes interpreters should translate/interpret into their L1.

All except (1) are contingent issues and they require that the question whether a second language learner can become a native speaker of a target language will only be answered by the further question: is it necessary to acquire a code in early childhood in order to be a native speaker of that code? As will be obvious, we are now into a circular definition such that we are forced to ask a yet further question, that is: what is it that the child acquires in acquiring his or her L1 ? We have however already answered that question in our criteria 2 to 6 above and so the question again becomes a contingent one.

Even the imperative, implicit in the intuitions criteria (numbers 2 and 3 above), to acquire the cultural (as well as formal) resources of the language early can be challenged. It is, after all, just not the case that all 'native speakers' share the same sociolinguistic competence. What of subcultural differences between, for example, the Scots and the English; of different cultures with the same standard language, for example, the Swiss and the Austrians and the former West Germans and East Germans; or of different cultures with different standard languages, for example, the British and the Americans? What too of International English and of an isolated L1 in a multilingual setting (for example, mother tongue English speakers of Indian English)? Given the interlingual differences and the lack of agreement about norms that certainly occur among all such groups, it does appear that the second language learner has a difficult but not an impossible task to become a native speaker of a target language.

Difficult but not impossible. Birdsong (1992) takes issue with researchers such as Long (1990b) who appear to make an absolute distinction between the native speaker and the non-native speaker, namely, that 'ultimate attainment' for the non-native speaker can never be equal to native speaker competence. Birdsong re-examines the Coppieters (1987) experiment with learners of French and reports also on his own parallel study. What he concludes is that while as a group his French language learners and the French native speaker subjects differed significantly, the large amount of overlap suggests that 'this general lack of difference is taken as evidence that ultimate attainment by non-natives can coincide with that of natives' (Birdsong 1992: 739). Of course those who overlap are, as Birdsong admits, 'exceptional learners'; but the implication here is that 'our attention should turn to the issue of trainability: what can be discovered from exceptional learners that could be applied to improve other learners' chances of attaining native norms' (ibid.: 742).

Our conclusion might therefore be that it is indeed possible—though difficult—for a post-pubertal second language learner to become a native speaker of English. But as we have just seen, our definition of native speaker is unstable. When we remove the criterial 'first language learnt' which is the bio-developmental definition, it appears that what we are left with is proficiency.

Which is precisely the point made by Paikeday (1985) in his diatribe against the unfairness of more traditional definitions of native speaker based on biography (on language first acquired), which in his view should be replaced by a proficiency definition. We may therefore suggest as a compromise between the native speaker and proficiency goals that the proper outcome for instruction is indeed the native speaker, realized or measured or established by a defined proficiency. In other words (which is not quite what Paikeday had in mind, but goes some way towards his position) we can recognize the native speaker— institutionally—by achieved proficiency.

Conclusion

The native speaker is a fine myth: we need it as a model, a goal, almost an inspiration. But it is useless as a measure; it will not help us define our goals. So in spite of my firm agreement with Birdsong and my conviction that there is a continuum between native speakers and non-native speakers, nevertheless, I recognize that for language teaching purposes what is crucial is the definability of partial proficiency.

We may summarize as follows: the native speaker is the construct, proficiency its metric. Or, metaphorically: the native speaker is the voyage or exploration, proficiency the chart or map; the native speaker is history, proficiency is geography.

Notes

1 A version of this paper was given as a plenary talk at the 33rd annual meeting of the Japan Association of College English Teachers in Nagoya, Japan, in September 1994.

2 The American Council on the Teaching of Foreign Languages (ACTFL) and the Inter-Agency Language Round Table (ILR), formerly the Foreign Service Institute (FSI) Rating Scales, in particular the Oral Proficiency Test.

10

Grammar and lexis in communicative competence

HEIKKI NYYSSÖNEN

Introduction

ALL GENERALIZATIONS ARE false, it is said. Yet we do, and indeed must, generalize. For instance: where a native speaker (NS) may, owing to a misjudgement in performance, commit a pragmatic failure, a language learner is apt, owing to a gap in competence, to commit a grammatical error (Corder 1973).

According to this generalization, there is a fundamental difference between the competence and the resulting performance of the NS and the learner. Therefore, it is the task of language teaching to reduce the difference, at least to a difference which won't make a difference. As a result, the learner will be less likely to commit errors—which will improve intelligibility—and more apt to perform appropriately, which will increase the likelihood of smooth and effective interaction.

It is the purpose of this paper to reassess the notion of the underlying competence as an ingredient of communicative competence, and to relate the reassessment to concerns of language teaching. The focus is, in particular, on the role of grammar and lexis, or 'lexicogrammar'. Interspersed with the discussion there are also a few illustrative analyses of language data.

Communicative competence

So performance depends on competence, but what does competence depend on? According to the Chomskyan view, competence means

[159]

grammatical competence, the knowledge of grammar of an ideal speaker. This may be called the formalist view. It contrasts with the functionalist approach, associated with pragmatics and sociolinguistics, according to which competence suggests all the abilities of an actual speaker (Hymes 1972). Competence is communicative competence, the ability to perform. As Corder says (1973: 92):

> It is just as much a matter of 'competence' in language to be able to produce appropriate utterances as grammatical ones . . . The learner must . . . develop the ability to produce and understand grammatical utterances . . . but he must also know when to select a particular grammatical sequence, the one which is appropriate to the context, both linguistic and situational.

The selection of the appropriate sequence depends on a knowledge of 'speaking rules' prevalent in the culture or language community. These rules are sociolinguistic and discoursal: they ensure social acceptability, on the one hand, and discourse coherence, on the other (Canale and Swain 1980).

Since communicative competence includes discourse competence, the notion of fluency must be added to the 'abilities of an actual speaker'. According to Stubbs, fluency is the ability to handle connected discourse in real time without prior rehearsal; it is the ability to

> improvise, maintain continuity in speech and comprehension, respond immediately to unexpected utterances, make rapid changes of topic and speaker, and so on.
> (Stubbs 1983: 36)

Thus communicative competence is a highly complex ability. It includes grammatical accuracy, intelligibility and acceptability, contextual appropriateness and fluency. It is far more than the grammatical competence of an ideal speaker. However, it is, in practice, not the same as the abilities of an actual speaker, for the actual speaker, even an NS, may commit failures in performance, i.e. mistakes in the use of the code, such as social gaffes, choices of the wrong term, choices of the wrong style or register, and so on.

Lexis in text and discourse

NSs are occasionally non-fluent, especially in unplanned discourse, i.e. talk which is not thought out prior to its expression (Stubbs 1983: 34). 'Normal' non-fluencies include hesitations, filled pauses, repetitions, false starts, etc. The following example is from Corder (1973: 257):

It's a bit—it hasn't—I mean, *I wouldn't really care to have one just like that* . . .

What is important to note is that the false starts at the beginning of the utterance are followed by a completely fluent sequence, a pre-thought element in what is otherwise an unplanned discourse. It seems that this sequence, selected with a view to its contextual appropriateness, is a pre-assembled pattern, a syntactically combined sequence of words (Widdowson 1990a: 91).

It is one of the fundamental insights of computer-assisted corpus research (for example, the Cobuild project) that by far the majority of text in English is made of 'the occurrence of common words in common patterns or in slight variants of those common patterns' (Sinclair 1991a: 108). Thus it seems that text is not produced according to the formalist 'slot and filler principle' which separates grammar and lexis, but according to the 'idiom principle' which severely limits the choices of what comes next.

We can observe the idiom principle in practice in the above example. It is obvious that the false starts at the beginning of the utterance remain false, because if they had been pursued, the speaker would have produced an 'undesirable', i.e. contextually inappropriate, speech act. No context is given, but we may assume that the illocutionary force of the utterance is 'refusal', that the speaker is 'saying no' to an offer. It seems that the false starts, *it's a bit* . . . and *it hasn't* . . ., would have led to speech acts directly critical of the thing offered, and indirectly critical of the person who had made the offer. This may be why the speaker hesitated: he felt that he was going to be critical, which might have been socially unacceptable, and sought a more tactful way of voicing his opinion. In this search for a more appropriate sequence the idiom principle seems to have served as a useful resource by allowing the speaker to monitor and repair his linguistic output.

The chosen sequence makes use of the pattern:

I wouldn't + a verb denoting liking + *to* + a main verb

Here the grammatical subject and the main verb are contextually determined, but there is some choice concerning the verb denoting liking, and the item *care* is selected, perhaps because it is a milder variant of *like*. The same mitigating purpose is evident in the use of the hedge *really*, as an 'optional' element.

We can also observe that the non-fluencies serve a useful purpose, for instance by helping the speaker to select an appropriate lexicogrammatical sequence. The false starts and filled pauses serve as aids in the negotiation of meaning in other ways, by allowing the speaker to repair his speech and by giving him time to think ahead. Thus the nonfluencies function as stepping-stones, or as means of trying out candidate expressions and as means of judging their potential effects in the context.

Reassessing competence

The frequent use of fluent culturally popular lexical sequences (for example, *I wouldn't care to . . .*) leads us to a reassessment of the linguistic ability underlying communicative competence. The traditional view of this ability is based on a particular view of linguistic communication according to which such communication is, basically, a semantic affair, the transfer of information from the speaker to the hearer. The relevant kind of meaning is semantic, the result of a compositional process whereby words are combined into sentences. This view may indeed correspond to the facts in planned discourse, such as some kinds of formal writing where there is time to compose and make careful use of grammar.

The alternative view, which is more in tune with the facts of linguistic communication in everyday conversation and other types of unplanned discourse, is that the relevant meaning is pragmatic, the result of a contextual adjustment called 'negotiation' (Widdowson 1990a: 99–114). Pragmatic meaning is based on semantic or grammatical meaning, but its interpretation requires the invoking of contextual or 'schematic' knowledge, to the extent that is necessary for the purpose in hand.

Some culturally popular lexical sequences are frozen idioms and as such already part of schematic knowledge. One example is the idiom

I couldn't care less. In contrast, the adjustable pattern *I wouldn't (really) care to* . . ., in the above example, is not quite as immediately accessible; some inferencing is required, to recover the particular meaning which is intended in the context.

Grammar as index

In the traditional model of linguistic communication the role of grammar is clear. Meaning is semantic, and semantic meaning is grammatical meaning. It is what the *language means*, not what *people mean* by the language, that counts. Of course, what the language means does count, but it is not the whole story. Consider the process of comprehension as an example. According to Widdowson (1990a: 102), there are two kinds of comprehension: understanding sentences and understanding language in use. The first is a semantic matter of deciphering 'symbolic' meanings, i.e. the senses of linguistic signs. However, this knowledge alone will not enable us to understand language in use, for this is always a matter of realizing particular meanings of signs in association with the context. These particular meanings are 'indexical', in that the sign which is used will indicate 'where we must look in the world we know or can perceive in order to discover meaning' (Widdowson 1990a: 102).

Consider, as an example, the following utterance from the British National Corpus (BNC), made in casual conversation (Leech 1993: 14):

A to B: Smart brake lights aren't they on *that* (B: yes) car in front

Here, obviously, an indexical meaning is carried by the premodifier *that*, allowing reference to be achieved. This meaning, which is a kind of verbal pointing (possibly accompanied by a nod, gaze, and gesture), is a conventional function of the form in question, i.e. the premodifier *that* which (together with the nod, gaze, and gesture) directs the hearer to pay attention to the car in front.

The final indexical noun phrase is, however, only a kind of 'background' feature; it comes after the marked theme as a kind of afterthought. The 'foreground' feature consists of the brake lights, which is the focus of the second kind of indexical meaning, namely illocutionary force (Widdowson 1992c: 334). Like reference, illocutionary force

[163]

is ultimately determined by the observable conditions and the context (Leech 1983: 30). While the indexical clue in the referential expression *that car* consists of the premodifier *that*, the clue as to the illocutionary force consists of the truncated form of the sentence used by A. It is a form which is associated with a particular rhetorical schema, namely that of casual talk and especially casual opening moves in such talk, i.e. moves which introduce a topic and aim to elicit a response from the hearer. It is this rhetorical schema of casual talk that is here invoked by the form of the utterance while its content circumscribes the topical framework, i.e. the *brake lights* (McCarthy 1991: 52).

Examples of this kind show that competence clearly has a pragmatic component: the grammatical form and meaning of an utterance interact with the world we know or can perceive, and this world is internalized as formal and content schemata (Widdowson 1990a: 104). The meaning born in interaction is pragmatic—reference, illocutionary force, and effect (Widdowson 1992c: 335).

It is a feature of pragmatic meaning that it is 'publicly available' (Leech 1983: 35) in the text that precedes or follows the utterance. Thus we find empirical proof for our interpretation of A's utterance in B's response, which is as follows:

B to A: I was just thinking what an intriguing colour they were (A: yeah).

B's utterance is clearly a response to A's comment and accepts the topical framework introduced in the comment. B also makes a contribution to the topic within this framework by means of commenting on a specific feature of the brake lights, namely their colour.

As regards the social acceptability of B's response, even a 'minimal response' would have been appropriate, but B also signals involvement and solidarity, among other things, by his use of the 'gushing' attribute *intriguing*.

This example of the exchange about the brake lights points to the role of grammar and lexis in the negotiation of pragmatic meaning. In this process of making and interpreting meaning, grammar and lexis serve as directions, instructing discourse participants to make a particular kind of connection between the linguistic sign and the relevant aspect of their schematic knowledge (Widdowson 1990a: 104). Interpretation is always ultimately a matter of guesswork, an informal problem-solving strategy (Leech 1983: 31). In this case, for instance, B could be reasoning as follows: 'obviously A is referring to those brake lights on the car in front of us, obviously he thinks they are 'smart', worth noticing and worth talking about, obviously he wishes me to say what *I* think of them; well, I will pay him the compliment of agreeing that the lights are indeed remarkable and deserve to be discussed, even at this length and in this detail . . .' This is at least one hypothetical interpretation compatible with the textual evidence. It is possible, of course, that B had indeed been already thinking of the brake lights before A spoke, and that he was really of the opinion that they were an 'intriguing' colour.

Grammar as regulative

Widdowson (1992c) refers to another function of grammar in communicative competence. This is its regulative function. Widdowson says, for instance:

> Over recent years we have seen the restoration of grammar from its temporary exile. But we surely do not want it restored under the old dispensation. We need to enquire into the way it relates to lexis, how it operates as a complement to context in the achievement of pragmatic meaning, how it functions in the regulation of language use. (Widdowson 1992c: 334)

In the above discussion of the extract from the BNC the analytical focus is specifically on the way grammar relates to lexis and the way it operates as a complement to context. As regards the regulative function of grammar, it is also apparent in the example. Regulation refers to the adjustment of syntactically combined lexical sequences, by means of the rules of grammar, for the purpose of achieving a good contextual fit (Widdowson 1990a: 91).

Under 'the new dispensation' the rules of grammar are no longer seen as constitutive, as formation rules in the sense of Corder (1973). However, the analytical power of grammar rules comes in handy when a particular sequence requires some contextual adaptation. This may involve modification of the syntax or wording or both. It may be a case of regulating reference, illocutionary force, or interpersonal effect.

In the above example from the BNC, the phrase *I was just thinking* is an alternative to *I think*, while the rest of B's utterance is a contextual

[165]

modification of '*what* + *a/an* + adjective + *colour*'. The pragmatic force achieved by use of this pattern may be compared with the following weak alternative version:

Yeah, they're a nice colour.

Acquisition

The above discussion suggests that it may be possible to reduce the difference between NS and learner competences if more attention is paid to the communicative role of grammar and lexis as resources in the achievement of pragmatic meaning. One of the distinct merits of this approach to communicative competence is its strong emphasis on the close integration of grammar and lexis, in performance and also in underlying competence. If the learner could make more, and more effective, use of culturally popular lexical sequences, which are routinely employed by NSs in large quantities, the gap would already be closing. If the learner could also make more use of grammar in its regulative function, to adapt the patterns if necessary, to achieve contextual fit, the gap would be reduced even further. As a result, the learner's chances of talking coherently and to the point as well as talking fluently would be greatly improved, and he or she would be less likely to commit grammatical errors and pragmatic failures.

The learner would make fewer grammatical errors, because the syntactically combined sequences of words are, by definition, grammatical. What is more, they are also idiomatic. From the pedagogic point of view, their manner of combination provides the learner with an insight into the ways in which grammar and lexis interact. These insights can then be utilized in practising the regulation of the learner's linguistic output in speech and writing.

The learner would also commit fewer pragmatic failures, because the lexical phrases are, specifically, *culturally popular* patterns and therefore, provided they are used in appropriate contexts, tailor-made for socially acceptable use—first, as polite ways of speaking and, secondly, as established elements of 'the community's code', i.e. the prevailing and current speech habits in the target-language culture (Loveday 1982: 83).

The process of acquiring this kind of competence should start, as always, with the study of the commonest patterns in the commonest uses as these patterns and uses are also structurally the simplest and functionally the most familiar. However, it is important that there is, as early as possible, a clear focus on the study of the patterns in extended speech, in connected discourse. This will make learners aware of the formal and functional role of the patterns in the information structure of the sentence, in topic development and conversational organization, in the performance of illocutions and in the choice and consistent use of an appropriate style and register. Last but not least, the study of lexical sequences will help learners to extend their vocabulary and their knowledge of speaking rules.

Vocabulary enrichment and the acquisition of speaking rules are closely connected. We can use the term 'pragmalinguistic' to refer to the linguistic resources a given language provides for conveying particular illocutions with an appropriate rhetorical force. Rhetorical force refers to the interpersonal implications that are conveyed by an utterance in a context, irrespective of whether they are intended or not.

Pragmalinguistic studies are language-specific. 'Socio-pragmatic' studies, on the other hand, are culture-specific (Leech 1983: 10; Thomas 1983). They investigate the variable use of pragmatic principles such as the politeness principle in different cultures and in different social situations. In one culture, for instance, it may be quite in order, or even preferable, to remain silent in a situation in which the norm of another culture calls for some sociable talk. When a person coming from the first type of culture and a person coming from the second type of culture meet in such a situation, misunderstanding is likely to arise if both behave in accordance with their native norms. If, for some reason, it is the norm of the talkative culture that prevails, people coming from the silent culture have to conform, or may think it wise to conform. However, they may be unable to do so if they have not the required pragmalinguistic resources—grammar, vocabulary, and a repertoire of lexical phrases—at their disposal. So even in this case the end result may be misunderstanding or, perhaps, a communication breakdown.

It has been suggested (McCarthy 1991: 71) that to behave in a natural way in a foreign language, learners need a fairly rich vocabulary, and need to have at their fingertips the synonyms, antonyms, etc. of the words that are 'in play'. In addition, a learner's vocabulary should also form a system, so that the lexical items and lexical phrases would be easily retrievable, for sustaining talk on different topics, for setting up cohesive links, for signalling effect, for maintaining fluency, etc. A particular lexical selection in a text or conversation may have to perform all of these things at once, as a simultaneous signal of ideational, textual, and interpersonal meaning. One example of this is the word *intriguing*, in the extract from the BNC. There is no synonymous relation, no relation of equivalence, between *smart* (in A's initiation) and *intriguing* (in B's response), and yet these adjectives in their context, as tokens used in the negotiation of meaning, set up a meaningful lexical relation across the two speaking turns, producing a sense of social accomplishment and of a satisfactory conversational outcome.

Whereas the learning of lexical phrases starts with the commonest patterns in the commonest uses, the acquisition of lexical items begins with the commonest items in the commonest patterns, making it possible to learn and practise items and patterns in parallel from the start.

The commonest lexical items, or 'core words' (Carter 1987: 33–46), share the feature of having little specific content and, as a consequence, a wide range of applications. In contrast, the less frequent items, which are 'non-core', share the characteristic of having considerable specific content but a narrower range. Consider, as an example, the words *enjoy* and *savour*. There is a wide variety of things that may be enjoyed but only an exclusive number of things that are savoured, lingeringly and with appreciation.

Vocabulary acquisition is a long and gradual process consisting of the acquisition of more and more uses for the common items, and a parallel learning of more and more of the less common ones. The latter may be used infrequently, compared with the former, but they are used in meanings in which they can only be replaced at a price, if at all. Thus both types of words are useful, each in its own way. It is a virtue of the core word that it can take on meaning from the context, and a merit of the non-core word that it can bring in context by virtue of its meaning.

A fairly rich vocabulary, in the form of an accessible and extendable system, including both individual content items, core and non-core, in suitable proportions, and a fair number of the commoner culturally popular patterns, form a good basis for a working communicative competence. This kind of vocabulary cannot be derived from word lists; it can only be derived 'textually', through the painstaking study of a large number of well-chosen and carefully graded texts, spoken as well as written.

This painstaking study can take many forms. It has already been mentioned that the manner in which words are combined syntactically into lexical patterns provides an insight into the operation of grammar and lexis in language use. The following is just one example of this kind of 'awareness-raising'. We know that language is used to perform illocutions in accordance with speaking rules. For instance, the sentence *I bet he'll turn up tomorrow* (from Widdowson 1990a: 36) may be used as an emphatic assertion, a commissive, or for some other function, depending on the context. In this illocution the item *I bet* conveys a discourse meaning which is related to the canonical meaning of the verb, i.e. 'to lay a wager', and obviously has a specific grammatical form. As a carrier of the discourse meaning, however, *I bet* is not a form of grammar but a form conceived at the level of 'assembly', i.e. in the interface or transition between grammar and discourse (Sinclair and Coulthard 1975: 134). The assembly is a level of language in the form of 'syntagms' such as the various kinds of collocational sequences and collocational frameworks. As for the cultural origin of this culturally popular pattern, it may be traceable to the popular social institution of betting as a part of the British way of life!

As for the speaking rules themselves, the rules used to select a pattern on a particular occasion to perform a particular illocution, or some other discourse function, they are partly universal and partly 'local', i.e. specific local conditions on language use (Leech 1983: 10). The local variation means, for instance (going back to a previous example), that a learner coming from a 'silent' culture (for example, Finnish) might want to acquire a repertoire of small-talk patterns and to learn to use them, in order to perform appropriately with members of a more 'talkative' culture (for example, American).

Conclusion

This paper has made reference to computer-assisted corpus research and to the facts revealed by the computer concerning lexical patterning in English. As Widdowson says (1992c: 336), these facts are incontestable. However, Widdowson goes on, facts are not factors: they bear no guarantee of relevance. The criteria for the description of actually occurring language are not necessarily the same as those for the prescription of language for learning.

There is, indeed, a difference between language use and language teaching. Words, for instance, cannot be learnt, truly learnt, from word lists. The words must be internalized: the learner must acquire the rules which govern the formation and use of words. Then the words must be stored in the mind in the form of an organized system for fluent access. The computer can tell us which words and word combinations are the most frequent; it does not tell us *why* they are the most frequent, why this word or word combination is chosen instead of that. There are, on the one hand, the strategies and goals of language users, and on the other, the principles and constraints of linguistic communication. It is these sometimes conflicting pressures which determine the choice of one word or combination instead of another.

It is only by means of a careful analysis of discourse that we can find out about the 'whys and wherefores' of particular language choices and develop prescriptions from descriptions. It is only by a study of the negotiation of meaning in actually occurring language that we can establish the factors that are pedagogically relevant.

11

Cultural meaning and rhetorical styles: toward a framework for Contrastive Rhetoric

YAMUNA KACHRU

Introduction

THE FIELD OF enquiry now established as Contrastive Rhetoric (CR, henceforth) developed out of pedagogical concerns related to writing in English as a Second Language (ESL). In his study that began the cross-language comparison of rhetorical styles, Kaplan concluded that 'contrastive rhetoric must be taught in the same sense that contrastive grammar is presently taught' (1966 [1980]: 409). Although the concern is no longer purely pedagogical, language teaching/learning is still a strong motivation for such studies. Also, the interpretations and the resultant claims of the 1966 study have been modified by Kaplan himself, and seriously questioned by others, in many respects.

Whatever the controversy surrounding the Contrastive Rhetoric Hypothesis (CRH, henceforth) may be, it is undeniable that it has had an enormous impact on research on writing across cultures, and on the teaching of writing in English to speakers of other languages (Leki 1991). This is obvious if one looks at studies comparing writing in several languages with writing in English, for example, Choi (1988), Clyne (1983, 1987a), Connor (1987), Eggington (1987), Hinds (1980, 1983a, 1983b, 1987), Johnstone-Koch (1983), Y. Kachru (1983, 1988), Kaplan (1988), Katchen (1982), Ostler (1987), Pandharipande

(1983), Reynolds (1993), Tsao (1983), among others. Also, any claims and assumptions made in CR studies are increasingly being presented as universally valid. There is, therefore, an urgent need to look at CR research closely and examine its theoretical foundations and methodological approaches. A beginning has already been made in this direction (see, for example, Y. Kachru 1983; Martin 1992, among others), but no coherent theory has yet emerged to guide this area of research in all aspects.

In order to progress toward theory building, it is necessary to understand clearly what the claims, assumptions, and implications of CR are. The major theoretical claim of the CRH is that different speech communities have different ways of organizing ideas in writing, which reflect their 'cultural thought patterns'. A related claim, relevant for language teaching, especially for the teaching of ESL, is that non-native users of English employ 'a rhetoric and a sequence of thought which violate the expectations of the native reader' (Kaplan 1972). Hence, their writing is perceived as 'out of focus', 'lacking organization', or 'lacking cohesion' (Kaplan 1966). This claim is based on the assumption that there *is* a native English norm of writing which is clearly identifiable. The claim and the assumption naturally lead to the conclusion that it is both necessary and desirable to teach this model of writing to non-native users of English, since there are clear benefits to be derived from changing the 'rhetoric and sequence of thought' of non-native users of English.

This paper focuses on issues relevant to CR and ESL, particularly from the point of view of users of English in the Outer Circle (B. Kachru 1985).[1] It questions the claim, the assumption, and the conclusion of the CRH on the basis of (a) research on American, Australian, and British norms of writing; (b) CR studies and their methodologies inspired by Kaplan (1966); (c) recent research on the acquisition of language and literacy; and (d) studies of writing in English in the Outer Circle. The theoretical perspective in this discussion is that of 'socially realistic linguistics' (Labov 1972a: xiii), as represented by Halliday (1978), Hymes (1974), B. Kachru (1981a), and Labov (1988), among others. Following the theoretical discussion, I propose a framework for CR research which is based on the notion of sociocultural meaning of rhetorical styles. Finally, I will suggest an orientation to pedagogy which exploits the 'meaning potential' (Halliday 1973) of different

[172]

rhetorical styles to enrich the writing experience of all learners, native or non-native.

Cultural meaning

Before I proceed with the detailed discussion of CR as outlined above, let me clarify what I mean by 'cultural meaning'. The term 'culture' has been defined in various ways in different disciplines. I would like to define culture as shared knowledge, that is, what people 'must know in order to *act* as they do, make the things they make, and interpret their experience in the distinctive way they do' (Quinn and Holland 1987; emphasis added). 'Act' in this sense includes verbal acts—whether in the spoken or the written mode. People who share a common language and culture have an easier time 'making sense' of each other's utterances and actions. Everyone readily recognizes the fact that only very restricted communication is possible without a shared language. However, the realization that, even with a shared language, successful communication may depend upon sociocultural factors is just beginning to dawn. This understanding has led to renewed interest in investigating the interface of language and culture. One such area of investigation, obviously, is CR.

Norms of composition in the Inner Circle

The assumption that there are clearly identifiable norms of written composition in English in the countries of the Inner Circle (i.e., Australia, Canada, New Zealand, the UK, and the USA) is problematic. Studies that have compared persuasive writing in the native varieties have found clear differences among them (for example, Connor and Lauer 1985). No research is available on styles of writing within the USA, though research on literacy (Heath 1983), conversational styles (for example, Tannen 1981, 1984) and narratives (for example, Labov 1972b) shows clear differences among communities. Also, as Leki (1991) points out, studies in CR have largely relied on style manuals or textbooks in rhetoric for characterizing English patterns rather than an actual examination of English writing. This means that in CR studies, ESL/EFL student writing is compared with some idealized notion of writing in English. What is even more unsettling is that it is not clear that there is a well-defined text type such as 'expository prose' in English (Grabe 1987) or, for that matter, in any language, though it has been the focus of much research in these studies.[2]

Contrastive Rhetorical studies

Research in CR has had many different strands, and it is not possible to discuss all of them in any detail here. The studies that have investigated the interplay of culture and rhetorical mode have resulted in certain findings which may or may not be corroborated by further research. At present, it seems to be uncontroversial that native varieties of English such as American, Australian, British, and New Zealand differ significantly from each other (for example, Connor and Lauer 1985, which deals with persuasive compositions produced by American, British, and New Zealand writers). Also, languages such as Arabic (Johnstone-Koch 1983; Ostler 1987; Reynolds 1993), Chinese (Tsao 1983), German (Clyne 1983, 1987a), Hindi (Y. Kachru 1983, 1987, 1988, forthcoming), Japanese (Hinds 1980, 1983a, 1983b, 1987), Korean (Choi 1988; Eggington 1987), Marathi (Pandharipande 1983), and Persian (Katchen 1982) have characteristic rhetorical organizations of 'expository' and 'argumentative' prose not shared by the native varieties of English. Note, however, that most of these studies have employed methodologies based essentially on a Western rhetorical tradition. It is possible that the resultant differences are an artefact of the methodology followed in a particular study (Kenkel 1991).

Studies in language acquisition and literacy

The evidence from research in language acquisition, language use, and literacy in the field of sociolinguistics/ethnographic linguistics raises a number of issues relevant to language pedagogy. Since studies of the acquisition of language and literacy and use of English in writing in the Outer Circle are the most relevant for our purposes, I will discuss the research in these areas in some detail.

First, I would like to situate the discussion of language acquisition in the theoretical framework of systemic linguistics as developed by Halliday. In this framework, the central notion is 'meaning potential' defined in terms of culture: what people can mean and can do.

[174]

Biologically, all humans are alike in their capacity for language acquisition. However, we learn our first language(s) 'in the context of behavioural settings where the norms of the culture are acted out and enunciated' (Halliday 1978: 23). Language is thus the primary means of cultural transmission whereby social groups are integrated and the individual finds a personal and, subsequently, a social identity. The 'context of culture' defines the potential, or the range of possibilities, and the 'context of situation' determines the actual, or the choice that takes place (Firth 1964; Halliday 1973).

This view of language is corroborated by research in first language acquisition (for example, Halliday 1975; Ochs 1988), acquisition of literacy in the mother tongue (for example, Heath 1983; Scribner and Cole 1981), and research on writing in the Outer Circle of the English-using world (B. Kachru 1985). Work on the acquisition of literacy in different communities has shown that even within a well-defined cultural group (for example, American culture), communities may differ with regard to the functions of literacy, the domains of literacy, the roles of literacy in the communities' lives, and the value attached to literacy (Heath 1983). It is not surprising, then, that communities that belong to different cultural groups will show greater variation in their views on and practice of literacy (Scribner and Cole 1981). Note that it is not enough to have access to a writing system, or printing, or other devices to produce and reproduce written texts. Ancient India had a well-developed writing system prior to the Buddhist period (500 BC), as is evident from inscriptions and tablets found in various locations within and outside India. There was also a well-developed tradition not only of creative literature, both prose and poetry, but also of arithmetic, algebra, astronomy, grammar, logic, and philosophy; but there is no evidence that written texts played an important role in the transmission of this body of knowledge. Instead, most of the accumulated knowledge was passed on orally, by a dedicated teacher to committed students. Thus, the claim that Western rhetoric resulted from the development of writing, and subsequently, of printing, and from the rapid diffusion of literacy following the industrial revolution needs to be further examined. The same is true of the claim that literacy contributes to 'logical' thinking.[3] Studies such as Scribner and Cole (1981: 36–37) have arrived at the conclusion that 'nothing in our data would support the statement . . . that reading and writing entail fundamental "cognitive restructurings" that control intellectual performance in all domains'.

It is evident that a variety of cultural considerations, in addition to a large literate population, play a role in the development of rhetorical patterns. Also, there does not seem to be a necessary cause–effect relationship between a straight linear thought or rhetorical pattern, and the development of scientific and technological ideas. This becomes clear if one considers the evidence of the history of non-Western thought, for example, in China and India.

Writing in English in the Outer Circle

The concept of meaning potential discussed above is equally relevant to linguistic structure and rhetorical patterns. According to Halliday (1985), language is not a set of isolated sentences; rather, it is an interrelated set of texts in which meaning potential is actualized: people express meanings to realize some social goal. Evaluation of texts rests on interpretation of the context of situation and the context of culture.

That cultural considerations play a role in the development of linguistic structures and rhetorical patterns is corroborated from the history of writing in English in the Outer Circle, too. It has been shown in several studies that the institutionalized varieties of English used in the countries of the Outer Circle have developed their own grammatical and textual forms to express their contexts of culture (for example, Dissanayake 1985, 1990; B. Kachru 1987, 1992d; Y. Kachru 1987, 1988, 1992; Nelson 1991; Smith 1987; Thumboo 1985, 1990; Valentine 1988, 1991). For instance, in Indian English, the categorization of verbs in terms of stative vs. dynamic is not significant; instead, verbs are categorized in terms of volitionality, as in Indian languages such as Hindi, Marathi, Kashmiri, etc.[4] Also, it has been suggested that Indian English texts have stylistic features that recreate the Sanskritic noetics (Y. Kachru 1992). As has been emphasized in studies on world varieties of English (for example, Dissanayake 1985, 1990; B. Kachru 1987, 1992c; Strevens 1980; and Thumboo 1985, 1990, among others), users of these varieties are bilinguals or even multilinguals; English is one code in their code repertoire. The lexicogrammar and discoursal patterns they use represent their ways of saying and meaning, to use Halliday's terms; as Strevens (1980: 68–69) states so succinctly:

[176]

The pragmatics of discourse seem to be prone to display features transferred from the local culture in the same way as pronunciation does. This is perhaps not surprising: the pragmatics of discourse constitute a major part of our rules for regulating both interpersonal relations in general and at the same time the subtle ways in which we express our own requirements and understand what other human beings are doing. Such rules are learned within our particular culture from a very early age—certainly before mastery of language—and over a long period, perhaps one's entire lifetime. The point at issue is that local forms of English vary in the detail of their discoursal rules; the appropriate set of detailed rules is an essential defining feature.

A framework for research

In view of the above discussion, research in CR has to be much more sensitive to criteria establishing comparability of data from languages under focus. As has been pointed out by Vähäpassi (1988), it is not easy to establish the congruency of writing tasks, or to determine the comparability of the genres of writing (argumentative, persuasive, narrative, etc.). What needs to be done is to study the traditions of writing in different cultures, and to establish clear criteria for comparability across genres (Bhatia 1993) and registers (Halliday and Hasan 1976). Both of these bases for research are important because (a) there may be genres which are unique to a language and culture, and (b) there may be different rhetorical patterns associated with different genres. To illustrate, the Anglo-American genre of written directions for accomplishing various tasks, such as recipes for cooking, patterns for knitting, instructions for upholstering and assembling furniture, etc., has no parallel in the traditional Indian context. These sorts of writing have been borrowed from the English patterns and 'nativized' in Indian languages such as Hindi. Even the intricate designs one sees in rugs, silk materials, etc., are orally recited or sung out as several weavers work on a piece. An example of specific rhetorical patterns associated with particular genres in Hindi is the preference for circular or spiral rhetorical patterns of expository prose as compared to the straight linear pattern of scientific-technical writing (Y. Kachru 1988). The latter style may or may not be the result of India's colonial experience, as suggested in Leki (1991).[5] More research is needed in the Indian, especially Sanskrit, tradition of argumentation before any conclusions can be arrived at on this point. Hinds (1987) suggests that the non-linear pattern of Japanese expository prose is in harmony with the expectation that the listener/reader has the primary responsibility for effective communication, which contrasts with the expectation in English that the speaker/writer has the primary responsibility for effective communication. This suggests that if according to the conventions of a speech community, the writers have the primary responsibility for effective communication, they have to be explicit and direct, so that the readers have to make the least amount of effort to figure out what the writers' intentions are. Hinds then goes on to suggest a typology of listener/reader- vs. speaker/writer-responsibility languages. If we apply this typology to Indian languages such as Hindi, they will turn out to be shared responsibility languages in that both non-linear and linear patterns are used for communication in these languages (Y. Kachru 1988, forthcoming).

In addition to the criteria of comparability, the framework of CR needs to be based on a theoretical model that takes into account the social meaning and the intertextuality of texts, since texts derive their meaning not only from the social context, but also from other texts in the tradition. The concepts needed for such a model are already available as a result of research in pragmatics, sociolinguistics, and ethnography of speaking. Research in pragmatics has yielded valuable insights in how we use language to express our intents and get other people to act for the realization of our own or mutually desirable goals. Research in sociolingusitics and ethnography of speaking has demonstrated the relevance of variables pertaining to sociocultural situations, events, participants, purposes, norms of interaction, and language varieties. All these need to be exploited in proposing a framework for research in CR. This must be done in addition to the theory of textuality aimed at in Martin (1992), if CR is to achieve explanatory and predictive power.

Pedagogical implications

Most studies that deal with pedagogical implications of CR studies suggest that it is desirable to teach ESL students the preferred 'rhetorical mode(s)' of English (for example, papers by Connor, Eggington, Hinds, and Kaplan in Connor and Kaplan 1987). Although it is recognized that several languages have more than one rhetorical mode (for example, English, Hindi, Japanese, Korean), the concern remains that '. . . while all forms are possible, all forms do not occur with equal frequency or in parallel distribution' (Kaplan 1987: 10). Native speakers are aware not only of the forms, but also of the sociolinguistic constraints associated with the forms, and the consequences of selecting a particular form. Non-native users of a language do not necessarily possess the same competence (Kaplan 1987). Another major concern is that unless the non-native users of English become competent in the English rhetorical patterns, the vast body of scientific and technical information stored in English will remain inaccessible to them.

These concerns arise because of the narrow perspective adopted by most researchers in CR—the perspective of ESL as the teaching of academic English to international students in Inner Circle universities. An awareness of the wider perspective of ESL as relevant to the Outer Circle has so far been totally absent. If we take the wider perspective, the view of CR presented in this paper does not support the above concerns with regard to the pedagogical implications of CR research findings to ESL.

Let me present an alternative view of what the needs of the field of ESL relevant to the Outer Circle are. While it is perfectly legitimate to raise the consciousness of ESL writers regarding preferred English rhetorical patterns, it is equally legitimate and desirable to raise the consciousness of ESL professionals regarding the different rhetorical conventions of learners of English. Just as no language is more or less logical than another, so no rhetorical pattern is more or less logical. For example, the following are examples of two different traditions of syllogistic thinking (quoted from Basham 1954: 501–2):

1 a Where there is smoke there is fire.
  b There is smoke above the mountain.
  c There is fire on the mountain.

2 a There is fire on the mountain.
  b There is smoke above it.
  c Where there is smoke there is fire, as, for instance, in a kitchen.
  d Such is the case with the mountain.
  e Therefore, there is fire on the mountain.

[179]

Both are equally logical and contain the same essential elements; the second contains an extra element, an example. The first represents the traditional Western syllogism; the second, the Indian. Once the equivalences are made apparent, it is clear that neither one is superior to the other. In fact, the Indian syllogistic thinking is more explicit in some sense, in that, according to Datta (1967: 126–7), '. . . we do not have a mere formal syllogism, but also an attempt to establish its material validity by the citation of concrete instances supporting the universal major premise'.

The suggestion to foster an awareness of different rhetorical styles among ESL professionals is motivated by two major considerations. First, in view of the findings of the research on socialization through language mentioned above, it is not possible to train the entire English-using population of the world to the way of thinking and writing in American, British, or any other variety of English. As Halliday observes, even the 'mode', the rhetorical channel with its associated strategies, though more immediately reflected in linguistic patterns, has its origin in the social structure; it is the social structure that generates the semiotic tensions and the rhetorical styles and genres that express them (1978: 113). Obviously, not all the English-using world can become identical to Anglo-American society; nevertheless, it would be a pity to deny large numbers of people of the Western *and* non-Western worlds the opportunity to participate in contributing to the development of knowledge in all fields, including science and technology. A narrow view of what constitutes good writing may shut out a large number of original studies from publication and dissemination, since most information technology is controlled in the Inner Circle. Any view of rhetoric that keeps a majority of people from contributing to the world's knowledge base, and legitimizes such exclusion on the basis of writing conventions, hurts not only those who are excluded, but also those who would benefit from such contributions. It is worth remembering that the bases for the modern scientific and technological revolutions were laid in the mathematical and scientific thinking of many non-Western cultures, for example, the Indian and Arab tradition of mathematical investigations.

Secondly, it is clear that within native English-speaking conventions of writing, there is a difference between the two major traditions: the American and British. For instance, while Hoey (1983: 68) discusses examples of discourse which contain paragraphs with more than a single unit, Smith and Liedlich (1980: 21) insist that 'the paragraph is a unit of thought concerned with the exposition of a single idea, and if it is to communicate that idea clearly and concisely, it must possess oneness. That is, all the details—the reasons, illustrations, facts—used to develop it must pertain to one controlling idea.'

Additionally, the teaching of rhetoric—an American institution not shared by all native English-speaking countries—seems to have an idealized notion of what an ideal English paragraph or composition is. Most real texts, even within the American culture, exhibit variation from the idealized pattern(s). The repetitions of Arabic and the circularity of Indian writing occur in native English writing as well.[6] If academic writing in general is not to become a sterile, formula-oriented activity, we have to encourage individual creativity in writing. It is the tension between received conventions and the innovative spirit of the individual that produces good writing in academic disciplines, as well as in creative literature.

However, this does not mean that I am advocating neglecting the readers and their expectations. As Barthes (1977: 148) observes, 'The reader is the space on which all the quotations that make up a writing are inscribed without any of them being lost; a text's unity lies not in its origin but its destination . . .' What I am suggesting is that it is as desirable to educate the readers of texts produced by international users of English as it is to educate the international writers to be sensitive to the expectations of the Inner Circle readers. Instead of putting all the responsibility on the writers from the wider English-using world, it is desirable that the readers from the Inner Circle be willing to share the responsibility of making meaning. This will enrich the available and acceptable range of linguistic structures and rhetorical modes, and serve the cultural diversity of which we are becoming increasingly aware. After all, it is already happening in creative literature: a large number of the major literary prizes in recent years have been awarded to multilingual, multicultural writers, for example, the Booker Prize of Britain to the Maori writer Keri Hulme in 1985, the Neustadt Prize of the USA to the Indian writer Raja Rao in 1988, and, of course, the Nobel Prize to the Nigerian writer Wole Soyinka in 1987, and to the St. Lucian writer Derek Walcott in 1992. This has happened because though the novel is a Western form, critics seem to agree that 'its most

[181]

spectacular reinventions over the past several decades have come from the non-Western world' (Jussawalla and Dasenbrock 1992: 3). It is time for the multilingual, multicultural world to be welcomed to contributing to writing in general, not just creative literature.

Conclusion

To conclude, the CRH, as presently conceived, is not compatible with the pluricentricity of English. Contrasting rhetorical patterns is as legitimate an activity as contrasting linguistic structures but should aim at arriving at a typology and a set of universals of rhetorical patterns. Contrasting rhetoric with the aim of changing the behavior of users of English who are not native speakers is a form of Behaviorism no longer acceptable in linguistic research or language teaching. Instead, contrasting rhetorical styles to discover the meaning potential realized in texts is a legitimate activity for fostering cross-cultural understanding via an appreciation of cultural differences. Teacher education[7] programs in the Inner and Outer Circle universities are ideally situated to take the lead in this venture.

Notes

I am pleased to have this opportunity to show my regard for my dear friend, Henry Widdowson, by dedicating this paper to him.

1 B. Kachru (1985) divides the English-using world into three concentric circles: the Inner Circle consists of the native English-speaking countries, i.e. Australia, Canada, New Zealand, the UK, and the USA. The Outer Circle comprises the former colonies or spheres of influence of the UK and the USA; for example, India, Kenya, Nigeria, the Philippines, and Singapore, among others. In these countries, nativized varieties of English have achieved the status of either an official language, or of a language widely used in education, administration, the legal system, etc. The Expanding Circle consists of countries where English is fast becoming a dominant second language in the domains of education, science, and technology; for example, China, Japan, Taiwan, Thailand, and the countries of Europe.

2 Grabe (1987: 133–135) makes it clear that while there seems to be a clear basis for positing a text genre of expository prose, within the genre there are several text types, 'including at least two types of Science texts, a type of Humanities text, and another type yet to be labelled'.

3 Kaplan (1987: 1) contends that:

> In societies in which information is held in living memory, simply because information is variably retrieved (depending on the condition of the owner of memory and the nature of the audience for whom retrieval is accomplished), fact is inevitably somewhat flexible and truth mutable. But once the capacity to fix information in invariable form exists, and once the capacity to retrieve information invariably across time and space exists, the nature of fact and truth changes, fact becoming invariable as the form in which it is stored and truth becoming invariable. These features make possible the whole structure of science—an activity absolutely dependent upon invariable, easily retrieved information.

4 That is why it is perfectly grammatical to use verbs such as *know, see, hear,* etc. as dynamic verbs in South Asian English. This is also true of South East Asian and African varieties of English.

5 The Hindi term for essay, *nibandh,* comes from the Sanskrit root meaning 'to tie down'. The term *nibandh,* it has been suggested (Navalkishore, n.d.), was used in Sanskrit in the context of philosophical treatises where arguments were tied down in composition or writing.

6 The paragraph quoted here from F. David Peat's *Superstrings and the Search for The Theory of Everything* (Chicago: Contemporary Books, 1988: 240–241) illustrates the occurrence of the Arabic pattern (the repeated parts are in italic):

> Penrose was able to show that each of the massless fields of nature can be created out of nothing more than a function of a single twistor. This is a truly remarkable result. It means that it is possible to write down *a relatively simple mathematical function in twistor space that is so powerful it contains all the*

[183]

information that physicists need to know about the field at every point in space and for all time. In place of the differential field equations of nineteenth-century physics, Penrose has substituted *a simple function in twistor space. The power of twistor mathematics is sufficient to define the field for all time and at all points in space.*

I would like to add here that this is not an isolated instance; there are many such passages in the book. Also, see Tannen (1989) for the role that repetition plays in English dialogue and creative literature.

7 For a discussion of the concept of teacher education see Widdowson 1983b: 16ff. and 1990a: 61ff.

12

The paralinguistics of reference: representation in reported discourse

GEORGE YULE

Introduction

DESPITE THE FACT that more than two decades have passed since Henry Widdowson pointed out that 'there is a need to take discourse into account in our teaching of language' (1972d), there continues to be a substantial mismatch between what tends to be presented to learners as classroom experiences of the target language and the actual use of that language as discourse outside the classroom. It is, for example, still relatively common for most second language learners of English to be presented with the use of reported discourse solely in terms of mechanical conversion exercises whereby written direct speech forms, as in (1a), are to be transformed, via a set of backshifting operations, into written indirect speech forms, as in (1b).

1a Henry: 'I'm in the bath.'

1b Henry said that he was in the bath.

Exercises designed to practice this transformational skill continue to be characteristic of both new and revised editions of ELT texts (Murphy 1989; Azar 1992).

However, opportunities to apply this transformational skill, once thoroughly learned, would appear to be rather limited in the everyday conversational business of representing what was previously said. Like any classroom activity that has a narrow focus on form, such exercises will not provide opportunities for learning what those forms are normally used for, i.e. their function. Typically, direct speech has a quite different discourse function from indirect speech and, consequently, one form simply does not take the place of the other (Haiman and Thompson 1984; Li 1986; Mayes 1990; Yule 1993). Indeed, the paratactic nature of quoted speech structures is often cited as a crucial feature distinguishing them from their indirect speech 'equivalents', both syntactically and semantically (Quine 1960; Partee 1973; Mittwoch 1985; Bertolet 1990). At the formal level, there appears to be a continuum, and not a binary choice, of forms available in English for reporting discourse (Yule, Mathis, and HopKins 1992). There is also a crucial relationship, in terms of interpretation, between the reported speech and the reporting context (Bakhtin 1981; Yule and Mathis 1992) which will necessarily be missed in contextless structural exercises. While other disadvantages of standard textbook exercises could no doubt be enumerated, it may be more useful for current pedagogy to devote our attention to describing those features of reported discourse which actually occur in contemporary English and which our learners might be made aware of.

In pursuing that goal, we can certainly select our data from a wide range of sources, including what Widdowson (1987b) distinguished as literary and conventional discourse. I will present examples from conventional discourse, but following Widdowson's inspiration to focus on the language user's 'essential capacity for creativity' (1987b: 18), I will attempt to include a consideration of how that special 'representational use', sometimes assumed to be restricted to literary discourse, is also discernible in the poetics of everyday talk.

In the discussion that follows, I would like to focus on some features of reported direct (or quoted) speech in the recorded conversations of American women. I will be particularly concerned with the use of intonation (fundamental frequency) to mark shifts in voicing by a reporting speaker. Those shifts can be characterized as 'intonational quotation marks' (Bakhtin 1981: 44) which are used to present an image of a reported speaker's style. In contrast to the prosaic impersonal versions of direct speech generally found in language teaching exercises, the conversational occurrence of direct speech reporting is always contextualized within a reported scenario and inevitably loaded with some characterization of the attributed speaker. Thus, the paralinguistic marking that I shall be most concerned with is the pitch height and movement found in the reporting speaker's intonation within a particular discourse context. The referential function considered will be related to the identification of the reported character whose speech is ostensibly being represented in the scenario.

Quoted speech

The orthographic markers of quoted speech used in written discourse, such as the punctuation shown in (1a), are simply not present in spoken discourse. Instead, speakers can use a variety of paralinguistic markers, with pauses, pitch change and voice quality shifts being the most salient (Poyatos 1991; Mathis and Yule 1994). We might also include that special gesture involving two fingers of each raised hand which is used to mimic punctuation marks in the air (digital quotation marks, perhaps). These paralinguistic markers accompanying direct speech forms tend to communicate a version of what is being reported as a showing rather than as a telling. Direct speech reporting is an attempt to demonstrate what happened rather than to describe, as in indirect speech (Clark and Gerrig 1990). This distinction is present in a contrast proposed by Plato (c. 400 BC) between the mimetic, or showing, and the diegetic, or summarizing, forms of discourse. Indeed, in Book III of *The Republic*, Plato provides the original, prescriptively negative, view of imitating, that is, of direct quotation: 'It appears, then, that a man skilled in mimicry and able to imitate many things will hardly be suited to the pursuit of some serious occupation.' (trans. Sterling and Scott 1985: 92).

The more positive value accorded to the diegetic, or indirect, reporting style actually leads Plato to rewrite parts of Homer, changing the direct speech forms to indirect. Clearly, the ELT conversion exercise creators have an illustrious antecedent. (It is worth noting, however, that Homer's original does seem to have survived without Plato's 'improvement'.)

Rather than adopt such a prescriptive view, we can simply note, as several writers have done (for example, Wierzbicka 1974; Tannen 1989; Yule 1993), that indirect speech forms, backshifted and subordinated under quotative frames, have much in common with narrative telling, whereas direct speech forms are more like dramatic representation. Indeed, a particular scenario can be recreated, as in several of the examples to be presented later, with some elements in indirect speech, functioning as background, and other elements in direct speech, foregrounded. This foregrounding, or highlighting, function of quoted speech has been noted in discourse studies of a number of languages (for example, Larson 1978; Sherzer 1983; Maynard 1984; Glock 1986; Brody 1991; Macauley 1991; Besnier 1993). Moreover, as Plato recognized, that highlighting function often results in a 'performance' by the reporting speaker which, in many situations (*contra* Plato), appears to be given a highly positive value (Hymes 1975; Sternberg 1982; Bauman 1986; Yule and Mathis 1992).

Constructed, not recalled

In keeping with the 'performance' aspect of quoted speech, we must also recognize that the direct speech being quoted is typically constructed by the reporter rather than the result of verbatim recall (Tannen 1986). It is speech attributed to a speaker as a persona in a scenario. There is typically no distinction made in the reporting format whether the 'persona' is a human, a body part, a car, a dog, an insect, or whatever. In the following example, from Yule (forthcoming), the reporting speaker gives voice to some caterpillars she saw on the back of her friend's shirt.

> 2 she turned around and she had four of them clung to the back of her shirt—they were hanging all over and I was like, 'Ahh—what are those?' and I went to brush them off and they're like, 'No— don't touch me.'

It is worth noting, in (2), that not only are nonhumans reported as speaking, they are also somehow presented as if speaking in chorus, with a plural pronoun used to identify the attributed source of the constructed dialogue. A similarly unlikely choral response is attributed, in example (3), from data in Schiffrin (1987a: 289), to the parents of one reported speaker.

> 3 and she said t'her parents, 'D'you know, I'm a person.'
> And they said, 'Yeh, we know.'
> 'No. Really. I am a person in my own right.'

In the constructed dialogue shown in (3), there is an instance of zero quotative use in the last turn, where we assume that it is the first reported speaker responding to her parents, but no introductory quotative frame (for example, 'she replied') is included. This pattern is not unusual in reported interaction (Mathis and Yule 1994), but the absence of a clearly attributed speaker for the last line means that some conventional paralinguistic marking for change of speaker was probably recognized in the speech, but is not indicated in the transcript.

It has also been noted that quoted speech can be presented, not as recalled talk, but as a means of giving voice to thoughts, feelings, and attitudes (Schourup 1982). In example (4), from data in Schiffrin (1987a: 277), the quoted speech is clearly a future possible thought rather than a reported utterance.

4 She could go through a year, and then maybe, figure 'I'm tired of studying.'

In example (5), from Mathis and Yule (1994), the reporting speaker first describes her attitude towards another person and then 'performs' that attitude as if the person were there to be directly addressed. The performance of the direct speech is accompanied by a 'creaky' voice quality (Laver 1980), distinguishing paralinguistically what is not marked by a quotative frame.

5 and now she's gonna marry Mike I mean—I don't like him at all—
   (creaky voice) 'I don't like you at all'

Quoted speech can also be co-constructed (Ochs, Taylor, Rudolph, and Smith 1992). In example (6), from Mathis and Yule (1994), one speaker is in the middle of reporting (i.e. reconstructing) a previous interaction with an acquaintance when she seems to hesitate and her current conversational partner immediately provides an appropriate expression to use.

6 A: well I'll call you some other time and she's like, 'Yeah—right.'
      And I'm like, 'Don't start it—don't honey—don't=
   B: =don't throw attitude
   A: don't throw attitude and don't start and don't call me up and
      say "Yeah right" at me.'

Notice that, in (6), it is the friend, not present during the previous interaction, who provides an expression (*don't throw attitude*) that is incorporated into the reporting speaker's quoted speech account of the previous interaction.

In addition to zero quotatives, contemporary conversational English has a number of other quotative forms which are not included in the ELT textbook version of the language encountered by most learners. In example (6), the reporting speaker uses versions of *be like* twice as a quotative. As noted by several writers (for example, DuBois 1989; Blyth, Recktenwald, and Wang 1990; Ferrara and Bell 1991; Romaine and Lange 1991), this form is increasingly used in American English spoken discourse to introduce quoted speech. Other forms currently being used in a similar way are the verbs *go, be,* and *be all.* In example (7), the speaker uses *go* to introduce the other woman's quoted speech, then a form of *be* (i.e. *I'm*) to introduce her response. In (8), the speaker is discussing her friend's boyfriend and uses *be all* to introduce the quoted speech.

> 7 she's just really cool and it breaks my heart to watch her just go, 'Oh my life sucks—my husband's dead—my life is over—my son doesn't live here—I can't take care of him anymore'—you know—I'm, 'Get a grip on yourself and go do something fun.'
>
> 8 Sarah was trying to get him to stop doing drugs and he was all, 'Hey, that's me—that's me—okay?'

It is worth noting that the structure of (8) consists of a background context, with past tense and progressive aspect used to summarize (at the diegetic end of the reporting scale), prior to the presentation of the foregrounded direct speech quote. That quote also seems to be too neat, too directly representative of someone's egocentricity, to have been uttered exactly as reported. We might recognize more than one voice in this apparent quotation—that of the reported speaker, of course, but also the tone and influence of the reporting speaker's voice. This duality of voicing in quoted speech makes the identification of reference a relatively complex process (i.e. whose voice are we hearing?) and one that will be explored further in the examples which follow.

Data and analysis

Having established some of the basic aspects of quoted speech in contemporary English conversational discourse, I would like to present evidence from a more fine-grained analysis of the speech signal to show

how vocalization clues are used to represent different characters in reported scenarios. The data consists of recorded informal conversations between American women who are white, lower middle-class, college educated, Southern, in their mid-twenties, and who apparently enjoy talking to each other. I shall concentrate on pitch height and movement in this analysis, but it should be kept in mind that a large range of voice quality differences are also used by speakers to indicate different characters (and characteristics). Some discussion of these shifts in laryngeal mode (for example, creaky voice, harsh voice, etc.) is presented in Mathis and Yule (1994). The fundamental frequency measurements (in hertz) were made from narrow band spectrograms using MacSpeech Lab 2.0 software on a Macintosh Plus microcomputer linked to a TEAC V–707 RX stereo cassette deck. Those measurements are represented graphically in a stave format accompanying examples (9)–(14). Gaps in reported levels occur when there is overlapping talk and separate measurements for each speaker could not be made.

Example 9

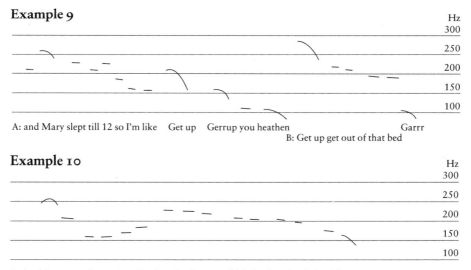

Example 10

B: the thing was – she was just like I can't take care of this dog I can't take it with me

Example 11

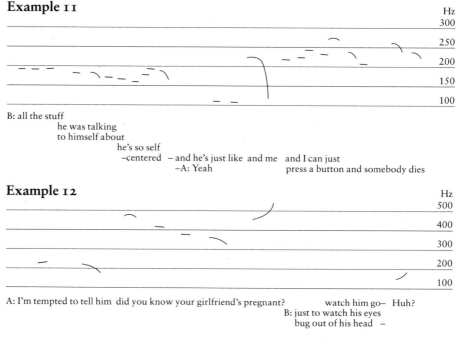

Hz
300
250
200
150
100

B: all the stuff
    he was talking
    to himself about
        he's so self
        –centered – and he's just like and me and I can just
          –A: Yeah   press a button and somebody dies

Example 12

Hz
500
400
300
200
100

A: I'm tempted to tell him did you know your girlfriend's pregnant?   watch him go– Huh?
                                    B: just to watch his eyes
                                    bug out of his head –

Example 13

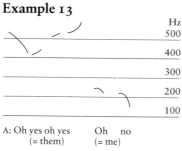

Hz
500
400
300
200
100

A: Oh yes oh yes   Oh   no
    (= them)   (= me)

Who said that and how do we know?

In example (9), there are two speakers, with A as the primary speaker describing some past events and reporting an occasion when she wanted a friend to get out of bed. Speaker B was not present on the occasion being reported. Speaker B's utterance echoes the reported utterance of speaker A, so that the effect is of two speakers sharing a single dramatic persona. That persona, however, has two distinct voices in terms of the intonation used. Speaker A reports her reaction, going low in her range at *heathen* and staying very low for her final expression of annoyance, *Garrr*. Speaker B echoes the same message in terms of content, but goes high in her pitch range, marking how she would do it if she were in that situation. Notice that speaker B uses no introductory quotative frame such as 'You're like' or 'I would say'. The question then is: to whom is this reported utterance being attributed? Who is the referent? The answer seems to be that it is a combination of the persona (or dramatic character in the scenario) created by speaker A and the voice of speaker B if she had been in that dramatic role. We should also note that, although it is a face-to-face interaction and speaker B utters a direct imperative form with no other indication of intended addressee, the actual addressee of that imperative is NOT speaker A. The addressee is the non-present sleeper called Mary who exists in the scenario created by speaker A.

In example (10), speaker B uses raised pitch for the start of the quoted speech, but does not maintain high pitch, instead falling towards the end of the utterance as in standard paratonic structure (Brown and Yule 1983). Thus, a distinct voice is initially introduced by the quotative frame (*she was just like*) and a shift up in pitch to start the quote. The question then is: which speaker is this utterance being attributed to? The nominal referent is someone called Bonnie, but the referent as understood by the participants is the persona created for Bonnie by speaker B in this dramatic presentation where Bonnie's perceived lack of concern for her dog is being articulated by speaker B in her characterization of Bonnie. The referent, then, is speaker B's caricature of Bonnie. A related phenomenon involving irony has been described in terms of 'echoic mention' (Sperber and Wilson 1981).

A similarly parodic effect is achieved in example (11) as speaker B overtly dramatizes a character in a scenario. In order to have that character express himself in a way that illustrates her description (i.e. *self-centered*), his attributed utterance is raised very high in the pitch range, giving a high-pitched maniacal quality to the character. It is worth noting that the sequence is first narrative, containing description (lower pitch, restricted pitch range), followed by dramatic demonstration (higher pitch, extended pitch range, and movement). The referent is this self-centered male character as *performed* by speaker B.

Example (12) illustrates speaker A creating two characters in a scenario. Note that the quotative frame (*tempted to tell him*) marks these utterances as not possibly being reported speech, because they haven't been uttered yet. In the scenario, speaker A will perform one character, with exaggerated final rising intonation on the highlighted word (*pregnant*), and then perform the male character's role with a low pitch, slightly rising response (*Huh?*). While speaker A is performing the scenario (dramatic mode), speaker B offers a description (narrative mode) of the same reaction. This type of mutual recognition of where the other is going in a collaborative interaction is strikingly convergent behavior (Mathis and Yule 1994 for a fuller discussion).

Example (13) follows a description by the speaker of two friends who make a lot of noise during sexual intercourse in a room adjoining hers. There are no introductory quotative frames for these utterances, but the marked difference in pitch in the utterances of *yes* from the utterance of *no* is a clear paralinguistic signal that the *no* must be attributed to a different persona (or referent) from the *yes* in this scenario. As already noted in example (9), the representation of annoyance by a persona in the dramatic scene is expressed by low falling pitch. Widdowson's observation (1987b: 15) that the linguistic sign in representational uses is necessarily iconic is certainly supported by the high-rising pitch on *yes* for sexual fervor, contrasted with the low-falling pitch of *no* for annoyance in this dramatic performance.

Example (14) is presented as an extended turn by one speaker in which pitch range is manipulated to report a reconstructed scenario involving the speaker and her mother. There is a general range for narrative segments from 194 Hz to about 300 Hz, in blocks 1, 3, 5, and 7, counting from left to right. Background information, as in the aside (the second block), is presented with lower phonation and reduced pitch range. The dramatic representation of the personae is accomplished via shifts away from this restricted narrative range. It should be emphasized that it is the shift, not the direction, that marks a dramatic voice in this scenario. The utterances attributed to the mom character can shift lower (as in the fourth block) and higher (in the ninth block). The utterances attributed to the reporting speaker's character shift higher (in blocks six and ten).

In example (14), once the dramatic scenario has been established and the mom character's first question has been introduced by a quotative (*she's like*), no other quotative frames are used. Identifying what is

Example 14

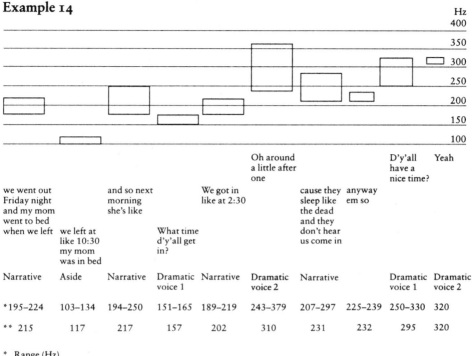

					Oh around a little after one			D'y'all have a nice time?	Yeah
we went out Friday night and my mom went to bed when we left		and so next morning she's like		We got in like at 2:30		cause they sleep like the dead and they don't hear us come in	anyway em so		
	we left at like 10:30 my mom was in bed		What time d'y'all get in?						
Narrative	Aside	Narrative	Dramatic voice 1	Narrative	Dramatic voice 2	Narrative		Dramatic voice 1	Dramatic voice 2
*195–224	103–134	194–250	151–165	189–219	243–379	207–297	225–239	250–330	320
** 215	117	217	157	202	310	231	232	295	320

* Range (Hz)
** Mean (Hz)

narrative and what is drama in this report is made possible in part by the pitch range clues. Identifying the referents (the characters in the scene) is also partly accomplished via pitch, but supported by inferences from simple turn-taking expectations (of adjacency pairs) as each character speaks in turn through the two question–answer sequences presented as quoted speech.

Conclusion

I hope that I have presented sufficient evidence to support a number of proposals regarding the nature of quoted speech forms in contemporary English discourse. Even in what may be termed 'conventional' discourse, direct speech can have a representational use and must be recognized as such in order to be interpreted appropriately. Many first and second person references within quoted speech have to be identified as dramatic personae within created scenarios rather than as the reporting speaker and the immediate face-to-face addressee. The ability to recognize the creation of those personae, via paralinguistic signals and different quotative frames, would appear to be a more useful and potentially more absorbing exercise for language learners than mechanically converting contextless direct speech forms to indirect. The fact that direct speech forms are generally used for similar highlighting functions in many languages may mean that presenting such constructions in their discourse contexts could allow learners to recognize and understand the representational function of the forms as an aid to acquiring them, rather than mechanically manipulating such forms with no obvious discourse function.

13

Grammar in discourse: attitude and deniability

ROB BATSTONE

Grammar and meaning: the notional and the attitudinal

WRITING SOME EIGHTEEN years ago, Bolinger had this to say about the meanings which are signalled through language:

> Linguistic meaning covers a great deal more than reports of events in the real world. It expresses, sometimes in very obvious ways, other times in ways that are hard to ferret out, such things as what . . . our attitudes are towards the person we are speaking to, how we feel about the reliability of our message, how we situate ourselves in the events we report, and many other things that make our messages not merely a recital of facts but a complex of facts and comments. (Bolinger 1977: 4)

Over the last twenty years or more, there has been growing interest in exactly the phenomenon which Bolinger describes: an interest not merely in how events (and states) are reported, but also in how attitude is signalled through language.

Take, for instance, the following invented example:

1 Smith (1980) *argued* that Britain *was* no longer a country in which freedom of speech *was* seriously *maintained*. Johnson (1983), though, *argues* that Britain *remains* a citadel of individual liberty.

Concentrating on the writer's use of tense, I suggest that there are two levels of meaning here. The first level has to do with the reporting of states and events: we can say with some certainty that past time is being signalled with respect to Smith, and present time with respect to Johnson. I refer to these as *notional* meanings: they constitute two of the fundamental notions involved in the reporting of states and events. Such meanings are the common currency of semantic idealization in pedagogic grammars, and they have found their way into the very metalanguage we use to distinguish tenses—the 'present tense', the 'past tense'. And of course, this metalinguistic convention is not accidental. There are form/meaning pairings here which recur with great regularity across many different contexts of use, and they are relatively stable in that they are difficult to contest or to deny.

The picture is very different, though, with my second level of meaning, which has to do with the expression of *attitude*. We could say, for instance, that the past tense in example 1 signals that Smith's argument is no longer worthy of current interest, that it is (in two significant senses) 'passé'. In contrast, Johnson's argument is held to be of real and continuing relevance (hence the present tense). Present and past tense, then, are being used to express the writer's attitude: his subjective distribution of approval and disapproval. Very often, attitudinal meanings are signalled covertly (as is the case with example 1) so that—as Bolinger puts it—they are not always easy to 'ferret out'. We cannot infer a particular attitudinal meaning simply by 'reading it off' from the grammar, but by taking bearings on the discourse as a whole. This involves paying close attention to the interdependency between grammar and lexis. Had example 1 been 'Smith (1980) *demonstrated* that . . .' then our perception might be changed very considerably. Our reading of the writer's viewpoint will also be affected by the preconceptions which we (as readers) bring with us in any discourse encounter. In short, the covert signalling of attitude is much more delicate (and more context-sensitive) than the relatively explicit grammatical signalling of notional meanings.

The expression of attitude is a central concern in Critical Discourse Analysis (for an overview, see Fairclough 1989; Kress 1991). Critical Discourse Analysts seek to reveal how texts are constructed so that particular (and potentially indoctrinating) perspectives can be expressed delicately and covertly; because they are covert, they are elusive of direct challenge, facilitating what Kress calls the 'retreat into mystification and impersonality' (1989: 57). In discussing the expression of attitude, I will refer to a number of examples taken from Critical Discourse Analysis.

Various issues arise out of this initial discussion. Later in this paper I suggest that the notional/attitudinal distinction is useful in formulating relationships between grammar and discourse, and in understanding how writers and speakers can effectively deny certain attributions of attitude—a matter of some importance, particularly for Critical Discourse Analysis.

Firstly, though, I examine the conceptual relationship between notional and attitudinal meanings. We are dealing here with a relationship between the semantic and the pragmatic, whereby what I call the 'notional semantic' gives us basic conceptual parameters within which pragmatic inferences of attitude become plausible[1]. Widdowson sees the relationship between the two in the following way:

> The meanings which are provided in grammars and dictionaries are records of conventional encodings . . . They are the general semantic bearings from which language users can take their particular pragmatic fix.
> (Widdowson 1994e: 15–16)

Grammar provides us with a semantic resource which establishes certain (albeit broad) constraints on what we can mean with grammar: constraints on what Halliday calls 'meaning potential'.

Projection in discourse grammar: elaboration, extension, and expansion

In this section I propose a framework to help explain the connection between these notional/semantic bearings and certain attitudinal/pragmatic 'fixes' which can be made in the discourse context. The kind of 'semantic bearings' to which Widdowson refers involves, I suggest, making a *projection* from the general semantic into features of the particular discourse context. In example 1, for instance, the inference that it is Johnson's and not Smith's work which is approved of involves a projection from the semantic notions of past time (linked to disapproval) and present time (linked to approval). I examine how links are made between some of the notional semantic parameters of states and events (past and present time, sequence and simultaneity, location and agency) and attitudinal inferences of responsibility, blame, interpersonal control, approval, and disapproval. In so doing, I will outline three kinds of projection: elaboration, extension, and expansion.

Elaboration

We have already seen an example of elaboration (in 1), where notions of 'pastness' and 'presentness' are used to convey a connected sense of the presence or absence of current relevance. How exactly is the connection made between these two levels? It is not that these notions of past and present are being entirely discarded. Rather, they are built upon or 'elaborated' in some way. Elaboration involves taking some element of the semantic notional meaning, and giving it a particular but related attitudinal orientation, so that the two bear a very close conceptual relationship with each other.

Tense and metaphor: distance

In example 1 above, notions of past and present time are being elaborated metaphorically. There is something in the temporal notion of 'presentness' which has taken on a closely related meaning: that what Johnson *says* is present in the sense of being relevant, of being part of the 'here and now', and part of our current concerns. Conversely, what Smith *said* is perceived as being complete and finished, and thus not a valid component of contemporary debate. There is a metaphorical link between the two levels of meaning: between the broad temporal semantic and the delicate inference concerning approval and relevance. What is temporally past and so distant is seen as being *psychologically distant* and irrelevant and remote, and vice versa[2] (for further discussion of psychological distance, see Batstone 1994: 19–21). There may be an ideological element here, because there is an intricate connection between implying that something is 'not relevant' and thereby signalling that it is 'not approved of'. In particular contexts, of course, the tenses used in reported speech may imply any number of delicate meanings (see Harman 1990; Yule, Mathis, and HopKins 1992).

The expression of psychological distance does not, though, equate simply with the expression of approval and disapproval. Riddle (1986: 271) gives a very different kind of example:

2 ANNE: Jane just bought a Volvo.
   JOHN: Maureen *has* one.
   ANNE: John, you've got to quit talking about Maureen as if you
             were still going together. You broke up three months ago.

John's use of the present tense seems to be expressing a kind of 'psycho-logical closeness'. As Riddle (ibid.) puts it, he 'is still emotionally attached to his former girlfriend and is reluctant to break the psycho-logical tie'.

Other forms of distance operate in a similar way. The best known is probably *social distance*. Here, past forms can be used to signal defer-ence to an interlocutor ('I *was* wondering if you *could* . . .?'), thereby expressing a measure of social distance between participants involved in the discourse. Just as past time denotes temporal distance, so defer-ence can mark social distance. And there are many other kinds of dis-tance which involve 'past' and 'present' forms[3].

Subjects and agents: intentionality and blame

It has been known for a long time that the notion of subject in English is a complex one, and that it can be conceived of in very different ways (for a relatively recent discussion, see Halliday 1985: 32–37). Of most interest here is what Halliday calls the 'logical subject', which he defines as the 'doer of the action' (1985: 34), equivalent to the 'agent' in terms of case grammar (Fillmore 1968).

But the notion of the agent as 'doer of the action' is a very broad and unrefined one. People 'do' actions in all kinds of ways, and the particu-lar circumstances of this 'doing' will inevitably affect the way we con-ceive of their agency. In example 3 it is obvious that Jane does the spilling in some sense, but in what sense precisely?

3 Jane spilled the milk.

In fact this sentence is ambiguous. It may be that she spilled the milk accidentally:

4 Jane, unable to see where she was going, spilled the milk over her mother.

Or it may be that her action was deliberate, pre-meditated, and intentional:

5 Jane, sick of maternal dominance, spilled the milk over her mother.

The highly idealized notion of the 'doer of the action' gets *elaborated* in various ways as it is contextually refined by reference (for example) to this connected notion of intentionality. Sometimes, intentionality is left open to contextual inference (as with example 3). At other times it is signalled by reference to the surrounding co-text (as with examples 4 and 5).

In Critical Discourse Analysis there is a particular interest in agency, and it is not difficult to see why. We can easily construct a context where example 3 is uttered by someone wishing to indicate where responsibility and blame should be directed—a child pointing accusingly at her sister, perhaps. In English, the grammatical signalling of responsible agency can reside purely in word order, so that there may be no explicit linguistic marking which would reveal the writer's perspective.

Stubbs, in an analysis of a newspaper report dealing with events surrounding the release of Nelson Mandela, points out that 'when Blacks are reported as doing things, committing violence or issuing threats, they are in subject position, and at the beginning of the clause' (1990: 6). Here are two examples from the newspaper report:

6 Jubilant blacks clashed with police . . .

7 . . . ANC supporters have been feuding with a more conservative black group . . .

In 6 and 7 one might argue (as Stubbs does) that the choice of verb and adjunct helps to mystify the whole issue of intention and responsibility. The role of agent (let alone the more delicate notion of intention) is indeterminate, and the writer could easily enough argue that this is merely a report of 'clashes' and 'feuds' in which blacks and police were inseparably involved. In the context, though, Stubbs sees a clear implication that 'the Blacks are the cause of the violence' (1990: 7). Such texts are not ideologically neutral, so that there may be an ideological difference between saying 'blacks clashed with whites' (with blacks as agents and a deniable implication of responsibility) and saying 'whites clashed with blacks'.

At the semantic level, all that can be said is that agents are in some way the 'doers' of the action. But this broad idealization raises key questions which can only be answered in the discourse context. In what sense the 'doers'? Is the action direct or indirect? Are the agents responsible, and can they be held to blame? Answers (or partial answers) to these questions are *elaborated* contextually and co-textually, where the delicate level of attitude comes into focus. We could continue to elaborate more finely tuned accounts, relying increasingly on lexical and contextual cues, until we reach the point where we are dealing with rich elaborations with respect to a single and unique discourse.

Aspect and change

I was involved not long ago in a discussion about gathering friends together for an outing, during which I heard the following very particular use of the progressive form in reported speech:

8 Sheila's saying she doesn't want to come.

The conversation then quickly shifted to how we could persuade Sheila to change her mind. The implication of this particular discourse fragment, then, is that Sheila might not have been firmly resolved, but instead open to change. In part, such an interpretation can be supported by the present tense used in the reporting clause. It expresses a kind of psychological closeness, so that what Sheila says is seen as relevant and current, rather than past and beyond reach.

More to the point, though, is the use of the progressive form. Semantic idealizations about the progressive invariably make reference to something which is 'in progress', and to 'something that is temporary' (Leech 1989: 393). Other idealizations make similar observations, emphasizing the incompleteness of an action or state (Celce-Murcia and Larsen-Freeman 1983). Changing the emphasis slightly, Bland (1988: 56) argues that the progressive often 'focuses on a *change* (or changes) of state'.

In example 8, the speaker is using the progressive to present Sheila's state of mind as changeable, and hence open to modification. So the concept of change or temporariness captured in the semantic idealization is *elaborated* in context to infer specific attitudes, including the possibility of change through persuasion (though the added inference of persuasion is particularly context-dependent). This link between progressive, change, and persuasion represents an increasingly delicate level of interpretation.

Extension: from time and place to cause in subordinate clauses

I am concerned here with the grammatical linking of events (and events and states) by explicit reference to place and time in subordinate clause structures. Here is an example (Stubbs 1990: 27) taken from the text about South Africa referred to earlier:

9 Mobs of his [Mandela's] followers ran wild and looted shops in Capetown, where police fired on the crowd.

A semantic description of this clause structure has to be quite brief: it is a clause of place, linking two events by reference to a location in which they both occurred, probably at or about the same time. Shifting to a much more delicate and context-sensitive level, we can say in addition that there is a relationship of cause/effect which may be implied here. But it is fundamentally ambiguous: either police fired in justifiable response to the provocative and causal behaviour of Mandela's followers, or Mandela's followers ran wild as a result of firing from police. The grammar itself does not and cannot tell us which interpretation is more plausible, although the positioning of the police in the subordinate clause may be significant, giving them less prominence and so reinforcing the idea that they are seen as respondents in the interaction rather than instigating agents.

Here is another example from the same text (Stubbs 1990: 27):

10 The situation in Capetown was highly volatile throughout the day as thousands massed in Grand Parade in front of City Hall where Mandela was due to make his freedom speech.

Concentrating on the first two clauses, a notional/semantic gloss would say that a state and an event existed at approximately the same time. The second clause is an adverbial clause of time, and specifically of simultaneity. More delicately, there is again an inference of causality. Was the volatility of the situation a result of the massing crowd, or was it a consequence of a more intricate mix of factors involving both the crowd and the authorities? The close syntactic linking of clauses through subordination alerts us to an intimate connection between them.

Once again different levels of meaning are at work here. The broadest semantic idealization captures the 'surface' and least deniable meanings (to do with location in example 9, and time in example 10). More delicately, relations of cause/effect shift into view, and more delicately still there are attitudinal implications of responsibility and blame which are so often covertly attached to agent roles. These notional/semantic and attitudinal/pragmatic levels of meaning are linked, I suggest, by a relationship of *extension*. In relations of extension, the meanings which emerge in context cluster round a specific and (in principle) a self-standing notional category (here, cause/effect) which is quite conceptually distinct from the notions of time and location which lie more on the surface. In actual discourse, though, this distinction all but dissolves, and the link between (for instance) sequence and *con*sequence is close as well as pervasive in many contexts of use. Relationships of extension, then, involve connections between distinct notional categories; in this case, a semantic signalling of time and location linked to a pragmatic inference of cause/effect. Consequently, there is a greater conceptual divergence between the semantic and the pragmatic in extension than there is in relationships of elaboration.

Expansion: reduced forms and mystification

There is always some balance to be struck, in discourse, between language and context in the sharing and distribution of information. In the case of transitive clauses, a lot of information is signalled linguistically, as with 'the man broke the window with a hammer' (where agent, process, affected object, and instrument roles are all encoded). But the grammar also provides us with reduced forms which allow certain deletions to be made. With the passive we can delete the agent role ('the picture was destroyed'). Nominalization deletes yet more information, including time references (as with 'the picture's destruction' or even 'this destruction. . .'), and there are many other forms which permit deletions of this kind (such as non-finites: see Kress 1989: 57–59).

In terms of semantic meaning, our capacity to draw on notional idealization is similarly reduced. The passive 'allows us to omit the actor if we want to' (Leech 1989: 332), and nominalizations enable us to pretend 'to see the action as a static thing' (Quirk and Greenbaum 1973: 21). This paucity of information is inevitable given that these forms are so context-dependent. It is only in specific contexts that participants and time references may be inferred. The relationship between semantic idealizations of meaning and specific meanings inferred in context is one of *expansion*: the grammar provides, so to speak, empty slots which are 'expanded' by reference and inference so that participants and the temporal context can be supplied. Expansion is distinct from elaboration and extension in that there is so little information discernible at the broadest semantic level, and consequently so much more work to be done, by way of inference, in context.

Such forms are discussed a great deal in Critical Discourse Analysis, because the deletion of information can be motivated by power. Sources of authority can be concealed, and a sense of inaccessibility or impersonality can be conveyed (as in academic or scientific genres). Such language can also be used to evade or manipulate responsibility, as with 'this place hasn't been cleaned for ages', where the passive may be used to imply that someone else should do the cleaning. Because it allows such a thoroughgoing series of deletions, nominalization is said to be particularly well suited to the expression of power through the mystification of time and participants (see Fowler and Kress 1978: 207–209).

But the intrinsic context-dependence of these forms means that they tend to be open to multiple interpretations in discourse. Often they get used for purposes of communicative economy, where the deleted references are clear and where it would be tedious to spell them out. Often, too, they arise in part because of the way the surrounding text has been constructed. The passive, for example, is often motivated by the distribution of given and new information (see Rutherford 1987).

Grammar, constraint, and deniability

In the rest of this paper I will consider some of the issues which arise out of the foregoing discussion, and which have to do with the nature and role of grammar in discourse.

Freedom and constraint: the stability of meanings

Notional and attitudinal meanings are distinct in terms of their relative stability. Very often, notional meanings reside on the surface of discourse: they are stable and explicit, and in most cases it would be hard to deny them. Attitudinal meanings, however, are frequently much more delicate because they depend so much more on particular alliances of grammar, lexis, and context. They are, then, relatively unstable and thus hard to 'ferret out'. So, for example, I have suggested that in adverbial clauses of place and time (examples 9 and 10) it is the notional/semantic level (location and time reference) which is comparatively explicit and stable, while attitudinally the implication of cause and responsibility is more ambiguous and unstable. With psychological distance (example 1), references to the notions of past and present time are undeniable, but the underlying implication of relevance and (yet more subtly) of disapproval is unstable. With notional subjects, the notion of a 'doer' of the action is clear enough, while conceptions of responsibility and blame are much less stable or overt.

Some stability in the functioning of discourse grammar is essential, in order to provide relatively clear and mutually accessible bearings without which communication would be absurdly hit and miss. Semantic stability is a prerequisite for pragmatic creativity in language use. Constraint and freedom are necessary partners, for it is only by reference to some relatively fixed conceptual parameters that language users can fashion their own particular projections in the discourse context. As Widdowson puts it, conventional limits on independent initiative 'operate negatively as constraints, but positively as enabling conditions' (1990a: 5).

Constraints on meaning and on the role of grammar

There are two kinds of constraint on the meaning potential of grammatical forms—on what can be meant, and on what can be perceived to be meant. One constraint is semantic, defining what Widdowson calls 'the conventional limits of common and communal agreement' (1994e: 16). The other constraint is pragmatic, where features of context may implicitly direct readers and listeners towards one interpretation in favour of another. In actual contexts, then, certain meanings

[207]

will appear to be more or less stable, more or less apparent and plausible, so that the degree of constraint on meaning potential will be variable, rather than an absolute.

This notion of constraint on interpretation is of considerable relevance in Critical Discourse Analysis. Although in principle texts are open to multiple interpretations, Critical Discourse Analysts maintain that our interpretative capacity can be seriously constrained in actual contexts. It is argued that the repeated deployment of certain linguistic forms helps both to maintain and to conceal existing power structures by delimiting the interpretations actually available to us, thus shaping the way we see the world: 'if people and things are repeatedly talked about in certain ways, then there is a good chance that this will affect how they are thought of' (Stubbs 1990: 8).

It is important to identify both the scope and the limitations on grammar in this process of constraint. Clearly, Widdowson's 'particular pragmatic fix' cannot reasonably be taken in the absence of some semantic and linguistic warrant. Grammar sets certain limits on meaning potential, yet within these limits there are pragmatic constraints (relating in part to those prior social experiences which interlocutors bring with them in any discourse encounter) which will delimit our actual freedom of interpretation.

What is certain is that it is not the grammar in itself which constrains us to interpret texts in certain ways. In the previous section, my concern was with how certain projections are made possible in principle, but I am not arguing that grammar can in some way pre-empt any particular projection relationship. The perception of attitude—when it is covertly signalled—cannot be determined solely on linguistic grounds.

We should, therefore, be cautious in making statements which suggest that grammar contains its own pre-coded attitudinal meanings. Stubbs, in discussing the article about South Africa referred to earlier, seems to push the role of grammar beyond its natural limits:

> The article does not anywhere say explicitly that the Blacks are the cause of the violence, but *the grammar expresses this message.* (Stubbs 1990: 7, emphasis mine)

My own reading of this newspaper article (and this is in itself an important delimitation) is that there are features of the text which may justify the notion that the 'Blacks' are covertly presented as instigators. But

[208]

this interpretation is not a product of grammatical factors in isolation. It is influenced by grammar in association with lexis, and by the way in which lexico-grammatical patterns are progressively built up through the text as a whole.[4] Stubbs' definition of grammar as 'the syntactic mechanisms which a language has for encoding experience' (1990: 21) appears to ride roughshod over the very important distinction between the notional/semantic and the attitudinal/pragmatic. It is a definition which we can apply with some accuracy to semantic meanings, but it would be seriously deficient as a definition of our subjective experience and perception of the attitude with which events are reported. The very term 'encode' (together with other related metaphors—'embody', 'contain') suggests a narrow and self-contained relationship between grammar and meaning.

In Critical Discourse Analysis, then, there is a danger of overplaying the role of grammar in discourse, and of implying that grammatical forms can themselves 'encode' ways of seeing the world, thus leading to indoctrination and to the maintenance of discrimination and existing power relations in society. To be fair, there is some recognition of this. Fairclough, for example, comments that:

> ... in analysis, the relationship between textual features and social meanings tends to be portrayed as straightforward and transparent ... in practice, values are attributed to particular structures (such as passive clauses without agents) in a rather mechanical way. (1992a: 28)

Deniability and power

The fact that notional meanings are often so explicit and stable (in contrast with attitudinal meanings) is highly significant for critical interpretations of discourse. In terms borrowed from Brown and Levinson (1978), the notional dimension is *on record*—open to explicit examination and relatively incontestable—whereas the attitudinal dimension is often *off record*, hidden behind the attestable surface of discourse and difficult to pin down. An impartial rendering of such texts will of necessity focus on notional/semantic meanings. If we were to focus only on those semantic meanings which are most clearly 'on record' in the newspaper article about South Africa, then we could maintain that much of the text constitutes no more than an objective account of events in the real world. This appearance of objectivity is of great interest in Critical Discourse Analysis. Foucault, for example, discusses 'how effects of truth are produced within discourses' (1980: 118), and Stubbs describes the appearance of many discourses as 'factual, literal, objective, authoritative and independent of the author' (1990: 10).

The relationship between the notional/semantic and the attitudinal/ pragmatic is central here, because writers and speakers can effectively deny any interpretation of attitude by reference to the more explicit level of notional meaning. If, for instance, we challenge the writer for signalling unfair disapproval in example 1, he can simply claim that it was only the notional meaning (the temporal sense of pastness) which he had in mind. Smith's work is reported in the past, he may say, because he no longer reads Smith's work, or because Smith has ceased publishing, or because Smith has passed away, or perhaps because Smith's article was published earlier than that of Johnson. Challenged about the implication that Mandela's followers are the cause of the violence and killing, the writer of examples 9 and 10 can retreat into the notional, asserting that it was only the most general notion of agency that he intended, or that the element of time or place was uppermost in his thoughts. In short, the text producer can deny the attitudinal by referring to the notional, with the latter (residing so much more on the surface of things) acting as camouflage for the former. He may also, of course, deny one attitudinal interpretation by asserting another.

So while Critical Discourse Analysis is open to criticism for underplaying the flexibility with which texts can be interpreted, it is precisely this flexibility (and particularly the tension between notional and attitudinal interpretations) which fuels the expression and maintenance of power.

Conceptions of grammar and discourse

Much of this paper has been concerned with conceptions of grammar and of discourse, and it seems appropriate to conclude by making these conceptions explicit. There are three positions which are relevant:

a) Grammar is seen as independent of discourse

b) Grammar is seen as a dependent and inseparable component of discourse

c) Grammar is both dependent on and independent of discourse, so that the relationship between grammar and discourse is reciprocal.

The first conception of grammar—as independent of discourse—presupposes a degree of idealization which characterizes semantic study. It involves, that is, formulating statements about meaning which appear to attach to self-standing grammatical forms. The aim is to capture a kind of conceptual 'common core', sufficiently generalized to apply across a range of actual instances. In the terms presented in this paper, it is the notional/semantic level of meaning which is most relevant here. Such idealizations are only possible because grammar serves to encode semantic parameters which are not strongly discourse determined[5].

The second conception of grammar—as a dependent and inseparable component of discourse—relates most directly to the kinds of attitudinal meaning discussed here. This level of analysis focuses on the interdependence between grammar, lexis, and the wider discourse context. We are concerned here, then, with implicit or covert meanings, and because these meanings are strongly discourse determined we cannot sustain a rigid separation of 'grammar' from 'discourse'.

There is a danger of blurring these two conceptions, so that the stability of grammatical meaning in semantic idealization is seen (erroneously) to characterize the function of grammar in the signalling of attitudinal meaning. This leads to the notion that it is 'the grammar' which independently 'encodes' perceptions of experience, attitude, and power.

The third conception of grammar is the one I have been outlining in much of this paper. It utilizes insights from the first two conceptions, while maintaining that neither of these is adequate on its own. In other words, grammar is distinct from discourse in that it encodes conceptual bearings necessary for effective and creative communication. At this level (which includes the notional semantic), discourse interpretation is *informed by grammar*, providing a necessary conceptual constraint. But at the same time grammar is also a dependent, an interacting component of discourse. At this level (which includes the attitudinal pragmatic) grammar is *informed by the discourse context.* These two levels act on each other, so that semantic and pragmatic dimensions are mutually informing. Relationships of projection (of elaboration, extension, and expansion) are struck between the two, but they can also be exploited by language users in the operation and exploitation of ambiguity and deniability. This third conception could be a useful one for Critical Linguistics, where there is a need both to observe and to detach from the particulars of any specific textual inter-pretation, and to make more systematic reference to a broad frame-work of linguistic analysis[6].

To conclude with a brief critical analysis, the term 'discourse gram-mar' itself creates a slightly mystifying sense of duality: there is gram-mar, and there is discourse. In one sense this is a valid and a necessary distinction. In another sense, though, the distinct terms conceal their interdependency. I have tried, in this paper, to suggest that there is something to be gained by maintaining both senses, so that we can bet-ter appreciate the reciprocal relationship between the two.

Notes

1 My interest here is with cases where notional meanings are clearly signalled by the grammar (and so are part of semantics), and where attitudinal meanings are much more context-dependent (and so part of pragmatics). On many occasions, of course, the situation is quite different, with notional meanings needing to be inferred from context, and with attitudinal meanings explicitly marked in the language (particularly through lexis).

2 For a discussion of relationships between tense and metaphor, see Kress 1977.

3 Kress (1989: 53) discusses how present tense can signal certainty/ confidence, and how past tense modals may signal uncertainty, insecurity, and powerlessness.

4 The lexical choices in the newspaper article discussed by Stubbs are very strongly suggestive of an unsympathetic attitude towards ANC members (words like 'mobs', 'wild', and phrases including 'an ecstatic black ANC follower' and 'one sickening scene of sav-

agery' in reference to how Mandela supporters 'knifed a man repeat-edly'). Attitude is not always signalled implicitly, and these examples appear to be explicit markers of attitude which (consequently) are so much less open to pragmatic variation in interpretation.

5 Stability is always a matter of degree, and even broad semantic idealizations (however carefully formulated) will be subject to some degree of modification in context (see Widdowson 1984a: 42–3; Batstone 1994: 11–15).

6 There are references in Critical Discourse Analysis to a broader and less contextually dependent conception of grammar, and most often it is Halliday's conception (particularly 1985) which is referred to. What is lacking, though, is a systematic framework for relating (for example) Halliday's broader conception to the more pragmatic inferences drawn by some Critical Linguists.

14

Field-guides in strange tongues: a workshop for Henry Widdowson

JOHN M. SWALES

The final measure of intellectual achievement is in terms of its contribution to the conversation in which all universes of discourse meet. (OAKESHOTT 1959: 491)

Prologue

To THE LIKELY readers of this book, Henry Widdowson will be well known as a figure who has indeed contributed to many universes of discourse. At the very least, these contributions cover appropriate principles for language learning and teaching, the uses and abuses of linguistic analysis, the role of literature in language and literacy education, and the theory and practice of Languages for Specific Purposes. Others will doubtless be talking about the first three of these universes of discourse and of Widdowson's scholarly contributions to them. I will focus on the last. However, all our conversations with Widdowson's work constitute that distinctive kind of wide-ranging intertextuality that a *festschrift* uniquely provides. Very appropriately so, since intertextuality has itself become an increasingly pervasive theme in Widdowson's more recent writing. And in this context, it is no accident, I suppose, that my opening epigraph is taken from an essay entitled 'The Voice of Poetry in the Conversation of Mankind'. I trust Widdowson will approve.

Widdowson has, in fact, paid relatively little attention to ESP/LSP affairs since the appearance of the *Learning Purpose and Language*

Use monograph in 1983, presumably as a result of his heavy involvement with teacher education at the University of London Institute of Education and elsewhere. Indeed, his absence from the ESP arena provides at least part of the underlying reason for Waters' recent lament (1994) that there have been few significant advances in ESP thinking during the last several years. However, his absence has not been total: I know of at least one recent and notable ESP/LSP paper. This is entitled 'The relevant conditions of language use and learning' and was published in a volume called *Language and Content: Discipline- and Content-based Approaches to Language Study* (Krueger and Ryan 1993). The minimally necessary background to this volume is that it constitutes the edited proceedings of a conference on foreign languages across the curriculum (FLAC) held at Brown University in Providence, Rhode Island, in 1992. FLAC courses have developed in the United States in order to offer students some useful and continuing foreign language experience *after* they have satisfied their institution's basic foreign language requirements. These courses have proved particularly attractive for students who are not interested in majoring in a foreign language (with its traditionally heavy emphasis on literature). The courses are typically discipline- or content-based, wherein, for example, the history of the Weimar Republic might be taught and studied partly or wholly through the medium of German. In effect, what the FLAC approach seems to be after is additional, and initially often quite circumscribed, authentic foreign language literacies—literacies conceived of as interacting with, interpreting, and responding to texts chosen from areas of disciplinary expertise. Hence the affinity of such developments with ESP/LSP.

A first point to note about the Widdowson paper (1993c), however, is that it carefully and consistently declines to offer support for the 'content-based' aspects of the proceedings and, indeed, of the volume's title. Not for Widdowson is there any simple division between *language* and *content*; not for him any simple conduit metaphor of how language works to convey meaning by 'carrying' content (Lakoff and Johnson 1980). His refusal to align his essay with the terminology of the *soi-disant* 'content-based' movement is, of course, very much what we might expect of him; additionally, however, his loud silence on 'content' has also been highly salutary for its particular time and place. In my view, nothing has hindered the acceptance of FLAC in the Arts and

Sciences colleges of American universities more than this advocacy of a crude language/content dichotomy. While this division may be sufficiently straightforward and 'catchy' to appeal to deans and college-wide curriculum committees, it also looks down-home simplistic (as yet another language teacher reductionism) to those who wield power and influence in departments of foreign languages and literatures—the professors who teach culture, literature or linguistics. Widdowson's paper thus stands apart as offering a subtler and more nuanced vision of what FLAC/LSP might be.

The value of a somewhat different approach can be illustrated by the Wesche article from the same volume. Although, in terms of research substance, this article is arguably the strongest in the book, it remains symptomatic of an approach that Widdowson (and I) will have trouble with. Consider this statement from Wesche's opening section (my emphasis): 'Essential to all content-based language teaching is a view of language acquisition which emphasizes the *incidental* internalization of new knowledge by the learner from rich target language data, while focusing on the meaning being communicated' (1993: 57–58). Later, Wesche expands upon this view by listing four features that she believes are shared by content- or discipline-based approaches:

1 Content as the curriculum organizing principle;

2 Double objectives: content mastery and second language development;

3 Authentic language materials and tasks (i.e. created for other, non-pedagogical purposes), with teacher adaptation as required;

4 Accommodation to the needs of second language learners (e.g. increased redundancy and exemplification, use of advanced organizers, initial emphasis on receptive skills).
(Wesche 1993: 61)

Although this amplification does suggest that the *incidental* in the earlier quotation is better glossed as 'concomitant' rather than 'accidental', it still remains clear that linguistic self-consciousness and linguistic sensitivity are attributes to be expected of teachers (features 3 and 4), but not of the student learners, who are expected to give their full attention to the content. In contrast, Widdowson's contribution to the 1993 volume is largely taken up with the ways and means of

developing *foreign language students'* linguistic and textual awareness. He offers, after seven pages of preliminary argument, this first
shot as an answer to the didactic problem as he sees it:

> It can be argued, then, that the advantage of a discipline-based
> approach to language teaching is that it shifts from a contextual to
> an intertextual perspective. In drawing attention to genre as a media-
> tion between code and context, it facilitates the process of abstrac-
> tion upon which language learning depends. Students can be
> induced to notice form because it plays a crucial part in realizing
> conventions of communication.
> (Widdowson 1993c: 34)

However, admirers of Widdowson's writing—and there are many—
will immediately recognize the phenomenon that his first answers are
never his last. Indeed, there are eight paragraphs to go yet. The first
potential difficulty he foresees is 'the obvious point that if the genres of
particular disciplines, professions, occupations are already known and
practised, then they will not need to be learned by being noticed, and so
the language which realizes them will not need to be noticed either'
(ibid.: 34). However, if we recollect that the target groups are undergraduates in their third or fourth year, then it is unlikely that the genre
acquisition process will have become consolidated even in the first language. Moreover, intertextuality functions *across* the L1 and L2 borders as well as within them. As a result, FLAC courses will still need to
help senior undergraduates and junior graduates 'notice' cross-cultural
differences, 'appreciate' national academic traditions (such as Clyne's
(1987b) discussion of scholarly digressions in German), and 'recognize' other generic and stylistic features. Widdowson's *difficulty* seems
unlikely to arise in the FLAC context.

Widdowson then raises the issue of how we can attain the necessary
condition of abstraction, especially if genres are highly specific in their
disciplinary conventions and so inhibit acquisition of more general—
and more generally useful—rhetorical patterns. 'One way', he coun-
ters, 'is to engage students in activities which are not directly *derived*
from disciplines, but *contrived* from them in reference to their basic
principles of design and more general generic features' (1993c: 35).
Another is to focus on linguistic features of disciplinary genres that
might pass the students by, not only in terms of the features themselves

but also as a way of showing how conventions have evolved—and can indeed be challenged. Widdowson then concludes his paper by suggesting the kind of genre-based disciplinary activities he has been discussing (ones that are 'discipline referred rather than discipline determined', ibid.: 35) have clear possibilities, but need careful appraisal.

In the next section of this piece, I hope to offer a demonstration of much of the thinking underlying Widdowson's 'The relevant conditions of language use and learning' chapter. These activities are, I trust, sufficiently explicit and specific for Widdowson to, indeed, appraise them (if he should so wish). I shall certainly take a final opportunity to comment on his recent LSP paper in their light. The materials take the form of a workshop (itself very much a Widdowsonian genre) which, after a trial run at Michigan, I first offered at Brown University in 1993. (I suspect that Henry Widdowson himself suggested that Brown invite me. Intertextuality rules OK?)

Entr'acte

I have so far conducted my conversation with Widdowson's work within the context of disciplinary literacies. However, it is also well known that those with hobbies or special interests often have expert amateur knowledge of the technical genres that these hobbies or special interests have developed. Collectors can read catalogues, price guides, and auction lot descriptions; chess or bridge enthusiasts can follow game commentaries in newspapers; modelers, gastronomes, and quilters can handle very complex instructions. Typically, the writers of such genres engage in extensive ellipsis, making much use of sentence fragments and abbreviations. Sentence subjects, complements, articles, and prepositions may be omitted, since they are thought to be recoverable by members of the discourse communities. Indeed, experience with these genres often allows enthusiasts to cope with specialized material in languages they know little, even though the vocabulary used may be extensive and, in terms of general frequency, rare.

One widely used group of such genres are nature field-guides (or pocket handbooks) that are designed to aid the identification of wild flowers, butterflies, trees, birds, seashells, and so on. So, *cher lecteur*, here is your first assignment:

Task One

Complete the following table:

Faced with an entry in a typical field-guide written in one of the following languages, I would anticipate that I would . . .

	English	French	Italian	Swedish
understand everything				
understand most of it				
puzzle out some of it				
be able to get a few words				
understand almost nothing				

In fact, the material used for this demonstration consists of entries from field-guides designed to help observers identify birds. Here is a typical entry for a common bird from a North American guide, except that I have 'exploded' the text to facilitate analysis:

A CANADA GOOSE *Branta canadensis* 25–43" (63–108cm)

B The most widespread goose in N. America.

C Note the black head and neck or 'stocking' that contrasts sharply with the pale breast and the *white patch or chinstrap* that runs onto the side of the head.

D Flocks travel in long strings in V formation, announcing their approach by musical honking or barking.

E **Voice:** A deep musical honking or barking *ka-ronk* or *ka-lunk*.

F **Range:** Alaska, Canada, n. U.S. Winters to Mexico. **East:** Map 21.

G **Habitat:** Lakes, ponds, bays, marshes, fields

(Peterson, page 44)

In the above entry, then, the information is given in the following order:

A Common name + Latin name + size

B   Abundance (common, local, rare, etc.)

C   Identification features

D   Typical behavior

E   Voice

F   Range (summer and winter)

G   Habitat (where typically found)

Other common elements that a field-guide entry might contain include:

H   Distinguishing the species from a similar one

I   Food

J   Nest, eggs, young, etc.

Task Two

Now here is the entry from a French-language edition of a North American field-guide for a famous but rare species, the Golden Eagle. Using the key above (A–J), place the appropriate letter at the beginning of each element.

- **Aigle royal** *Aquila chrysaëtos* L: 76–102cm; E: 203–224cm
- Brun; cou et nuque variablement teintés de doré; bec foncé; queue discrètement barrée. L'imm. en vol, vu de dessous: zone blanche et nette à la base des primaires, queue blanche à bande terminale sombre.
- Plane souvent les ailes un peu relevées.
- Le Pygargue à tête blanche de première année a le dessous de l'aile plus barbouillé, la tête plus grosse et la queue plus courte.
- Habite les terrains montagneux ou montueux . . .
- . . . et chasse petits mammifères, serpents et oiseaux en terrain découvert; il est aussi charognard.
- Niche dans un escarpement ou un arbre.
- Peu commun à rare dans l'Est; assez commun dans l'Ouest.

(National Geographic Society, page 184)

Task Three

Answer the following questions:

1 How is the order of elements different between the two entries you have seen so far?

2 Which elements (if any) in the Aigle royal entry might be moved; and to where?

3 Can you translate the last four elements in English, guessing (wherever necessary) as you go?

Task Four

Now here are two more entries for the Golden Eagle: the first from a British guide, the second from an Italian one. This time, however, the texts have not been broken down into elements. If you read the two entries *together*, you should be able to answer the questions which follow:

GOLDEN EAGLE *Aquila chrysaëtos* 80 cm, but variable. Widespread but rare resident (order 3). Large, glides with wings in shallow 'V'; young and immatures have white at base of tail. VOICE fairly quiet, but can produce loud nasal yelps and screams. HAB mountains, open plains. NEST on cliff or in large tree; may be large as used over many years; twigs. EGGS 2, whitish, usually blotched with brown. FOOD wide range of birds and mammals, carrion. (Perrins and Attenborough, page 92, slightly abridged)

AQUILA REALE *(Aquila chrysaëtos)* 75–88
Localmente stazionaria e nidificante, immaturi parzialmente erratici. Abita le regioni montuose. Ha sagome poderosa ma slanciata con la coda ampia e arrotondata ed il capo prominente. Rotea ad alta quota tenendo le ali alte sul dorso a 'V' (unica fra le Aquile), poi plana con le ali semichiuse e poche potenti battute. Il bianco degli immaturi scompare progressivamente con l'età al 4–5 anno, mentre negli esemplari molto vecchi le copritrici diventano pallide e fulve. VOCE: un alto e miagolante 'kee-ooo' e un rapido, abbaiante 'ka ka ka'. SPECIE SIMILI: (adulto) le altre Aquile, 83 e 105. (Chelini and Petretti, page 120)

1 What is the range in size of the Golden Eagle (in centimeters)?
2 When does it glide with its wings in a 'V'?
3 Why is this a good identification feature?
4 At what age do young birds lose their white?

Task Five

The final entry is from a Swedish field-guide entitled *Fåglar: En Fälthändbok*. (Sverige = Sweden)

KUNGSÖRN *Aquila chrysaëtos*

Fältkännetecken: 76–90 cm. Mörkbrun rovfågel med kraftig näbb, breda vingar och helt fjäderklädda tarser. Hjässa och nacke guldgula, hos ungfågeln är stjärten vit med svartbrun spets. Flykt tung, handpennor spretande rakt ut. Stjärt bred, tvärskuren.

Biotop: skogsmark i bergig terräng, gärna intill sjöar och myrar, och klippiga kuster. Ungfåglarna vintertid i odlingsbygder.

Föda: renkadaver, hare, ripa, lämlar, smågnagare, någon gång lamm. Jagar på låg höjd över marken och överraskar bytet. Spanar stundom från sten eller trädtopp.

Häckning: bo på klipphylla eller i grovtall av grenar och kvistar, fodrat med gräs och mossa. Ägg 1–3, ruvas i 6 veckor. Ungarna i boet 12 veckor.

De äldre *stannfåglar*, de yngre *flyttfåglar* till södra Sverige.
(Gidstam and Wahlin, page 73, slightly abridged)

1 Using the letter codes, what do you think the following refer to?
   Fältkännetecken
   Biotop
   Föda
   Häckning
2 How would you translate the title of the Swedish book?
3 The first phrase in the entry is 'mörkbrun rovfågel med kraftig näbb'. What do you think this might mean?
4 You should be able to translate the last sentence in the Swedish text (yes, a whole sentence!). In fact, the first line of the Italian entry is quite helpful here. Well?

Task Six

Using the information in the texts, where do you think the Golden Eagle is most and least common? Re-arrange in increasing order of rarity: Britain, eastern North America, Italy, Sweden, western North America.

Epilogue

I have so far given versions of this workshop-type demonstration about half a dozen times, both to student groups and to ESP practitioners (including those attending seminars in Brazil and Tunisia). I have yet to find groups (typically working in pairs) who cannot, on the whole, make much good sense out of these specialized and authentic texts often written in languages they profess to hardly know. It has, in fact, been the case that most of the participants to date have knowledge of at least one Germanic and one Romance language and so can avail themselves of cognates. Notwithstanding, many find themselves amazed at being able to translate the last line of the Swedish text: 'the elder are stay-birds, the younger are flight-birds to southern Sweden' (i.e. 'adults are resident; immatures are migrants to southern Sweden'). When I ask them, at the close of play, to re-evaluate their reading comprehension of field-guide entries by reviewing how they assessed themselves on the opening chart, two things typically happen. First, they upgrade their capacity to cope with languages they hardly know; secondly, they tend to downgrade their reading comprehension in the language they know best (usually English). These responses, I suspect, are symptomatic of all our encounters with genres that we are getting to know.

At this point it might be objected that these mini-texts from field-guides are mundane and idiosyncratic creations of little real use to language learners. The first part of my answer to such complaints relies on Widdowson's argument about engaging 'students in activities which are not directly *derived* from disciplines, but *contrived* from them in reference to their basic principles of design and more general generic features' (1993c: 35). Obviously, my little demonstration is neither directly derived from nor designed for an ornithology class. So far, so good. But are there any basic principles of design that underpin a wider academic, or indeed any academic, context? Despite appearances to the contrary, I think there are. We can start with a paper by a pair of sociologists, John Law and Michael Lynch, which turns out to have the surprisingly pertinent title 'Lists, field guides, and the descriptive organization of seeing: Bird-watching as an exemplary observational activity' (1990). Law and Lynch start with the observation that bird-watching is a particular kind of seeing, from which novices are largely excluded through 'aspect blindness' (Wittgenstein 1968: 213–214). They go on to argue that field observations are, in essence, a 'literary language game' that is strongly shaped and structured by entries and illustrations in field-guides. They also observe that 'the activity of bird-watching is also an exemplar for studying the place of an instructional text in the order of practice' (Law and Lynch 1990: 293) as this is carried out on a routine basis. For Law and Lynch there is, additionally, methodological value in using such 'homely' examples as field-guides since they are comparable to but more accessible than the arcane observations and cryptic documentations of professional scientists and scholars. While I might not want to go so far, the genre of the species entry, in its shaping and prioritizing of the reader's perceptions, performs functions very similar to those of other texts that encourage the reader to 'read' (say) a mediaeval cathedral, a Parisian street, a fossil specimen, an African mask, or a Tuscan landscape in ways that have been normed by the professional discourse communities. Classifying, coding, and perceiving are always educationally and historically constructed, whether we are on a nature walk, in a museum, or strolling down a famous street. The 'mundane' species-entry thus turns out to be a useful piece of a larger and more truly academic picture.

But, to use a common Widdowson metaphor, we are not quite out of the woods yet. There remains the issue of different languages, in their differently evolved disciplinary and generic traditions, carrying different cultural loads and values. Alas, we seem to see little of this in the field-guides (except perhaps for the attention given in the European guides—for better or worse—to nests and eggs). One likely reason is the near-universal preservation of a Linnean mode of species description. As it happens, we *would* find those desired differences if it had been possible to compare the work of the field-guide bird illustrators; particularly if we had compared the two most famous exponents of this genre in recent times: the American, Roger Tory Peterson, and the Swede, Lars Jonsson. For Peterson, the illustration is a schematic diagram with all 'unnecessary clutter' ruthlessly stripped away; for Jonsson, the aim is to capture the poise, attitude, and personality typical of the species. Thus, we see two cultural traditions here: one of mapping, the other of 'inscape'. More centrally, however, we need to remember that the demonstration is designed in such a way that one or more languages will likely be unknown to participants. It is hardly reasonable to expect such debutants (even Widdowson) to be capable of tracing subtle differences in cross-cultural academic styles, even if I had been able to assemble a set of short texts that illustrated them. At this level, the Contrastive Rhetoric aspect could only be handled in translated texts—itself a clear denial of FLAC principles.

The apparent success of the short demonstration can, I think, be assigned to three factors. Let me mention two immediately and turn to the third in my conclusion. One of the 'relevant conditions of language use and learning' is the interplay of text and task, whereby difficulty in the former is balanced by simplicity in the latter (and vice versa). A second is the attention given to form, broadly understood as comprising rhetorical structure and its linguistic realization, in order to make this form/structure both visible to the learner/user and to make it understandable as an evolved response to a recurring context of situation. Widdowson puts this better than I can:

> . . . to instruct people in a discipline, or subject, or profession is to make them aware of its typical genres, to present them in such a way that they are *noticed*. And now to put in the last piece to complete the pattern of argument: since the rhetorical features of genres are realized by linguistic means, then the language will be noticed as well, and so the necessary condition for learning will be met accordingly (1993c: 34).

To those who might argue that this attention to form is over-done and largely unnecessary, I would offer the following well-known anecdote about Mozart. One day a man came up to Mozart on the street and asked 'Can you tell me, Herr Mozart, how to write a symphony?' 'Sure,' replied Mozart, 'this is what you do: first you write a piece for solo piano, then a duet, then a quartet, next a piece for a wind ensemble, then a concerto, and finally a symphony.' As the man on the Vienna street was writing all this down, he observed, 'But, Herr Mozart, that is not what you did.' 'Ah, well, you see,' the genius responded, 'the big difference between us is that I didn't have to ask the question.' Now, doubtless, there are some language learners who are like Mozart: natural auto-didacts who can learn to read a foreign literature with nothing more than a grammar and a dictionary. But most of us are more like Mozart's questioner, people who need a staged process, a structure with a visible scaffolding, the provision of feedback, and the regularized and institutional arrangement of having a teacher to keep our attention selectively focused on form in all its multi-layered manifestations.

The third and final factor for success I take to be the restriction to a single genre. It is this which allows exposure to texts in different languages to be a coherent rather than disruptive set of activities, since now the better-known languages can come to the direct assistance of the lesser-known ones as the participants explore themes and variations, and models and instances, in a mutually supportive enterprise. Indeed, I would argue that, as we strive to 'bias for success' (Dvorak, personal communication) in our attempts to foster additional foreign language literacies, we would do well to concentrate on limited sets of genres. And here, at the very end, I at last part company with Widdowson's 1993c paper, since therein he writes 'one might hazard the generality that the more specific you can be about genres, the more enabling it is for teaching the subject, the less enabling for teaching the language' (1993c: 35). While this proposition may be yet another example of Widdowson's capacity for crisp logical argument, I am less sure that it is very sound psychology. After all, engendered genre-specific achievements (in all or any of the skill areas) run consistently ahead of general proficiency levels and so provide motivating landmarks of success. As this piece has, indeed, tried to demonstrate.

Notes

The extracts from field-guides are taken from:

A Field Guide to the Birds East of the Rockies by R. T. Peterson (1980, Houghton Mifflin, Boston);

Guide d'identification des oiseaux de l'Amérique du Nord by the National Geographic Society (1987, Éditions Marcel Broquet, La Prairie, Québec);

New Generation Guide to the Birds of Britain and Europe by C. Perrins and D. Attenborough (1980, Collins, London);

Manuale per il Riconoscimento degli Uccelli Italiani by A. Chelini and F. Petretti (1984, Editoriale Olimpia, Florence);

Fåglar: En Fälthändbok by B. Gidstam and B. Wahlin (1990, Page A. Norstedt, Stockholm).

Acknowledgements

I am grateful to Sunny Hyon for valuable comments on an earlier draft of this paper.

15

Explorations in applied linguistics 3: forensic stylistics

MALCOLM COULTHARD

This [article] might be described as an exercise in applied stylistic analysis. (WIDDOWSON 1975:1)

Introduction

IT WAS WITH some trepidation that I began writing this my contribution to *Principle and Practice in Applied Linguistics*. A *festschrift* is a natural present to give to most colleagues, but to offer one to the master of communication is a risky undertaking. I briefly contemplated attempting an article in Widdowsonian style, but soon desisted—Henry has written not only well but extensively and thus it should be possible to begin to isolate the basic features of his style; but the wit, the authority, and the breadth of knowledge and reference could not be simulated. So, instead, I decided to write about the burgeoning area of forensic stylistics in order to give Henry an idea of how he might set about exposing anyone who does have the temerity to attribute a text to him.

The linguistic investigation of authorship

Several years ago the novelist Margaret Drabble, concerned that her books might be being published simply because they carried her name, sent a manuscript to her publisher under a pseudonym. It was rejected. Other rejections followed in quick succession, until one publisher sent the manuscript to a reader in New York who read it overnight and phoned next morning to ask, 'Who are you trying to deceive? Surely, this is by Margaret Drabble'. The concealing and discovery of authorship has a long and fascinating history (see Davis, forthcoming), but one which until recently has been the province rather of the biblical and the literary scholar than of the linguist.

The linguistic concept of *idiolect*, the claim that all speakers have their own individual version of the language(s) they speak and write, allows for the possibility that linguists might be able to devise a method of *linguistic fingerprinting*—in other words that the linguistic 'impressions' created by any given speaker/writer could be used to identify them. So far, however, practice is a long way behind theory and no one has begun even to speculate about how much and what kind of data would be needed to characterize a single *idiolect*, nor how the data once collected would be analysed and stored—indeed work on the very much simpler task of identifying the linguistic characteristics or 'fingerprints' of *genres* is still in its early stages (Biber 1988).

In fact, the concept of the linguistic fingerprint is an unhelpful if not misleading metaphor, at least when used in the context of investigations of authorship, because it leads us to imagine the creation of massive databanks consisting of representative linguistic samples (or summary analyses) of very large numbers of idiolects, against which a given text can be matched and tested. In reality such an enterprise is and will always be impractical, if not impossible. The value of the fingerprint is that each sample is both identical and complete, that is, it contains all the necessary and unique information, whereas, by contrast, any text sample provides only very partial information about its creator's idiolect; a situation compounded by the fact that many of the texts the forensic linguist is asked to examine are very short indeed—most suicide notes and many threatening letters for example are under two hundred words long.

However, the situation is not as bad as first appears because the forensic requirements of textual evidence are much less rigorous: forensic texts are usually accompanied by information or clues which massively restrict the number of possible composers. Thus the task of the linguistic detective is never to identify an author from millions of candidates on the basis of the linguistic fingerprint alone, but rather to identify (or of course discount if working for the defence) one author from a very small number of candidates, usually fewer than a dozen and in many cases only two. To continue the analogy with fingerprinting, in forensic stylistics one is in fact focusing on only one small part of one line, i.e. a fraction of the total set of features of the idiolect and, for this reason, in some cases no distinguishing features may be found.

Forensic stylistics, just like literary stylistics in its early days, is currently still developing its methodology, almost case by case or text by text. Only when it is clear on which linguistic features it is useful to focus will it be possible to create a battery of tests and begin to automate the analysis.

In what follows I will exemplify some of the current analytic approaches (others are reported in Coulthard 1992, 1993, 1994a, 1994b). All of the extracts and examples are authentic, although sometimes the names of people and places have been changed to preserve anonymity when there is a possibility of an appeal.

Mistakes and errors

It is a basic tenet of linguistics that not only is language rule-governed, but that so also is its production in written or spoken form, although, of course, any spoken or written text may display items which break the rules of the standard language. We can divide such rule-breaking into two categories: 'performance' *mistakes*, where speakers/writers know that they have broken a rule, which, of course, doesn't prevent them from breaking it again, (and again, as learners of foreign languages know to their chagrin); and 'competence' *errors*, where speakers/writers are working with a non-standard set of rules, but rules which they nevertheless follow consistently, even though they may still make performance mistakes which break their own rules. In the short texts which are typically the focus of the forensic linguist it is usually only possible to focus on the grammatical and orthographical rule-breaking, because in order to examine characteristic vocabulary choices one needs a great deal of textual data.

The most difficult author-identification cases for the forensic linguist to handle are those involving anonymous letters, as there is usually a fairly large number of potential authors and only a small amount of written text to analyse, often a single letter. For this reason, success is in the main limited to those cases which involve semi-literate authors, who necessarily provide a comparatively large number of idiolectal mistakes and errors in a comparatively small amount of text. (Obviously all intending anonymous letter writers should learn to wordprocess, to use a spell-checking system, and to exploit the style-improver options available in the latest programs in order to homogenize and thereby disguise their idiolect!)

Below I reproduce a few short extracts from a typed anonymous letter, which the addressee-company suspected was written by one of its own employees. The words containing non-standard features are in italic type (there are many more instances of these particular phenomena in the rest of the letter).

> . . . I hope you appreciate that *i* am *enable* to give my true *idenitity* as this *wolud* ultimately jeopardize my position . . .

> . . . *l* would like to *high light* my greatest concern . . .

> . . . have so far *deened* it unnecessary to *investegate* these *issus* . . .

There are several interesting non-standard features immediately evident, although one of the problems of dealing with a typewritten text is that error and mistake may be confused and compounded—one may not know, for a given 'misspelling', particularly if it only occurs once, whether the 'wrong' form is the product of a mis-typing or a non-standard rule. If, for instance, the text includes the word 'color', is this a typing mistake or a (British English) spelling error?

In examining the non-standard items above we note: firstly, the writer is an inexperienced typist; the first-person pronoun 'I' appears not only as 'I' but also as 'i', and the very unusual 'l'. Secondly, some of the words have metathesized (reversed) letters and others incorrect, additional, or omitted letters. Thirdly, the writer has serious problems when spelling words containing the reduced (unstressed) vowel—thus we have the following spellings: *enable* ('unable'), *investegate* ('investigate'), and elsewhere *except* ('accept'). Fourthly, the writer is unsure about when to write certain sequences of morphemes as a single word and when as two separate words—thus *high light* and elsewhere *with out*. In addition, but not exemplified here, there are homonym problems, *weather* appears for 'whether' and *there* for 'their'. Finally, the writer has some grammatical problems: the frequent omission of markers of past tense and third-person singular present tense, and even of articles—*have now [a] firm intention*. Collectively, these mistakes and errors are idiosyncratic and distinctive and proved to be instanced in the authenticated letters of only one of the eight employees who, according to the company, were the only ones who had access to the information contained in the threatening letter. This employee was in fact the suspect the company had identified on other grounds.

Contextual variation

The basic facts of the next case are as follows. An armed robbery took place at an estate agent's which doubled as a sub-branch of the Halifax Building Society. A man with a record of previous, less serious, offences was arrested and accused of the robbery. When questioned he denied any involvement, though he admitted having been in the vicinity at the time. He claimed he had left the immediate area some ten to fifteen minutes before the robbery and had gone to a 'bookies' not very far away where he had spent the rest of the afternoon.

The police did not believe his story and therefore asked him to go with them in a police car and show them his previous day's itinerary. He sat in the back of the car handcuffed to a police constable and gave instructions to the driver. In the front passenger seat sat an officer with a single sheet of lined paper, secured to a clipboard, on which he noted where they went and what was said during the journey. On returning to the police station the suspect was invited to read what the officer had written and then to sign it as a true and accurate record, which he duly did after making one small correction, namely, the addition of 'or Iti' to line 28 on the first side of the paper.

At trial the accused claimed and the police strenuously denied that the record which was presented to the Court had been substantially altered; indeed that roughly half of the text had been added *after* he had signed it, and that all the incriminating parts were later additions. However, despite all his protestations the jury convicted him and he was sentenced to fifteen years' imprisonment. At the time of writing he is beginning his eighth year in custody.

Below is a transcript made from the original handwritten record of the journey as it was presented in Court by the police—only the line numbers have been added for ease of reference:

1.1   5 pm O/S P. Station
1.2   I/think/ came past here yesterday I then
1.3   turned left. Up there (towards Suttonway).
1.4   but I'll know for sure after
1.5   5 06 pm At Mercury towards Stanlow (not
1.6   Little Sutton) as I first said
1.7   this morning
1.8   Left on A5302, Chester Rd, Whitby
1.9   and went towards town centre
1.10 Through T/L (Overpool Rd)
1.11 and carried straight on
1.12 Stopped near Offleys—looked at
1.13 some of the cars down left side and some of the
1.14 cars down right hand side. I got back
1.15 into car then.
1.16 (Pointed out Patsy Ang.) that's where
1.17 I get my dinner.
1.18 Pointed out Halifax. I might have
1.19 looked in the window there.
1.20 Stopped on Sportsman car parking and
1.21 that's where I walked back.
1.22 Went to Manny Cooks—no bet—
1.23 I know Manny very well but I
1.24 didn't speak to any staff. Manny
1.25 wasn't in.
1.26 Chippy further up—a bloke.—
1.27 might have seen me in there he was a
1.28 Chineese maybe—half caste bloke or Iti
1.29 I can't say.
1.30 Back to car.—started driving off
1.31 that's when the woman saw me I suppose
1.32 Left back to P.S. left into
1.33 Sutton way.
1.34 Turn Flatt lane—U—turn.

2.1   Back to lights turn right and back
2.2   past the Estate agent.
2.3   Back to Strawberry Roundabout,

2.4   no deviation
2.5   Turn right towards Mercury
2.6   or the Ladbroke's I know it as.
2.7   Turn right towards Little Sutton (A41)
2.8   I was looking at houses there.
2.9   Turn left at Lights Ledsham Rd.,
2.10 where I was going to park and hide but
2.11 PC in car on public car pk. (—op H Jones)
2.12 saw me and I thought he was going to follow.
2.13 Turn at Black Lion Lane and I saw
2.14 PC was making some notes up
2.15 Back to lights but turned around /left/
2.16 went down the road a bit and came back
2.17 to Travellers Rest car park where I
2.18 parked the car up
2.19 Into Henry Jones Betting Office where I
2.20 spent some of the money. I won £200 and
2.21 stayed to 5 pm or after 5 pm.

I re-present the text below with all the items which the accused contests moved to the right-hand side of the page. It will be noted that there remains on the left-hand side of the page roughly half of the text and also, surprisingly, that this half is apparently fully coherent.

Claimed original text	Claimed later additions
1.1 5 pm O/S P. Station	
1.2	I/think/ came past here yesterday I then
1.3	turned left. Up there (towards Suttonway).
1.4	but I'll know for sure after
1.5 5 06 pm At Mercury towards Stanlow (not	
1.6 Little Sutton)	as I first said
1.7	this morning
1.8 Left on A5302, Chester Rd, Whitby	
1.9	and went towards town centre
1.10 Through T/L (Overpool Rd)	
1.11	and carried straight on
1.12 Stopped near Offleys	—looked at
1.13	some of the cars down left side and some of the
1.14 cars down right hand side.	I got back
1.15	into car then.
1.16 (Pointed out Patsy Ang.)	that's where

1.17		I get my dinner.
1.18	Pointed out Halifax.	I might have
1.19		looked in the window there.
1.20	Stopped on Sportsman car parking	and
1.21		that's where I walked back.
1.22	Went to Manny Cooks—no bet—	
1.23		I know Manny very well but I
1.24	didn't speak to any staff.	Manny
1.25		wasn't in.
1.26	Chippy further up—a bloke.—	
1.27		might have seen me in there he was a
1.28	Chineese maybe—half caste bloke or Iti	
1.29		I can't say.
1.30	Back to car.	—started driving off
1.31		that's when the woman saw me I suppose
1.32	Left back to P.S.	left into
1.33		Sutton way.
1.34	Turn Flatt lane—U—turn.	
2.1	Back to lights	turn right and back
2.2		past the Estate agent.
2.3	Back to Strawberry Roundabout,	
2.4		no deviation
2.5	Turn right towards Mercury	
2.6		or the Ladbroke's I know it as.
2.7	Turn right towards Little Sutton (A41)	
2.8		I was looking at houses there.
2.9	Turn left at Lights Ledsham Rd.,	
2.10		where I was going to park and hide but
2.11	PC in car on public car pk. (—op H Jones)	
2.12		saw me and I thought he was going to follow
2.13	Turn at Black Lion Lane	and I saw
2.14		PC was making some notes up
2.15	Back to lights	but turned around /left/
2.16		went down the road a bit and came back
2.17	to Travellers Rest car park	where I
2.18		parked the car up
2.19	Into Henry Jones Betting Office	where I
2.20		spent some of the money. I won £200 and
2.21	stayed to 5 pm or after 5 pm.	

What is even more surprising is that the text becomes more consistent linguistically. From the left-hand and claimed authentic text we can derive a 'note-taking grammar' which has the following features:

1 verbs without subjects, e.g.
   1.18 'Pointed out Halifax', 2.5 'Turn right towards Mercury'

2 an absence of definite and indefinite articles, e.g.
   1.10 'Through T/L', 1.32 'Left back to P.S.'

3 verbless clauses, e.g.
   1.8 'Left on A5302', 2.1 'Back to lights'

4 verb forms restricted to the present imperative or simple past, e.g.
   2.5 'turn right', 2.7 'turn right', 2.9 'turn left',
   2.13 'turn at', 1.12 'stopped', 1.18 'pointed',
   1.22 'went', 2.21 'stayed'

By contrast, for the entries in the right-hand column, which comprise the claimed additions, we note:

1 a large number of the verbs have explicit subjects, e.g.
   1.14–15 'I got back into car', 1.17 'I get my dinner',
   1.31 'the woman saw me', 1.21 'I walked back',
   2.14 'PC was making some notes up', 2.20 'I won £200'

2 use of definite articles, e.g.
   1.13 'some of the cars', 1.19 'looked in the window',
   1.31 'the woman saw me', 2.2 'the Estate agent',
   2.16 'down the road', 2.20 'some of the money'

3 the majority of the clauses have verbs, e.g.
   1.9 'went towards town centre', 1.11 'carried straight on',
   2.12 'I thought he was going', 2.10 'I was going to park'

4 auxiliary verbs are used to make continuous and future tenses, e.g.
   1.4 'I'll know', 2.8 I was looking', 2.10 'I was going to',
   2.12 'he was going to', 2.14 'PC was making'

5 there are subordinate time and place clauses, e.g.
   1.16–17 'where I get my dinner', 1.21 'where I walked back',
   1.31 'when the woman saw me', 2.10 'where I was going to park',
   2.19–20 'where I spent some of the money'

6 modal and other verbs are used to express uncertainty, e.g.
   1.18–19 'I might have looked', 1.27 'might have seen me',
   1.2 'I think', 1.29 'I can't say', 1.31 'I suppose'

Thus we have two markedly different styles arguably appropriate to and claimed to have been created in two different contexts. If we accept the accused's claim that the right-hand column was created by later insertion, we would expect to find evidence of three compositional problems. Firstly, at times it would be difficult to insert something which was both coherent and also advanced the narrative. In this respect it is important to look at the sequences 1.10–1.12 and 2.3–2.5 where the intervening lines seem to add very little:

1.10   Through T/L (Overpool Rd)
1.11   **and carried straight on**
1.12   Stopped near Offleys + **looked at**

2.3   Back to Strawberry Roundabout
2.4   **no deviation**
2.5   Turn right towards Mercury

Secondly, as it is always easier to link backwards than to link forwards and/or to introduce completely new material, one would expect a tendency for the majority of insertions to be backward links. Indeed we notice that whereas almost all the lines which are claimed to be authentic begin with a capital letter and are new topic beginnings, almost all the lines which are claimed by the accused to be insertions begin with lower-case letters and are specifically linked back to a claimed authentic item by **and, where** or **there**.

1.8   Left on A5302, Chester Rd. Whitby
1.9   **and** went towards town centre
1.10   Through T/L (Overpool Rd)
1.11   **and** carried straight on

1.16   (Pointed out Patsy Ang.) **that's where**
1.17   I get my dinner
1.18   Pointed out Halifax, I might have
1.19   looked in the window **there**

Thirdly, there would at times be concord mistakes where the grammar of the inserted text fails to fit with the original. I will use the following extract from page 2 to illustrate:

2.5   *Turn* right towards Mercury
2.6   **or the Ladbroke's I know it as.**
2.7   *Turn* right towards Little Sutton (A41)

[238]

2.8 I was looking at houses **there.**

2.9 *Turn* left at Lights Ledsham Rd.,

2.10 **where** *I was going* to park and hide but

2.11 PC in car on public car pk. (—op H Jones)

2.12 *saw* me and I *thought* he *was going* to follow.

2.13 *Turn* at Black Lion Lane **and** I *saw*

2.14 PC *was making* some notes up

In 2.6 and 2.8 we can see 'successful' links back to 2.5 and 2.7 respectively. In each there is an instruction to the driver of the police car to 'turn', followed by a (claimed) comment on the place mentioned in the instruction. However, there are problems with 2.9–2.10 and 2.13–2.14. In both these cases the second clauses are *grammatically* linked backwards, the first by 'where' and the second by 'and', but this linking turns the sequence 2.9 to 2.14 into a past tense narrative and therefore would require *past tense* verbs in the clauses in 2.9 and 2.13 as well, i.e. 'turned' instead of 'turn'. The most incongruous sequence is 2.13 'Turn . . . and I saw'.

Taking into account all the points made above, it is difficult to dispute that the document was written on two separate occasions. It is of course still possible that the interlineations were made after the journey was completed but before the accused was asked to read and sign the document. However, the fact that this procedure was never acknowledged, let alone explained by the officers involved, leads one to believe that the interlineations were made, as the accused claimed, after he had signed the document.

Falsified text

There are many occasions when someone claims that a text is in part or entirely falsified—that is, that the real author is different from the purported author. In this context the fabricator, whatever he or she is creating, be it an interview record, a confession statement, or a suicide note, is acting as an amateur dramatist or novelist and imagining what the purported speaker/author would have produced in the same circumstances. As with any fabrication, be it bank notes or texts, the quality of the finished product will depend on the degree of (mis)understanding that the falsifier has of the nature of what he or she is falsifying and thus the specialist can usually discover mistakes in the finished product. Depending on the nature of the text being fabricated, different linguistic approaches are suitable.

Register variation

One of the component features of an idiolect is obviously the set of registers of which the speaker has command. Sometimes one can demonstrate that a given individual could not have been the (sole) author of a text because it contains features of a register to which he or she does not have access. This was the approach I took when analysing a statement from the case in the 1950s in which the teenagers Craig and Bentley were convicted of killing a policeman. The statement attributed to Bentley by the police was claimed by him to be in fact a joint production, with considerable input by the police. I compared it with a) statements made by other lay witnesses; b) statements made by police officers; and c) a mixed corpus of 1.5 million words of spoken English, and it was indeed possible to discover traces of police register in the text. The evidence was both lexical and grammatical, but the most compelling was the very frequent occurrence of time and place adjuncts (see Svartvik 1968) and, in particular, non-clause initial 'then' in structures like 'I then', 'the policeman then', 'Chris then' which were non-existent in the lay witness statements, extremely rare in the spoken corpus, but very frequent in the police and Bentley statements (for further details see Coulthard 1992).

Genre variation

There are many linguistic differences between spoken and written texts and thus sometimes it is possible to dispute authorship because a text which is supposedly a verbatim record of what was said is in fact in written style. In a recent case in Northern Ireland an accused claimed, like Bentley in the example above, that a statement attributed to him was in fact only partly an authentic record of what he had said; the rest he alleged had been invented and simply written down by the interviewing officers. The first sentence reads:

> I wish to make a further statement explaining my complete involvement in the hijacking of the Ford Escort van from John Smith on

Tuesday 28 March 1981 on behalf of the A.B.C. which was later used in the murder of three person (*sic*) in Avon that night.

In arguing that, whatever else it was, this sentence (and of course several others which occurred later) was not a verbatim record of something that had been said, I drew on Halliday's analysis of the differences between spoken and written English, which he suggests can be characterized in part in terms of differences in *lexical density*—the proportion of lexical items per clause:

> On the basis of various samples, I have found that a typical average lexical density for spoken English is between 1.5 and 2, whereas the figure for written English settles down somewhere between 3 and 6 [lexical items per clause], depending on the formality of the writing. (Halliday 1989: 80)

Thus the lexical density of the sentence below, which is taken from the same statement and is one which the accused accepted had been transcribed as spoken, does conform to Halliday's 'typical average':

> I drove down to the flats & I saw him up on the roof & I shouted to him & he said that he would be down in a couple of minutes.

It has eight lexical items spread over five clauses, giving a lexical density of 1.6. By contrast, the disputed initial sentence has some twenty-five lexical items (depending how one counts '28 March 1981', which I chose to regard as three but could have counted as six), spread over three clauses, giving a lexical density of 8.3.

In addition, many of the disputed sentences of the statement display other features which corpora show to be more typical of written text, marked themes, cleft sentences, and a substantial amount of what Halliday (1989) calls *grammatical metaphorization*; that is, the representation of *processes*, which are typically reported by verbs in spoken English as *products*, which are encoded as nominal(ization)s. As we can see, the first sentence contains four such grammatical metaphors: 'make a *statement*', 'complete *involvement*', 'the *hijacking*', 'the *murder*'. Thus it was possible to argue that this was not as the police claimed a verbatim record of what the accused had said. On cross-examination the police officer/scribe conceded that the statement may not after all have been verbatim, but continued to maintain that all the words were indeed spoken by the accused, though 'perhaps not in that order'!

Automated analysis

Although no two cases are ever the same it would be useful to have a battery of computer-assisted measures which could provide the forensic linguist with an initial profile of the style of both the questioned text(s) and of the candidate authors. Results so far suggest that the following measures are useful ones to begin with.

1 *Lexical density*
   As we saw above in the Northern Ireland terrorist case, lexical density can be used to distinguish genres; we now need to see to what extent it can also reliably distinguish individual authors.

2 *Lexical novelty*
   One of the interesting discoveries of computational linguistics is that in any text or corpus of whatever length—150, 150 thousand, or even 150 million words—roughly half of the word-types occur only once. However, there are sometimes interesting individual deviations from this norm: on the one hand, Winter (personal communication) has shown that a highly articulate speaker/writer may use a disproportionately and therefore distinctively large percentage of once-only words, while on the other hand the unauthentic Northern Ireland statement analysed above, whose main function is to convict by frequent reference to and repetition of the main aspects of the crime, displays an unusually low proportion of lexical novelty.

3 *Word frequency*
   Word frequency lists give the forensic linguist the means to discover author- and/or register-specific use and frequency of vocabulary items. In the Bentley case discussed above, the marked use of 'then', originally noticed almost by chance and calculated manually, would have been immediately and strikingly obvious had a word frequency list been prepared by computer. Other texts display idiosyncratic choices of clause subordinators, while research by Collins (1994) suggests that the use and choice of modals and modalisers can also be distinctive.

[242]

4 Collocation

A concordancing program like Scott and Johns (1993) allows the investigator to examine not simply frequencies of occurrence of individual words like 'then', but also frequent and/or idiosyncratic collocations and colligations. Thus in the Bentley case the occurrences of 'then I' were much more significant than the frequency of 'then' alone, while in a suicide/murder case currently going to appeal it is the frequent co-occurrence of 'cause' and 'pain' with 'heartache' and 'suffering' which is significant.

5 Stylistic structures

Occasionally an examination of frequent words or collocations throws up distinctive stylistic structures. Thus in the same suicide case a list of the stylistic preferences of one of the candidate authors includes the frequent use of the paired-item structure 'X and Y': 'hurt and suffering', 'hurt and pain', 'hurt and greaf' (*sic*), 'pain and heartache', 'lied and cheated', 'physically and emotionally'.

Concluding remarks

Any branch of applied linguistics depends essentially upon but also raises interesting questions for descriptive linguistics. The future of forensic stylistics is inextricably linked to the development by descriptive linguists of more sophisticated means of identifying and isolating regularities in texts. Even so, forensic stylistics, like its older brother literary stylistics, is likely to remain for the foreseeable future more of an art than a science.

16

Corpus evidence for norms of lexical collocation

MICHAEL STUBBS

HENRY WIDDOWSON IS well known for his influential work in language teaching and stylistics. In this paper, I will discuss a method of linguistic analysis which has considerable implications for both these areas. More specifically, Widdowson (for example, 1976) is known for his careful analysis of the concepts of language use and of authenticity in language teaching materials. I will use authentic data to present findings about language use.

Collocations and semantic prosodies

I will discuss some lexical collocations which are frequent or typical in English. (More below on these terms.) The only way to investigate norms of use is to study corpora of naturally occurring data. I will therefore demonstrate a corpus-based method of establishing norms of lexical collocation.

There are various areas of applied linguistics where information about such norms is essential. For example, language teachers are interested in what learners are likely to encounter or likely to need; and collocations are a notoriously difficult area for language learners. And stylisticians are interested in how a particular text under study might follow or depart from patterns of expectation in the language as a whole. All the descriptive statements below concern expectations and probabilities.

The analysis requires a few technical terms. By *collocation* I mean the habitual co-occurrence of words. I will talk of a *node* word and its *collocates* within a given *span*, for example, four words to both left and right. Collocation, in this use, is a purely lexical relation between words in linear sequence, irrespective of any intervening syntactic boundaries. The node might be an individual *word form*, such as *cause*, *causes*, *caused*, or *causing*; or it might be a lemma (= lexeme or dictionary head word), for example, CAUSE.

The other term I will use is *semantic prosody*. This is a term used by Louw (1993) to refer to a type of linguistic relation which has not previously been clearly documented. *Prosody* has its Firthian sense of a phenomenon which extends over more than one linguistic unit, in this case over a span of words. For example, Sinclair (1991a) points out that the phrasal verb SET IN commonly collocates with unpleasant states of affairs: what typically sets in is *bad weather, decay, despair, rot*, and *rigor mortis*. Similarly, things which BREAK OUT are usually unpleasant, and include *disagreements, riots, sweat, violence*, and *war*. *Miracles* HAPPEN, but not frequently: things which frequently HAPPEN include *accidents, quarrels, tragedies*, and *something untoward*. (Like all the examples in this article, these are attested examples of collocates from corpus data.) In such cases, I will talk of 'unpleasant' or 'negative' semantic prosodies.

It is easy to find other examples of words with unpleasant or negative prosodies. People COMMIT *adultery, crimes, murder, offences, sins, suicide*. Things can UNDERGO *changes, transformations*, and *modifications*, which can be *considerable, extensive, radical*, or *rapid*; people often undergo *crises, difficulties, ordeals*, and *risks*, or *medical treatments* or *tests* and *surgical procedures* which can be *traumatic*. And I will show in detail below that CAUSE (both noun and verb) has a strongly negative prosody.

But some lemmas do have positive prosodies: an example is PROVIDE. Contrast the collocations CAUSE–*work* and PROVIDE–*work*. The first is probably bad news: causing (extra) work is not usually welcome. But the second is probably good news, and would probably be interpreted as 'providing employment'.

I will now structure the argument as follows. I will give examples of frequent collocates of CAUSE and PROVIDE, with some following commentary. This will give more detailed examples of semantic prosodies. Then I will give details of the corpora and computational methods used to establish the findings.

[246]

CAUSE *and* PROVIDE

Exactly how such collocational information should be presented will depend on the purpose, such as dictionaries for beginners or advanced learners, or base-line comparative data for stylistic analysis. However, the following format displays findings in a convenient way for the present argument. The opening definitions are simplified from the Cobuild Dictionary (Sinclair, Hanks, *et al.* 1987), the rest are my own suggestions.

1   CAUSE: A *cause* is something that makes something happen. To *cause* something means to make it happen.

  1a   Most frequently, > 90%, the circumstances are *unpleasant*. Typically, what is caused is: an accident, cancer, concern, damage, death, disease, pain, a problem, problems, trouble.

  1b   The circumstances can include a wide range of *unpleasant* things, mostly expressed as *abstract nouns*, such as: alarm, anger, anxiety, chaos, commotion, confusion, crisis, delay, difficulty, distress, embarrassment, errors, explosion, harm, loss, inconvenience, nuisance, suspicion, uneasiness.

  1c   Frequently, the unpleasant collocates are *medical*: Aids, blood, cancer, death, deaths, disease, heart, illness, injury, pain, suffering, symptoms, stress, virus.

  1d   Frequent accompanying adjectives include: common, considerable, great, major, root, serious, severe.

  1e   Occasionally, however, the circumstances can be pleasant: a cause for celebration; cause for confidence.

  1f   Typical semi-fixed phrases are: cause for great concern; death caused by reckless driving; death from natural causes; cause grievous bodily harm; cause irreparable damage; cause untold damage; cause untold heartache.

  1g   Other typical examples are
     – the rush hour causes problems for London's transport
     – dryness can cause trouble if plants are neglected
     – considerable damage has been caused to buildings
     – I didn't see anything to cause immediate concern
     – some clumsy movement might have caused the accident.

2 PROVIDE: If you *provide* something for someone, you give it to them so that they have it when they need it. If something *provides* a feature, it provides a desirable and valuable quality that you can benefit from.

2a What is provided can be *neutral*, or *positive* and *valuable* (but not negative or undesirable). Typical collocates are from the semantic fields of *care, food, help, money* and *shelter*. The most frequent object nouns are: aid, assistance, care, employment, facilities, food, funds, housing, jobs, money, opportunities, protection, relief, security, services, support, training.

2b The most frequent accompanying adjectives are positive: additional, adequate, enough, extra, free, necessary, useful. Though things provided may also be: inadequate, etc.

2c Neutral cases (though often with a positive adjective: see below) typically include *linguistic events*. One can also provide: an answer, a basis for, a copy, a definition, evidence, figures, a framework, information, an overview, a summary.

2d Fixed phrases are: provide grist to the mill; provide the wherewithal.

2e Typical examples are:
  - they provide social services, nutrition, and education
  - this enabled him to provide better health benefits
  - he had the foresight to provide funds to rebuild their temple
  - the government cannot afford to provide housing
  - the claim to provide an easily comprehensible explanation
  - he provided a particularly vivid example
  - the study will provide an objective and thorough evaluation
  - this will provide your doctor with valuable information.

2f Note: to *provide for* someone (with no following object) can only mean to provide someone with money, shelter, and things that they need.

Note some features of these findings.

The simplest sense of 'typical' in such statements (for example, 1a) is 'high raw frequency', and it is a good idea to keep clearly in view the kind of frequencies that we are talking about. For example, in a 120 million running words (from the Cobuild corpus), CAUSE itself occurred some 38,000 times, and it occurred (in a span of 3:3) with the following collocates: *problem(s)* 1806, *damage* 1519, *death(s)* 1109, *disease* 591, *concern* 589, *cancer* 572, *pain* 514, *trouble* 471. There were no 'pleasant' words at all amongst the top dozen collocates ordered by frequency. (CAUSE also has a different sense of 'aim' or 'principle', as in *a good cause* or *plead a cause*. Such causes can be *glorious* and *worthy*, but also *lost* and *foolish*. This sense is relatively infrequent, and does not affect the findings.)

Within sets of collocates (for example, 1a, 1b, 2a, 2b), I have listed word forms alphabetically. The frequency of even fairly common words differs considerably across different corpora, and is very dependent on the topic of the texts which have been included. The precise frequency order would be a mere artefact of the data used. The collocation CAUSE–*problem* is frequent in all the corpora and in all the genres which I have looked at. The collocation CAUSE–*blindness* was not frequent or evenly distributed, though it clearly fits the overall 'unpleasant' pattern.

Semantic prosodies may be of a very general kind: such as the shared semantic feature 'unpleasant' (1a, 1b). Alternatively, one may be able to predict that a node will most likely co-occur with collocates from a restricted lexical set: for example, from the semantic field of 'care' (2b).

The identification of such lexical sets cannot be entirely automatic. I am not arguing that intuitions have no place in such analysis, but that intuitions are often inaccurate or very incomplete, and that they should be firmly based on attested data. For example, with PROVIDE, all the computer can do is to identify the most frequent collocates in a given corpus. It is up to the human analyst to spot that a set of collocates (for example, *answer, definition*, etc., in 2c) are from the lexical set 'linguistic events'. The occurrence of any single word form may be quite low, and will be missed in a simple list of descending frequencies. What is significant is the summed frequency of semantically related items; and this can be spotted only by a human being. (One can envisage that an outcome of such work may eventually be the establishment of lexical sets, which would allow the automatic recognition of such semantic fields, but we are a long way from such automatic procedures at present.)

The statements are mostly probabilistic. It is possible to use CAUSE in neutral or positive collocations (for example, 1e). But such uses are rare (see 1a). And such strikingly asymmetric semantic patterns should be represented in statements about word meaning.

Statements about chains of collocations are beyond the methods discussed here. For example, *considerable* (1d) is a frequent collocate of CAUSE, due to phrases such as *cause considerable damage*. Similarly, *driving* (1f) is a frequent collocate, due to phrases such as *death caused by reckless driving*.

The concept of a 'typical example' (1g, 2e) is a strange one. No specific concordance line can be typical—it can only be specific! It will almost certainly be a unique utterance and will reflect unique features of its specific co-text. So by this contradictory phrase, I mean an example which includes frequent collocates, and which is understandable in a short concordance line.

A corpus can give information only about what does actually occur, not about what might occur (and of course not about what cannot occur). But the statements are refutable. If you find attested examples of PROVIDE with negative or unpleasant collocates (see 2a), then my statements about this lemma will have to be revised. (But they must be attested examples, not examples which you have invented!)

In retrospect, such lists of collocates may seem intuitively obvious to a native speaker. And there may be the illusion that they could have been provided, after a bit of thought, by intuition alone. But this is indeed an illusion. Intuition certainly cannot provide reliable facts about frequency and typicality. And whilst a native speaker may be able to provide some examples of collocates (which may or may not be accurate), only a corpus can provide thorough documentation. If you are not convinced, then I recommend two courses of action:

- Check the entries for CAUSE and PROVIDE in several dictionaries. You will find that the examples given (if any) may well match the findings above. But the word definitions will not give explicit information on the patterns of lexical co-occurrence which I have identified.

- Consider, intuitively, whether the word SOMEWHAT has a semantic prosody. Is it neutral, or clearly positive or negative? Can you list its most frequent collocates one word to the right? You may consult any dictionary you have (this probably will not help much). But don't look at the end of the article until you have written down your intuitive response!

Corpus data and computer-assisted methods

I will now say something about the methods I have used to establish such findings.

I have used two main corpora. One corpus, held at Trier in Germany, contains some 3.5 million words of running text, comprising over 1,000 samples of written and spoken English from many different genres. Most findings below are also based on 120 million words from the Bank of English corpus, held at Cobuild in Birmingham, which comprises samples from British newspapers and the BBC, books from many different genres, and some spoken language.

The most basic research strategy of corpus linguistics is to look for regular patterns across dozens or, ideally, hundreds or thousands of concordance lines. If one is investigating a small corpus, of one million words or so, then it may be quite possible to extract concordance lines, scan them by eye, and identify patterns of the type I have discussed. But if one has 120 million words of data, and some 38,000 examples of a lemma (as is the case with CAUSE in the Cobuild corpus), this is clearly no longer possible. One requires software which reads in a corpus and identifies all occurrences of a specified node, counts the frequency of the node, records all collocates within a given span, and counts the frequency of each collocation. It should also count the absolute frequency of each collocate in the corpus (independent of the node).

There is considerable discussion in the literature of various statistics which can then be calculated from such information. Clear (1993) describes such software which he has written for working with the Cobuild corpus. Church and Hanks (1990), and Church, Gale, Hanks, and Hindle (1991) propose various formulae. I discuss these formulae in detail (Stubbs 1995), and argue that they are over-complex and misleading in various ways.

Here, I will use two statistics which are based on this literature, but which are much simpler. First, we need to know the absolute (raw) frequency of a collocation, relative to corpus size. This raw figure needs some downward adjustment in the case where node and/or collocate are themselves very frequent (for example, because they are common grammatical words), since in such a case they might co-occur merely by chance. Second, we need to know the frequency of a collocation relative to the independent frequency of the node or collocate in the corpus.

The need for this second statistic is easiest to see with a simple example. Consider the phrase *quintessentially English*, from the point of view of *English* as the node, and of *quintessentially* as the collocate. In a corpus of 130 million words, *English* occurred some 30,000 times. The commonest collocates, in a span of 4:4, included *language* 1,300, *French* 800, *speaking* 770, and *football* 700. The phrase *quintessentially English* occurred only 55 times, and would be missed by a method which searches only for collocations with high raw frequencies. But, of course, the word *quintessentially* is itself rather rare: only 170 occurrences in 130 million words. However, of these 170 occurrences, 55 were collocations with *English*: a third of its use. A further 54 occurrences were with other nationality adjectives. Looked at from this point of view, the collocation *quintessentially English* is therefore linguistically significant. So, we need a statistic which catches words which are relatively rare, but which (when they do occur) have a tendency to be restricted in their collocates. (For the precise formulae used to calculate such statistics, see Stubbs 1995.)

Comparative semantic profiles

We now have a method which can be used to compare and contrast the characteristic uses of semantically related words. Again, how such comparative profiles are best presented will depend on the purpose: say, a dictionary for learners themselves, information for writers of teaching materials, or comparative information for a stylistic analysis. Here, I will simply give some very brief and informally presented examples of the kind of findings which arise. The collocates which I cite here are high on one or both of the statistics discussed above, and in that sense 'typical'.

Consider, then, a selection of words in the semantic field of 'cause and effect'. CAUSE, as I have shown, has a predominantly negative prosody. By contrast, CREATE has a mixed prosody. One can create *havoc* but also *a good impression*. Collocates include *conditions, havoc, illusion, image, problems*. REASON has no very clear prosody, though it is more positive than its rough synonym CAUSE. Collocates include *altruistic, apparent, cogent, compelling, different, earthly, good, main, obvious, political*. (*Earthly* occurs, of course, due to the fixed phrase *no earthly reason*.) RESULT is also rather mixed or neutral. Collocates include *disappointing, end, expected, final, inconclusive, interim, preliminary, unintended.* AFFECT is very negative. Something is typically affected *adversely, badly, directly, negatively, seriously.* Hence, if we hear that something *affected the accuracy of the solution,* we are likely to interpret this as 'adversely affected'. EFFECT is also very negative. Effects are typically *adverse, deleterious, devastating, dramatic, harmful, ill, negative, profound, toxic.* CONSEQUENCE is also very negative. Consequences are often to be *feared,* and are typically *catastrophic, devastating, dire, disastrous, grave, negative.*

Cultural key words

This powerful technique for comparing words can also be applied to lexical sets which are culturally important. Firth (1935) proposed such a study of 'the detailed contextual distribution of sociologically important words', what he called focal or pivotal words, for example:

> such words as *work, labour, trade, employ, occupy, play, leisure, time, hours, means, self-respect* in all their derivatives and compounds in sociologically significant contexts during the last twenty years . . .

Firth did not carry out this project, and indeed it would require access to large corpora and computational resources which he did not have. Again, I will provide just some brief notes on some lemmas in this semantic field.

A feature of the lemma WORK itself, which is very striking from concordance data, is that it occurs in a very large number of compound words and fixed phrases, many of which are new formations:

– workaholic, workforce, workload, workplace, worksheet
– aid worker, factory worker, office worker, social worker.

JOB can be positive: one can do a *good job* or have *job satisfaction.* But it is often negative, and frequent collocates include *botched, crummy, hard, hatchet, menial, wangled.* By contrast, CAREER has a very positive prosody and a very sharply defined profile. People have careers in high prestige professions. Collocates include *acting, director, film, international, literary.* Careers are typically described as *brilliant, distinguished, glittering, illustrious*, although, against expectation, careers can also be *blighted* and *thwarted*. LABOUR is largely negative. Collocates include *casual, cheap, deskilling, manual, unproductive*. EMPLOYMENT is typically talked about in legal terms. Frequent collocates include *conditions, contract, discrimination, rights*. UNEMPLOYMENT is typically talked about in statistical terms. Collocates include *average, fall, grow, increase, rocket, soar*.

In his well-known book, Raymond Williams (1976) also discusses the history and implications of such cultural 'keywords'. I discuss the 'work' examples, and possibilities of such ideological analysis, in more detail in Stubbs (forthcoming). (See also Channell 1994.)

Somewhat

If you are still somewhat sceptical about such work, consider the collocates of *somewhat*. In the 3.5 million word corpus, *somewhat* occurred 150 times. There were two main sets of word forms immediately to the right.

1 A few individual words, which themselves occurred several times each, concerned comparisons. All words which occurred 3 or more times were

   – analogous 4, different 7, greater 3, higher 3, less 3, more 3, similar 4.

   Many other collocates were comparatives:

   – better, clearer, earlier, older, simpler, younger.

   Other collocates to the right included *comparable, like*. And collocates to the left also confirm the 'comparison' pattern: for example, *changed, declined, differ, figure, increase*.

2 Other words one place to the right occurred only once or twice each, but, of those, the majority were clearly negative. They included

   – arbitrary, biased, bleak, complacent, confused, cramped, curious, cynical, depressed, dim, dirty, disturbed, embarrassing, extravagant, futile, grubby, haughtily, hazily, hypersensitive, ignominiously, imprecise, inaccurate, incoherently, laboriously, limited, misleading, nasty, nervously, neurotic, opaque,

[254]

out of date, peculiar, priggish, provincial, repetitive, resentful, shabby, simplistic, sullen, uncertain, unusual, unwillingly, vulgar, worried.

Other occurrences of *somewhat* were preceded by negative words: for example, *her fears were somewhat lulled*.

These collocation data make clear two predominant uses of *somewhat*: (1) a 'neutral' use involving comparisons, including comparisons of quantities; and (2) a use which mitigates a disparaging reference, often to a person. This second pragmatic meaning is not recorded in any of the well-known dictionaries which I have consulted. (These findings are from a corpus of mainly British English data, and I have not checked whether the same patterns occur in other varieties of English.)

Conclusions and implications: principles and practice

In conclusion, a few implications for principles and practice in both descriptive linguistics and in language teaching.

A semantic prosody is a linguistic relation between a node word and a lexical set. This relation is defined by a very general semantic feature (for example, 'unpleasant'), or by a more specific semantic field (for example, 'care') whose members are established from corpus data. This type of linguistic relation may, in the past, have been recognized in isolated instances. But it is currently not recorded systematically in either dictionaries or grammars. It is a purely lexical, yet syntagmatic, relation, of a type which cannot be captured by current descriptive theory. Indeed it undermines conventional views of the relation between syntagmatic and paradigmatic. In addition, the descriptive statements which I have given are probabilistic. Again, conventional linguistic description usually assumes categorical relations between units, and has no theory of typicality.

These descriptive methods and findings have many implications for language teaching. Exactly how such findings should best be turned into teaching materials and presented to students is a topic which will require long-term experimentation, and I do not intend here to jump prematurely from a few findings on a few words to such pedagogical

[255]

prescriptions. However, at the very least, it seems to me that language teachers would find such reliable information about collocations useful. It raises questions about the balance in a language between creativity and fixed phrases. And it is also easy to see, at least in general terms, how one might start to use such descriptive methods for integrating semantic, pragmatic, and cultural information into language teaching materials.

I hope this article has *provided convincing examples* of the *extensive and radical changes* which linguistics is *undergoing* as a result of corpus-based methods. Such work also *creates the conditions* for major innovations in teaching materials, although I have been *somewhat more cautious* in making large claims here.

Acknowledgements

I am very grateful to the following friends and colleagues for help with data and software: staff at Cobuild, especially the director Gwynneth Fox, for permission to use the Bank of English corpus; Oliver Jakobs who wrote collocational software for use in Trier; Susan Hunston who provided me with the PROVIDE example; Wolfram Bublitz who pointed out to me the interest of the SOMEWHAT example; Joanna Channell, Andrea Gerbig, and Gabi Keck who provided other data and helpful discussion.

17

Corpora in language pedagogy: matching theory and practice

GUY ASTON

IN TODAY'S WORLD computers increasingly provide access to information, and are thus by definition a potential instrument of learning. In the field of language, their use mainly involves access to collections of free text (free speech still poses problems of storage space, not to mention transcription: Edwards and Lampert 1993), or else to elaborated materials, particularly electronic reference works such as spellers, grammars, dictionaries, and thesauri. The latter are increasingly being produced through computerized analysis of the former. Tens or hundreds of millions of words of text, selected to capture the variety of uses and users of the language on the one hand (representative corpora) and the variety of its instantiations on the other (monitor corpora: Clear 1987; Sinclair 1991a), are subjected to concordancing to display the contexts of occurrence of particular forms and to calculate their frequencies, and these analyses have produced a wide range of descriptive and theoretical insights into language use (Altenberg 1991; Sinclair 1991a). With the growth of standardized formats for machine-readable text (Sperberg-McQueen and Burnard 1994) and the development of cheap and simple software for concordancing (Chandler 1989; Scott and Johns 1993), teachers and learners seem set to have an enormous quantity of material at their fingertips, with obvious implications (at least in theory) for greater democratization and autonomy of learning. This paper aims to consider some criteria for the design and use of text corpora in pedagogy, also in the light of some recent work by Henry Widdowson addressing these issues (1991b, 1993d).

The relevance of corpora to language teaching can be examined from two perspectives, corresponding to the distinction made by Widdowson (1980a) between two interpretations of the term *applied linguistics*. The first, that of 'linguistics applied', attempts to examine how insights deriving from linguistic research can be transferred to language teaching. For instance, it has been extensively argued by Sinclair (1987b, 1991a, 1991b) that the improved descriptions of the language made possible by corpus-based research provide a basis for improved pedagogy, both by providing better reference tools (grammars and dictionaries such as those developed in the Cobuild project: Sinclair *et al.* 1987, 1990), and by enabling better decisions as to which lexical items, senses, and grammatical structures should be included in the syllabus (for exemplification, see Willis and Willis 1987; Sinclair and Renouf 1988; Willis 1990). Many of the findings of corpus-based research are in fact in contrast with traditional pedagogic priorities: metaphorical uses of many common words are more frequent in reality than the literal senses which dominate textbooks, and commonly occurring grammatical patterns often receive less emphasis in pedagogy than ones of which it may be doubted 'whether beginning students will ever need to produce or comprehend [. . .] outside the language classroom' (Biber, Conrad, and Reppen 1994: 174). The argument has been extended to ESP: corpus-based register analysis (Biber 1988, 1989; Biber and Finegan 1991) provides descriptions of the distinguishing characteristics of different registers which, it is claimed, should lie at the basis of ESP syllabuses, since

> the markedly different patterns of linguistic form and function that occur across registers indicate that there is no single set of linguistic features that should be emphasized for all students, once they have mastered the rudiments of English grammar.
> (Biber *et al.* 1994: 174)

As well as the findings of corpus-based research, it has been proposed that certain methods of this research can have applications in the language classroom, with concordances listing the contexts of occurrence of particular expressions in a corpus providing data from which learners can infer or test the rules which govern their use (for example, Tribble and Jones 1990; Johns and King 1991). Johns (1986, 1988, 1991) argues that concordances allow for 'data-driven learning', where students take the role of researchers constructing their own lexicogrammatical descriptions, inferring rules from examples rather than simply being told them by teacher or textbook.

While sharing a perspective of 'corpus linguistics applied', these proposals are not in practice compatible. The suggestion that the findings of linguistic research should be transferred to pedagogy in no way entails that learners should use the linguist's same methods: corpus linguists draw on very large corpora to which teachers and learners cannot easily obtain direct access, and in interpreting this data they rely heavily upon their intuition as native speakers and their professional training (Sinclair 1991b: 494). Sinclair does not see the corpus as a source of data for use by students themselves, but as a source of lists and concordances relating to particular linguistic features (Francis and Sinclair 1994), 'a database for teachers' reference, a repository of facts about English on which new syllabi and materials can be based' (Sinclair 1987c: 158). The methods by which these facts are to be taught are left up to pedagogy. The proposal that concordancing should be used by learners, on the other hand, in no way entails that the content to be taught should correspond to the linguist's facts. Work with classroom concordancing is generally based on very small corpora, often carefully selected to facilitate interpretation by learners (for example, Johns 1994), but which do not permit inferences of similar descriptive reliability to those of corpus linguistics. Both applications, in other words, are contaminated by pedagogic reality.

Widdowson's second (and preferred) interpretation of the term 'applied linguistics' instead starts from the pedagogic context, considering that developments in linguistics and other related fields have to be evaluated and interpreted on the basis of independent criteria of relevance, grounded in the actual processes of teaching and learning. Thus in a recent paper (1991b) he criticizes Sinclair's assumption that the improved descriptions of the language provided by corpus linguistics necessarily provide a better basis for language teaching: he notes that while corpus-based descriptions may reveal new facts about the frequency and distribution of particular forms and meanings, we need only hark back to Halliday, McIntosh, and Strevens' work on principles of vocabulary selection and grading (1964: 190ff.) to recognize that other criteria—availability, teachability, and classroom needs—are involved in selecting items for inclusion in a syllabus:

[259]

Language prescriptions for the inducement of learning cannot be based on a database. They cannot be modelled on the description of externalised language, the frequency profiles of text analysis. Such analysis provides us with facts, hitherto unknown, or ignored, but they do not of themselves carry any guarantee of pedagogic relevance.

(Widdowson 1991b: 20–21)

An essentially similar argument can be made concerning the transfer of corpus-based methods to pedagogy. The fact that concordancing has proved a useful tool in formulating descriptive generalizations by linguists is no guarantee that it can be usefully transferred to the classroom. In particular, it can be argued that in so far as it involves the decontextualization of individual instances from their original communicative setting, concordance analysis fails to engage the learner in those processes of negotiating meaning in its pragmatic aspects, illocutionary and perlocutionary, which, Widdowson has argued (1984a, 1990a: chapter 7), are central to acquisition. In this respect the idea of concordance-based 'data-driven learning' seems at odds not only with a major premise of the communicative approach in pedagogy, that of 'using English to learn it' (Howatt 1984: 279), but also with findings in those areas of computational linguistics which are more concerned with language learning than language description:

To understand how language is used in performing tasks such as speaking and comprehending [. . .] entails understanding how innate structures and experience contribute to the acquisition of these capacities. Linguistic representations do not reflect generalisations derived from samples of adult utterances drawn from within and across languages; rather they develop in the service of solving the acquisition problem [. . .]
(Seidenberg 1994: 397–398)

This is not to imply that the findings and methods of corpus linguistics are necessarily irrelevant to language pedagogy: Widdowson's point is simply that it is up to pedagogy to determine whether and what uses such findings and methods may have, on the basis of its own principles and criteria, and there is no a priori reason why such uses should simply ape those of other fields. In this paper I shall outline some ways

[260]

in which corpus-based work appears theoretically compatible with current language teaching practice, arguing that even if the case for corpus-based learning *tout court* (in terms of determining the syllabus, the methodology, or both) seems weak, corpora constitute resources which, placed in the hands of teachers and learners who are aware of their potentials and limits, can significantly enrich the pedagogic environment.

Schemata in corpora and pedagogy

Recent developments in corpus linguistics and in language pedagogy have one substantial point of overlap. Both have come to assume an idiomatic or schematic view of language competence and use. Thus rather than seeing the production and interpretation of discourse as rigidly componential, with morphemes being selected and combined according to complex sets of grammatical and pragmatic rules, both tend to see it as exploiting ready-made memorized building blocks or 'pre-fabs', put together using simpler 'jerrybuilding' operations (Bolinger 1975). Pawley and Syder (1983) argue that the retrieval of memorized chunks which are instantiated as wholes accounts for both 'nativelike selection', where the number of routinely occurring realizations of a particular meaning is far smaller than that of the potentially rule-conformant ones, and for 'nativelike fluency', enabling extensive segments to be produced as single units. Along with multi-word phraseological units, Bolinger suggests that lexis itself is largely known schematically rather than being generated componentially from the morphology; Widdowson (1983b, 1984a) has argued that schematic knowledge also includes more abstract conceptual, propositional, and rhetorical associative structures, such as membership categorization devices (Sacks 1972), frames (Minsky 1975; van Dijk 1977), and scripts (Schank and Abelson 1977; Schank 1980). The use of ready-made schemata is reflected in that aspect of communicative competence concerned with whether something 'actually occurs', as opposed to simply being grammatically correct, psychologically feasible, and situationally appropriate (Hymes 1972).

Sinclair, in reviewing corpus-based work on lexicogrammar, makes an argument which is in many respects similar to Pawley and Syder's. He notes how, to a far greater degree than a componential view would imply, lexical items and grammatical structures appear to be co-selected as idiomatic colligations, so that particular senses of particular lemmas have idiosyncratic environments (Sinclair 1987b: 110). The use of these ready-made combinations speeds processing in reception as well as production, with systematic grammatical knowledge only being used as a last resort:

> The first mode to be applied is the idiom principle since most of the text will be interpretable by this principle. Whenever there is good reason, the interpretive process switches to the open choice principle, and quickly back again.
> (Sinclair 1987d: 324)

Corpus linguistics sees such schemata primarily as social facts of language, evidenced in patterns of use in the community as a whole. A pedagogic perspective instead treats them primarily as psychological constructs, which may vary both within and across users, including obviously learners. A schematic view of competence implies multiple representations in memory, in the sense that the 'same' behaviour may be produced or interpreted in various manners on different occasions or by different users, in reference to schemata of differing sizes and degrees of generality (Winograd 1977). At a phraseological level, the expression 'I don't know' might be available to its user as a fixed formula for answering questions, as a partly fixed 'I don't' + main verb colligation usable with a class of stative verbs to perform expressive speech acts, as well as being generable from its morphemes by applying rules for person, tense, aspect, and negation, along with the necessary pragmatic components. The use of multiple representations entails that new schemata may be acquired through the composition and decomposition of existing ones. Larger, more context-specific schemata, where subject to variation for use in other contexts, may undergo a process of analysis leading to the creation of smaller and more generalized ones (approximating more closely, on the phraseological level, to systematic knowledge of the lexicogrammar: Fillmore 1979; Peters 1983; Pine and Lieven 1993). Conversely, where smaller, more generalized schemata are repeatedly combined in a recurrent context this may lead to their synthesis as a single ready-made schema—in phraseological terms, a relexicalization (Skehan 1992) or, on the level of rhetorical structure, a script (Schank 1980). These processes involve

[262]

what Skehan terms the 'restructuring' of knowledge, adding schemata of different sizes and generality to the user's repertoire.

This view implies that contextual repetition (leading to synthesis) and variation (leading to analysis) are key to acquisition. Learners need to acquire schemata not simply as a set of routine formulae and scripts for use in repetitive situations (following the 'idiom principle'), nor simply as an analytic rule-based system with associated 'rules of use' (following the 'open-choice principle'). While particular pedagogic contexts and individual learning preferences may privilege one or other approach, undue emphasis on the former risks fossilization and non-acquisition of aspects of the lexicogrammar (Harley and Swain 1984; Celce-Murcia 1991a), while undue emphasis on the latter risks ignorance of what 'actually occurs' in native-like production (for instance, routine collocational patterns: Bahns and Eldaw 1993). The learner needs to be presented with materials and methods which encourage restructuring, allowing the formation of schemata which may progressively approximate the varied (and varying) multiple representations of native speakers.

Corpus-based methods have proved to be a powerful means of highlighting patterns of repetition and variation in text. Whether these methods can be of value for learning depends on the extent to which the patterns highlighted are relevant to the learner, emerging in contexts which facilitate the restructuring of knowledge, and in such a manner as to make this knowledge available for use. On the one hand the patterns highlighted may not correspond to the schemata which learners need to internalize. Not only is manifest use not in a one-to-one relationship with native-speaker competence (Aarts 1991; Widdowson 1991b, 1993d), but most descriptive approaches emphasize maximally analytic generalizations rather than the partially analytic or synthetic ones which the view outlined would suggest are equally important to acquisition. On the other hand, it cannot be assumed that observation of recurrent patterns is sufficient to enable their use. We have so far glossed over any distinction between declarative knowledge of how the language is used, and procedural ability to use the language (Færch and Kasper 1984; Widdowson 1989c). As well as establishing the kinds of observations in corpus data which may be appropriate for the restructuring of knowledge, we need to ask what procedures can help activate this knowledge as ability.

Using corpora to acquire schematic knowledge

The account of schematic knowledge and its acquisition outlined points to a need for learners to seek out recurrences and variants in corpus data rather than simply trying to infer or test generalized rules. To remain at a lexicogrammatical level, Jordan (1992) suggests that learners might use concordancing to investigate the rule that *for* and *since* in time adjuncts are respectively associated with periods and points of time. By using *MicroConcord*'s blank-out facility (Scott and Johns 1993), learners can try to reinstate the appropriate preposition in each context and then check their answers (Murison-Bowie 1993: 10). However, a concordance of *since* from the *MicroConcord* newspaper corpus also highlights the recurrence of *since* in particular phraseologies. Excluding cases where it is used as a causal conjunction, and with specific dates (*since Tuesday*, etc.), we find three or more occurrences of these expressions following *since*: *become, been, he (was), his, its, the, then (there has/have been), they*. If we instead sort the concordance to examine the phraseology which precedes *since*, we find multiple examples (shown below) of *and since then, ever since, (and/which) has/have since (been), (have/has) long since*:

```
wpipes to the guerrillas in 1986 and since then there have been no reports of ad
esituation has changed greatly, and since then we have made a significant move
roduce a memorable body of work, and since then she has appeared, as if in penan
ical issues he has been ducking ever since the ructions of 1968. <p> The feature
referred privacy to flamboyance ever since his public companies had the stuffing
out against Mr Le Pen's group. 'Ever since the elections they have been revealin
, the musical establishment has ever since accused him of selling out politicall
k. Controversy has followed him ever since, encouraged by his own unpredictabili
sed of being a Nazi sympathiser ever since. The Speer book has enabled critics o
closer to Welney at Yarmouth and has since won easily at Brighton. Despite the p
group lost £1.368m last year and has since radically slimmed down to three
condemn Peking for its butchery, has since acknowledged that 'at the end of the
food prices on 1 August: butter has since then gone up 1,000 per cent, meat by
ust's Hellerman Deutsch Classic, has since suffered some unexpected defeats, win
Os by Warren Gummow, Royal Foods has since been owned and managed by him and his
sh resources". <p> A £215m fraud has since been discovered at ISC which has brou
years between 1975 and 1985, he has, since losing the title, been doggedly pursu
at Stoke Mandeville Hospital. He has since been granted temporary leave to stay
ilander was No. 1 a year ago. He has since lost the Australian, French and US Op
st Midlands. <p> The Shoe People has since been televised in 52 countries and ha
angdong operations. The province has since been in the forefront of China's effo
ping. The definition of a second has since officially been the time it takes a c
e Scottish Philharmonic Singers, has since sung with several other orchestras an
ce on the wings. But that theory has since been discredited, and many critics, p
y was quickly invested and there has since been a stream of rights issues, parti
dollar to the US currency, which has since worked perfectly. Thus, whatever cons
t to publicise the report, which has since been backed up by an internal report
he 'dance house" movement, which has since subsided. Their search for authentici
anged in a peculiar manner which has since become known as 'Residential". <p> Me
lled spares company Alpex, which has since been wound up. The case arose through
, presented by a party chief who has since been redeployed. <p> Alfred Yu, a uni
men Square massacre in June and have since provided donations to Chinese groups
```

```
ved in the May coup attempt and have since been executed. Without their influenc
r observer status, the eyeballs have since become valuable rock icons themselves
it any more." The old eyeballs have since been retired, being replaced, for the
e Athletic Ground. <p> Richmond have since sought help from Middlesex in pursuin
t Ninagawa to join him and they have since produced an extraordinary row of clas
egion's cities and ports, which have since had much of their former life and gla
tage. <p> Nature, we learn, has long since sickened and died. The 'leafy screens
used very little damage and has long since ceded its title to the great earthqua
cused in the first place _ have long since become obsolescent. But the film gets
nfield about his judgement have long since been swept away. If Dalglish ever lef
hey ever existed, have probably long since been destroyed. <sect> Foreign News P
```

A closer look reveals that some of these recurrent phraseologies are associated with particular syntactic or semantic contexts. *Since then*, for instance, is largely clause-initial (sometimes preceded by *and/but*) or clause-final; *long since* is medially positioned between the auxiliary *have/has* and the past participles of semantically similar verbs, all indicating demise or fall from grace.

Noting such partial regularities seems a way of helping learners synthesize larger, context-specific schemata, rather than just the generalized analytic rules traditionally presented in grammars and textbooks. These schemata may well differ from those proposed in corpus-based descriptive studies. The criteria of concordance analysis and of corpus design adopted here differ from those invoked by corpus linguistics, which seeks to establish descriptively adequate rules on the basis of much larger quantities of data. We are not exposed to representative samples when we learn languages, but to highly biased selections, and what we learn from them is not definitive, being subject to refinement in the light of future observations. What would seem important is that these selections have those characteristics of repetition and variation which enable schemata to be formed and restructured on a variety of levels.

From this perspective, it seems arguable that corpora for language teaching should be composed of texts which are relatively homogeneous, deriving from similar contexts. A further desirable feature seems that of limited size, which may facilitate identification of recurrent patterns of a semantic and a pragmatic nature. Concordancing generally highlights recurrences which have clear lexical and/or morphological correlates, a fact reflected in the emphasis of corpus linguistics on essentially lexicogrammatical phenomena of collocation, colligation, and connotation (Sinclair 1991a). Unless annotated corpora are used (and any tagging is generally limited to grammatical features: Leech 1991), more abstract categories can rarely be located

[265]

automatically. Nor are they evident to the observer: the relatively short contexts provided in most concordances may be adequate to arrive at a semantic interpretation of the current clause, but they give next to no idea of the ongoing discourse and the role of this clause in its development. With relatively small corpora, however, we can partly overcome these limits by comparing the texts manually or by adding simple annotation prior to concordancing. For instance, using the retrieval software provided with CD-ROM collections of text, it is possible (given some filtering of the output) to create small subcorpora of texts of the same genre and/or on the same topic. If these texts are reasonably short, their rhetorical and informational structures and their realizations can then be compared by inspection. For instance, eight short articles, all dealing with the same murder trial, were retrieved from *The Independent* for a classroom exercise where learners were asked to seek similarities in the information given and the way it was presented. Among the regularities they noted were:

- many initial sentences took a routine form 'A [profession-descriptor] [witnessed some event potentially related to the murder of a woman], a jury/court heard/was told yesterday';
- these sentences were followed by an expanded description of the event witnessed, the witness this time being identified by name, age, and geographical origin in that order;
- the location of the trial was specified, in a subsequent sentence, as *Shrewsbury Crown Court* (rather than, say, 'the Crown Court in Shrewsbury');
- if this fact had not been previously mentioned, the final sentence stated that the accused had denied the murder;
- the murderer was consistently referred to as the *killer*—murder is the charge, killing the event giving rise to it.

The use of a few structurally similar texts also enables the identification of some higher-level regularities through concordancing. In another exercise, a corpus of twelve medical research articles on hepatitis C was concordanced following division of the texts into sections. This demonstrated not only such recurrent collocations as that of *recent* with *study/studies/reports*, and of *patients* with *were tested*, but also

[266]

that these phraseologies were concentrated in the introductory and methods sections respectively.

Corpora and communicative language teaching

The examples just discussed presume access to whole texts rather than brief extracts, contextualizing regularities in similar discourses. Relatively small, homogeneous corpora also offer other advantages. The observation of regularities in multiple texts in itself offers little guarantee that the learner will be able to use this knowledge for communication. Communicative language teaching holds that the prime condition for acquisition of ability for use is participatory experience, as provided by information-gap, reasoning-gap, opinion-gap, and rapport-gap tasks (Johnson 1982; Howatt 1984; Prabhu 1987; Aston 1988), and that declarative knowledge is relevant to this development in so far as it can be related to current communicative concerns (Brumfit 1984; Prabhu 1987). From this point of view tasks of observation and analysis need to be embedded in tasks of communication, so that learners derive from the data information as to how current communicative goals are or can be achieved (Aston 1988; McCarthy and Carter 1994).

To achieve such embedding, two procedures suggest themselves. One, widely proposed in the literature (for example, Louw 1993; Murison-Bowie 1993), is to treat the corpus as a reference tool for the solution of problems which emerge in the performance of other tasks. The collection of hepatitis research articles mentioned above was developed for use by learners in preparing for and carrying out translations of similar articles. Faced with a particular problem, the learner could turn to the corpus for evidence that a particular form could have a particular meaning in a particular context, the similarity of the corpus texts to that involved in the task making it relatively likely that models and analogies would be found. For instance, a problematic reference to ELISA was clarified by a concordance for this term in the corpus as a whole, which included the fully spelt-out formulation *Ortho HCV enzyme-linked immunosorbent assay (ELISA)*.

An alternative procedure is to treat the corpus not just as an aid to

[267]

task performance, but as a source of communicative tasks. Texts retrieved from a corpus can provide opportunities for learners to participate in discourse from a variety of perspectives. Newspaper corpora can be used to find out about people, places, events, and attitudes towards them: in the murder trial example mentioned above, the selected texts were first read by learners to find out about the murder in question, as a jigsaw reading activity (Geddes and Sturtridge 1982). The corpus of hepatitis articles could be used to find out about hepatitis C, the methods used to investigate it, and the main problems in the field. The teacher or learner retrieves a subcorpus of texts to be read for the purpose of a particular communicative task. The same subcorpus provides a reference tool to assist with difficulties in comprehension, providing information which, in so far as learners have become familiar with its component texts during performance of the task, is more readily interpretable.

Corpora seem a particularly rich source of reading-based activities. Where a number of similar texts can be retrieved, there is wide potential for information exchange and discussion as well as linguistic comparison. Learners can independently seek out groups of texts on topics of interest to them. As well as the prespecified task, there is often an impromptu element: since text retrieval and concordancing are inaccurate processes from a semantic or pragmatic perspective, being based mainly upon orthographic features, they often give rise to unforeseen distractions. The concordance below not only highlights the use of *dire* with *need* as well as *trouble, situation*, and the like, but introduced this user to Dire Dawa and its role in the khat trade:

```
East Berlin </bl> <st> <p> AROUND the dire brick pile which is Gethsemane Church
ks have suggested that there could be dire consequences for the City should the
with bombs and rockets, take off from Dire Dawa and head west. <p> The estimated
light from Addis Ababa had stopped at Dire Dawa but had picked up no passengers.
n civil servant said he would stay in Dire Dawa, for a week if necessary, rather
legal. The arrival of the flight from Dire Dawa, where the khat is grown, is met
6-9, 9-6, 9-5, 9-5 on Saturday, is in dire need of a rest. <p> Had Beeson lost t
test time, when 'they were in the most dire need of calm, clear orders, when ever
have done nothing. Irish racing is in dire peril," Jonathan Irwin, the showman o
s. <p> 'It is an accepted practice in dire situations such as this that the boar
bels, including Fine Young Cannibals, Dire Straits and Bon Jovi as well as perfo
r in what one fanzine has dubbed the 'Dire Straits and lager guide". In it, the
ing areas like Wallis and Horne and a dire time in housebuilding to limit the de
ure on continued reaction to August's dire trade figures, fell to a low against
```

In this manner corpora can invite the user to browse through texts in an autonomous manner (Aston, forthcoming b)—which, for many learners, may be just as motivating as using them to carry out linguistic analysis (Sinclair 1991b).

Conclusions

The proposals outlined differ from practice in corpus linguistics in a number of ways. While similarly assuming the importance of noticing regularities in discourse, a pedagogic emphasis must be on the relevance of these for learning rather than on the descriptive adequacy of the analysis. This legitimates the use of limited, non-representative but relatively homogeneous and understandable corpora in order to facilitate restructuring through repetition and relatively controlled variation. Communicative tasks entail specific uses of language, and limited subcorpora from a specific domain make it easier for the learner to observe regularities which relate to those uses, and to interpret data where 'the word works indexically to key in with and complement a context of shared knowledge' (Widdowson 1993d: 309). Such subcorpora also enable learners to go beyond a lexicogrammatical level to consider aspects of informational and rhetorical structure which can only be observed through comparison of extended texts. Of course the regularities found within such a corpus do not come with any guarantee of generality, and many regularities (including, of course, those associated with other context-types) will be excluded. Learners need to be aware of this, appreciating that learning is a process of approximation, and it may make sense for them to build up a bank of subcorpora, gradually increasing the size of the overall text-base to which reference can be made, and learning to select an appropriate subcorpus for the analysis of a particular problem.

While providing opportunities for the progressive acquisition of schematic knowledge, as currently conceived corpora would not seem able to aspire to replace learning tools which explain meaning analytically. Corpus linguistics has played a major role in bringing to light the extent of patternings in collocation, colligation, and connotation, areas to which pedagogy has traditionally paid little attention, but there are other areas of competence for which corpora fail to provide positive evidence. The regularities underlined by corpus linguistics fail to match up with native-speaker intuitions concerning prototypes (Aarts 1991), knowledge of which seems highly relevant to the learner (Widdowson 1991b). This may not be instantiated directly in corpus data, precisely because it is generally taken for granted. As Sinclair notes, 'if something is obvious it is optional. The more obvious it is, the less likely it is to occur, and the more marked for meaning is its occurrence' (1991b: 497). Thus proverbs and clichés are very rarely reproduced verbatim in a newspaper corpus, but the fact that they frequently form the basis of modified citations demonstrates that their prototypical forms are assumed to be available (indeed we can perhaps most readily imagine the prototype being used to explain such a citation to a learner). The learner clearly needs to acquire the prototype, but to do so can hardly rely upon 'authentic' corpus data. One, as yet largely unexplored avenue, might be to use collections of 'unauthentic' texts as a learning resource (a possibility hinted at by Willis 1993, who suggests that an accessible corpus for elementary learners might consist of those texts so far encountered in learning the foreign language). On the other hand, authentic data seem more likely to help the learner understand how reference to prototypes is made in a particular area of practice, illustrating how, for instance, newspapers use *a bridge too far* either with a pun on the literal sense of *bridge*, or in allusive variants such as *a call / a fridge too far* (Aston, forthcoming a).

Above all, I would argue that corpora should be seen as providing opportunities to engage in discourse as well as to analyse it. The growing amount of machine-readable text available, and the increasing sophistication of retrieval software, means that teachers and learners can put together their own subcorpora as a hypertextual environment in which to move from one text or concordance to another, switching between roles of participant and analyst. Widdowson has recently questioned the assumption that experience of use can provide an adequate basis for language learning, stressing the need for learners to notice linguistic patternings (Schmidt 1990), and proposing the use of activities which are 'contrived to bring linguistic features to conscious awareness' (Widdowson 1993d: 313). Because of the facility with which discourse participation can be combined with the analysis of textual recurrences, corpus use seems to offer one means whereby this requirement can be indirectly met.

18

Transcultural creativity in world Englishes and literary canons

BRAJ B. KACHRU

Introduction

THE *ṢAṢṬIPŪRTI* CELEBRATION of Henry Widdowson is an appropriate occasion on which to consider his various insightful contributions to several dimensions of applied linguistics. One major dimension of his research has been his important studies in literary creativity and stylistics. This paper[1] is an attempt to provide another perspective on stylistics: that of the multilingual's creativity in world English literatures. My first aim is to argue that the generally held view that the 'mother tongue' is the main medium for literary creativity is only partially true, and the second aim is to show that the role of 'translation' and 'transcreation'[2] in the bilingual's creativity has usually been underestimated. The texture of the bilingual's creativity is essentially the result of the processes of translation and transcreation, and insightful approaches to stylistics—its theory and methodology—must take this fact into consideration. This is particularly true of transcultural creativity in world Englishes.

In recent years there has been a vibrant debate on literary creativity in the *mother* tongue, as opposed to the *other* tongue. The debate is essentially concerned with the 'transculturational process', its manifestations in world Englishes, and the resultant canon formation.[3] At the root of this debate is the generally held view that literary creativity is essentially undertaken in one's mother tongue, and that creativity in the other tongue is an exception—a rare activity, and a break from the norm. This view of creativity is prevalent in the societies that prefer to view themselves as monolingual, as opposed to bi- or multilingual. This perception is also present in what may be termed the folk view of literary creativity.

The view that literary creativity in the other tongue is an exception is not restricted to lay persons—that would perhaps be understandable—but is also a widely held view in the scholarly community. One excerpt from a distinguished North American social scientist, Edward Shills, and a second from a respected British linguist, David Crystal, will illustrate the point. Shills (1988: 560) claims that:

> The national language of literary creation is almost always the *language of the author's original nationality*; there are, of course, exceptions, such as Conrad, and, at a lower level, Nabokov and Koestler, Apollonaire and Julien Green. But for writing about public or political matters, a foreign language is often used effectively [emphasis added].[4]

Crystal's response to a question concerning the difference between people who have native-speaker awareness of a language and those who do not is more mystifying. Crystal asserts (cited in Paikeday 1985: 66–67) that 'it is quite unclear what to make of cases like Nabokov and the others George Steiner (*Extraterritorial papers*) talks about as having no native language. But these are marginal cases.' And, elaborating on who is a 'native speaker' (of English), Crystal continues (ibid.: 68):

> I know several foreigners whose command of English I could not fault, but they themselves deny they are native speakers. When pressed on this point, they draw attention to . . . their lack of childhood associations, their limited passive knowledge of varieties, the fact that there are some topics which they are more 'comfortable' discussing in their first language. 'I couldn't make love in English,' said one man to me.

The views of Shills and Crystal only partially reflect the contexts of literary creativity across speech communities, particularly in the multilingual societies. The attitude towards one's mother tongue (however the term is defined) depends on a variety of factors: the role of the mother tongue in various domains, the status of the mother tongue in the hierarchy of languages, and questions of identity.

[272]

And let me illustrate the question of identity from my own mother tongue—Kashmiri. One might ask: why has the Kashmiri language traditionally not been used in literary creativity? Why have the creative writers from Kashmir preferred another language for such creativity, for example, Sanskrit, Persian, Urdu, Hindi, and English? It is not for lack of a literary tradition in Kashmiri. Actually, good specimens of literary creativity in Kashmiri date back to the fourteenth century, in Lalleshwarī's (born c.1335) *vāks* ('verse-sayings'). A partial answer to the question is found in a *masnavī*[5] composed by Lachman Rainā (d. 1898), who adopted Persian for composing poetry:

Writing verse in Kashmiri
   is groping in the dark.
If you would shine as candle-flame,
   write in Persian verse;
You merely waste your talent if
   you write in Kashmiri.
For you would not the jasmine hide
   in a nettle bush,
nor edible oil or spices waste
   on a dish of mallow wild.
But times have changed and Persian is
   no longer read,
and radish and loaf-sugar is
   relished alike.[6]

It is not only that at one time the language of literary creativity in Kashmir was Persian (see Tikku 1971), but Persian also provided the standards of comparison for Kashmiri writers, a sort of a literary yardstick: Maḥmūd Gāmī of Shāhābād, a Kashmiri poet, was called the Niẓāmī of Kashmir, and Waḥab Pare, another Kashmiri poet, was considered the Firdausī of Kashmir (Kachru 1981b: 34–5).[7]

In such multilingual societies, as the language of creativity changes, the models for creativity and experimentation also change: one sees this in the creativity of Kashmiris in Sanskrit, Hindi, Urdu, and in English. Kashmiri, of course, provides an example of a minority language. But what applies to Kashmiri can also be seen on a larger scale in several major languages in South Asia or other multilingual regions of the world. The language of literary creativity—even a transplanted language—has traditionally been élitist and in most of the world an élitist language has generally been the mother tongue of a mere fraction of the population of the users of that language.

Transcultural creativity and types of cultural crossover

In transcultural creativity, cultural crossover entails a cline. There are essentially three types of crossover. The first type occurs within a speech fellowship: the members of a speech fellowship generally have shared underlying sociocultural resources. The linguistic resources may be somewhat different, though to a large extent there is mutual intelligibility (for example, in India between the speakers of Dogri and Punjabi, Hindi and Awadhi,[8] regional dialects of English and educated English).

The second type of crossover occurs within speech communities sharing broadly identical literary, cultural, and religious canons, as is generally the case between the Dravidian south and the Indo-Aryan north in India. One might label this situation as linguistic divergence but underlying cultural identity. In such contexts, although there are linguistic differences, several processes of convergence may be identical, as is the case with the processes of Sanskritization, Persianization, and the ongoing process of Englishization in this region.

The third type of crossover takes place within speech communities which are culturally, sociolinguistically, and linguistically divergent. Their cultural, linguistic, and literary canons are distinct. The transcultural creativity in the Outer Circle[9] of world Englishes is of this type.

Measuring intercultural crossover

The existence of intercultural crossover and its various manifestations in transcultural creativity is not in doubt. The question which is yet unanswered to full satisfaction is how to measure intercultural crossover.

A number of criteria have been used to characterize the complexities of such crossover in a literary text. Smith has proposed the use of three key concepts: *intelligibility*, *comprehensibility*, and *interpretability* (see Smith 1992; Smith and Nelson 1985). The Smith triad may be explained as follows.

The term *intelligibility* refers to surface decoding of a linguistic utterance. It has been shown that in several varieties of world Englishes a number of lexical items present no problem in decoding the denotative meaning, but that what is essential is to comprehend the extended meaning, which involves the crossover in literary texts.

The second stage of the triad is termed *comprehensibility*—that is, comprehension of a text of one variety of English within the context of situation of another variety. Consider, for example, the following formations: *cowdung cakes, salt giver*, and *twice-born* in their extended meaning in Indian English. One has to go beyond the lexical meaning—from denotation to connotation. One has to focus on the culture-specific meanings which the above formations have acquired in Indian English. At this level, *cowdung cakes* has a functional and ritualistic meaning among Hindus; *salt giver* expresses gratitude in the sense that 'one has done a good deed for you'; and *twice-born* conveys a vital stage in one's initiation into Brahminhood, from one's natural birth to a second 'birth' as a Brahmin. In other words, an intelligible linguistic item acquires a function within a specific sociocultural context. Consider, for example, the translation of *hazūr kā namak khātē hain* in Indian novelist Premchand's (1881–1939) short story 'Shatranj ke khilārī' ('The chess players').[10] Three renderings of this construction in English are as follows (see Gargesh 1989: 67–8):

1 We are your devoted slaves.

2 We have eaten your salt.

3 We are loyal to our master.

The third stage is that of *interpretability*: contextualization of the text within the variables which are appropriate for it within the context of its source language. This goal for making text explicit has traditionally been accomplished by adding commentaries to translations, for example, those of sacred texts such as the Bible, the Bhagwad Gita, and so on. It is at the level of interpretability that one establishes the relationship of a text with an appropriate context-language seen as an exponent of culture. In the case of world English literatures, it would mean 'reincarnating' English into *local* culture.

Text types and contexts

It is this 'reincarnated' culture-specificity of world Englishes that has contributed to the institutionalization of canons of English literatures in Asia and Africa. It is again due to these processes that claims of the 'decolonization' of English have been made (see, for example, Dissanayake 1985; Kachru 1992a; Thumboo 1992). A number of aspects of such culture-specific texts, particularly of politeness, class and caste hierarchy, persuasion, and apologies in world Englishes, have been insightfully discussed by Y. Kachru (1991). Let me go back to Kashmiri and present an example of the speech act of *greeting* in that language:

A *kɔt chivɨ gatshān*
where are (HON.) going?
'where are you (HON.) going?'

B *bas yɔt tām*
just here up to
'just up to here'

A *kyah karni?*
what to do?
'For what?'

B *bas yithay*
just for nothing
'nothing'

Contrast this speech act with American or British English greetings. This 'inquisitive' and 'probing' speech act is not only unacceptable, but also conveys 'nosiness' from the English or North American perspective. And now, multiply a variety of such culture-specific speech acts in a large text, a short story, a novel, and add to that the underlying cultural and literary assumptions from India, Singapore, and Nigeria: the result is a shared medium but divergent cultural manifestations (see Kachru 1995). Two examples of this divergence are Shashi Tharoor's novel *The Great Indian Story* (1989) and the recent, much acclaimed novel of Vikram Seth, *A Suitable Boy* (1993).

Linguistic and cultural issues in transcreating a text

Whatever underlying theoretical and methodological frameworks one adopts, it is clear that transcreating a text poses a variety of challenges. Let me again revert to Kashmiri to illustrate this point by giving my own translation[11] of a sonnet entitled 'Zūn' ('The Moon'), composed by Dīnā Nāth Nādim (1916–1988).

The moon rose like a tsoṭ

That day, the *tsoṭ*-like moon ascended behind the hills
looking
wan and worn like a gown of Pompur tweed
with a tattered collar and loose collar-bands,
revealing
sad scars over her silvery skin.
She was weary and tired
and lusterless
as a counterfeit pallid rupee-coin
deceitfully given to an unsuspecting woman labourer
by a wily master.
The *tsoṭ*-like moon ascended
and the hills grew hungry.
The clouds were slowly putting out their cooking fires.
But the forest nymphs began to kindle their oven fires.
And steaming rice seemed to shoot up
over the hill tops.
And, murmuring hope to my starving belly,
I gazed and gazed at the promising sky.

What this translation illustrates is that cultural and linguistic crossover is a cline and the linguistic and cultural 'distance' of a text may increase or decrease in terms of the three variables in the Smith triad discussed above.

The task of contextualization becomes progressively more complex as one crosses the shared, and partially shared literary, cultural, and sociolinguistic canons, and the shared knowledge concerning such canons. One has to go through a process of, as it were, redefining and recontextualizing the text with each crossover.

The genre of sonnet in Kashmiri is patterned on the English sonnet, and it is a recent literary innovation in Kashmiri in which Nādim excelled. The Kashmiriization of the sonnet form is obvious in many ways. First, by the use of what may be termed 'culture-dependent' lexis; for example, *tsoṭ* 'Kashmiri nān'; *tani* 'collar-band'; *mɔzrəñ* 'a female laborer'; *ṭhēkidār* 'contractor'; *gɔ̌* 'a traditional place for cooking'; *vɔthidān* 'a traditional portable oven for cooking'. Second, by the use of fixed collocations which entail shared knowledge of the local (in this case Kashmiri) context, for example, *põmpur poṭ* 'tweed made in Pompur town'. Third, the use of language-specific fixed collocations and idioms. Consider, for example, the following:

> *batɨkul' khasɨñ*
> cooked rice trees (plural) to grow
> 'to have trees resembling cooked rice'

> *šech bāvɨñ*
> 'to share a secret'

> *əch phər' phər' vuchun*
> eyes turn turn to see
> 'to gaze incessantly'

> *pani pani gatshun*
> thread thread to happen
> 'to fall apart (to be very tired)'

> *phākɨ phor*
> hungry stomach
> 'to be hungry'

Fourth, the use of phonaesthetic features, for example, as in the following line in Kashmiri.

> *rɔpɨ tani hani hani pani pani gãmɨts põmpɨr' poṭ hiš.*

There is no way this phonaesthetic effect can be created in a translation.

This much about the segmentation. Now let me explain some other features of the text. The metaphor *zūn* ('the moon') as *tsoṭ* (Kashmiri nān 'bread') is very potent and suggestive. The personification of the moon is consistent with Indian mythology and literary tradition. But, in Nādim, there is a shift in such personification. In this sonnet, the depiction of the moon as *tsoṭ* acquires centrality. It evokes the feelings which are traditionally associated with the moon in Indian literature and folklore. But there the similarity ends. Consider also the range of lexis which occupies the modifier position: 'the collar-bands are loose' is a sign of grief; among the Kashmiri Pandits 'loose collar-bands' are indicators of mourning. The moon is lusterless 'like a counterfeit pallid rupee-coin' deceitfully passed on with other coins to an unsuspecting woman laborer by a wily contractor. The skyscape further intensifies the suggestion of unsatisfied hunger: the clouds 'put out their cooking fires', the forest nymphs 'kindle their oven fires' and steaming rice seems to 'shoot up over the hill tops'. And what does the laborer do? 'Murmuring hope to her starving belly, she gazes at the promising sky.'

There are several questions one can ask about the underlying context of the sonnet. How relevant is it to mention that Nādim was an active member of the Progressive Writers Association, a leftist political and cultural organization, which dominated the literary scene of South Asia in the post-1930s, and to note that in this sonnet there is a conscious effort to neutralize his style—not to use Persianized or Sanskritized varieties of Kashmiri? And the major point is: how does transcreation in Punjabi, Hindi, Tamil, or, in our specific case in English, recreate the devices and strategies used for 'foregrounding'[12] by Nādim? These questions have faced translators—and creative writers—since the first cross-linguistic translation was attempted, or since literary creativity in the 'other' tongue was attempted.

The English version of Nādim's poem given above illustrates that the transcreation of the text results in marginal crossover—it is mere approximation. The complexities are at the lexical, collocational, syntactic, phonaesthetic, and sociocultural levels. And this limitation of 'translation' is generally well recognized.

And now, turning to transcultural creativity in world Englishes, we see that the 'in-betweenness' of two or more languages and of two or more sociocultural contexts has not been explored with methodological rigor in stylistics.

World English literatures and transcultural canons

Let me go back to the above observations of Shills and Crystal. Their claim actually is that literary creativity as an artistic manifestation is restricted to one's 'mother tongue', or to one's 'native language'. This claim is close to the position of the Romantics, who emphasized that 'each language has its mystery and its soul, and that these are very sacred things' (Forster 1970: 7). In the Romantic view, the secret to this mystery is available only to the 'native speaker'. That there is not enough evidence to support such a hypothesis about the 'mother tongue' and its relationship to literary creativity is a different story, and I will not go into that here.

However, there is another manifestation of literary creativity—more widespread than the first type—that is common among bi- and multi-linguals who engage in creativity in two or more languages. There are a number of creative writers who write in more than one language— their 'mother' tongue and the 'other' tongue. In India, for example, as Paranjape (1993: 5) observes, '. . . most of the Indian poets in English have been bilingual or have at least translated from Indian languages.' The creativity of such multilingual writers is based on conflation of two or more languages, and the basic ingredients are 'translation', 'transfer', and 'transcreation', used in the broadest senses of those processes.[13]

There are several explanations why, in linguistics, literary criticism, and stylistics, the 'native language' and its 'pure' form have been considered as the 'norm' and as the 'expected' tools for literary creativity. In reality, this view is in conflict with what actually has been the tradition of literary creativity in most of the multilingual world, involving large parts of Europe. In Forster's brief but well-argued study he has shown that it is not difficult to see that 'the idea of polyglot poets should seem rather less strange than it may well have done at first' (1970: 7).

I have yet to explain what motivated my long digression on translation and transcreation, and on the Smith triad concerning intelligibility. My explanation is that there are several unique characteristics in transcultural creativity in world Englishes which may be explained with reference to these processes. In such texts one first notices that

[280]

there is an underlying scaffolding, as it were, for formal patterning of the text from another language. In the case of the Nigerian novelist Amos Tutuola, it is Yoruba, and in the case of the Indian novelists Raja Rao and Mulk Raj Anand, it is Kannada and Punjabi respectively. One also sees that the formal patterning and linguistic conflation is not always conscious. In establishing such an equivalence, a creative writer obviously has to make several choices. The writer can do what Amos Tutuola and Mulk Raj Anand have done in terms of equivalence to keep the English text close to Yoruba and Punjabi-Hindustani respectively. A writer may take another track, for example, that of Raja Rao, and establish equivalence not at the lexical level or in terms of just the speech functions; Rao goes much beyond lexis and creates a distinct discourse.

This strategy is evident in Rao's *Kanthapura* and *The Serpent and the Rope*—one representing the vernacular style of the mother tongue, and the other of Sanskritization. It is almost a case of recreation or transfer of the diglossic situation of his 'mother tongue' into English. In such literary creation much depends on how close the bilingual writer wants to remain to the formal patterning of the *other* language.

The third aspect of such texts relates to the type of link a creative writer desires to establish with the earlier native literary traditions— oral and/or written. In the case of Amos Tutuola, the link is essentially with the oral Nigerian tradition, and in Raja Rao's *The Serpent and the Rope* the link is with the classical (High) Sanskritic tradition. In both cases, the desire is to establish an ancestral link between one's creativity and the past tradition. And this connection with the past is essential, as T. S. Eliot (1951) reminds us:

> [. . .] we shall often find that not only the best, but the most individual parts of his [a poet's] work may be those in which the dead poets, his ancestors, assert their immortality most vigorously [. . .] No poet, no artist of any art, has his complete meaning alone.

It is by establishing such a connection with the past—with the 'ancestors'—that an African or Asian creative writer in English introduces the native literary and cultural tradition to the 'other' language. It is through such strategies that the process of 'decolonization' of English is initiated and accelerated, and its distinctness in terms of new canons is established.

Transcreation as a tool of power

The translator's task is far from innocent. We see translation as a tool of power in many contexts. FitzGerald's translation of the *rubais* of Omar Khayyam is a good example of the use of such power. In this translation, he demonstrates immense artistic capacity for transcreation, and reveals his attitude towards the Persians as people and as creative writers. FitzGerald's originality as an unsurpassed translator is widely acclaimed. However, what is less well known is his ethnocentricity and his disdain for the Persians as masters of the art of poetry. While discussing the 'liberties' he took in his translation of Omar Khayyam, FitzGerald (cited in Lefevere 1990: 19) wrote to a friend:

> It is an amusement for me to take what Liberties I like with these Persians who (as I think) are not Poets enough to frighten me from such excursions, and who really want a little Art to shape them.

And, commenting on this outpouring of FitzGerald, Lefevere warns us that 'FitzGerald would never have taken the same liberties with Greek or Roman authors' (ibid.: 19).

Perhaps not. However, Lefevere is making a broad generalization. That is evident when we read T. S. Eliot's attack on the translation of Euripides by Gilbert Murray (see Eliot 1960 and Murray 1910). Eliot feels strongly that in Murray's translation of *Medea*, 'the Greek brevity' is sacrificed 'to fit the loose frame of William Morris, and blurs the Greek lyric to the fluid haze of Swinburne' (cited in Das 1989: 34).

What a translator does to a specific text depends on the translator's creativity. Das, discussing the English version of *Medea*, is right in saying (1989: 33) that it 'does not belong to English literature, nor does it belong to Greek, though in some sense it belongs to both'. Das is right. A translator functions between languages, between two or more formal systems and their contextual connotations. The translator makes choices in creating a desired effect. In crossover and 'blending' of two or more systems a text is reincarnated.

The situation in creativity in world Englishes is not different from this. It is in this formal and contextual 'in-betweenness' that a bilingual writer in world Englishes creates complexities in relation to Smith's three levels of intelligibility, comprehensibility, and interpretability.

BRAJ B. KACHRU

Transcultural creativity as a linguistic 'weapon'

The stylistic innovations in transcultural varieties of world Englishes have yet another dimension which remains to be studied in detail. That is using various stylistic devices as a linguistic 'weapon', as it were, to alter the 'colonial' language to give it a new identity, and as Soyinka says ([1978] 1993: 88), to turn English into 'a new medium'. Soyinka explains it thus:

> The unaccustomed role which such a language is forced to play turns it indeed into a new medium of communication and simultaneously forges a new organic series of mores, social goals, relationships, universal awareness—all of which go into the creating of a new culture.

And he is, of course, right to emphasize that

> where language is involved, we have at our disposal evidence of the revolutionary use to which the language of the oppressor has been put in oppressed societies.
> (ibid.: 88)

The list of such users is extensive indeed, both in historical terms and in terms of the countries it covers. The list includes African, African-American, and South and East Asian writers, political thinkers and social reformers. In their hands we see, as Soyinka asserts, 'the conversion of the enslaving medium into an insurgent weapon'. And Soyinka uses a powerful image to convey his point:

> Black people twisted the linguistic blade in the hands of the traditional cultural castrator and carved new concepts onto the flesh of white supremacy. The customary linguistic usage was rejected outright and a new, raw, urgent and revolutionary syntax was given to this medium which had become the greatest single repository of racist concepts.
> (ibid.: 88)

In the perception of the colonized creative writer, then, the English language was to be redeemed from its exhaustion; it had to be revived with fresh linguistic energy, and it needed planned strategies for stylistic innovations to answer African, Asian, and Caribbean challenges. The linguistic 'weapon' had to be redefined. In Bhabha's view (1994: 166):

[283]

[. . .] Salman Rushdie's *The Satanic Verses* attempts to redefine the boundaries of the Western nation, so that the 'foreignness of languages' becomes the inescapable cultural condition for the enunciation of the mother-tongue. In the 'Rosa Diamond' section of *The Satanic Verses* Rushdie seems to suggest that it is only through the process of *dissemiNation*—of meaning, time, peoples, cultural boundaries and historical traditions—that the radical alterity of the national culture will create new forms of living and writing.

Stylistic studies of transcultural texts have only marginally analyzed such writing in world Englishes from these perspectives.

World Englishes and stylistics

The honoree of this volume, Henry Widdowson, has explored several dimensions of applied stylistics. In his usual insightful way, he has discussed the relationship between the linguistic sciences and stylistics, and has provided useful guiding-points to a teacher of literature (Widdowson 1975, 1992a). However, we have yet to develop appropriate theoretical and methodological frameworks for the study of transcultural creativity in non-Western world Englishes. This fast-expanding and well-established body of writing has yet to attain the status it deserves in the departments of English language and literature, and in the ESL curricula. The types of questions raised by the translation of Nādim's 'Zūn' ('The Moon') into English concerning cultural crossover are to a large extent identical to those we need to answer in explaining the creativity of bilingual writers in world Englishes. The conceptualization of stylistics must go beyond the confines of monolingual paradigms. Literary creativity in Englishes is as much a part of the West African or South Asian canon as it is a part of world Englishes. In understanding these canons, and various strategies of canon formation, one cannot underestimate *translation* as one of the significant ingredients of such creativity.

One has to agree with Lefevere (1990: 24) that there are two major reasons why the role of translation in the creative process has generally been ignored or underestimated. The first reason, as Lefevere says, is that 'for the literary historian translation had to do with "language" only, not with literature'. That, of course, is a very restricted view of creativity. The second reason is 'another pernicious outgrowth of the "monolingualization" of literary history by Romantic historiographers intent on "national" literatures preferably as *uncontaminated* as possible by foreign influence' (emphasis added).

And viewed from these perspectives, transcultural creativity in English is 'contaminated' on many counts: it is not a part of a 'national' literature as the term is generally understood; it shows deep linguistic and cultural convergence and contact—actually, it may reflect more than one 'influence'—as is true of many literary traditions of South Asia, to give just one example of such traditions. These attitudinal concerns are only part of the story. A more fundamental reason for this inattention to processes of translation is that we have shown no interest in formulating approaches to stylistics which would account for the bilingual's creativity, and for transcultural creativity.

The story in this case is not much different when we compare it to our understanding of the bilingual's grammar. World English literatures essentially manifest the diversity view of literary creativity and canon formation. Our approaches to linguistic and literary creativity of bilinguals must be based on such perspectives. And I am using the term 'diversity view' without any political connotations.[14]

Conclusion

In conclusion, then, this paper makes three claims. The first claim is that the bilingual's creativity is the result of a textual and contextual blend of two literary and cultural canons—that of the 'native' language and culture and that of the 'other' tongue. The result of this bi-ness is another canon of creativity, as we see, for example, in West African English and South Asian English (see Kachru 1995). The second claim is that the conscious or unconscious processes of translation at various levels play a very vital role in establishing the cultural and linguistic distinctiveness in the text. And finally, that the 'monolingualization' of approaches to stylistics is inadequate to provide insightful analyses of texts in world Englishes. Our approaches have to be liberated from the prison of monolingual biases in order to provide theoretical and methodological answers to the challenges which the bilingual's creativity poses.[15]

Notes

1 In this paper I have attempted to elaborate some of the arguments presented in Kachru 1995. In a sense, then, this paper is a follow-up of the earlier paper. I am grateful to Cecil L. Nelson for his comments on this paper.

2 Following the Indian English poet P. Lal, I use the term 'translation' to refer to a one-to-one correspondence between source and target language, and the term 'transcreation' to refer to an attempt to recreate the source language text in the target language.

3 I will not explain the elusive concept 'canon' or 'canon formation' in this paper. I have briefly discussed this concept with reference to world Englishes in Kachru 1995.

4 Perhaps by 'language of the author's original nationality' Shills is referring to the 'mother tongue'. It is obvious that in multilingual societies—for example, in India—national language(s), and the language of literary creativity are not necessarily identical.

5 *Masnavī* is a Persian literary form borrowed by Kashmiri writers.

6 See Kaul (1945: 175), from which this translation is taken.

7 Firdausī (d. AD 1020–1026) and Niẓāmī (AD c.1250–1300) are two of the most distinguished Persian poets. The yardsticks for comparison provide valuable clues to the attitudes toward one's own language and the language of comparison.

8 Dogri is spoken in the Jammu province of the Jammu and Kashmir state of India. Awadhi is traditionally considered a dialect of Hindi; it is spoken in eastern Uttar Pradesh.

9 For discussion of the term 'Outer Circle' see note 1 on page 182.

10 Premchand was one of the most innovative novelists in Hindi and Urdu.

11 Published in Kachru 1981b.

12 The term 'foregrounding' is used here in the sense in which it is used in the Prague School of linguistics.

13 Paranjape's list (1993: 5) includes the following names: Toru Dutt, Manmohan Ghose, Sri Aurobindo, Rabindranath Tagore, Puran Singh, Sri Ananda Acharya, Nissim Ezekiel, A. K. Ramanujan, R. Parthasarathy, Pritish Nandy, A. K. Mehrotra, Arun Kolatkar, Jayanta Mahapatra, Dilip Chitre, Saleem Peeradina, and Agha Shahid Ali. The situation is not much different in Africa or other parts of Asia.

14 Discussing the creativity of Indian writer C. V. Desani, Anthony Burgess refers to his use of language as 'a sort of creative chaos'. He says:

> It is the language that makes the book a sort of creative chaos that grumbles at the restraining banks. It is what may be termed whole language in which philosophical terms, the colloquialism of Calcutta and London, Shakespearean archaisms, bazar writings, quack spiels, references to the Hindu pantheon, the jargon of litigation, and shrill babu irritability seethe together. It is not pure English; it is like the English of Shakespeare, Joyce, Kipling, gloriously impure (cited in Dissanayake 1989: xviii).

15 See, for example, B. Kachru 1992b, Y. Kachru 1994, and Sridhar and Sridhar 1992.

19

An approach to the teaching and learning of poetry in Nigeria

JOSEPH O. BISONG

IN HIS PAPER, 'The teaching, learning and study of literature' (Widdowson 1985b), Widdowson makes a distinction between *learning* literature and *studying* literature. Learning literature he defines as getting to know how to read literature, a performance that ensures that the student comes to grips with the way language is deployed in literature to create a different order of reality. Studying literature he sees as a rational enquiry aimed at acquiring knowledge of and about literature. The study of literature can be done successfully, he argues, only when the student has first learnt how to read it. 'The task for literature teaching, then,' he writes, 'is . . . to develop a pedagogy which will guide learners towards an independent ability to read literature for themselves, as a precondition for subsequent study' (Widdowson 1985b: 186). This distinction between study and learning is for Widdowson of crucial importance, and he believes that 'the lack of progress in literature teaching can in large part be attributed to a failure to recognize it' (ibid.: 184).

I want to explore some of the implications of this distinction for the teaching and learning of poetry at secondary and tertiary levels in Nigeria. I shall begin by detailing what the current situation is with regard to the teaching and learning of literature in English, particularly poetry, and then go on to examine critically the sorts of changes that a serious consideration of the distinction might lead to. In the process I shall be revisiting some familiar issues: the integration of language and literature in teaching, the relevance of translation, the aim of teaching poetry, what is involved in experiencing a poem, and the value of such experience. In the course of discussing these matters, I shall also suggest and attempt to justify a particular approach to the teaching of poetry.

First, some background information that may be useful for the discussion. The present structure of the education system in the country expects pupils to spend six years in the primary school, three in the junior secondary school, three in the senior secondary school, and four in the university. The transition from mother tongue to English is effected in the last three years of the primary school. Thereafter English takes over as the medium of instruction and the pupil expects to pursue the rest of his or her education in English. Thus after the first three years of primary school, English becomes both a subject in the curriculum and the language in which all subsequent formal learning takes place. This at any rate is what is outlined in the national policy on education. It is probably fair to say that in the main the policy is adhered to, subject to the availability of English teachers in some parts of the country.

Teaching and learning literature in English: the current situation

Literature teaching in secondary and tertiary institutions in Nigeria, as in a number of other ESL countries, is still very much an uncertain business. Now and again concerns are voiced about what literature to teach at school and how to teach it. These concerns have over the years resulted in certain changes in the English literature curriculum in secondary schools. Texts by African authors now feature prominently in the list from which selections are made. This no doubt reflects the prevailing mood of freedom from linguistic and cultural imperialism and the need to assert cultural identity. But it seems to me that the more important question about how to initiate learners into the activity of reading and appreciating works of literature for themselves has not been properly addressed. Nor has there been a serious consideration of the use of literature, particularly poetry, in language learning. The school syllabus attempts to give some direction. *The National Curriculum for Junior Secondary Schools*, for instance, envisages an 'English studies' programme, requiring teachers of English at this level to provide a good blend of language and literature and achieve some form of integration in their teaching. It even suggests appropriate literary texts. But what actually happens in practice is another matter. Because of lack of confidence in their ability to handle literary texts in a language class, teachers at this level either avoid literature altogether or make half-hearted attempts to get pupils to read the texts in class. For more advanced students the teaching method employed, as some writers have observed (Rodger 1983; Banjo 1985; Widdowson 1985b), is mainly that inherited long ago from a first language context. The teachers *assume that the learners can read the literary work* and so proceed to discuss aspects of the work that should properly engage the attention of anyone *studying* it. In their teaching they lay emphasis on what they consider most important in the novel or poem and expect learners to study the work and come to their own conclusions based on their firsthand experience of the work. The approach is judged successful if in the end the learners are able to make critical judgements about the work. But of course the learners find it extremely difficult to make the expected judgements on their own because they have had no systematic training in how to read literary works. So, to get through the course and face their examinations with confidence they are tempted to rely on what Rodger (1983) aptly describes as 'the plethora of lucrative study guides marketed by some of the more economically enterprising but less academically illustrious former alumni'. The situation is sometimes reminiscent of Chinua Achebe's description of Onitsha as 'a self-confident place where a man would not be deterred even by insufficient learning from aspiring to teach and improve his fellows—and making a little profit as well'. As substitutes for the firsthand experience of literary works, these study guides and notes have over the years become so popular with learners that teachers have themselves resorted to producing them in order to get a share of the lucrative market. In the universities, lecturers' 'handouts' (a curious but popular name for their notes, which students are usually under pressure to buy) are threatening to become the main instrument for teaching and learning, with dire consequences for education (see Bisong 1991).

Poetry presents particular difficulties for learners in this environment. Although they may be familiar with proverbs, riddles, and praise songs in the oral tradition, learners find written poetry complex and difficult. Part of the problem lies in the unfamiliarity of the written form. 'Written literature', Banjo (1985) observes, 'is still something fairly strange to the Nigerian cultures.' Even where learners are used to reading novels or short stories, they still have difficulties with the form of printed verse. In discussing the case of printed lyric poetry Widdowson (1987a) puts his finger on the problem. He writes:

> The arrangement of language into parallel lines, the patterns of verse form and rhyme scheme all conspire to deny the ordinary procedures of online processing. Instead of the single dimension of temporal sequence, we have a two-dimensional spatial disposition of language. The lines in a poem vertically arrayed, counteract linearity. These prosodic constituents do not correspond with the syntactic devices which are conventionally used for the organisation of meaning. (Widdowson 1987a: 243)

The 'prosodic constituents' of verse may not inhibit learners' initial access to meaning. It is the *appearance* of the printed words on the page, the strangeness of this arrangement and the complex demands it makes on the reader, that leaves some Nigerian learners, who are unused to processing written poetry, discouraged from the start. The initial shocked reaction of 'What is this and why must I bother with it?' stubbornly remains with most learners with each new encounter even after considerable progress has been made with a few poems by both teachers and learners. The latter somehow remain unconvinced that the effort necessary to understand and appreciate poems is worth making. Consequently, the uphill task faced by teachers in this situation often discourages all but the most dedicated.

But while lack of familiarity with the genre may be the reason for the difficulties learners have with poetry, a good number of them are put off by fear. Poetry for speakers of English as a second language has unfortunately acquired the reputation of being difficult, so that young learners suffer from a psychological barrier when they encounter it. What these learners have heard from their peers are mostly discouraging comments about the problems encountered in the attempt to read poems. So they have come to believe that poetry is a region of knowledge and experience that is impenetrable because of its inherent difficulty. We now have a situation in Nigeria in which learners who want to get through their study of English with the minimum of unpleasantness instinctively avoid poetry in the sincere belief that in doing so they are escaping from one of life's unnecessary problems! These are perhaps the kinds of people that Wole Soyinka describes as

Grey presences of head and hands
Who wander still
Adrift from understanding.
(From 'In Memory of Segun Awolowo')

It is probably fair to add that a contributing factor to the avoidance of poetry by young learners is the fact that the language and imagery of a lot of Nigerian poetry in English presents problems which even adult readers have difficulty coming to terms with. 'Most good Nigerian poetry written in English', argues Banjo (1985), '. . . turns out to be a conundrum for most highly educated Nigerians, for the act of literary creation in a second language situation is necessarily a bicultural and bilingual process for which few consumers are adequately prepared.'

Learning poetry: some implications of Widdowson's distinction

What changes in the teaching and learning of poetry will a serious consideration of Widdowson's distinction between learning literature and studying literature lead to? Widdowson, we had earlier pointed out, sees the literature teacher's task as that of guiding learners 'towards an independent ability to read literature for themselves, as a precondition for subsequent study'. I would want to argue that the inability of learners to read poetry for themselves is the main reason why they seek to avoid poetry and conclude that the effort required to process the text and experience the work at first hand is not worth it. The lack of ability to read poetry and experience it first hand is also the reason why many learners resort to packaged ready-made critical judgements culled from the ever popular 'notes'. We should also keep in mind the fact that most learners in this environment come from societies and cultures that are still severely traditional in the sense that respect for authority is strong. Thus it is easy for learners here to have undue reverence for the printed text, teachers' notes, and received critical opinion. Such learners see their role as one of unquestioning submission to the pronouncements of teachers or the stipulations of textbooks.

How should teachers seek to develop in learners the desire to read poetry and the willingness to learn how to read it? One way could be to start off young learners with simple printed poetry of the traditional cut where a straightforward acknowledgement of the rhythm is all the response that is often required. This would be drawing on territory familiar to the learner. An example:

A chain-rhyme

If a jackal bothers you, show him a hyena,
If a hyena bothers you, show him a lion,
If a lion bothers you, show him an elephant,
If an elephant bothers you, show him a hunter,
If a hunter bothers you, show him a snake,
If a snake bothers you, show him a stick,
If a stick bothers you, show it a fire,
If a fire bothers you, show it a river,
If a river bothers you, show it a wind,
If a wind bothers you, show it God.
(Traditional Fulani)

The lines give advice on how to overcome particular problems. This advice, couched in the form of a song, embodies the collective experience, beliefs, and wisdom of a people which are often transmitted orally from one generation to another. Learners may be led to note the repeated structure of each of the conditional sentences that make up the poem. The first half of each line is what the lead singer would sing, and the second half is the refrain or chorus that would come from other singers in the group or everyone else around. Thus:

LEAD SINGER: If a jackal bothers you . . .
CHORUS: . . . show him a hyena.
LEAD SINGER: If a hyena bothers you . . .
CHORUS: . . . show him a lion.
    (and so on)

The fairly regular beat of each line would lend the song easily to a dance accompaniment. This is in fact a typical example of a traditional song usually acccompanied by drumming and dancing. Young learners are likely to be attracted by the easy response which this sort of poem invites and they would be pleasantly surprised to discover that poetry can be enjoyed. This would go a long way towards reducing the dread of poetry. Something else is gained which is crucial for the reading of poetry: since the lines are presented on the page as a poem—the appearance does after all achieve what Widdowson (1987a) describes as 'the culmination of graphological craft, the very apotheosis of print'—learners without realizing it begin to consider them as having representational significance rather than referential meaning (see Widdowson 1992a). Each of the conditional clauses can now be seen as implying more than what the words actually state, an instance of any of life's myriad problems rather than a particular problem. Understood in this way, the poem takes on greater significance: every problem in life has a solution. The game of life is to confront the problem and find a solution. This move from referential to representational meaning, although it may be embryonic at this stage, is an important step for learners in this environment because it leads to an understanding of the way all verbal art functions.

It is easy for learners to offer other examples of traditional songs from their individual cultures. Teachers could then move on from this sort of rhythmic verse to examples that invite discussion and a somewhat more complex response. The following would fit the bill.

> Young lady, you are:
> A mirror that must not go out in the sun
> A child that must not be touched by dew
> One that is dressed up in hair
> A lamp with which people find their way
> Moon that shines bright
> An eagle feather won by a husband
> A straight line drawn by God.
> (Traditional Ibo)

As Moody (1983) points out in his discussion of the poem, this is 'a series of attributes of female charm in increasing order of power, leading to a climax which is powerful enough to leave nothing more to be said'. Yet the structure is simple. In teaching learners to read the poem, teachers should lead them to analyse the single sentence that comprises the poem and examine each of the metaphors that make up the seven assertions. This would be a way of achieving the integration of language and literature. Learners in a class usually have several languages and cultures between them. These could be tapped for examples of similar praise songs that could first be given in the native language and then translated into English. Other cross-cultural issues could be taken up. Attention could be drawn, for example, to the fact that in praising the young lady, the poem singles out her youth, femininity, and desirability but makes no mention of other qualities to do with strength of character and personal achievement. Is this perhaps a limited African male view of womanhood? Learners should be challenged to try to contradict this perception by more comprehensive examples of praise songs. The discussion which the attendant comparisons would lead to should generate a healthy scepticism about the values of the society in which the learners live. This is one way of allowing poetry, even humble examples of it as provided by the two selections above, to achieve the subversive force which, Widdowson (1987a) argues, is the essential educational value of lyric poetry. It would then be easy to move from these sorts of examples to lyric poetry proper, to the kind illustrated by J. P. Clark's poem, 'Ibadan':

> Ibadan,
> running splash of rust
> and gold—flung and scattered
> among seven hills like broken
> china in the sun.

Here the evocative choice of words and imagery combine to suggest a powerful picture of the planlessness and internal contradiction of a Nigerian city. With more advanced readers a comparison could be made between the picture and message suggested by this poem and that suggested by Ezra Pound's famous poem:

In a Station of the Metro

The apparition of these faces in the crowd;
Petals on a wet, black bough.

Both poets use nearly the same number of words to create their vastly different worlds—Clark's nineteen to Pound's twenty.

I have mentioned the use of translation in the discussion of examples of praise songs in the native language. This would be translation from an indigenous language into English. But a case could be made not only for a more general use of translation as a method of teaching poetry, but also as a way of viewing the entire process of artistic creation in an ESL context. In 'Partial meaning and pragmatic correspondence' Widdowson (1994f) argues that translation 'is a special case of a more general pragmatic process' and that it would be a mistake to see translation exclusively as a process of rendering a text from one language into another. We could take this argument a step further and suggest that there is a sense in which artistic creation could be seen as a process of translation. Verbal artists, especially those operating in an ESL context, could then be viewed as translators of experience into words. The struggle to find the right word in a second language that best captures the experience could then be seen as comparable to the attempt by the ordinary translator to find the right expression that captures the meaning of the original. Support for this view can be found in Achebe:

> For an African, writing in English is not without its serious setbacks. He often finds himself describing situations and modes of thought which have no direct equivalent in the English way of life.
> (Achebe: *Morning Yet on Creation Day*)

This, I submit, is not unlike the kind of problem faced by the translator who has to render a literary text in a foreign language into English. He too often has to find expressions in English for situations and modes of thought that are very different and often untranslatable.

> Caught in that situation he can do one of two things. He can try and contain what he has to say within the limits of conventional English or he can try and push back those limits to accommodate his idea. The first method produces competent, uninspired and rather flat work. The second method will produce something new and valuable to the English language as well as to the material he is trying to put over.
> (Ibid.)

Examples of 'something new and valuable to the English language' can be found not only in Achebe's own work but in modern African poetry. The third and last verse of Gabriel Okara's 'The Snowflakes Sail Gently Down' reads:

> Then I awoke. I awoke
> to the silently falling snow
> and bent-backed elms bowing and

swaying to the winter wind like
white-robed Moslems salaaming at evening
prayer, and the earth lying inscrutable
like the face of a god in a shrine.

The central image of elms which had occurred earlier in the first and second verses of the poem is here modified and the 'bent-backed elms' bow and sway to the wind 'like white-robed Moslems salaaming at evening prayer'. This visual image is given additional emphasis, as Roscoe (1971) notes, by the resonantly poetic word 'salaaming', an image and a word which clearly add 'something new and valuable to the English language'. Numerous other examples could be found in the poetry of Okigbo, Soyinka, Clark, and others. They show poets pushing the 'limits of conventional English' to produce work which is new and original. And this is good not just for the development of literature in English but for the extension of linguistic and cross-cultural awareness. There is nothing more reassuring to students in a second language situation faced with the task of reading and interpreting poetry in cold print than to have some of it translated into their first language. Comparisons can then be made between expressions of the same sentiments or ideas in the two languages. Such comparisons will in many cases be actual discussions of the way particular poets have rendered indigenous cultural ideas in English. When learners in a second language situation are able to make such comparisons, they are already making fruitful responses to poetry. In developing a strategy for the teaching and reading of such work, teachers must give a central place to the use of translation.

The position I have sought to maintain in this paper is that Nigerian students must first be taught to read poetry before they can profit from the study of it. The eagerness with which all learners accept and use critical judgements handed down by teachers or culled from 'notes' is not just an indication of their laziness—they can't all be lazy. It says something about their inability to read the original text for themselves. And if they have problems reading the text, then of course all talk of experiencing the work firsthand goes out of the window. For if poetry is a particular use of language, it also creates a world of the imagination, an alternative world to the existing reality and it is this world that readers enter imaginatively when they experience a poem. The aesthetic experience of a work can only begin when the reader is in the world of the work. In order to have access to such experience learners must first be taught to read poetry. The bicultural nature of the poetry they are likely to encounter does not make life easy for learners. But they can be taught to make their own secret pacts even with this sort of poetry. The trick is to get learners to employ some of the techniques of ordinary discourse processing such as the use of contextual clues to guess at meanings or allusions that are not immediately obvious. But this, as Widdowson (1985b) recognizes, 'calls for a much closer attention to the actual language than would customarily be the case when reading'. Soyinka's poem 'Death in the Dawn' affords us a good example. The poet's prefatory note to the poem states the main events on which the poem is based: *Driving to Lagos one morning a white cockerel flew out of the dusk and smashed itself against my windscreen. A mile further I came across a motor accident and a freshly dead man in the smash.* The poem starts with a dramatic but casual tone using the rhythm of ordinary speech:

> Traveller, you must set out
> At dawn. And wipe your feet upon
> The dog-nose wetness of the earth.

Then follows the painting of the scene and the establishment of the mood of the traveller who has 'joys and apprehensions for / A naked day'. After this comes the description of the sacrifice of the cock and the mother's prayer, amidst references to Yoruba belief and culture:

> On this
> Counterpane, it was—
> Sudden winter at the death
> Of dawn's lone trumpeter, cascades
> Of white feather-flakes, but it proved
> A futile rite. Propitiation sped
> Grimly on, before.

> The right foot for joy, the left, dread
> And the mother prayed, Child
> May you never walk
> When the road waits, famished.
> Traveller you must set forth
> At dawn.

[299]

The sacrifice of the cock and the mother's advice and prayer do not, however, guarantee a safe journey for the traveller. The god of the road remains unappeased. Waiting, famished, he must have human sacrifice. In the Yoruba system of belief which Soyinka is employing, Ogun, the god of the road, is an insatiable deity and is ever present and watchful over travellers on the road. The last two verses of the poem show the grim price that the traveller finally pays:

> I promise marvels of the holy hour
> Presages as the white cock's flapped
> Perverse impalement—as who would dare
> The wrathful wings of man's Progression . . .
>
> But such another Wraith! Brother,
> Silenced in the startled hug of
> Your invention—is this mocked grimace
> This closed contortion—I?

The traveller meets his inevitable end suddenly—'Silenced in the startled hug of [his] invention'. But the poem also pursues another theme. The earlier death of the cock—its 'perverse impalement'—came about because the poor fowl got in the way of the symbol of human progress. The traveller's death too is seen in the same light. The lines that describe the earlier sacrifice and prayer give us a good illustration of the way Soyinka's poetry works. There is the allusion to Shakespeare's *Hamlet* with 'dawn's lone trumpeter' echoing Horatio's

> I have heard,
> The cock, that is the trumpet to the morn,
> Doth with his lofty and shrill-sounding throat
> Awake the god of day . . .
> (*Hamlet* I.1)

In Shakespeare's world the god of day arrives to frighten away creatures of the night, including ghosts. In Soyinka's, the famished but patiently waiting god of the road must be satisfied with nothing less than human flesh, and unwary travellers oblige. This kind of allusion, which adds richness and density to Soyinka's poetry, is something which learners may not pick up at a first reading. But if they are engaged in what Widdowson (1985b) calls 'creative reading', they would get enough from the surrounding words, setting, and tone to build their own complex picture. Other cultural references in the poem would of course be familiar and the idea of human progress towards self-destruction as mirrored in the poet's identification with the accident victim's 'mocked grimace' and 'closed contortion' would immediately be appreciated as a withering, sarcastic comment on society. But creative reading of the kind being envisaged should ultimately lead to an imaginal entrance into the world of the poem, where readers identify with the events of the poem as if they were actual participants, the kind of imaginary encounter which Elliott (1967) describes as experiencing a poem 'from within'. With certain kinds of poems—and this is true of a lot of lyric poetry—this kind of imaginal entrance is the only way that the poems will yield their full meaning and effect, or the only way readers can negotiate meaning and arrive at their optimal interpretation of the poems.

Among the activities that will help students to learn to read poetry Widdowson (1985b) mentions getting learners to choose—giving reasons—alternative linguistic expressions within the context of the poem from a list provided by the teacher. Particularly useful in an ESL context is Widdowson's (1992a) suggestion that learners be led to compare prose passages and poems with the same or similar propositional content. Activities involving such comparisons should enable students to learn what makes referential prose descriptions of phenomena different from poetic representations. They would in the process also learn how words and phrases in a referential description could be selected and combined to produce a poetic effect. Such lessons should go a long way towards abolishing the undue reverence for the poetic text and the general fear of poetry mentioned earlier. *Practical Stylistics* (Widdowson 1992a) is rich in suggestions of this kind and the teacher could usefully try out with learners the activities that involve deriving and comparing different poetic variants, all designed to sharpen learners' awareness of the way 'language can be used to express different aspects of reality'. To these we could add some of the word and picture exercises that Maley and Duff (1989) discuss in the first three chapters of their book. These include writing out the text of a poem in which lines are given out of order and requiring learners to put the lines back into their original order; presenting learners with three or four poems and requiring them to adopt the role of editors and choose one of the poems for publication in the school magazine and the award of a prize; and dramatizing the events in a poem. 'Death in the Dawn', for example, could easily be dramatized, with learners taking the roles of narrator, car driver, and mother.

It is important to keep in mind that one of the purposes of teaching students to read poetry is to get them to want to read other poems besides the ones they have to study as part of the set texts for their examinations. At the end of an undergraduate course when successful students are awarded their degrees, it should be possible to ask, without causing embarrassment, not 'What texts did you study?' but 'How much poetry have you *read*?' The chances are that if students are able to answer the latter question without hesitation, they are likely to go on reading poetry for pleasure, beyond the requirement of formal study. And that is a goal worth pursuing in education.

Notes

1 The three extracts by Chinua Achebe are from *Morning Yet on Creation Day: Essays* (1975, Heinemann, London).

2 Poets whose works are quoted in this paper are:
J. P. Clark: 'Ibadan' (from *A Reed in the Tide*, 1965);
Gabriel Okara: 'The Snowflakes Sail Gently Down' (from *The Fisherman's Invocation*, 1978);
Ezra Pound: 'In a Station of the Metro' (from *Ezra Pound: Collected Shorter Poems*, 1952);
Wole Soyinka: 'In Memory of Segun Awolowo' and 'Death in the Dawn' (from *Idanre and Other Poems*, 1967).

20

Discourse and creativity: bridging the gap between language and literature

RONALD CARTER &
MICHAEL MCCARTHY

Introduction

THIS PAPER EXAMINES some practical issues in the design and implementation of materials at the interface of language and literature. In order to achieve this practical focus, theoretical issues are necessarily never far from the forefront of discussion. In the paper there are therefore core questions such as: What is literature? What is literary competence? What kind of materials development is best suited to teaching which enhances both linguistic and literary competence? Such questions are not new but answers to the questions, however preliminary and provisional, must continue to form the basis for any prospectus for further development in this field.

In this paper we argue that an extension of *language awareness* and the enhanced interpretive skills which should go with that fuller language awareness are instrumental to a prospectus for future materials development. In particular, we argue that main-line course books should exploit the opportunities provided by recent work in the domain of language awareness and that, if language awareness becomes a more central component in all course books, then the need for *separate* books which seek to integrate language and literature will not exist to the same degree. As we argue in the final section, a move to greater language awareness will also have implications for the ways in which future language and literature tests are constructed and in turn used as a measure of a student's proficiency in a language. In order to build the overall argument the paper begins with a review of relevant materials development during the past ten years.

Literary materials 1983–1993

During the 1980s and early 1990s materials for the teaching of literature in the context of English language teaching have operated according to a number of common theoretical and strategic principles. Among the underlying theoretical assumptions are firstly that literature is made from language, and that sensitivity to language use is a strong basis for the development of an understanding of literary texts and, particularly in the case of non-native users of a language, often a secure and practical way to unlocking the different levels of meaning in such texts. Secondly, suitably selected literary texts can provide a motivating and stimulating source of content in the language classroom, serving as a basis for discussion and interpretation in which the response of the individual learner is encouraged. Thirdly, the skills of decoding literary texts are transferable to most language learning contexts in which meanings, because they are not always immediately transparent, have to be experienced, negotiated, or read between the lines. Such principles stress the mutual reinforcement and support of literary and linguistic skills and underlie an essentially integrated view of language and literature.

Pedagogically, two main principles can be isolated: an activity principle and a process principle. An activity principle means that students are more than merely passive recipients of interpretations generated by a teacher or assimilated from books of literary criticism. Instead, students actively participate in making the text mean. In this activity they are supported pedagogically by a range of strategies of the kind widely used in the EFL classroom: rewriting, cloze-procedures, jumbling texts, role-play, prediction tasks, and so on. A process principle means that students are more likely to appreciate and understand texts if they experience them directly as part of a process of meaning creation. Process-based approaches are learner-centred and seek to encourage students to respond to the text not exclusively as a complete artefact or finished product but rather more to the text as an unfolding process in which the relationship between form and meaning is shown to be central, as in Widdowson (1992a). Such learner-centred activities serve also to stress the unfolding and evolving nature of reading and inter-pretation of literary texts. Skills in interpretation are likely to be more successfully fostered if both activity and process principles operate at the same time (for further discussion see Carter and Long 1991: chapter 1).

The materials developed during these years have had different inflec-tions according to context, purpose, and audience. For example, some more advanced materials have involved learners in more linguistic-stylistic analysis (Carter and Long 1987); some materials (Gower and Pearson 1986; Gower 1990) have been more traditionally literary in orientation, providing detailed reference to literary and cultural his-tory. Some materials have been more eclectic, drawing on a wider range of literary and non-literary texts to encourage the building up of liter-ary competence through interaction with the text, the textbook, and others in the class (for example, Boardman and McRae 1984; McRae and Pantaleoni 1991). All have taken inspiration from Widdowson's seminal *Stylistics and the Teaching of Literature* (1975).

All these materials are characterized, however, by being additional or supplementary to main-line language course books. They reflect a teaching context in which language courses and literature courses are taught separately and in which integrated courses in language and literature are not integral to either. In the remainder of this paper we shall argue for the need to build upon the advances of the past decade but at the same time switch the focus to the place of language aware-ness in language and literacy development and to the place of literary texts in all language course materials.

Some core questions

In order to provide such a focus, some core questions have to be posed. The main ones are: What *is* a literary text and how does it differ from other kinds of text? What is the relationship between literary uses of lan-guage and everyday uses? What is literary competence and how does it differ from general linguistic competence? What is literacy development and are there major differences between literacy development in a first language and literacy development in a second or foreign language? Is there such a thing as pre-literary competence (that is, a set of skills basic to the development of a subsequent fuller literary competence)?

[305]

The provision of answers to such leading and complex questions depends on many more years of extensive research than have currently been undertaken, but continually to pose the questions is a necessary part of all processes of text selection, materials design, and of competence testing in relation to language and literature in language learning.

Basic material: the arbitrariness of the sign

It can be safely assumed that colour words are among the first words learned in a language (Wyler 1992: 43ff.), allowing as they do a necessary contact with the identity of things and providing the language user with a vital means for distinguishing and differentiating within the material world. *Red, yellow, green, black, white, brown,* and *blue* are thus central to the semantic structure of the lexicon of English, and the words are normally assimilated both early in a learning sequence and with relative ease. The centrality and coreness of such words often means, however, that they are extended into a range of compounds and combinations which result in changes in meaning. It also means that such words are available as basic signs for states of mind and feeling, for marking core cultural properties and for shaping attitudes and interactions, usually through processes of idiomatic extension. Taking a core word such as *green*, therefore, we can have the meaning of green as a core colour, as in the first example, but also:

green	= basic colour of something
green	= grassed area (for example, village green)
Green Cross Code	= set of guidelines for safety in crossing the road
green light	= the go-ahead to do something
greens	= green vegetables
greens	= the Green party in politics
greenhouse	= place for cultivating plants; also the expression 'the greenhouse effect'
green	= innocent, inexperienced
green	= envious
green	= the colour of Catholic Republicanism in Northern Ireland

In a first language learning environment such meaning extensions to the word *green* and its morphological derivatives are learned in the process of naturalistic exposure to the language in its cultural contexts; in most second or foreign language learning environments the specifically cultural, idiomatic and, to a considerable extent, simply *arbitrary* meanings of the sign are normally withheld on the grounds that they are problematic for learners, for the most part re-appearing only in upper-intermediate and advanced learning contexts. However, to tidy up the language to this extent may be to remove opportunities for recognizing and interpreting non-literal forms and meanings in ways which lay a valuable basis for reading and interpreting a variety of texts, including literary texts. McRae (1991) has explored this domain with particular reference to differences and distinctions between referential and representational language. And as we shall see later, the productivity that results in the derivatives of *green* within prevailing sociocultural frameworks is immanent in everyday conversational interaction, not just in literary creation.

One essential element in the literariness of language is that there is no single or simple one-to-one correlation between the language used and the meanings produced. Meanings have to be read from the language. Such a process of negotiation also pays due attention to the arbitrariness inherent in many language forms, which may require a re-orientation to what was supposed to be their point of reference in the world, even a re-learning of the frames of reference within which differently possible worlds are created. The process may also require an understanding that more than one meaning can exist as part of the message. To know the word *yellow* is also to know its associations with cowardice; to know the word *blue* is also to know that in English its plural in nominal form (*the blues*) is connected with feelings of depression; to know the word *green* is to know the colour, its natural, vegetative associations, *and* its additional considerably more non-literal, representational and arbitrary meanings.

Idioms, metaphors, proverbs, and other extensions to what is assumed to be the core of a language are frequent across all languages and may, indeed, be in themselves more core than the construction of language courses would suggest. They are often embedded within the cultures which are intrinsic to that language and therefore do not readily translate between and across languages. But awareness of such features and interpretations of them allow access to these cultural embeddings, providing in the process opportunities for interpreting

[307]

meanings which are communicated with varying degrees of indirectness and obliqueness.

As a preparation for subsequent reading of complete literary texts such awareness is valuable in this connection but the language learner is also learning that words have extended meanings as well as learning those meanings themselves, that meanings often have to be negotiated, that a language is something to be learned *about* as well as learned, and that a language is a productive resource of great creative potential, not just a fossilized code.

Playing with words

The simultaneous holding of more than one meaning within the communicative layers of a message is basic to a very wide variety of language use, from everyday conversation to the most elaborated literary texts, and in the context of language and literacy development may therefore be better included in the language course and not separated off into the literature course or into more advanced supplementary materials. Very young children possess the capacity for telling and receiving jokes which depend on a recognition of creative play with patterns of meaning. For example:

Q: What is black and white and read all over?

A: A newspaper.

They can also give varying explanations for a newspaper headline such as:

Giant Waves Down Tunnel

Both examples depend on recognizing dual meanings created by the phonology (*read/red*) and syntax of English (*giant* is both a noun and a modifier; *waves* can be both a verb and a noun).

Advertising language also depends crucially on creative play with language and on the cultural discourses of society within which the language is embedded (see, in particular, Cook 1992; also Moeran 1984; Tanaka 1992). For example, an advertisement for a motor car which states that it is

A Car for the 90°s

[308]

holds simultaneously together the possibility that it is a car in which you can travel at great speeds (90 m.p.h.), that it is particularly suited to very hot weather (90° Fahrenheit), and that it is modern (the 1990s). To provide learners with such a text and working collaboratively with them to decode it is also to provide them with an especially rich set of possibilities for learning language, for learning about language, and for literacy development.

Creativity in conversation

It is not just in the more contrived contexts such as journalism and advertising that we find embedded cultural references, extended uses of linguistic forms, metaphors and idioms, and language generally being creatively manipulated. Everyday conversation reveals uses of language that are strongly associated with criteria for 'literariness', that is, with the uses of language that characterize texts held by members of given speech communities to be 'literary'. One of the more negative aspects of the communicative movement in language teaching that has dominated the last couple of decades is an over-emphasis on the transactional uses of language (i.e. the transacting of information, goods, and services) at the expense of interactional uses (i.e. for the creation and reinforcement of social relationships) and creative uses. (We have criticized that trend in McCarthy and Carter 1994, a book which attempts to formulate what a language teaching syllabus based on a notion of language as discourse would entail.) However, the communicative urge has been a double-edged sword, and the very desire for authenticity in communication has led language practitioners to look more and more towards real spoken data, where day-to-day creativity and cultural embedding leap to the fore again.

One kind of creativity students of literature have to contend with, especially in modern poetry, is *morphological* creativity, whereby derivational potential is creatively exploited. Vizmuller-Zocco (1985) sees lexical derivation as belonging to 'that linguistic competence which is based on creativity', while Howden (1984) sees the native speaker's knowledge of existing derived words and what the potential for choice is as centrally important; she also stresses the interrelationships of meaning set up by new combinations of stems and affixes. Such creativity is surprisingly common in everyday talk, and can be used as the basis of a bridge towards its more daunting manifestations in literary texts. Here are some examples from the Nottingham University Spoken English Corpus of speakers exploiting the –y suffix in non-institutionalized word forms to create diffuse and evaluative meaning:

[B, who is preparing food, has asked A to get her a bowl]
A: You said you wanted the little ones as well. Want the little ones?
B: Not really . . . sort of *salady* . . . that fruit bowl would be ideal

[A is describing some new-fangled shoelaces she has bought]
A: They're well sort of like lycra, *elasticky* sort of stuff

[A and B are deciding where to go for the evening]
A: Cos there's a really nice place me and Myra go to
B: Oh I don't want a romantic *mewsy* pub

Later in this paper, we present some examples of creativity with the –y suffix in poetry.

On another occasion, using the –*ing* inflexion, a speaker 'derives' a verb from a noun while telling a story of a dangerous game he and his friends played as children, rolling down industrial spoil heaps inside old lorry tyres. He intensifies the nightmarish rolling movement:

A: And you'd just roll, like *circusing* right the way down and get right up the top

This is not inherently different from the poet Seamus Heaney's morphological creativity in describing the flight of a snipe: 'as he *corkscrews* away / into the vaults / that we live off' ('The Backward Look').

In another extract in our corpus, two women are assembling a portable baby-cot which involves twisting the metal parts until they become rigid. Note how speaker B uses morphological creativity, this time with a prefix (instead of using the more conventional 'loose' or 'slack'), to satirize her own mistake in the twisting movement:

A: There, that's solid now
B: I think I've made it *unsolid* . . . sorry . . . I've done it the wrong way round, have I

We find parallels of this in poetry, with the 'hot *unasking* sun' and 'the friendless and *unhated* stone' in W. H. Auden's poem 'As He Is'. To make such parallels between conversation and literary text is, as we always maintain, not to demean literary text in any way. As Widdowson (1975: 36) points out, it is the randomness of such occurrences in conversation as opposed to their *patterning* in literary text which is the significant difference. What the literary and conversational contexts cited have in common is their ability to bring together elements that are normally separated in the language code, to borrow again an observation from Widdowson (ibid.: 57). It is this common property that the teaching of literature and language can exploit.

Morphological creativity can be combined with satirical cultural reference too, as in this extract where a hostess (speaker A) is apologizing to her dinner guests (one of whom is speaker B) that they are a little short of home-grown vegetables. The extract reinforces with real data our comments above on the breadth of lexical extension and shared cultural reference that accrues to a basic term such as *green*:

A: And so I'm afraid we're a bit sort of erm challenged *greenwise*

B: *Greenly* challenged

A: We're *greenly* challenged so erm sorry about that

Here we have the morphological creativity of *greenwise* and *greenly* combined with an oblique cultural reference to phrases such as *visually challenged, physically challenged*, etc., as current 'politically correct' euphemisms for 'blind' and 'disabled', just as being 'green' (growing one's own vegetables organically, etc.) is a politically correct stance. The pun works on several levels, and it is significant that the joke is jointly created by the two speakers, emphasizing the high degree of shared cultural knowledge and convergence. Between everyday conversational punning and literary text we find parallels in journalistic satire, as in the following example taken from a recent newspaper article on left-handedness:

These . . . figures come from a survey held by the Left-Handers' Club . . . the national mouthpiece of the *dexterously challenged*.
('The Left Protest', *The Observer 'Life' Magazine*: 21 August 1994)

We have also mentioned the importance of awareness of multiple meanings. Speakers play on these spontaneously by exploiting the real, immediate context for humorous effects, just as ready-made jokes exploit fictitious contexts. In the next conversational extract, a group

[311]

of young female students are taking tea together, and two such ambiguities are exploited within a very short stretch of text:

A: Yeah, did you ever do . . . erm erm . . . oh what was she called erm Cynthia

B: Did I ever do Cynthia

A: [Laughs]

B: [Laughs] Can't say, did you

. . .

A: Oh this is wonderful, Bakewell tarts

B: Tea and tarts

A: [Laughs] tea and tarts

B: [Laughs] tea with

A: Tea with tarts [laughs] . . . tarts with tea

'Do' is exploited for its sexual ambiguity, and 'tarts' for its meanings (in British English) of (a) a sweet pastry item and (b) a slang term for a prostitute.

These examples are some of the many kinds of linguistic creativity that one finds in a corpus of everyday conversation. They have in common with literary language that language is being made to 'stick out' from its context of use. Casual conversation is classically marked by a high degree of automatic and unconscious routine language use, but, now and again, speakers make their language draw attention to itself in some way, displacing it from its immediate context, a phenomenon Widdowson (1992a: 26) has argued to be a fundamental characteristic of poetic language. We would therefore argue that to use in the language class only those types of dialogue that are transparent and transactional and devoid of richness, cultural reference, and creativity is to misrepresent what speakers actually do and simultaneously to lose an opportunity for interesting language awareness work of the kind we believe to be an ideal precursor to enhanced literary awareness.

Semantic density: grading the text

It is clear that some instances of language require a greater processing effort. One reason for this is that they possess a greater semantic density. Stretches of language or texts such as the advertisement for 'A Car for the 90°s', involving as they do a greater element of creative play with language and a layering of patterns at different levels, generally demand more processing effort than the semantic re-ordering of the word green as a colour to the phrase 'on the green' in which the word refers to a stretch of (mostly) green parkland. Similarly, idioms such as 'bumper to bumper', as in 'the traffic was bumper to bumper', are semantically transparent when compared with idioms such as 'to smell a rat' or 'to be on the ball'. Proverbs such as 'don't cry over spilt milk' allow real-world analogies to be drawn or semantic extensions to be made in a relatively more straightforward way than is normally the case with proverbs such as 'every cloud has a silver lining', which involve more indirect and metaphoric processes of decoding and interpretation.

The following examples of the names of shopfronts for hairdressers' shops in Britain involve varying degrees of creative play with language (and are indeed essentially *literary* in such verbal play), and require a competence in recognizing a multi-layering of effects; but some names are more semantically dense and require a greater processing effort than others which are less oblique and less multi-layered in the creation of meaning:

Highlights	Brush Strokes
Way Ahead	Cutabove
Headlines	Hair Comes Linda
Shampers	Hair and Share Alike
Cut 'n' Dried	Headcase
New Wave	

'Way Ahead', for example, is more transparent in its straightforward link between hairdressing and 'head' and its suggestion that hair styling in this shop puts you at a social advantage over others, as does 'Cut above', from the idiom 'to be a cut above the rest', meaning to be superior, though this example demands more idiomatic knowledge, as does 'cut 'n' dried', a patterned semantic equation between the idiom and cultural behaviour (a confident, no-nonsense approach) as well as a literal link between cutting and drying hair. 'Shampers' too requires a specific cultural knowledge of the drinking of champagne (colloquial word 'shampers' and its phonetic analogy with shampoo) in contexts of high living. 'Brush strokes' obliquely suggests 'art', while 'Headcase' (meaning 'crazy', 'lunatic') suggests a zany, youthful environment, and so on.

Proverbs, idioms, metaphors, jokes, and texts such as newspaper headlines, advertisements, and some titles/names for shops involve language use which is central to the culture patterned in and through that language. A further processing effort is therefore required in the case of those texts which invoke specific frames of cultural reference, for without the relevant cultural knowledge interpretation becomes a much more testing procedure. For example, children's jokes such as:

Q: How do you make a Swiss roll?

A: Push him down a mountain.

or

Q: What's the difference between a teabag and Everton?

A: A teabag stays in the cup.

demand cultural knowledge which is specific to British culture (knowledge that Everton is a Liverpool-based football club with a poor FA Cup record; or knowledge that a Swiss roll is a kind of jam sponge cake), in addition to the linguistic knowledge that 'roll' can be both a verb and a noun and that Swiss can be both noun and noun modifier. And some texts allude in ways which require specific literary knowledge. For example, a camping shop with an advertising slogan:

Now is the discount of our winter tents

may only be processed on one level by readers not acquainted with a key speech from Shakespeare's *Richard III* (for this and further similar examples see McCarthy 1992).

On the other hand, some effects produced in poetry are less semantically dense. 'Fern Hill', a poem by Dylan Thomas, which contains phrases such as 'all the sun long' or 'once below a time' (based on the fixed phrases 'all the day long' or 'once upon a time'), obtains its effects from, for example, a basic substitution of 'sun' for 'day', creating a suggestion that the sun shone through the day. A title such as Dylan Thomas's 'A Grief Ago' allows grief to be measured in temporal terms by a substitution of a noun describing the emotion for the more usual noun measuring time such as hour, week, month, or year (Leech 1969:

30). Recognizing such patterns is instrumental to understanding the effects which such patterns produce. Producing them, as a British actress did recently in a television interview (commenting that a 1950s film she had appeared in was 'four husbands ago'), is a marker of a linguistic inventiveness and creativity which 'ordinary' language users possess.

In this section it has been suggested that texts from various sources can be utilized to promote the development of skills of interpreting, inference, reading between the lines, that such texts could be included as a natural and normal component in language teaching materials at all but the most elementary levels, and that such texts can be graded and thus appropriately sequenced according to the relative degrees of processing effort required of them.

Language awareness: opening a door to literary competence

The above arguments are for learners to engage earlier in second or foreign language learning processes with samples of non-literal, representational language. Such engagement entails processes of interaction with and interpretation of language use. A necessary prerequisite for this kind of interaction and interpretation is a fuller awareness of language itself as a medium. This awareness requires learners to become more reflective, that is, to become more conscious of texts and stretches of language as containing messages which need to be negotiated for meaning. In addition to interpreting language use they need to be aware of how they have made interpretations and to reflect on interpretative procedures, learning, in other words, how to learn better to interpret and engage with such texts as a result of more conscious operations.

The orientation here is parallel to that advocated by, among others, Ellis and Sinclair (1989) who have constructed teaching materials designed to enhance both awareness of the nature of the language system being learned and consciousness of the learner's own procedures for learning the language. Ellis and Sinclair's work underlines that a more conscious, reflective language learner is a more effective language learner. (A similar point is made by Swain in this volume.)

Testing language and literature

While the development of literary materials in the last ten years has been innovative and has led to closer integration between language and literature, the same cannot be said for developments in the assessment of literary competence. Tests have tended to be of a very traditional order and have in this respect tended to work to reinforce divisions between language and literature. Echoing Widdowson's (1985b) distinction between *learning* and *studying* literature (see Bisong in this volume), Carter and Long (1990, 1991) and Spiro (1991) have argued that the traditional literature test is characterized by an assessment of knowledge *about* literature (as a body of information, facts, dates, etc.) rather than by an assessment of knowledge *of* literature (as a set of personal responses to the meanings released for the individual reader by the text). There is additionally only minimal attention given to the language of the text.

There is insufficient space for detailed exemplification of traditional literary questions but Carter and Long (1990) illustrate three main question types: 'paraphrase and context'; 'describe and discuss', and 'evaluate and criticize'—all of which have advantages in that it is important to be acquainted with a range of facts and judgements in order to have studied a text, but all of which have a main disadvantage in taking students away both from responses to the language of the text and to the text as a particular kind of text.

Integrated language and literature tests

In this final section some examples are suggested which might form a basis for literary language development and testing. The test material is based on principles elaborated earlier in this paper and presupposes a language classroom which focuses neither on language nor on literary texts as separate components but rather on all texts as creatively constructed and as continuous rather than discontinuous with other texts.

1 Listed below are some well-known English proverbs. Write a brief explanation of the proverb, indicating in what situations you would expect it to be used.

a) Don't cry over spilt milk.

   b) A bird in the hand is worth two in the bush.

   c) Don't count your chickens until they're hatched.

   d) Every cloud has a silver lining.

   e) Out of the frying pan into the fire.

2 The following phrases are used frequently in English when describing people. Explain briefly what you think each phrase means.

   a) a real angel

   b) a closed book

   c) a lion

   d) a mouse

   e) a gem

   f) a mystery to me

3 The following are taken from recent newspaper headlines. They are meant to be amusing. Write brief notes on the way the language of the headlines is used to create comic effects.

   a) Giant waves down tunnel.

   b) Judge's speech ends in long sentences.

   c) Milk drinkers are turning to powder.

Next, two examples are suggested for more advanced learners of English which draw on the principle of rewriting in order to develop and/or assess an ability to compare and contrast alternative forms of a text. For further examples see Carter and Nash (1990) and Nash (1986).

4 'Upon Westminster Bridge' by William Wordsworth

> Earth has not anything to show more fair:
> Dull would he be of soul who could pass by
> A sight so touching in its majesty:
> This City now doth, like a garment, wear
> The beauty of the morning; silent, bare.
> Ships, towers, domes, theatres, and temples lie
> Open unto the fields, and to the sky;
> All bright and glittering in the smokeless air.
> Never did sun more beautifully steep
> In his first splendour, valley, rock, or hill;
> Ne'er saw I, never felt, a calm so deep!

The river glideth at his own sweet will:
Dear God! the very houses seem asleep;
And all that mighty heart is lying still!

a) Attempt a prose paraphrase; then study the compromises and necessary defects of paraphrase.

b) Make a prose version, faithful to the content of the poem but composed as though for an encyclopaedia entry ('the city is most advantageously viewed from one of the bridges, preferably in the early morning before traffic builds up'), or for a travel book ('we were struck by the almost rural calm of our surroundings'), or for a commercial ('you'll THRILL to the stupendous views!').

5 Here are two versions of the first stanza of Thomas Hardy's poem 'After A Journey'. Say which version is the one written by Hardy. Pay particular attention to choices in language, and give reasons for your decision.

a) Hereto I come to view a voiceless ghost;
      Whither, O whither will its whim now draw me?
Up the cliff, down, till I'm lonely, lost,
      And the unseen waters' ejaculations awe me.
Where you will next be there's no knowing,
      Facing round about me everywhere,
      With your nut-coloured hair,
And gray eyes, and rose-flush coming and going.

b) I have come to see a silent ghost.
Where will its whim now draw me?
Up the cliff, down, till I'm lonely and lost
And the crash and roar of the sea awe me.
I do not know where I will see you
Facing all about me everywhere
      With your nut-coloured hair
And gray eyes. Your blushes grew and grew.

Finally, an example is suggested of a literary exercise which could follow language-awareness activities involving conversational creativity with prefixes and suffixes, as exemplified earlier.

6 In these snippets from the works of poets, some of the words in italic are established English words, others are very unusual, and were created by the poets. Using a good dictionary if necessary, decide which of the words in italic you feel are original creations, and how the prefixes and suffixes affect the meaning of the words.

To-night, a first movement, a pulse,
As if the rain in bogland gathered head
To slip and flood: a bog-burst,
A gash breaking open the *ferny* bed.
(Seamus Heaney: 'Act of Union')

The plait of my hair,
a *slimy* birth-cord
of bog, had been cut
(Seamus Heaney: 'Bog Queen')

With the farming of a verse
Make a vineyard of the curse,
Sing of human *unsuccess*
In a rapture of distress;
(W. H. Auden: 'In Memory of W. B. Yeats')

The fire's between us.
Is there still no place
Turning and turning in the middle air,
Untouched and *untouchable*.
(Sylvia Plath: 'Getting There')

I am a miner. The light turns blue.
Waxy stalactites
Drip and thicken, tears

The earthen womb
Exudes from its dead boredom.
Black bat airs

Wrap me, *raggy* shawls,
Cold homicides.
(Sylvia Plath: 'Nick and the Candlestick')

Conclusion

One of the main theoretical and practical implications of this paper is that the term literature is not defined in any exclusive sense. The position adopted here is close to that established by Carter and Nash (1990), exemplified with comparisons of conversational data and literary texts by McCarthy (1993, 1994), and developed more fully in pedagogy by McRae (1991) and McCarthy and Carter (1994: chapter 4). It is that of recognizing the co-existence of literature with a capital 'L' (canonical literature) and of literature with a small 'l' (the latter is the title of McRae's 1991 book, which contains texts ranging from proverbs to jokes, to advertisements, which display an inherent literariness). Such a position may be felt by some, especially teachers of literature, to demean texts valued by a cultural community to be of canonical status; the argument here is that, far from demeaning literary texts, it reveals and endorses the creativity inherent in much 'ordinary' everyday language use.

Literary uses of language and the necessary skills for its interpretation go routinely with all kinds of text, spoken and written. Literature exists at many different levels for different people in different communities but it is argued here that literary language is not simply any use of language. The main argument in this paper is that literary language will always be patterned in some way and will involve a creative play with these patterns. The patterns may also involve words or structures which are representational and not intended to be read literally. The patterns invite involvement on the part of a reader or hearer who then has an option to interpret the text as the context and circumstances of the language use appear to him or her to demand. This patterned, representational 'literary' aspect of language is central to language use though it will of course occur with greater density in some texts than others. The sooner language learners can come to appreciate this central component of language, the sooner they appreciate that they themselves and other users of language are essentially creative users of language. In the future pedagogies and related tests for literary language development are likely to be all the richer for recognizing this reality.

Notes

Poets whose works are quoted in this paper are:

W. H. Auden: 'As He Is' and 'In Memory of W. B. Yeats' (from *Collected Poems*, 1976);

Thomas Hardy: 'After a Journey';

Seamus Heaney: 'The Backward Look' (from *Wintering Out*, 1972), 'Act of Union' and 'Bog Queen' (from *North*, 1975);

Sylvia Plath: 'Getting There' and 'Nick and the Candlestick' (from *Collected Poems*, 1981);

Dylan Thomas: 'Fern Hill' and 'A Grief Ago';

William Wordsworth: 'Upon Westminster Bridge'.

21

The impact of the Army Specialized Training Program: a reconsideration

BERNARD SPOLSKY

LANGUAGE TEACHING, IN spite of the wise words of scholars like Stern and Widdowson, continues its bent to descry and deify some magic 'methodology' that will make language learning both painless to the learner and easily manageable by the teacher. There remains, then, a duty not so much to debunk as to attempt to clarify any vestiges of belief in an empirical basis or implementable principle that can be found in the mythology of methodology. This paper, dedicated to the celebration of Henry Widdowson's major contributions to our field in introducing into it a principled but pertinent skepticism, deals with one such mythologized method.

The popular history of modern language teaching assigns a significant role to what is still mistakenly called the Army method, presented as the forerunner of the even more fabulous Audiolingual Method. In spite of the doubt expressed by Stern (1983: 102) that it was 'such a radical and successful innovation', this over-simplification has become so deeply ingrained into the common wisdom that we find it repeated in one of the first books to make a serious attempt at re-evaluating the history of English language teaching:

An earlier example of ELT [English Language Teaching] professionalism in operation was the American audiolingual doctrine which was widely disseminated in the post-war period [. . .] It is unthinkable that audiolingualism would have had such a significant impact globally without American economic might behind it. It is also possible that it would never have taken the form it did without its genesis in the Defense Language Institute, set up to teach foreign languages to US armed forces; learners were under military discipline and their promotion depended on success, which does wonders for motivation. (Phillipson 1992: 49)

Apart from his understandable confusion of the wartime Army Specialized Training Program (hereafter, ASTP) and the post-war Defense Language Institute, Phillipson's account is very close to what generations of applied linguists and language teachers have learned in their history of methods course. The published contemporary reports suggest a somewhat different story, which I will sketch here, in the hope that others will follow Barnwell (1992) in carrying out still-needed basic research.

What, I would like to ask, was the basis for the ASTP myth? Recent re-evaluations of the ASTP (of which the Foreign Language and Area Studies was one part) by Keefers (1988) and by Cardozier (1993) have made clear that the Army considered the program of little value, and felt it may have actually hurt the war effort by skimming off 150,000 highly qualified recruits from more useful employment. It did serve a useful function for the universities, in making up for the threatened wartime loss of students, and it did give the trainees a respite before they were sent, as most were, to regular infantry units where their language and other specially taught skills were not needed. But our interest is in the language teaching itself. How successful was language teaching in the ASTP? What contribution did the ASTP make directly to the changes in methodology in language teaching? Did this wartime emergency program, which was in active operation for barely a year, provide evidence that would have supported any revolution in language pedagogy? My answers on the value of the language program can only be tentative, for they are based on a limited number of published accounts I have come across in the course of reading with a different goal (see Spolsky 1995). But they will suggest, I hope, that the topic deserves more thorough study than it has so far received.

The outline is fairly clear. The exigencies of the Second World War exposed the major gap that had been left in American language teaching by the realistic if regrettable recommendation of the Modern Language Study, a decade earlier in 1924–28. Noting that most

American university students studied a foreign language for only two years, in classes that met for three hours a week, the authors of the study thought it wisest to reduce the goal of American foreign language teaching from the four skills that had been the aim of the earlier Direct Method to the reading ability that could be achieved in this limited allocation of time (Coleman 1928). The result was that most universities dropped their earlier interest in teaching the spoken language. This pragmatic decision fitted in well with the melting-pot philosophy that in the ethnocentrist and isolationist atmosphere of the United States after the First World War had led to the closing of bilingual education programs that would have encouraged the maintenance of national linguistic resources. Thus, in the early 1940s when the US Armed Forces started to gear up for a global war, its commanders quickly became aware of a shortage of recruits who could speak, understand, and read the large number of languages required for military purposes. Moreover, they found how inadequate was the ability of the current language teaching establishment to meet this demand and were forced to develop a completely new approach.

Their answer was the Army Specialized Training Division, created on December 18, 1942, under the jurisdiction of Lieutenant-General Brehon B. Somervell, Commanding General, Army Service Forces. One mission of the Division, under the direct command of Colonel Herman Beukema, was to produce soldiers with needed competence in all the languages and areas where the US armed forces could be reasonably expected to operate. By August 30, 1943, some nineteen different curricula had been established for language and area schools (Lind 1948).

The first Army Specialized Training Program language courses began their work in April 1943, with fifteen thousand non-commissioned trainees in courses offered at fifty-five different colleges and universities. In the absence of language aptitude tests of the kind that were to be developed a decade later, the trainees had been selected on the basis of their performance on the Army General Classification test, their proficiency in foreign languages, and their having completed one year of college (Agard, Clements, *et al.* 1944).

The language teaching curriculum was based on that developed for the Intensive Language Program of the American Council of Learned Societies (ACLS). The ACLS program had started some two years before, with two grants from the Rockefeller Foundation of $50,000 each, with the goal of teaching 'unusual' languages. It was directed by J. Milton Cowan, secretary of the Linguistic Society of America. Reflecting not just practical needs but also the ideological revolt of American structural linguists against the overriding concern of their philological predecessors and rivals with the written text and the literary language, the objective of the ACLS curriculum was to develop control of the spoken and vernacular variety of the target language. The goal of these structural linguists, as Widdowson (1990a: 11) points out, was communication, although their successors were later to claim the name 'communicative' for their own alternative methods.

The Army program endorsed the linguists' commitment to the specific goal of speaking the vernacular. In principle, any methodology was acceptable, provided that the teaching was 'intensive', which meant providing the recruit students with about fifteen hours a week of direct classroom instruction. Herbert Myron (1944), a teacher in the program, in a talk he gave while the program was in full operation, was clear that 'there is no such thing as the army method' but simply a directive insisting on emphasis on spoken fluency. Coming to the ASTP from more sheltered college teaching, Myron found his students to have generally poor attitudes to language learning (the high motivation induced by military discipline may also have been mythical), and described in some detail the modifications which he, as a traditional French teacher, had to make to fit the changed situation.

Public reception and evaluation of the ASTP

One immediate result of the wide publicity surrounding the program (see Angiolillo 1947) was a controversy between the supporters of the language teaching establishment and the linguists involved in the new development. In answering criticism that quickly appeared of extravagant claims being made for the new program, Cowan and Graves (1944) submitted a list of 'the modest "claims" which these advocates really do present'.

The first was that the 'dribble' method practiced in American colleges and universities of three hours of instruction a week, while it may have had other educational value, could not teach the 'practical speaking command' of the languages that the war situation demanded. This demanded a minimum of ten hours per week, conducted ideally by a trained technical linguist who was bilingual, and also an inspired and inspiring teacher. Their guess was that about twenty-five hours per week for three months or more would be desirable. While there was no new method, there were new materials needed for teaching spoken language, with grammar taught 'scientifically' as and when useful. Structural linguists, as Widdowson (1990a: 118) points out, were concerned with the medium of language and the process of learning. The fact that many structural linguists were involved in the teaching of the uncommon languages led to a belief that they developed a new scientific method of language teaching. Cowan and Graves downplayed this claim, which can be found repeated in such a recent treatment of the topic as Barnwell (1992). In their opinion, it was possible to employ teachers from many different pedagogic backgrounds. Their only proviso—and indeed assumption—was that all teachers were trained in 'scientific' linguistics.

The immodest and modest reports of the success of the new approach led to a call for more careful evaluation. At a meeting of the Commission on Trends in Education of the Modern Language Association of America in November 1943, Dr William Berrien (assistant director for humanities of the Rockefeller Foundation) passed on the suggestion of Elton Hocking of Northwestern University that a group of specialists should evaluate this new approach.

With funds provided by the Rockefeller Foundation, an evaluation team began its work on February 16, 1944, but only just in time, for on February 18 the War Department announced that by April 1, 1944, the Army Specialized Training Program would be suspended. Reinforcements for troops in Europe in preparation for the Normandy invasion had a higher priority than language specialists. Three of the field workers on the evaluation team had had some experience in ASTP programs; they spent two days preparing an outline of what they would look for. In the next six weeks, the six members of the project staff visited forty representative institutions across the country, saw 427 classes teaching sixteen different languages, met with program directors, teachers, and trainees, and talked to college and university administrators and faculty.

Their report (Agard, Clements, et al. 1944: 25) concluded modestly that for trainees for whom this was the first exposure to the target language, the results 'while by no means miraculous, were definitely

[327]

good, very satisfactory to the men in charge of the program, and very generally gratifying to the trainees themselves'. Wherever the program was well conducted (and they made no attempt to specify how many of the institutions met this criterion), a 'considerable percent' of the trainees developed ability to express themselves with fluency and a high level of ability to understand native speakers in normal conditions.

As a result of their survey, in a cautious statement issued in May, the Commission on Trends in Education of the Modern Language Association (1944) expressed 'deep satisfaction' with the results of the ASTP, which derived not from new methods but from well-tried practices that had been achieved not under the 'direction of linguistic magicians' but by regular foreign language teachers. These results, they stressed, were due to no 'miraculous formula' but to the liberal time allowed and to the use of small groups. Foreign language teachers would be happy to continue to work in these conditions, which would permit the 'creation of a body of American citizens whose knowledge of other languages would be adequate for our international contacts in post-war days' (Commission on Trends in Education 1944).

In spite of this belated interest in evaluation, there is little evidence of any attempt at a more general assessment of the results of the program. Agard and his colleagues (1944: 17) remarked on the absence of suitable tests of the spoken language. Most of the extensive debate, on one side or the other, depends on impressions and anecdotal evidence such as that recorded in Angiolillo (1947). Angiolillo, in the fullest but still incomplete account of the program, claimed that the Army desired tests and wanted the grading for them to be criterion referenced, and to indicate two levels of positive achievement: 'expert' and 'competent'.

1 Trainees who have satisfied the institutional authorities that they can both comprehend and speak the language as well as a person with the same amount of formal schooling should speak his mother tongue, will be graduated from Term 6 and will be designated on availability reports as expert.

2 Trainees who have satisfied the institutional authorities that they can readily comprehend the language as spoken by one adult native to another and can speak the language well enough to be intelligible to natives on non-technical subjects of military impor-

tance, will be graduated from Term 6 and will be designated on availability results as competent.

The wording of these criteria is interesting, appealing as they do to the native speaker comparison and setting up the distinction between the normal 'adult native' and the educated native that was maintained later in the Foreign Service Institute scale. The Army had two other grades, we are told by one commentator, non-competent and hopeless. In actual practice, however, institutions appear not to have used this system, but either a three-level system (fair, good, excellent) or a percentage score (Angiolillo 1947: 159).

There was a more elaborate test in use at Queens College, Angiolillo reported, on phonograph disks. This included vocabulary, idioms, sentences, paragraphs, conversations, and translator-situations but it was considered to be very difficult. Some of the other programs used standardized tests. At the University of North Carolina, three tests were given: the Cooperative French Test (both the Advanced Form and Form 19), and the Columbia Research Test (Form A) (Ghigo 1944). A set of tests for oral-aural skills in Russian and German was developed at Harvard by P. J. Rulon (1943, 1944a, 1944b, 1944c) under contract from the War Department. These tests, which Carroll (1954: 6) reported as existing on professionally produced phonograph records, were never used as the ASTP program for which they were prepared closed down before they were ready.

Post-war impact of the ASTP

After the war was over, in the lingering enthusiasm engendered by the wartime language-teaching experience, a number of US universities launched a program to reform their language instruction. One well-described case is Yale University, with a long tradition of an exceptional interest in teaching the spoken language (see Spolsky 1995).

At the beginning of 1944, a group of ten linguists at Yale (including such leaders in the field as Leonard Bloomfield, Bernard Bloch, William Moulton, and Edward Hall) wrote to the President of the University proposing that Yale adopt the ASTP methods for its elementary language classes. They suggested that all entering students should spend their first semester taking an intensive language program, with four hours a week in class meetings and ten hours a week in drill sessions, which would be three-fifths of their program. In the second semester they would go on to the reading of literary texts.

This proposal was referred to a faculty committee, which came up finally with a much more modest proposal. The committee (Pottle, Buck, *et al.* 1944) was enthusiastic about the effects of the Army courses, which required fifteen to seventeen hours a week rather than the old three to five hours a week. Instead of classes of twenty-five, there were three to five language structure lectures to the full group, accompanied by drill groups of six to eight. Many universities were contemplating adopting the system, but not to the extent of fifteen hours a week. The 'older literary and cultural teachers of foreign languages' remained skeptical (ibid.: 387). The method itself in its pure form was probably better for 'recondite languages' (ibid.: 388). A degree of intensity, the committee believed, would add a 'sense of steady growth and improvement' and so add to motivation. After interviewing numbers of supporters and opponents of the plan, they answered some of the major objections. Yale should not find it difficult to obtain native speakers 'whose speech is socially acceptable' (ibid.: 390). Literary goals were not ruled out. There was no danger of the 'natives' unbalancing the foreign language departments. Special provision could easily be made for the proportion of elementary language instructors, who must not be allowed to swamp the regular academic staff. The committee then recommended semi-intensive language classes meeting ten hours a week for all beginning language students, who would be encouraged to continue their studies and use the language skills obtained in courses in literature or other fields.

Another institution where the Army experience became a guiding light in the 'quest for curricular re-orientation' (Lind 1948: 5) was Mount Holyoke College, where Lind found 'much that is negative in the intensive language course as translated to the typical undergraduate campus' (ibid.: 7), but none the less appreciated its influence in encouraging a renewed enthusiasm for language learning. The approach was also influential as the basis for the organization of language instruction at Cornell University, but at most American universities, it tended to be restricted to the less commonly taught languages which continued for some time under the control of linguists and linguistic departments.

Despite the limitations on its diffusion to regular college teaching of the major foreign languages, the ASTP was influential in restoring American attention to oral teaching and testing. When Ralph W. Tyler, with support from the Rockefeller Foundation, conducted research at the University of Chicago (called *The investigation of the teaching of a second language*) on the effects of the new intensive programs, he found it necessary first to develop a testing program to measure the types and levels of skills that were objectives of the intensive instruction, so that in 1946 the project started to develop tests of oral and aural ability that would include among other materials a talking film (Agard and Dunkel 1948).

The Second World War might have been a critical period in the evolution of modern language tests in the US, but its effect was in fact limited, and as Barnwell (1992) concludes, 'no fundamental change in testing practices in high school or college grew out of the innovations brought about in the 1940s'. Barnwell (1992) does claim a direct line from the ASTP through Agard and Dunkel (1948) to modern practices, but deeper analysis suggests a more complex relationship. The absence of a formal centralized assessment for the ASTP lessened the potential impact of the wartime developments, but the change in curricular emphasis from reading to speaking added new urgency to the long-standing challenge of finding an acceptable way to assess proficiency in the spoken language. The old tests were not wrong; they just seemed irrelevant.

The experience of the ASTP, then, was limited. Its most important effect was in reasserting the emphasis, strong in 1913 but weakened after 1930, on the teaching of the spoken language, and thus reasserting the emphasis on face-to-face interaction which is usually associated with the communicative goal of language teaching.

The reputation of the ASTP a decade later

One of the later by-products of the interest in spoken communication was the language laboratory. William Riley Parker (1954), in the work paper he prepared for the citizen consultations initiated by the US National Commission for UNESCO on The National Interest and Foreign Languages, mentioned this debt.

> Although disc recordings for language learning had existed long
> before, the Army's use of a series (with a pause feature) especially and
> scientifically prepared for it during World War II did much to popu-
> larize this teaching or self-teaching device [. . .] At about the same
> time, Army experimentation with the magnetic wire recorder
> suggested infinite possibilities to some language instructors. Disc-
> recording laboratories were installed at Louisiana State and Cornell
> Universities; a few forward-looking teachers experimented with wire.
> (Parker 1954: 120)

It was only after the tape recorder became commercially available after
the Second World War that language laboratories started to burgeon,
with their new promise of a panacea for the frustrated language learner
and teacher.

The army experience also raised for the first time the challenge to
educational administrators of showing that there was real value in
clustering language teaching into intensive programs. As the account
of the Yale experience suggests, it took some time to move this idea into
regular educational settings (as in the immersion language programs
that spread out from Montreal) although it became the model for
military and government instruction.

Structural linguists and language teaching

While there was no direct methodology, the fact that a number of the
teachers in the program were trained in structural linguistics led them
to use some of the methods they used for linguistic analysis as the basis
for their teaching of the less commonly taught languages. It was this
approach, especially as developed at the School of Languages of the
Foreign Service Institute, that was to provide the false methodological
claims of the Audiolingual Method. But that is another myth, which
deserves a study of its own. Parker (1954) is a good place to start. In a
document making the case for language teaching to the general public,
he referred to the highly specialized meaning that had arisen for the
word *linguist*:

> persons who practice a certain technique of language learning
> and/or teaching (English or foreign) which may, in the case of an as
> yet unstudied exotic language, make it possible to instruct others in

that language without the personal ability to speak or read it with any skill.
(Parker 1954: 121)

This was, Parker noted, a 'recent phenomenon', and he noted that (in contrast to the 7500 members of the Modern Language Association of America which since 1883 had been comprised mainly of college teachers of English and modern foreign languages and literatures) there were only a thousand members of the more recently founded (1924) Linguistic Society of America, only a few of whom were 'structural linguists'. (He recommended using the adjective 'to save ourselves from the semantic asylum' of the confusion of terms.) He estimated that there were no more than a hundred or two such scholars, but noted that they formed 'an influential group. They are forward-thinking and enthusiastic; they have coherent views, which they express vigorously'. Most noticeably, they had been successful in achieving sponsorship and grants for their activities. In spite of this, Parker did not feel that their influence had been as wide as people feared.

Structural linguists first gained national prominence during World War II, when their constructive planning, their expertness, and their interest in exotic languages enabled them to assume a position of leadership in military teaching of language and 'area' programs. Their influence on foreign language teaching might today be considerably greater if they had been more numerous, but it so happened that most of the ASTP intensive language courses had to be taught by traditional language teachers, who modified their own methods in various degrees and produced as many variations of the 'Army method' as there were institutions involved.
(Parker 1954: 122)

From Parker's account, we can see evidence of the controversy that these structural linguists had produced, and I would like to quote one final paragraph from his monograph:

In this Work Paper it would be inappropriate to support either the 260 (say) who practice structural linguistics or the 26,000 foreign language teachers who do not. Common sense suggests, however, that if the 260 have something valuable to give the 26,000, as seems more than likely, they will not soon do it by ignoring or antagonizing

[333]

them, nor will the 26,000 help things by considering themselves beyond enlightenment.
(Parker 1954: 124)

This glimpse at what Parker called the 'troubled microcosm of language learning' leads us to appreciate the wisdom of Widdowson's arguments (1979a: 217) for the 'mediation' of an interpreter who can help language teaching realize the potential of insights about language. The attempt to find direct applications rather than to derive implications (Spolsky 1968) has been a regrettable tendency of our field, and we are grateful to Henry Widdowson for the elegant and polished ways in which he sets us on the wiser path.

Author's note

This is a revised version of an invited plenary address given at the 1994 annual meeting of the American Association of Applied Linguistics, Baltimore, Maryland. A modified version was read at the annual meeting of the Deseret Linguistic Association, Provo, Utah, and will appear in the proceedings of the meeting.

I am grateful to Nancy Fishberg for pointing out to me that the first patents for magnetic tape were issued in 1927 (in the US) and in 1928 (in Germany), and that the first public demonstration of the new medium was at the Berlin Radio Fair in 1936. Tape recorders made by the Magnetophone Company of Germany were used during the war.

I would like to take this opportunity to express my deepest thanks to Henry Widdowson for all his patient help and editorial guidance and warm friendship over the years, and to wish him, as one says in Yiddish, *biz hundert on tswantsik!*

22

'Reading with a suspicious eye': Critical Reading in the foreign language classroom

CATHERINE WALLACE

Introduction

HENRY WIDDOWSON HAS expressed reservations about work done in the field of Critical Discourse Analysis and Critical Language Awareness. None the less, it is discussion with him which has shaped much of the thinking in this paper. Many aspects of his work, particularly in stylistics and the reading process, have provided me with tools and insights for making sense of critical orientations to texts, readers, and classroom communication processes.

Over the past few years we have heard much talk of Critical Discourse Analysis, Critical Language Awareness, Critical Literacy, and Critical Pedagogy. I shall use the term Critical Language Awareness (CLA, henceforth), as the pedagogic arm of Critical Discourse Analysis, to cover all those aspects of classroom language work which aim to promote a critique of texts and language behaviour. It is the aim of this paper to explore the nature of this critique. The two broad questions to be addressed are: what does CLA mean in terms of classroom teaching, and what potential does it have as a tool for developing a new or differently focused pedagogy? In attempting to answer these questions, I shall look at key features of this field of enquiry, and describe how they come into play in the classroom context, in particular with foreign language learners.

The term 'Language Awareness' began to be used by Modern Language teachers and, to a lesser extent, by mother-tongue English teachers in the late seventies. This interest found expression in published Language Awareness materials, such as those devised by Hawkins (1984). The National Congress on Languages in Education report (1985) sees Language Awareness programmes (James and Garrett 1991: 4) as developing awareness within three broad parameters: a cognitive one which develops awareness of pattern in language; an affective one, relating to language attitudes; and a social one, for example, improving pupils' effectiveness as citizens and consumers.

Clark, Fairclough, *et al.* (1987), however, challenged the underlying aims of typical Language Awareness work, claiming that it took language conventions at face value and looked at language behaviour and phenomena only in global and general ways. Although issues of social diversity were addressed, they argued, there tended to be little or no consideration of the social influences which led to one variety or use of language being seen as more appropriate than any other for certain purposes. In particular, what was missing, it was claimed, was any consideration of how relations of power are implicated in the creation of linguistic conventions and are continually recreated in everyday discourse. Clark *et al.* set out an agenda for a CLA which would look at issues of diversity and inequality in more rigorous ways by promoting a closer and more critical analysis of both contextual and textual features of spoken and written language.

My aim here is to exemplify some of these principles through the description of a one-semester course taught to undergraduate students in a multilingual, multicultural class at Thames Valley University in West London. The focus of the course was on reading. The approach was 'critical', in the sense that students were encouraged to engage with reading as a practice and with texts as products in two major ways. First, they were invited to stand back from their own customary ways of reading texts and to reflect on reading practices which characterize different social groups, to see ways of reading (or what Heath (1983) has called 'ways with words') as socioculturally influenced. Secondly, they were given guidance in ways of critiquing particular written texts in order to reveal some of the otherwise covert relations of power embedded within them. There is a third level or layer of awareness which, as noted by Lankshear (1994), might emerge from such a way of looking at reading and at the nature of texts: the ability to relate specific readings of texts to wider readings of cultural practices or phenomena as observable, for instance, in other media such as television or film. Some of the students were beginning to articulate this kind of awareness by the end of the course.

In Critical Reading we are concerned both with the nature of texts and the nature of the reading process. And as this paper describes the attempt to *teach* something called Critical Reading in a course of that name, I am also concerned with the nature of classroom interaction—how meanings are negotiated not just between reader and writer but between all participants in a classroom setting. I shall therefore say something, in general and necessarily brief terms, about the role of the *text, readers*, and *classroom* setting as constituents in a series of discursive events we call 'lessons', before going on to describe the particular study.

The text

In the search for some set of principles or guiding framework to 'ground' textual analysis, like others working in the broad field of Critical Discourse Analysis, I looked to systemic/functional grammar. There are good reasons for this choice of model. Functional grammar offers the possibility of looking at whole texts in their social context. The ideational, interpersonal, and textual functions of language (Halliday 1970)—exemplified by features of grammar such as transitivity, mood, modality, and cohesion—are linked to features of the social situation in which the text arises, its content, the relationship between producer and receiver, and the overall function or rhetorical mode of the text, whether descriptive, narrative, or expository.

At the same time, Halliday (1990: 24–25) allows for depth as well as breadth of analysis. He talks of four levels of language use: the first and most readily perceived kind relating to obvious logical anomalies, such as 'eventually we will run out of food. We must learn to live with this'; the second, slightly less salient kind, relating to lexical effects as observed, for example, in ritualized collocations such as 'shedding jobs'; the third relating to what Halliday calls the 'outer layer' of grammar, as evidenced in function words such as pronouns; while the fourth is at the most concealed level of what Halliday calls 'the cryptogrammar', and relates to choices at clause level, which typically we are

[337]

less aware of. In other words, there is a gradient of linguistic options, along a cline from most to least accessible to consciousness.

Halliday takes the view that syntactic as well as lexical choices are socially motivated, in that they encode socially significant ways of looking at the world. 'Grammar creates the potential within which we act and enact our cultural being' (1990: 11); that is, the linguistic options exercised in texts will reflect taken-for-granted views of the world, assumed to be shared with the intended readership. As Stubbs (1994: 203) puts it: 'it is always possible to talk about the same thing in different ways and the systematic use of different syntactic patterns encodes different points of view.' (For a very different view of a similar point, made in Stubbs 1990, see Batstone in this volume.)

Stubbs and others seem to assume that all texts lend themselves to critical analysis. Is this the case, or do some texts or features of texts resist such analysis? According to Widdowson (personal communication), we do not question the ideological assumptions of a notice about a Fire Drill. Some kinds of text would seem to invite critical reading, most obviously discursive and expository texts. Invitation is signalled through the explicit nature of such texts, explicit because interaction may be specifically elicited by rhetorical questions, certain uses of modality, and cohesive features which give a recognizable rhetorical structure to the text. The avowed purpose of others (such as the Fire Drill text) is instrumental. These are texts which are supremely unopinionated, where interpersonal features such as modality are less apparent and ideological meaning is less salient.

Kress (1993: 174), in contrast, claims that all texts equally encode the ideological positions of their producers. 'The everyday, innocent and innocuous, the mundane text is as ideologically saturated as a text which wears its ideological constitution overtly.' This at first glance seems an absurdly strong claim. However, if we place the text in its context of production or reception, the point might be more readily taken. For example, the very decision to produce a text in the first place, or the presence of some kinds of texts in certain contexts rather than others, may indicate an assertion of power on the part of the producers of texts and their gate-keepers, related to the differing degree of prominence given to public texts such as those concerning entitlement to benefits, cigarette advertisements, and various kinds of health promotion campaigns.

Even when we look referentially at the content of the text itself, what is omitted is, arguably, ideologically significant, even in apparently uncontroversial texts. 'The absence of reference to shared information has led to the observation that it is what is omitted in discourse, the gaps within it, which constitute the shared ideology of the participants' (Cook 1992: 176). As no text can be fully informative, there must be omissions which are potentially prejudicial to particular groups or individuals.

None the less, there is a case for saying that there is simply more at stake, ideologically speaking, with some texts than others. There is what Eco (1992: 78) calls 'the transparent intention of the text'. Texts have a relatively stable, socially recognizable function and related kinds of content which it is perverse to disregard. Even if we later wish to use the text in different ways, to 'stand the text on its head', as Widdowson put it in a recent student seminar, we need first to acknowledge what the text is trying to do, that is, its generic identity. Culturally competent readers recognize the different jobs which texts are doing, and while the emergence of hybrid or mixed genres and the fudging of generic boundaries has been noted (for example, by Fairclough 1992a: 192), the fact that in general we can very readily name texts generically, as, for example, review, letter, pamphlet, or advertisement, testifies to some kind of consistency.

Finally, there is a case for saying that texts are not equally invested with power relations. As Eagleton (1991: 201) says, 'It is intellectually disingenuous to imagine that all language is rhetorical' (and therefore, he implies, ideologically invested) 'to exactly the same degree.' One imagines there is no covert persuasive function in the Fire Drill text; the producers of the text have, presumably, no ideological axes to grind.

Moreover, even if we compare texts from the same or comparable genres, texts do not, either through their manner of representation or reader address, reveal or mask their ideological provenance to the same degree. There are texts which, as indicated by the linguistic options taken up, invite a relative openness of response. To state this, however, suggests that some *aspects* of texts—as well as some *kinds* of texts—are implicated in the reproduction of power relations to a greater degree than others, and therefore carry greater ideological weight.

Widdowson (1991b) notes that while computers now offer comprehensiveness of analysis, linguists are still left with the job of selecting

[339]

which features to look for (see also Stubbs 1994: 218 and this volume, and Aston in this volume). And if the identification of ideologically significant features is hard for the critically oriented linguist, it is even more difficult for teachers to select particular features of texts on which to focus in critical language study in the classroom.

In the event, pragmatic factors play a major part in devising some kind of sequenced and rational linguistic analysis. These relate to the existing grammatical knowledge of the students, in particular their knowledge of metalanguage, the kinds of texts one wishes to work with, and the relative salience of linguistic features. Guided by Halliday's principle of the relative overtness or covertness of linguistic features (as discussed above), I decided, with the particular class described here, to give greater attention initially to interpersonal features, such as pronoun use and certain kinds of modality, as readily describable and observable, progressing later to ideational and textual features at the level of clause and textual structure manifested, for example, by transitivity and cohesion.

Readers and reading

We need a theory of reading as well as of texts. 'In critical linguistics there tends to be too much emphasis upon the text as product and too little emphasis upon the processes of producing and interpreting texts' (Fairclough 1992a: 28). In recent studies of reading, along with the granting of greater weight to the active role of the reader, there has been a move from 'comprehension' to 'interpretation'. Influential in this shift of emphasis has been Widdowson's work on the co-operative and negotiated nature of reader/writer dialogue (for example, Widdowson 1979c and 1984e). Readers do not simply receive or extract meaning from texts. They construct interpretations. Moreover, as Widdowson repeats in recent work (1992a), he would wish to offer legitimacy to a wide range of interpretations, at least in the case of poetry.

However, as Widdowson himself asks, 'how far does this licence run?' (1992a: 189). Do we wish to say that all interpretations are equally legitimate in all circumstances, especially if we look beyond literary texts to a wider range of text genres? Clearly the answer is no. I argue (Wallace 1992a) that some readers are in a stronger position than others to offer legitimate responses, for a number of different—even conflicting—

reasons. On the one hand there are readers (both L1 and L2) who are helped by a very full contextual and intertextual knowledge; they have considerable background knowledge to draw on, including knowledge of similar kinds of texts. However, some L2 readers who are reading texts originally written for an indigenous readership may be advantaged simply because they are reading from an outsider position; they are 'overhearing' rather than being directly addressed (see Mills 1992). Their overhearer status means that they are not invited to collude in a text's ideological assumptions. In other words, simply because a foreign language reader is not part of the text's intended or model readership, he or she may more readily observe and resist its positioning.

But (I hear my reader saying) what if the reader wishes not to resist? Critical reading is posited on the inevitability, albeit to varying degrees, of reader positioning and the consequent necessity of resistance. Resistance—a preparedness to challenge—is indeed the *raison d'être* of critical reading. This raises a number of questions and dilemmas. Firstly, a critical stance to texts arguably infringes Grice's co-operative principle (1975), running counter to the negotiated, jointly constructed nature of the reader/writer discourse, described in many places by Widdowson. In this sense, critical reading is indeed unnatural—it is posited on non-co-operativeness, a standing back momentarily to gain a different perspective, in ethnographic terms to 'make the familiar strange'.

A second, more substantial objection to critical reading relates more closely to the classroom context, and I shall turn my attention to this next.

The classroom

Critical reading pedagogy, its opponents argue, far from being emancipatory, is tyrannical, denying readers the option to submit—to position themselves, voluntarily and comfortably—among a text's model readership. Teachers in classrooms where resistance is unequivocally on the agenda are open to charges of demanding students' submission to their own (critical) purposes. The question then arises whether students are allowed to resist resistance. This may be even more of an issue when students come from cultural traditions where resisting either the text or the teacher is considered highly inappropriate.

However, as played out in the classroom setting, the initial reader roles adopted by both teacher and students become less polarized on the submissive/assertive continuum. So, although teachers will have favoured prior interpretations of the texts they introduce, all texts inevitably take on fresh and unpredictable meanings in the course of class debate. Even if the general orientation is one of resistance, in practice, interpretations are not so much submissively or assertively oriented, as layered and complex. In the course, for example, of revisiting a particular text (perhaps read casually at home), individual students will reassess initial responses—not necessarily to replace them, but to allow them to co-exist with subsequent ones. Moreover, any anticipated divide between affective and social/critical responses also tends to get fudged. Responses to texts will be both highly individual as well as socially influenced. Indeed, what individuals discover through critical analysis is more about the ways they are located in a complex nexus of social influences. This awareness is heightened by the impact of different cultural traditions and experiences which are particularly evident in multicultural classrooms.

A critical reading course: texts, readings, and classroom interaction

By way of illustration of how some of the principles so far discussed work out in practice, I shall describe a critical reading course which lasted for one semester of fifteen weeks. The students, in their early twenties, from Spain, France, and Germany, had chosen to do the course and most were first-year undergraduates doing a degree in Modern Foreign Languages. Among auditors attending the course were teachers from China, Indonesia, and Argentina. One of the teachers, from Germany, acted as a participant observer, in the sense that although, like the others, she took part in all class activities, she also advised me week by week about aspects of the course. This allowed me to gain some greater distance from—and thus a more critical perspective on—my own classroom practice.

Rationale of course

An initial 'consciousness-raising' phase lasted four weeks and looked at reading as a social practice and process. The aim was to draw on the resources of our multicultural group to share different perceptions about the ways in which texts are socially produced and interpreted. The second, longer phase involved detailed textual analysis of a range of texts where students worked in pairs and groups drawing on a framework adapted from Hallidayan grammar.

A key principle of the course was explicitness about features of both context and text. So, as well as presenting a set of grammatical terms as tools for text analysis, I offered terms for contextual analysis which preceded the more finely tuned work we did on the texts themselves. Thus terms such as 'knowledge of the world', 'intertextuality', 'model reader', and 'genre' were introduced.

The selection of texts

Both the students and myself brought texts into the classroom. I have one or two which I regularly use as and when they are likely to have a resonance for students. Indeed, some of these texts have accrued a history of layered interpretations through use with successive student groups. One is a newspaper text about violent behaviour by British tourists in Ibiza, which begins as follows:

EXPLOITATION THAT TURNED THE LAGER LOUT PROBLEM INTO A CRISIS

The blame that Spain must share

ROBBIE is not really a lager lout. He has been turned into one. He lives at home with his parents in a rather sleepy market town in Somerset. He's neat, quiet. He's got a job.

He's an enthusiastic supporter of his cricket club and his idea of a night out is a dance with his girlfriend, who was a bit upset he'd gone on holiday without her.

All of which makes the sight of him crumpled in a drunken heap among the cigarette ends on the floor of the Casa Padri Bar at 2.30 a.m. so depressing.

How many people back home in Frome would have recognised that livid face, reddened by the sun and an excess of alcohol? That slurred, thick voice hurling out mindless, four-letter insults: his soft West Country accent twisted into ugliness? The yellow singlet his mother had ironed before packing for him, torn and stained with beer?

'Why is it you English behave like this?' asked the bar's proprietor Paco Munoz as we dragged Robbie out on to the pavement, spewing curses at everyone, before he recovered enough to lurch into the nearest disco.

A hypocritical question for a Spaniard to ask. The Spanish wring their hands and rightfully complain about the shameless excesses of British youth: excesses which have not gone away, despite their disappearance from the news, excesses that this week in San Antonio, Ibiza, caused the murder of young waiter Jesus Moreno.

We should be ashamed. But so, too, should the Spanish. For it is their ruthless and cynical exploitation of young tourists, pouring alcohol down their albeit willingly open throats, that has turned a potential problem into disaster.

The Spanish have, whether they like it or not, created a factory for lager louts. Right across the Balearics and along the Costas they have nurtured a climate where drunken, outrageous behaviour is almost inevitable. Drink is so available, so ridiculously cheap . . .

Daily Mail 3rd August 1989

The institutionalized xenophobia of this report, while barely apparent to many native speaker readers, provokes outrage—articulated in varying ways—among foreign learners (see Wallace 1992b for a fuller discussion of this text).

Students brought in texts as a result of different kinds of motivation—anger, amusement, or bewilderment. The texts then formed a pool or resource and were drawn on, not necessarily immediately but when they could be maximally exploited, for example in conjunction with similar or contrasting texts. We began with texts where interpersonal features were dominant, such as advertisements, posters, letters, speeches, and manifestos. (One of the students was doing a project on the extreme right-wing British National Party, thus prompting the search for relevant texts.) We then progressed to descriptive texts such as travel brochures and magazine articles, report texts such as news reports, and concluded with expository texts, exemplified for instance in editorials and newspaper columns.

Contextual analysis

I approached the contextual analysis at the level of genre, using the term, as Kress (1989) does, to mean any socioculturally recognizable text type. As a category, genre is useful for students from diverse cultural backgrounds in underpinning discussion of the social and ideological factors involved in the emergence, disappearance, or reshaping of different kinds of texts in different social environments.

Specifically, we worked with the following set of questions adapted from Kress (1989). These guided us into progressively greater depth of analysis:

1 Why has this text been written?

2 What is this text about?

3 To whom is this text addressed?

4 How is the topic written about?

5 What other ways of writing about the topic are there?

Textual analysis

After four weeks the Hallidayan framework was given to students to support closer textual analysis. It was intended as a resource for students to draw on when they wished to show how particular readings are warranted by the linguistic features of the text (Widdowson 1992a: xiv). While earlier in the course we had looked at relatively salient features such as connotation at lexical level and at features of syntax such as pronoun usage, from week five we focused on, first, a wider range of interpersonal features which characterized the texts we had worked with early in the course, such as advertisements, manifestos, and speeches. We then moved on to attend to ideational features as evidenced through, for example, the nature of participants and processes in descriptive texts, and the representation of causation and agency in report texts.

Tasks

The tasks which were done in pairs or groups were designed to mediate between the text and the framework, and to become progressively more demanding in the detail of linguistic analysis which they invited. In one

[345]

very early task involving the identification of genre, for example, students sorted and categorized a whole range of everyday texts brought into the classroom. Another task encouraged them to observe the ways in which a reader is constructed by a text through the nature of the language used. It also invited students to judge whether they thought that they were part of the model readership of the text, and on what basis they formed their conclusions. Later tasks involved both greater depth and greater breadth of analysis. For example, students might pair up to focus in turn on the interpersonal, ideational, and textual aspects of a particular text before their observations were shared and further debated by the whole group.

Conclusion

How far do the kind of procedures described here develop awareness of what it means to be a reader in different social settings? To what extent are students offered understanding of the social nature of text production and reception, and greater insights into the ideological significance of the linguistic options exercised in texts?

Awareness may emerge in different ways through different channels and at different levels of generality. There is space here only for three illustrative examples. The first is an on-line verbal response as Blanca, a Spanish student, reflects on the possible significance of the linguistic options evident in a newspaper headline: MASKED MOB STONE POLICE.

> You notice how they're talking about violent events (this) 'Mob stone police' instead of 'Mob stones police'. They are emphasizing the size er . . . the number of people confronting the police.

In the following extract from the end-of-course evaluation, a French student, Aurelie, notes her awareness of how she feels her own reading has changed during the course.

> The course helped me to keep my distance in relation to the texts; to be careful and to pay attention to the writer's intentions. Now I read texts differently. I analyse words and construction of sentences more than before. Texts are more attractive and interesting when you read them with a suspicious eye, trying to catch key words, hidden messages and ideas between the lines.

[346]

I noted above how one or two students were beginning to move beyond the critique of particular texts to relate those readings to wider interpretations of ways of doing things, of cultural practices in specific social milieus. This, I take it, is what Virginia is engaged in here, as she draws on the text quoted above ('The blame which Spain must share'), relating this text to the general discourse of the news. The extract is taken from a much longer interaction between Virginia and myself three months after the end of the course:

> Also in the news but in the TV I pay attention to it . . . because it's a very very funny way of reporting news that you have here in England . . . you always look for a very specific example. Do you remember the Spanish text?—talking about the waiter, the text of the er . . . Englishman who went to Spain. The first lines of the article were the description of the guy and his mother and what he did on Saturdays and his girlfriend, and then once you have presented and described the person then you can tell the story . . . it's very personalized. It's everywhere—in the news, in the radio. You think it's natural . . . but it was new for me.

Final remarks: the personal and the political

Inevitably, unease and controversy will remain around the principles and practice of Critical Language Awareness, as we might expect from a committed pedagogy of this kind; there is a whiff of self-righteousness about it, a hint of missionary zeal. In its defence, I would argue that concern with the social and political does not preclude a role for the private and individual (see Cook 1994: 255). Indeed, it is often a student's strong and very personal initial response to a text which motivates the wish to explore more deeply the linguistic features which have combined to produce such powerful effects. Moreover, many students are liberated by the acknowledgement that apparently authoritative texts are open to challenge, that as foreign language readers their interpretations, for the very reasons that they are outsiders or 'overhearers', will be particularly welcomed. Critical reading thus has the potential to be affectively as well as intellectually and critically engaging.

23

What is this class about? Topic formulation in an L1 reading comprehension classroom

LUIZ PAULO DA MOITA LOPES

Introduction

CLASSROOMS AS SOCIAL events essentially operate on the basis of interactional procedures between teachers and pupils in which both try to construct meaning and knowledge. In contrast to other social events, classroom discursive practices are geared towards the construction of knowledge/learning between discourse participants[1] who are acting within asymmetrical social participation structures (Schultz, Florio, and Erickson 1982). In this paper[2], topic formulation in classroom interaction is investigated in an L1 reading classroom, from an ethnographic perspective, with a view to understanding how the topic as a crucial element in the organization of talk contributes to the construction of knowledge about reading comprehension in the classroom. First, the view of discourse and learning which underlies this paper is discussed. Then, the role played by topic formulation in classroom discourse is presented, the context and research instruments described, and the data analysed. The analysis reveals that, on the one hand, teachers' formulated topics are not perceived by learners as a way of orienting them towards what is to be learned and, on the other, teachers are not willing to accept pupils' topics.

Discourse and learning

Both discourse and learning are viewed here as the result of socio-interactional procedures between discourse participants in a joint effort to construct meaning and knowledge. This theoretical perspective, drawing attention to the centrality of interaction in human relationships and regarding it as the crucial element, now permeates different areas of investigation including discourse analysis, applied linguistics, education, and psychology. In all these areas, there has been concern with the study of language in contexts of interaction, with what Wertsch (1991: 8) refers to as 'the cultural, institutional and historical nature of mediated action'.

In the field of discourse analysis, several researchers (Widdowson 1983b; Duranti 1986; Fairclough 1989; Nystrand and Wiemelt 1991, among others) have argued for a dialogical perspective on both oral and written discourse which is taken as being constructed by participants in meaning negotiation and which is therefore socio-historically situated: '. . . meaning is always a negotiated, shared construct' (Nystrand and Wiemelt 1991: 32). That is to say, meaning is not inherent in language, but is, in fact, a social construction. Therefore, participants become involved and involve others in discourse through interaction in particular socio-historical circumstances. In other words, they construct discourse (i.e. the meanings by which they live) and, therefore, society. This view of the socio-historical nature of discourse implies that participants in discursive practices are positioned within power relations in which particular political and economic projects are in dispute (Fairclough 1992b). Therefore, discourse is represented here as having an intrinsic relationship with power.

Likewise, learning is taken here as being socio-interactionally determined. Several researchers (Wertsch 1985, 1991; Bruner 1986; Newman, Griffin, and Cole 1989; Lave and Wenger 1991, among others), all of whom follow a Vygotskian view of learning, have regarded learning as a form of social co-participation in which learners engage in a practice through interaction with a specialist, operating within what Vygotsky (1978) has called the 'zone of proximal development', and Newman, Griffin, and Cole (1989) the 'construction zone'. In this practice, learners operate peripherally in relation to the specialist until, little by little, his or her participation in the social act of learning becomes full and, as a result of learning, higher psychological processes are developed. In Bruner's words (1986), competence is handed over to the learner: intrapersonal processes are therefore seen as being generated by interpersonal processes. From this point of view, the basis of cognition is located in socio-interactional procedures.

Thus, as Duranti (1986: 239) says, the view of discourse presented here 'as a form of labour . . . which requires the coordination of several actors around a task . . . is consistent with a psychology in which higher psychological processes in the individual have their origin in social interaction'.

The issue of concern here is how the formulation of topic in a classroom discursive task in which teachers and pupils are co-participants relates to the construction of learning to read in L1.

Topic formulation

One of the central features of teacher talk is the formulation of topic, i.e. what learners have to attend to either in relation to what is going on, to what is to come next, or to what has already gone. According to Garfinkel and Sacks (1970), topic formulation in conversation is the moment when a participant describes the conversation, explains it, or provides its main point.

Following Brown and Yule (1983: 88), an interactive view of topic is adopted here. Participants are perceived as operating within a topic framework and contributing topics to the conversation which are then negotiated in the interactional process.[3]

In classroom interaction, however, due to the unequal knowledge distribution and the asymmetrical interactional relation between teacher and pupils, the teacher typically, as the more competent/ powerful member of the interaction, orients the organization of discourse by indicating the topic, hoping that this process will engage the student and be conducive to learning. Therefore, topic formulation has the function of organizing the interaction in the light of the teacher's agenda. That is to say that, contrary to most conversation, topics in classroom discourse are usually fixed beforehand (Brown and Yule 1983: 89). They call the pupils' attention to what they have to focus on to collaborate with the teacher interactionally. Pupils' engagement in

[351]

the teacher's topic constitutes a crucial point in the lesson since its development depends on teacher and students sharing a frame of reference on the basis of which common knowledge can be built (Edwards and Mercer 1987). 'Communication begins as an initial calibration of conversants' intentions and expectations *vis-à-vis* the topic and genre of the text . . .' (Nystrand and Wiemelt 1991: 36) so that the topic can be 'anchored'. It could be argued that one of the interactional procedures learners have to learn to use is exactly to subscribe to the suggested topic so that by developing a sense of meaning which is mutually constructed, teaching is made successful (Mehan 1979).

Learners, then, typically have to collaborate with the topics introduced by the teacher. Their interactional rights and obligations in classrooms imply that they have to operate in structures of social participation whose topics are, in general, suggested by the teacher's pedagogic agenda.

As Heyman (1986: 38) indicates, classroom topics are formulated in the form of statements or of questions. This leaves room for the learner to contribute a topic. That is, the teacher asks a question which, she or he hopes, may make the learner contribute to the topic she or he has in mind. Clearly, as I shall show in the data analysis below, these questions are actually a source of problems when the topics put forward by learners do not correspond to the teacher's agenda because learners are operating from different schematic knowledge structures (Rumelhart 1980) or from different learning agendas. In conversational contexts, where participants interact on the basis of more equal participation rights, this problem is more easily solved since participants negotiate their schemata and/or agendas with greater ease. In the classroom, however, teachers (as the more competent participants) are constantly evaluating and monitoring pupils' talk in the light of their teaching purpose: 'In almost any classroom teachers . . . exercise rights with regard to topic selection, topic change, turn taking and openings and closings, which pupils do not share' (Heyman 1986: 50). In view of the unequal social relations within which classroom discourse develops and the fact that topic formulation is a source of trouble, it seems essential to investigate how topic formulation relates to the construction of learning to read.

Research context and methodology

The investigation reported in this paper involves data derived from the Portuguese as a Mother Tongue (PMT) Reading Research Project, which centred on the evaluation of a set of materials in public-sector schools in Rio de Janeiro. This set of materials was designed on the basis of the following theoretical principles: an ethnomethodological view of discourse (Psathas 1979; Widdowson 1983b), a socio-interactional view of reading (Rumelhart 1977; Widdowson 1984e) and a socio-interactional view of learning (as discussed above). This project represents an attempt to address a central area of educational concern in Brazilian public-sector schools: the improvement of reading performance (Moita Lopes 1995).

The project extended over a period of one year (two classes of forty-five minutes each a week for a period of nine months) in the Escola Eurico Gaspar Dutra, located in a working-class neighbourhood in Rio de Janeiro. The project investigated two fifth-grade groups with the same teacher—group 501 (about eleven years old) and group 504 (about fifteen years old). The two groups had about thirty-five pupils each, but were different in terms of their members. While group 501 was considered the good-learner group, group 504 consisted of so-called 'repeaters' and was thought of as the poor-learner group in the school context. The groups were chosen because their teacher volunteered to participate in the projects. The classrooms were organized in a traditional way: pupils were seated in rows, facing the teacher.

The classes in each group were tape-recorded and observed with field-notes being taken by a research assistant and by the project co-ordinator. Four of the classes were also video-recorded for the purpose of ethnographic micro-analysis (Erickson 1992), including the class whose initial sequences are examined in this paper. At the end of the school year, semi-structured interviews were conducted with the teacher and three pupils from each group, chosen on the basis of the teacher's informal evaluation of their motivation as high, middle, or low level. The data presented in this paper are mainly derived from the transcription of a video- and tape-recorded class which was taught on 10th August 1992. Interview data derived from reviewing tape sessions with the teacher are also used. The ethnographic micro-analysis of the interaction to be discussed here is derived from just one class taught in group 504 (the so-called bad-learner group).

Analysis and discussion of data

The two research questions addressed in this paper are: 1) how the topic formulated by the teacher is taken up by learners in the joint effort of constructing common knowledge about reading comprehension; and 2) how this affects the task of learning to read. To carry out this analysis, I will focus on who formulates the topic and how it is developed by discourse participants. The sequences of the class below were selected because they typically indicate teacher and pupil involvement with topic formulation at the opening of a class when the teacher is pointing out what is going to happen in class. The data under focus are the initial sequences of the class (the first ten minutes). Since the classes were taught in Portuguese, I have translated the sequences of the lesson analysed below for the purpose of this paper. Although translation may affect the analysis or actually change the data, the analysis undertaken here follows the Portuguese transcriptions. I have tried to preserve the information found in these transcriptions in the English version presented below.

Analysis

Before I proceed to the analysis of the class, it is essential to contextualize the sequences. These are the opening sequences of the class when the teacher is trying to activate, in the pupils' minds, the content schematic area (Carrell 1983) of the text which she is going to use to teach reading comprehension on that particular day. With this purpose in her teaching agenda, she requires pupils to tell a story with fictional characters. The pupils, however, choose to talk about another issue, namely the impeachment of the President.

In lines 1–3 (Sequence 1), the teacher begins by formulating the topic of the class.

Sequence 1: the opening

1 T: Well, class, today we are going to work on our reading
2   material. And the title of the text we are going to study
3   is as follows . . .

[354]

Then, in lines 4–5 (Sequence 2), there is a short interruption of the teacher's topic formulation by a latecomer, but in lines 6–8 she resumes her talk and concludes the formulation by asking a pupil to read the title of the text aloud.

Sequence 2: concluding the opening

4   P1:   Good morning, Mrs S.

5   T: Good morning.

6   [T writes the title of the text on the blackboard] Well,

7   this is the title of our text . . . ehhh

8   P2, could you read the title aloud?

9   P2:   It is necessary to transform the world.

In lines 10–17 (Sequence 3), the teacher goes on specifying what is to happen in the class and the way she wants the pedagogic task to be developed. In other words, she goes into more detail about the topic. This reflects how she wants the content schema of the text to be activated in the pupils' minds. She requires them to invent a story with the same title as the text: 'It is necessary to transform the world'.

Sequence 3: the pedagogic task

10 T: It is necessary to transform the world. Then let's see

11   what kind of story I could give this title to. Let's

12   imagine a situation in which I write a story . . . tell

13   a story. And the facts presented in this story will

14   have as title . . . or better, the story will have as

15   title: 'It is necessary to transform the world'. Let's

16   think a bit. Then, ideas will come to your minds. You

17   tell the story to me.

In lines 18–23 (Sequence 4), P3 tries to engage in the formulated topic (lines 18 and 20), but the teacher does not accept her interpretation of the task and repeats how she wants pupils to tell the story (lines 21–23).

Sequence 4: trying to engage in the topic

18 P3: . . . [a story in which] something good . . .

19 T: Yes.

20 P3: which has to do with the title.

21 T: No, I want you to imagine a situation, a story whose

22   title could be this: 'It is necessary to transform

23   the world'.

In lines 24–41 (Sequence 5), P3 is still negotiating with the teacher. Finally, she seems to have understood that the story demanded by the teacher has to involve something bad which has to be transformed into something good. Accordingly, she chooses a topic which, at that time, was being widely discussed in the country—the impeachment of the President. From now on, this topic suggested by P3 will constitute a source of trouble for what is to come next. The pupil's topic is this political issue (P4 in lines 42–43 and P6 in line 49) while the teacher does not want to talk about it. She goes on insisting on a story with fictional characters (lines 36–38, lines 44–46, and line 50). In other words, she is formulating a topic which pupils do not seem to engage in. As she actually indicated in a retrospective interview about this class, her teaching agenda required the telling of a story to activate the content schema of the text they were to start reading. However, the pupils' learning agenda led them to discuss the political event. This would, in fact, have been adequate for her teaching agenda: activating a content schema which would facilitate the reading comprehension of the text entitled 'It is necessary to transform the world'.

Sequence 5: the source of trouble—the impeachment

24 P3: . . . something bad . . . to transform the world into

25   something good.

26 T: Yes, but I want a situation. You . . .

27 P3: The Congress Inquiry Commission, a fraud. It is

28   necessary to transform all this.

29 T: OK. You are telling me a fact which . . . eh . . . has

30   eh has to do with this conclusion here. After listening

31   to all these stories, you come to the conclusion that it

32   is necessary to transform the world. However, from these

33   recollections, imagine a story which involves the

34   Congress Inquiry Commission since you remember this.

35 P3:   The fake bank accounts.

36 T: OK, but let's try to create some characters who found

37   out about this situation . . . some characters who found out

38   about this piece of news. How did they react? While P3

39   thinks about a story . . ., would anyone have a situation

40   which could have as a conclusion that it is necessary to

41   transform the world?

42 P4:   If there is a fake bank account, there is someone

43   involved with it.

44 T: Yes, I know, but listen, we are not discussing the fact

45   itself. What I want is a story, i.e. a situation in which

46   people . . .

47 P5:   people

48 T: Right! Talk about this fact.

49 P6:   Yes, Paulo Cesar Farias [one of the people accused in the inquiry]

50 T: No, was the fact in the news?

51 P5:   Yes.

In lines 52–66 (Sequence 6), the pupils seem to have finally grasped what the teacher wants them to do: to invent a story (lines 57, 59, 62 and 64). At last they have engaged in her topic and seem willing to collaborate with her.

Sequence 6: the story, at last

52 T: This fact was published in the paper.

53 P7:   It was on TV, on the radio.

54 T: Everywhere. So, let's . . . think about some

55   characters who became aware of this fact via TV, for

56   example.

57 **P8:** Carlos and Pedro [two characters in the reading texts]

58 **T:** Aha. Who . . . would our characters be?

59 **P5:** Carlos, Pedro and Bia [another character in the texts]

60 **T:** You think they could be our characters? OK, Carlos,

61   Pedro and Bia. They are at home . . . doing what?

62 **P2:** Watching television.

63 **T:** Watching television.

64 **P2:** Listening to the radio.

65 **T:** Listening to the radio. [Pupils go on imagining what the

66   characters would do.]

Nevertheless, once again in lines 67–82 (Sequence 7), the pupils resume their topic (lines 70–79), i.e. they want to talk about a fact related to their lives (the impeachment of the President), although this is a source of trouble in their interaction with the teacher. P3 actually takes a turn and elaborates on the topic she wants to talk about (lines 70–79), but the teacher once again does not accept this topic. She does, however, frame it in such a way as to make the pupil's topic actually serve her own interactional purpose or teaching agenda (lines 79–82).

Sequence 7: trouble again—the impeachment

67 **T:** Yes, but what would their solutions be?

68 **Ps:** . . . [inaudible]

69 **T:** So, what should be done?

70 **Ps:** Look, there should be demonstrations.

71 **P3:** They should all lose their jobs and new people who

72   could transform the world should get them. People

73   could transform things differently. Because not

74   everybody who is getting into the congress now is

75   doing something. Everybody has to do something,

76   otherwise they should all lose their jobs, the

77   President included. Collor [the impeached President]

78   was one of the bosses. If all of them lost their

79   jobs, there could perhaps be some positive outcome . . .

80 T: So you think this was the discussion of the two brothers,

81   [Carlos and Pedro], that the transformation of the world

82   would be like that in our case. P8, do you have another idea?

In lines 83–89 (Sequence 8), the task (activating the content schema of the text) comes to an end. (The teacher conducts this sequence holding the reading texts which are going to be distributed, and moves on to another task—line 89.) But the same source of trouble persists: the pupils go back to their topic, the impeachment of the President (line 85), though once again this is not accepted by the teacher (lines 86–87). In fact, the teacher's pedagogic task set in Sequence 3 is simply not done because of the trouble created by the different topic.

Sequence 8: the closing—trouble once more

83 T: yes, P8? . . .

84   How do you think things could change?

85 P8: Impeaching the President.

86 T: No, let's talk in general terms about our everyday life.

87   We are always blaming people who are far from us . . .

88   This transformation of the world can start with ourselves,

89   can't it? Now, I am going to give out the texts.

Discussion

The question that needs to be addressed is why the teacher does not accept the pupils' topic, even when this seems to be totally adequate for her agenda. The conflict between the teacher's teaching agenda, expressed in her topic, and the pupils' learning agenda, made clear in their topic, persists thoughout the various sequences. Apparently, the pupils wanted to learn by discussing a fact related to their political lives—the impeachment of the President—whereas the teacher was concerned with having them tell a story to illustrate the title of the text.

This conflict constitutes a source of trouble in the interaction because teacher and pupils refer to two different bodies of knowledge:

[359]

the story and the impeachment respectively. In normal conversation, this trouble could be easily negotiated; here, however, because of the asymmetrical social participation structures within which pupils and teacher interact, the teacher exercises her right to open the interaction by formulating the topic of the pedagogic task, and to close it even when it has not been completed as planned. The teacher is exercising a kind of pedagogical tyranny by not allowing the pupils to contribute interactionally to the construction of meaning even when the pupils' topic is suitable for her teaching agenda and does not threaten to disrupt the order of the lesson. As made evident in the development of the sequences above, the teacher's refusal to accept the pupils' topic adds trouble to the interaction itself and to the completion of the task: 'since formulations are always a potential trouble source we can suggest that teacher formulation which does not allow space for pupil response can only add to the trouble' (Heyman 1986: 53).

The analysis of the data above seems to indicate that: a) the teacher's formulated topics may not be perceived by learners as orientation to what is to be learned (i.e. the topic of the class); and b) the teacher, in order to avoid disruption of her pedagogical agenda, may not be willing to accept learners' topic contribution. In view of the fact that the group of learners involved in the interaction analysed above are considered poor learners, this paper draws attention to the need to consider whether their reluctance to accept the teacher's topic, as more passive pupils would do, could be one of the reasons for their lack of success at school. They do not seem as willing to comply with the typical classroom interactional rules. In an earlier paper (Moita Lopes 1993), a similar issue was raised in connection with the less traditional interactional pattern of this group if compared with the so-called good-learner group.

Conclusion

The implications of the research presented in this paper relate to the construction of knowledge about reading comprehension and to the act of learning itself.

If the interaction analysed here aimed at the teaching of reading comprehension, it is essential to consider how the interactional role played by the teacher (when she does not accept the pupils' topic) may be affecting their perceptions of reading comprehension since she was actually directing their comprehension of the text to be read by indicating the content schema she wished them to activate.

While the pupils wanted to activate a schema related to their political context, which would then initiate their projection of schematic knowledge on the text and, therefore, their participation in the social construction of meaning, the teacher seemed to be guiding their reading from the perspective of her pedagogical agenda. This strategy in a reading class may lead pupils to perceive meaning not as socially constructed but as constructed by someone in authority—the teacher (Moita Lopes 1995). The danger, then, is that in such reading classes pupils may be learning that learning to read is learning to respect someone who has textual authority (Aronowitz and Giroux 1991).

Furthermore, by not having their topics accepted in classroom discursive practices, learners are learning to use language in contexts where their contribution to meaning is not taken into account, and therefore, in the last analysis, they may be learning to discount their own political effectiveness. This point becomes even more crucial when we consider that the pupils participating in this research belong to the oppressed social classes: the possibility of social transformation may be annihilated in schools through the interactional roles played by the teacher and the pupils. Perhaps, in this context, concern with interactional patterns on the part of teachers, leading learners as it does into the social construction of both oral and written meaning—including formulating and discussing topics—may be as important as issues related to pedagogical content and procedures.

As regards the act of learning itself, the analysis undertaken in this paper seems to indicate that the teacher's difficulty in accepting the topic introduced by learners may be harmful to the development of a shared mental context (Edwards and Mercer 1987) between the teacher and learners in which common knowledge about reading comprehension could be socio-interactionally constructed.

Finally, this research seems to show that topic formulation in classrooms requires learners to operate as pupils by accepting teachers' topics, but it also draws attention to the need to develop teachers' awareness of the necessity to integrate learners' roles as pupils—their institutional roles—with their roles as citizens (Ribeiro 1994, in which a similar point is made about the roles of patients as citizens and patients). This paper indicates that teachers, student-teachers, and researchers need to pay far more attention to the micro-analysis of teacher–pupil interaction than has been done so far.

Notes

1 Although, in principle, one could think of any interactional encounter (doctor–patient, salesperson–client, etc.) as an act of knowledge/meaning construction since questions and answers can be respectively framed as problems ('I don't know this; do you have a solution?') and solutions, ultimately teacher–pupil encounters are socially justifiable as learning encounters.

2 The research reported on here was made possible by CNPq (300194–86/2) and FUJB (3825–3) grants.

3 For a different approach to topic, see Schiffrin 1987b.

24

Discourse analysis and the teaching of listening

MARIANNE CELCE-MURCIA

Introduction

WHEN PEOPLE LISTEN—whether they are listening to a lecture, a news broadcast, a joke, or are engaging in a conversation—they are listening to discourse. In fact, listening is the most frequently used language skill in everyday life. Researchers (for example, Weaver 1972; Rivers 1981; Morley 1991) estimate that we listen twice as much as we speak, four times as much as we read, and five times as much as we write! It is thus remarkable that several of the otherwise excellent publications that have appeared over the past several years with the purpose of informing language teachers about discourse analysis and its pedagogical applications (for example, G. Cook 1989; McCarthy 1991; Hatch 1992) have had little to say about the listening process (but see Anderson and Lynch 1988; Dalton and Seidlhofer 1994). This paper, I hope, will begin to fill the gap.

Both L1 and L2 models of the listening process (Anderson and Lynch 1988) acknowledge that listening has both top-down and bottom-up aspects. Top-down listening processes, which are sometimes referred to as macroprocessing, involve activation of schematic knowledge and contextual knowledge. Schematic knowledge is generally thought to be of two types (Carrell and Eisterhold 1983): (1) content schemata, which are the background information on the topic and relevant sociocultural knowledge, and (2) formal schemata, which are knowledge of how discourse is organized with respect to different genres, different topics, or different purposes (for example, transactional vs. interactional). Contextual knowledge involves both an understanding of the specific listening situation (i.e. who the participants are, what the setting is, what the topic and purpose are) and an understanding of the ongoing discourse or co-text (i.e. what has already been said and what is likely to be said next).

The bottom-up listening process involves knowledge of the language system that allows the listener to segment and interpret the acoustic signal as sounds that form words, words that form phrases or clauses with a unifying intonation contour, and phrases or clauses that form cohesive and coherent texts such that all levels of language analysis come into play. When we put both perspectives on listening together, we come up with an interactive model such as the one shown opposite in Figure 1.

The bottom-up processing is where the initial signals or clues come from; however, it is generally acknowledged that this level cannot operate with any accuracy or efficiency on its own and that it requires the benefit of, and interaction with, top-down information in order to be comprehensible. For native speakers and skilled L2 speakers the bottom-up skills are assumed to be automatic whereas they are not automatic and can be the source of serious problems for beginning and less-than-expert L2 learners.

The listening process

In the early 1980s it was popular to assume that only top-down skills needed to be enhanced to improve L2 listening comprehension; however, it is now more generally acknowledged (Peterson 1991) that both top-down and bottom-up listening skills should be integrated and explicitly treated pedagogically to improve L2 listening comprehension. The discourse level is in fact where top-down and bottom-up listening intersect and where complex and simultaneous processing of background information, contextual information, and linguistic information permit comprehension and interpretation to take place.

Given such a model of the listening process, we can see that many factors related to the L2 listener are relevant to his or her success or failure: among these are factors capturing language-learning experience such as L2 proficiency in general and L2 listening ability in particular,

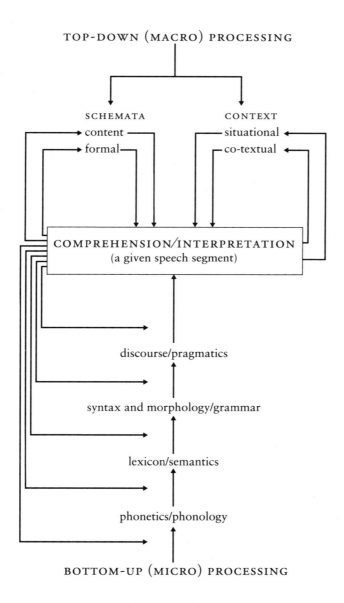

TOP-DOWN (MACRO) PROCESSING

SCHEMATA   CONTEXT

content   situational

formal   co-textual

COMPREHENSION/INTERPRETATION
(a given speech segment)

discourse/pragmatics

syntax and morphology/grammar

lexicon/semantics

phonetics/phonology

BOTTOM-UP (MICRO) PROCESSING

FIGURE I

including experiences with listening to a variety of speakers with differ-ent accents and in different speech situations (lectures, movies, face-to-face conversations, telephone conversations, etc.). Also relevant are factors such as the listener's background knowledge (topic content schemata, sociocultural information, etc.), the listener's memory and attention, and his or her verbal intelligence (i.e. ability to come up with the best interpretation out of several possible ones in a given context, and ability to predict what might come next or later in a given instance of oral discourse). We must also consider the compensatory strategies which good L2 listeners have and which weak ones lack: strategies such as ask-ing questions, slowing down the speaker, tape recording and relistening to a lecture, watching a movie a second or third time. In ongoing conver-sation, good listeners are able to recognize a problem and to signal the speaker in some appropriate way if they have not processed the input well enough to make an interpretation; they are thus in a position to elicit a repetition and/or clarification. Ability to implement such strategies helps the listener whose listening comprehension is not yet nativelike.

There are of course also situation-specific factors external to the listener: the quality of the acoustic signal and the amount of background noise. Similarly, there are non-linguistic situation-specific factors (such as room temperature, being involved in a test) and listener-internal fac-tors (such as lack of interest in the speaker or topic, inattention). In any given situation, these factors may impair listening comprehension, which is something complex, dynamic, and rather fragile to begin with because of the transitory non-permanent nature of the speech signal. Widdowson (1990a: 108) has stated the problem as follows:

> It is unlikely that we ever achieve an exact match between intention and interpretation, and we probably would not know it if we did. We arrive at the degree of convergence necessary to the purpose of inter-action and no more. Comprehension is never complete: it is always only approximate, and relative to purpose.

Another very important factor in L2 listening is task flexibility. As the situation and the task demand, can the listener get the overall gist of an oral communication? Can she or he accurately comprehend impor-tant details such as names, numbers, times, dates, etc.? In other words, Nida's (1953) notions of general vs. selective listening are still very rel-evant today.

[366]

Based on the assumption that one can discover much about how a process works by examining cases of its malfunction, Garnes and Bond (1980) analyzed a corpus of 890 'mishearings' committed by native speakers of English while the speakers engaged in everyday conversation. Based on their analysis of these hearing errors, Garnes and Bond proposed that listeners process incoming speech by employing the following four microprocessing strategies (holding the stream of speech in short-term memory would, of course, underlie all of these):

1. attending to stress and intonation and constructing a metrical template or pattern to fit the utterance;

2. attending to stressed vowels;

3. segmenting the speech stream into words that correspond to the stressed vowels and their adjacent consonants;

4. seeking a phrase—with grammar and meaning—compatible with the metrical template identified in the first strategy and the words identified in the third.

This is admittedly a bottom-up model. If we add—at the same time—the fact that the listener is actively attending to context (situational and co-textual) and calling up all relevant content and formal schemata, then we can begin to see where things might easily break down for the L2 listener. Interference from the sound system of the native language will make it hard to construct metrical templates and to identify stressed syllables and their vowel nuclei. Lack of a large receptive lexicon will impede segmentation of each intonation contour into words, and imperfect knowledge of morphology and syntax will make it difficult to identify phrase or clause boundaries and assign meanings.

An examination of data from written transcripts of oral discourse prepared by second language learners at UCLA confirms that words are commonly misheard (for example, *thought* for *fraught*) as are names (for example, *down the reed* instead of *Donna Reed*) and idioms (for example, *more stuff and barrel* for *lock, stock, and barrel*). Names and idioms are in fact prime candidates for mishearing even among native speakers (Celce-Murcia 1980). These are the types of errors that intermediate and advanced L2 learners make based on lack of lexical, grammatical, and cultural knowledge as much as on difficulties with

[367]

the L2 sound system. Lower-level learners can even misconstrue the hesitation phenomena produced by native speakers as words (Voss 1979; Griffiths 1991):

uh heard as *a*
huh? heard as *up?*
hmm heard as *him*

To see what problems low-intermediate L2 listeners of English had with aural comprehension, Martin (1982) had five native speakers of Spanish listen to short radio-broadcast segments and then give immediate paraphrases (in English or Spanish) of what they had heard. Martin also asked them to introspect and report back on their problems. Here are two samples of her data:

1 *Original radio segment* (p.78)
New York. A presidential economic expert says the current recession will linger for at least a few more months.
Learner's report (p.45)
I understood something about one expert, economy in relation with the president. I didn't understand that very well.

2 *Original radio segment* (p.78)
Poland. The Communist government denies that Solidarity leader Lech Walesa will soon be free.
Learner's report (p.42)
I missed the very beginning. I don't know what said that. Someone in Poland.

Noting that places where comprehension broke down seemed to yield the best information about the learners' listening strategies, Martin followed the same procedure but with longer segments and then in examining all her data, she found that her consultants had used two different types of strategies: (1) word-level strategies (which associate meanings with specific words) and (2) idea-level strategies (which deal with the establishment of a topic and help relate all subsequent meaning bits to the main idea). Her data indicated that three stages seemed to underlie the listening process:

1 an initial orientation period when the listener gets used to the speaker's voice quality and pronunciation, rate of speech, and

vocabulary; this varies in length but the listener is not effective until she or he gets oriented to the speech signal;

2 a search for the main idea that begins with the listener taking in words, phrases, and/or clauses; these can then be decoded and pieced together to form a tentative message;

3 new incoming information is matched against the perceived main idea and/or the listener's previous knowledge; adjustments are made and problems of consistency are identified.

Martin speculated that the two strategies and the three stages interacted and probably were often used simultaneously by her consultants. Even though there were tendencies that all the listeners followed, there were also interesting differences. For three of her consultants, Martin developed in-depth profiles to demonstrate that they approached listening in very different ways in terms of the strategies they employed and frequency of strategy use. However, since she had so few consultants, Martin could not identify which strategies would lead to better listening comprehension.

Teaching listening from a discourse perspective

What can be done by teachers to encourage their students to engage in listening practice at the discourse level? In many instances where reduced speech or imperfect acoustic processing might obscure a message, an effective listener is able to use the situational context and/or the preceding and following discourse to disambiguate or to decide on the best interpretation. For example, the speaker says:

I'm lookin' fer Joe 'n Barney. Have ya seen 'm?

The effective listener will process *əm* as *them* rather than *him* given the prior mention of two people: *Joe* and *Barney*. Whether the speaker is native or non-native, there must be sufficient information in the situation or co-text to process the acoustic signal properly.

In North American English the reduced form *whaddaya* can represent either 'what do you' or 'what are you'. Again, training the listener to attend to the discourse context and the local grammar can help disambiguate such a reduced form. Imagine, for example, a dialog between two students:

A: I dunno what classes to take. *Whaddaya* think I should take?

B: It all depends. *Whaddaya* gonna do after you finish school?

The first occurrence of the reduced form corresponds to 'What do you' in the environment of the verb *think*. The second occurrence corresponds to 'What are you' in the environment of *gonna* ('going to').

Similarly, Bowen (1975) suggests we can give our students practice in segmenting words in otherwise identical sound sequences and intonation contours by providing oral texts with two possible segmentations of the ongoing text:

Tape/voice:
Urban violence is getting out of hand. We really need to stop . . .

Written choices for completion:
a) attacks on city buses
b) a tax on city buses

The effective listener will guess (a) and not (b) because (a) makes better sense given the context provided by the prior spoken discourse.

Sometimes the only difference between two possible interpretations is a hard-to-hear unstressed syllable. Again, the context, in this case what comes after the problematic sequence, can provide the information needed to choose correctly:

1 Maria (praised/appraised) the vase. She said it was gorgeous.

2 Jonathan (proved/approved) it. He gave me his okay yesterday.

In the first example, *praised* is selected by effective listeners and *approved* is selected in the second. Good listeners can store the speech signal long enough to use the information given in the subsequent intonation contour to help disambiguate the problematic string.

The above examples are all fairly local. They make use of information in the immediately surrounding discourse to disambiguate or select a reasonable interpretation for a problematic segment. In these cases we can still fairly confidently say that the co-text is helping the listener with bottom-up, data-driven processing. I emphasize this because for many practitioners the assumption has been that discourse-level information assists the listener only (or mainly) with top-down processing, and indeed, there are many convincing examples of discourse-level information being very helpful with top-down processing. My point is that both types of processing are useful and necessary for effective listening comprehension.

Moving on to top-down processing, I offer the example of a history professor who begins his lecture with the following statement, thereby providing his listeners with a useful organizer:

Today we're going to consider three forces that helped to shape the Carolingian Empire. We'll look at religion, we'll look at the prevailing social structure, and we'll consider economic factors.

With these opening words, the professor has verbally established the following topic or main idea for his lecture:

Three forces helped shape the Carolingian Empire.

The professor then lists the three forces on the board—each of which we now know will be discussed during the lecture:

1 religion
2 social structure
3 economic factors.

The L2 listener who has comprehended the opening statement (i.e. the topic) and its relationship to the list (which is in effect an outline) is in a much better position to understand and take notes on the lecture than the L2 listener who has missed the opening information about the topic. Second language learners in English-for-academic-purposes programs can be trained to process such material by listening to a variety of lecture openings and being told to write down the topic and to predict what the lecture will cover. Their written notes can be checked, and feedback and clarification can be provided as necessary.

Learners can also benefit from listening to longer segments extracted from authentic lectures by working at getting the gist (i.e. writing down the main topic). This can be complemented by then relistening to the same segments and jotting down the details (the facts, dates, names, etc.). Learners can also listen to a lecture while looking at a partial outline with their task being that of filling in the missing information.

To make practice in listening comprehension more clearly part of communicative language teaching, Geddes and Sturtridge (1979) suggest the use of 'jigsaw' listening activities where several small groups of learners each listen to a different part of a larger piece of discourse (for example, a story, a recipe, a mini-lecture, a news broadcast) and write down the important points. Later each group shares their information with another group and then another in order to piece together gradually the larger discourse segment.

With the proliferation of voice-mail systems and telephone answering-machines, second language listeners should be exposed to a variety of authentic voice-mail messages; after each message they should write down the essential information so that they would be able to answer the message had the call been intended for them. For example:

> Hi, this is Judy. Uh. It's Tuesday afternoon and I'm calling to see if you have notes from the Geography lecture today. I missed it because of a dental appointment; so if you have the notes, just bring them tomorrow so I can borrow them. Hmm. If not, call me back at 213-876- 4201 tonight so I can call someone else. OK, thanks. Bye.

The listeners (working individually or in small groups) should be asked to reconstruct two possible scenarios in terms of responding to this telephone message:

Scenario 1: (I have notes for the Geography lecture)

- Judy wants them
- I'll bring them to class tomorrow
- No need to call Judy back

Scenario 2: (I don't have the notes for the Geography lecture)

- Judy wants them
- I should call Judy (213–876–4201)
- I'll tell her I don't have the notes

Inexperience in dealing with live telephone conversation can also be a serious problem for second language learners. They need opportunities to listen to, interpret, and sum up what they hear in a series of authentic recorded phone conversations. Their listening skills can be greatly facilitated if they are taught the conversational structure and options that the work of Sacks, Schegloff, and Jefferson (1974) have shown typically manifest themselves in informal telephone conversations among speakers of North American English[1]:

Opening segment
(Summons: phone rings)
ANSWERER: Hello?
CALLER: Hi, may I speak with _____?
ANSWERER: This IS _____.
          She/he's not here. Can I take a message?
          Wait a minute. I'll call him/her.
(ADDRESSEE: Hello?)
CALLER: Hi, _____. This is _____.

The 'how-are-you' segment
ADDRESSEE: Hi, how ARE you?
CALLER: Fine thanks. And YOU?
ADDRESSEE: Pretty good / Just fine.

Topic establishment
(Direct)
CALLER: Hey, I'm calling because . . .
(Indirect)
CALLER: Are you free Friday night?
(Call proceeds: topics are established; topics change)

Preclosing
ADDRESSEE: You know, I'd like to talk a bit longer, but I've got a
            calculus exam tomorrow. Can I call you back?
CALLER: Oh sure.

Closing
ADDRESSEE: Talk to you later then.
CALLER: Yeah. Bye.
ADDRESSEE: Goodbye.

Such listening practice not only prepares second language learners for telephone conversation but will also assist in more effective face-to-face conversation. This is important because L2 students have often told us that they don't know how to end a conversation or to decline an invitation politely.

In fact the whole area of social functions or speech act sets can be a

[373]

source of problems for L2 listening as well as L2 speaking. Hawkins (1985b) used discourse analysis to teach a complaint 'script' (Schank and Abelson 1977) to high intermediate ESL students enrolled in an oral communication skills class at UCLA. The basic complaint script involves two goals:

1 call attention to objectionable behavior
2 change that behavior.

These goals present the speaker with a dilemma since she or he must strike a delicate balance and be polite yet assertive in calling attention to the objectionable behavior in order to get the person responsible to change his or her behavior. Whether or not the listener is the person responsible, she or he must recognize a complaint as such and respond appropriately. Responses to complaints are usually of three types[2]:

1 admit responsibility, apologize, and offer a remedy
(for example: I'm sorry. I'll give you a refund/replacement.)
2a deny responsibility
(for example: Sorry. I didn't do it/It's not my fault.)
2b transfer responsibility
(for example: Sorry. I can't help you. You'll have to see Mr X.).

To begin the unit on complaints Hawkins had her students produce and respond to six complaints. Then she had her students audio-record and transcribe complaints and responses to complaints that they elicited from native English speakers.

Based on work by Schaefer (1982) and others, Hawkins showed her students that a complaint can be analyzed into seven components (some may be missing or reordered in any given complaint):

1 *Opener*
an utterance which initiates the complaint
2 *Orientation*
an utterance that provides the addressee with information about the complainer's identity and/or intent in making the complaint
3 *Act statement*
an utterance which states the trouble source

4 *Justification*

  a) of the speaker—an utterance by the complainer that explains why she/he is making the complaint

  b) of the addressee—an utterance by the complainer that offers a reason for the addressee's behavior ('Maybe you didn't have time, but . . .')

5 *Remedy*

  an utterance that calls for an action to right the wrong; this may include an ultimatum or threat ('I'll take my business elsewhere')

6 *Closing*

  an utterance by the complainer that concludes the complaint

7 *Valuation*

  an utterance by the complainer that expresses feelings about either the addressee or the wrong that has been committed; this usually comes in combination with another component (for example: 'This pizza is terrible.')

Then the students analyzed the data that they had collected and transcribed by working in small groups and using the description of complaints Hawkins had provided. As a final step, they compared their original pre-unit complaints with those they had collected from native speakers.

This unit took almost four weeks; other class activities intervened. At the end of the unit the students simply repeated their pre-test. A qualified judge then rated all the students' complaints for effectiveness (the pre- and post-test complaints had been randomly ordered). Hawkins' subsequent statistical analysis of the ratings indicated that the students had very significantly improved the effectiveness of their complaints by following the instructional procedure outlined above.

Other experimental evidence (Anderson and Lynch 1988: 16) shows that learners who have had sufficient and focused task-based experience as listeners are able at some later time to perform an oral communication task better than other learners who had only been given prior speaking practice (i.e. giving practice only in listening was more effective than giving practice only in speaking). One can safely assume that giving practice with both skills—first listening, then speaking—would be the best possible preparation, but if the teacher does not have time to do both, then listening practice (with awareness-raising and analysis) should take precedence.

Short segments from radio or TV news broadcasts can be recorded and played back to students to give them an opportunity to experience multiple listenings (segments can be replayed as needed) and to carry out a variety of tasks:

- extract topic/gist
- get details of news item (who, what, when, where)
- evaluate emotional impact of news item; this can vary but the listener should give reasons for the choice (neutral report of information; information makes me happy/sad; information worries/surprises me; information annoys me, etc.).

It can be useful for second language listeners to look at a good transcript of a lecture or a conversation with the pauses, false starts, incomplete sentences, and so on, faithfully represented. Access to such transcripts helps make listeners aware of many things (including the fact that authentic speech is 'messy' much of the time). More specifically, it helps learners see the discourse function of items such as the following:

- cue words and discourse markers that signal what the main points and minor points are
- lexical and structural cues including lexical routines and chunks that signal a new term and/or a definition (or some other notional construct)
- discourse markers and text segments that serve as higher order organizers (like the opening segment from the history professor quoted above)
- words and phrases used to open or close a topic
- ways to ask a question or interrupt
- how to decide which forms are polite and which direct
- how reference, ellipsis, conjunction, and lexical chains are used by listeners to interpret cohesion in discourse (see Halliday and Hasan 1976).

Conclusion

In this paper I hope to have demonstrated that in addition to using acoustic information to perceive and segment the stream of speech (i.e. to do microprocessing) native listeners and—even more so—non-native listeners must use a variety of schemata and contextual clues, especially those clues in the ongoing discourse, to accurately interpret messages (i.e. to do macroprocessing). Phonological signals such as stress, pause, and intonation; lexico-grammatical signals such as discourse markers, lexical phrases, and word order; and higher-level organizers such as those we find in conversational structure are all critical in signalling information to the listener. These findings have implications for language pedagogy in terms of the primacy of listening in oral communicative competence and in using English for academic purposes. They also have implications for materials development in terms of the type and range of practice materials needed to teach listening comprehension effectively.

Notes

1 Widdowson (personal communication) suggests that the conversational conventions for informal phone calls among British English speakers would be quite different. A similar template could be prepared for British English that reflects the structure of phone conversations in that dialect.

2 Hawkins (1985b) actually dealt only with the production of complaints. I have added the responses.

Notes on the Contributors

GUY ASTON
Bologna University School for Interpreters and Translators, Italy

His research interests include the discourse of service encounters (the PIXI project) and the uses of computer corpora in language learning. Among his recent publications are papers on contrastive and interlanguage pragmatics in the collection *Interlanguage Pragmatics* and in the journal *Applied Linguistics*.

ROB BATSTONE
University of London Institute of Education, UK

Among his main research interests are grammar, discourse analysis, and psycholinguistics. His publications include *Grammar* (in the series *Language Teaching: A Scheme for Teacher Education*).

JOSEPH O. BISONG
University of Uyo, Nigeria

He has been Visiting Fellow at the University of London Institute of Education. His main interests are in the teaching of language and literature and in language planning, and he has published papers in *ELTJ* and other journals.

CHRISTOPHER BRUMFIT
University of Southampton, UK

He has published widely on language in education, literature teaching, and educational policy, including *Communicative Methodology in Language Teaching* and *Research in the Language Classroom* (with

[379]

Rosamond Mitchell). His next book will be *Language Education in the National Curriculum*.

RONALD CARTER
University of Nottingham, UK

He has published widely on applied linguistics, English language teaching, discourse studies, knowledge about language, vocabulary, and literary stylistics. Recent publications include *Seeing Through Language* (with Walter Nash) and *Language as Discourse: Perspectives for English Teaching* (with Michael McCarthy).

MARIANNE CELCE-MURCIA
University of California, Los Angeles, USA

She teaches methodology, pedagogical grammar, practical phonetics, and advanced seminars in grammar and discourse. Her publications include the edited collection *Teaching English as a Second or Foreign Language* and *The Grammar Book* (with Diane Larsen-Freeman).

GUY COOK
University of London Institute of Education, UK

His interests include discourse analysis, literature teaching and theory, translation, language art, language and biology. Among his publications are *Discourse* (in the series *Language Teaching: A Scheme for Teacher Education*), *The Discourse of Advertising*, and *Discourse and Literature: The Interplay of Form and Mind*.

MALCOLM COULTHARD
University of Birmingham, UK

Currently his main research interest is the application of linguistic description in forensic contexts. Recent publications include the edited collections *Advances in Spoken Discourse Analysis* and *Advances in Written Text Analysis*.

ALAN DAVIES
University of Edinburgh, UK

His main research interests are in language testing and applied sociolinguistics. His publications include *Principles of Language Testing* and *The Native Speaker in Applied Linguistics*. He is a former co-

[380]

editor of *Applied Linguistics* and is currently co-editor of *Language Testing*.

ROD ELLIS
College of Education, Temple University, Philadelphia, USA

His principal research interest is second language acquisition in relation to second language education. His publications in this area include *Understanding Second Language Acquisition, Instructed Second Language Acquisition*, and *The Study of Second Language Acquisition*.

BRAJ B. KACHRU
University of Illinois at Urbana, USA

His primary research areas are world Englishes, multilingualism, language in society, and South Asian languages and literatures. He has published widely in these areas, including the edited collections *The Other Tongue: English Across Cultures* and *Cultures, Ideologies, and the Dictionary*. He is founder and co-editor of *World Englishes*, and series editor of *English in the Global Context*.

YAMUNA KACHRU
University of Illinois at Urbana, USA

She has published extensively on syntax, semantics, pragmatics, typology of South Asian languages, and cross-cultural discourse. Her publications include *An Introduction to Hindi Syntax* and papers in *TESOL Quarterly, World Englishes*, and other journals. She is now working on a book on cross-cultural discourse.

CLAIRE KRAMSCH
University of California at Berkeley, USA

Her main area of research is the application of discourse analysis and cultural theory to the learning and teaching of foreign languages in institutional settings. Her more recent books are *Text and Context: Cross-Disciplinary Perspectives on Language Study* (with Sally McConnell-Ginet) and *Context and Culture in Language Teaching*.

GUO-QIANG LIU
Deakin University, Victoria, Australia

His main research interests are second language acquisition and Chinese as a second language pedagogy.

MICHAEL MCCARTHY
University of Nottingham, UK

His principal areas of research are spoken corpora, the grammar of everyday conversation, fixed expressions in everyday conversation, and teaching the spoken language. Among his many publications are *Vocabulary and Language Teaching* (with Ronald Carter), *Discourse Analysis for Language Teachers*, and *English Vocabulary in Use* (with Felicity O'Dell). He is currently co-editor of *Applied Linguistics*.

LUIZ PAULO DA MOITA LOPES
Federal University of Rio de Janeiro, Brazil

His research interests are written discourse, reading comprehension, and classroom interaction. His publications include 'Teacher-researchers at the pivot between tradition and innovation in the EFL classroom' in *Reflections on Language Learning* and 'Perceptions of language in L1 and L2 teacher–pupil interaction: the construction of readers' social identities' in *Language and Peace*.

HEIKKI NYYSSÖNEN
University of Oulu, Finland

His main research interests are discourse analysis, text accessibility, language teaching, and cross-cultural communication. His publications include *Towards a Pedagogically-Relevant Model of Discourse Analysis*.

N. S. PRABHU

He has most recently been teaching applied linguistics at the National University of Singapore. His main research areas are language teaching methodology and teacher education. His publications include *Second Language Pedagogy*, reporting on a five-year project of task-based language teaching. He now lives in Bangalore, India.

BARBARA SEIDLHOFER
University of Vienna, Austria

Her main area of research is the application of discourse analysis, pragmatics, phonetics, and sociolinguistics to second language education. Among her publications are *Pronunciation* (with Christiane Dalton),

[382]

in the series *Language Teaching: A Scheme for Teacher Education*, and *Approaches to Summarization: Discourse Analysis and Language Education*.

PETER SKEHAN
Thames Valley University, UK

His research interests are individual differences in language learning, language testing, second language acquisition, and task-based learning. His publications include *Individual Differences in Second Language Learning*, and papers on 'Language Testing: state of the art review' (in *Language Teaching*) and 'Second language acquisition strategies and task-based learning'.

BERNARD SPOLSKY
Bar-Ilan University, Israel

His main research interests are applied linguistics, sociolinguistics, language policy, second language learning theory, and language testing. His books include *Conditions for Second Language Learning* and *The Languages of Jerusalem* (with Robert Cooper). His next book will be *Measured Words: The Development of Objective Language Testing*. He was one of the three founding co-editors of *Applied Linguistics*.

MICHAEL STUBBS
University of Trier, Germany

His current research areas are text and discourse analysis, including computer-assisted corpus linguistics. His main publications include *Language, Schools and Classrooms*, *Language and Literacy*, *Discourse Analysis*, and *Educational Linguistics*. He was chair of the British Association for Applied Linguistics from 1988 to 1991.

MERRILL SWAIN
Ontario Institute for Studies in Education, Canada

Her research interests include communicative language learning and teaching, second language acquisition, and bilingual education. She is co-editor of *The Development of Second Language Proficiency*, and her many papers (as author or co-author) include 'Using collaborative language production tasks to promote students' language awareness' and 'French immersion and its offshoots: getting two for one'.

[383]

JOHN M. SWALES
University of Michigan, USA

Among his many interests are discourse analysis, genre analysis, professional communication, English for Academic Purposes, and birdwatching. His publications include *Genre Analysis: English in Academic and Research Settings*, and his most recent book is *Academic Writing for Graduate Students* (with Christine Feak).

ELAINE TARONE
University of Minnesota, USA

Her research interests include variation in interlanguage, strategic competence and communication strategy use in a second language, and topics in English for Specific Purposes. Among her recent publications are *Research Methodology in Second Language Acquisition* (with Susan Gass and Andrew Cohen) and 'A sociolinguistic perspective on second language use in immersion classrooms' (with Merrill Swain).

CATHERINE WALLACE
University of London Institute of Education, UK

Her research interests include critical literacy, and the teaching of reading and of early literacy for bilingual learners. Among her publications are *Learning to Read in a Multicultural Society: the Social Context of Second Language Literacy* and *Reading* (in the series *Language Teaching: A Scheme for Teacher Education*).

GEORGE YULE
Louisiana State University, USA

He teaches theoretical and applied linguistics. A recent publication is *Focus on the Language Learner* (with Elaine Tarone). His next book will be an introduction to pragmatics.

Bibliography

AARTS, J. 1991. 'Intuition-based and observation-based grammars' in Aijmer and Altenberg (eds.).

ACTFL. 1994. *National Standards in Foreign Language Education*. A draft. August 1, 1994. Yonkers, NY: American Council on the Teaching of Foreign Languages.

ADJEMIAN, C. 1976. 'On the nature of interlanguage systems.' *Language Learning* 26: 297–320.

AGARD, F. B. and H. B. DUNKEL. 1948. *An Investigation of Second-Language Teaching*. Boston: Ginn.

AGARD, F. B., R. J. CLEMENTS, W. S. HENDRIX, E. HOCKING, S. L. PITCHER, A. VAN ERNDEN, and H. G. DOULE. 1944. *A Survey of Language Classes in the Army Specialized Training Program*. New York: Commission on Trends in Education [of the Modern Language Association of America].

AIJMER, K. and B. ALTENBERG (eds.). 1991. *English Corpus Linguistics*. London: Longman.

ALATIS, J. E. (ed.). 1991. *Georgetown University Round Table on Language and Linguistics. Linguistics and Language Pedagogy: The State of the Art*. Washington DC: Georgetown University Press.

ALATIS, J. E. (ed.). 1993. *Georgetown University Round Table on Language and Linguistics. Language, Communication and Social Meaning*. Washington DC: Georgetown University Press.

ALLEN, J. P. B. and S. P. CORDER (eds.). 1974. *The Edinburgh Course in Applied Linguistics* (Vol. 3). Oxford: Oxford University Press.

ALLEN, J. P. B. and S. P. CORDER (eds.). 1975. *The Edinburgh Course in Applied Linguistics* (Vol. 2). Oxford: Oxford University Press.

ALLEN, J. P. B. and H. G. WIDDOWSON (eds.). 1973–1980. *English in*

Focus (10 vols.). Oxford: Oxford University Press.

ALLEN, J. P. B. and H. G. WIDDOWSON. 1974. 'Teaching the communicative use of English.' *International Review of Applied Linguistics* XII/1. (Reprinted in C. J. Brumfit and K. Johnson (eds.): *The Communicative Approach to Language Teaching*. 1979. Oxford: Oxford University Press.)

ALLEN, J. P. B. and H. G. WIDDOWSON. 1975. 'Grammar and language teaching' in Allen and Corder (eds.): 1975.

ALTENBERG, B. 1991. 'A bibliography of publications relating to English computer corpora' in S. Johansson and A.-B. Stenström (eds.): *English Computer Corpora: Selected Papers and Research Guide*. Berlin: Mouton de Gruyter.

ANDERSON, A. and T. LYNCH. 1988. *Listening*. Oxford: Oxford University Press.

ANGIOLILLO, P. F. 1947. *Armed Forces' Foreign Language Teaching: Critical Evaluation and Implications*. New York: S. F. Vanni.

ARONOWITZ, S. and H. A. GIROUX. 1991. *Postmodern Education. Politics, Culture and Social Criticism*. Minneapolis: University of Minnesota Press.

ASTON, G. 1988. *Learning Comity: An Approach to the Description and Pedagogy of Interactional Speech*. Bologna: Cooperativa Libraria Universitaria Editrice.

ASTON, G. (forthcoming a) 'Electronic newspaper corpora as a language learning resource' in E. Siciliani (ed.): *Atti del XVI congresso nazionale dell'AIA*. Bari.

ASTON, G. (forthcoming b) 'Involving learners in developing learning methods: exploiting text corpora in self-access' to appear in P. Benson and P. Voller (eds.): *Independent Language Learning: Principles and Practice*.

AZAR, B. 1992. *Fundamentals of English Grammar* (2nd edn.). New York: Prentice Hall Regents.

BACHMAN, L. F. 1990. *Fundamental Considerations in Language Testing*. Oxford: Oxford University Press.

BACHMAN, L. F. and A. PALMER. (forthcoming) *Language Testing in Practice*. Oxford: Oxford University Press.

BAHNS, J. and M. ELDAW. 1993. 'Should we teach EFL students collocations?' *System* 21/1: 101–14.

BAKER, M., G. FRANCIS, and E. TOGNINI-BONELLI (eds.). 1993. *Text and Technology*. Amsterdam: John Benjamins.

BAKHTIN, M. 1981. *The Dialogic Imagination*. Austin, TX: University of Texas Press.

BANJO, A. 1985. 'Issues in the teaching of English literature in Nigeria' in Quirk and Widdowson (eds.).

BARNWELL, D. 1992. 'Foreign language teaching and testing during World War II.' *Dialog on Language Instruction* 8/1 & 2: 29–34.

[386]

BARTHES, R. 1977. *Image–Music–Text*. New York: Hill and Wang.

BASHAM, A. L. 1954. *The Wonder That Was India*. London: Sidgwick and Jackson.

BATES, E., I. BRETHERTON, and L. SNYDER. 1988. *From First Words to Grammar*. Cambridge: Cambridge University Press.

BATSTONE, R. 1994. *Grammar*. Oxford: Oxford University Press.

BAUMAN, R. 1986. *Story, Performance and Event*. Cambridge: Cambridge University Press.

BAUSCH, K.-H. and F. KOENIGS. 1983. 'Lernt oder erwirbt man Fremdsprachen im Unterricht?' *Die Neueren Sprachen* 12/4: 308–36.

BEAUGRANDE, R. DE 1994. 'Function and form in language theory and research: the tide is turning.' *Functions of Language* 1/2: 163–200.

BEEBE, L. 1980. 'Sociolinguistic variation and style-shifting in second language acquisition.' *Language Learning* 30/2: 433–47.

BERETTA, A. 1991. 'Theory construction in SLA: complementarity and opposition.' *Studies in Second Language Acquisition* 13: 493–511.

BERLIN, I. 1957. *The Hedgehog and the Fox*. New York: Mentor Books.

BERTOLET, R. 1990. *What is Said*. Dordrecht: Kluwer.

BESNIER, N. 1993. 'Reported speech and affect on Nukulaelae' in J. Hill and J. Irvine (eds.): *Responsibility and Evidence in Oral Discourse*. Cambridge: Cambridge University Press.

BHABHA, H. K. 1994. *The Location of Culture*. London and New York: Routledge.

BHATIA, V. K. 1993. *Analysing Genre: Language Use in Professional Settings*. London: Longman.

BIALYSTOK, E. 1990. *Communication Strategies*. Oxford: Basil Blackwell.

BIALYSTOK, E. 1994. 'Analysis and control in the development of second language proficiency.' *Studies in Second Language Acquisition* 16/2: 157–68.

BIBER, D. 1988. *Variation across Speech and Writing*. Cambridge: Cambridge University Press.

BIBER, D. 1989. 'A typology of English texts.' *Linguistics* 27/1: 3–43.

BIBER, D. and E. FINEGAN. 1991. 'On the exploitation of computerized corpora in variation studies' in Aijmer and Altenberg (eds.).

BIBER, D., S. CONRAD, and R. REPPEN. 1994. 'Corpus-based approaches to issues in applied linguistics.' *Applied Linguistics* 15/2: 169–89.

BIRDSONG, D. 1992. 'Ultimate attainment in second language acquisition.' *Language* 68: 706–55.

BISONG, J. O. 1991. 'The "handout" as a basis of learning and teaching in the university: a philosophical analysis of the educational implications.' *Journal of Research in Education and the Humanities* 1/1, University of Uyo.

BLAND, S. K. 1988. 'The present progressive in discourse. Grammar versus

[387]

usage revisited.' *TESOL Quarterly* 22/1.

BLEY-VROMAN, R. 1989. 'The logical problem of second language learning' in Gass and Schachter (eds.).

BLEY-VROMAN, R., S. FELIX, and G. IOUP. 1988. 'The accessibility of Universal Grammar in adult language learning.' *Second Language Research* 4: 1–32.

BLYTH, C., S. RECKTENWALD, and J. WANG. 1990. 'I'm like, "Say what?!": a new quotative in American oral narrative.' *American Speech* 65: 215–27.

BOARDMAN, R. and J. MCRAE. 1984. *Reading Between the Lines*. Cambridge: Cambridge University Press.

BOLINGER, D. 1975. 'Meaning and memory.' *Forum Linguisticum* 1/1: 1–14.

BOLINGER, D. 1977. *Meaning and Form*. London: Longman.

BOWEN, J. D. 1975. *Patterns of English Pronunciation*. New York: Newbury House.

BREEN, M. and C. CANDLIN. 1980. 'The essentials of a communicative curriculum in language teaching.' *Applied Linguistics* 1: 89–112.

BRINDLEY, G. 1989. *Assessing Achievement in the Learner-centred Curriculum*. Sydney: National Centre for English Language Teaching and Research.

BRODY, J. 1991. 'Indirection in the negotiation of self in everyday Tojolab'al women's conversation.' *Journal of Linguistic Anthropology* 1: 78–96.

BROWN, G. and G. YULE. 1983. *Discourse Analysis*. Cambridge: Cambridge University Press.

BROWN, P. and S. LEVINSON. 1978. 'Universals in language usage: politeness phenomena' in E. N. Goody (ed.): *Questions and Politeness: Strategies in Social Interaction*. Cambridge: Cambridge University Press.

BRUMFIT, C. J. (ed.). 1983. *Teaching Literature Overseas: Language-based Approaches*. ELT Documents 114. London: Pergamon.

BRUMFIT, C. J. 1984. *Communicative Methodology in Language Teaching*. Cambridge: Cambridge University Press.

BRUMFIT, C. J. 1994. 'The linguist and the language teaching profession: ghost in a machine?' in R. Barasch and C. Vaughan James (eds.): *Beyond the Monitor Model: Comments on Current Theory and Practice in Second Language Acquisition*. Boston, MA: Heinle and Heinle.

BRUMFIT, C. J. and R. A. CARTER (eds.). 1986. *Literature and Language Teaching*. Oxford: Oxford University Press.

BRUMFIT, C. J. and H. G. WIDDOWSON. 1981. 'Issues in second language syllabus design' in J. E. Alatis, H. Altman, and P. M. Alatis (eds.): *The Second Language Classroom: Directions for the 1980s. Essays in honour of Mary Finnocchiaro*. New York: Oxford University Press.

BRUNER, J. S. 1986. *Actual Minds, Possible Worlds*. Cambridge, MA: Harvard University Press.

BYGATE, M. 1987. *Speaking*. Oxford: Oxford University Press.

CANALE, M. 1983. 'On some dimensions of language proficiency' in J. Oller (ed.): *Issues in Language Testing Research*. Rowley, MA: Newbury House.

CANALE, M. and M. SWAIN. 1980. 'Theoretical bases of communicative approaches to second language teaching and testing.' *Applied Linguistics* 1/1: 1–47.

CANDLIN, C. N. and H. G. WIDDOWSON (eds.). 1987–1996. *Language Teaching: A Scheme for Teacher Education*. Oxford: Oxford University Press.

CARDOZIER, V. R. 1993. *Colleges and Universities in World War II*. Westport CT: Praeger.

CARR, T. and T. CURREN. 1994. 'Cognitive factors in learning about structured sequences: applications to syntax.' *Studies in Second Language Acquisition* 16/2: 205–30.

CARRELL, P. L. 1983. 'Some issues in studying the role of schemata or background knowledge in second language comprehension.' *Reading in a Foreign Language* 1/2: 81–93.

CARRELL, P. L. and J. C. EISTERHOLD. 1983. 'Schema theory and ESL reading pedagogy.' *TESOL Quarterly* 17/4: 553–74.

CARROLL, J. B. 1954. 'Notes on the measurement of achievement in foreign languages.' Unpublished mimeo.

CARTER, R. A. (ed.). 1982. *Language and Literature: An Introductory Reader in Stylistics*. London: Allen and Unwin.

CARTER, R. A. 1987. *Vocabulary: Applied Linguistics Perspectives*. London: Allen and Unwin.

CARTER, R. A. and M. LONG. 1987. *The Web of Words*. Cambridge: Cambridge University Press.

CARTER, R. A. and M. LONG. 1990. 'Testing literature in EFL classes: tradition and innovation.' *ELT Journal* 44/3: 215–21.

CARTER, R. A. and M. LONG. 1991. *Teaching Literature*. London: Longman.

CARTER, R. A. and W. NASH. 1990. *Seeing Through Language*. Oxford: Basil Blackwell.

CELCE-MURCIA, M. 1980. 'On Meringer's corpus of "slips of the ear"' in Fromkin (ed.): 199–214.

CELCE-MURCIA, M. 1991a. 'Language and communication: a time for equilibrium and integration' in Alatis (ed.): 1991.

CELCE-MURCIA, M. (ed.). 1991b. *Teaching English as a Second or Foreign Language* (2nd edn.). Boston: Heinle and Heinle.

CELCE-MURCIA, M. and D. LARSEN-FREEMAN. 1983. *The Grammar Book*. Rowley, MA: Newbury House.

CHANDLER, B. 1989. *Longman Mini-concordancer*. London: Longman.

CHANNELL, J. 1994. 'British culture and cultural assumptions in dictionaries.' Paper presented at the BAAL Annual Meeting, Leeds.

CHOI, Y-H. 1988. 'Text structure in Korean students' argumentative writing in English.' *World Englishes* 7/2: 129–42.

CHOMSKY, N. 1965. *Aspects of the Theory of Syntax*. Cambridge, MA: MIT Press.

CHOMSKY, N. 1976. *Reflections on Language*. London: Temple Smith.

CHOMSKY, N. 1979. *Language and Responsibility: Dialogues with Mitsou Ronat*. Sussex: Harvester.

CHOMSKY, N. 1981a. 'Principles and parameters in syntactic theory' in N. Hornstein and D. Lightfoot (eds.): *Explanation in Linguistics: the Logical Problem of Language Acquisition*. 1981. London: Longman.

CHOMSKY, N. 1981b. *Lectures on Government and Binding*. Dordrecht: Foris.

CHURCH, K. and P. HANKS. 1990. 'Word association norms, mutual information and lexicography.' *Computational Linguistics* 16/1: 22–29.

CHURCH, K., W. GALE, P. HANKS, and D. HINDLE. 1991. 'Using statistics in lexical analysis' in U. Zernik (ed.): *Lexical Acquisition*: 115–64. Englewood Cliffs, NJ: Lawrence Erlbaum.

CLAHSEN, H. and P. MUYSKEN. 1986. 'The availability of Universal Grammar to adult and child learners – the study of the acquisition of German word order.' *Second Language Research* 2: 93–119.

CLAHSEN, H., J. MEISEL, and M. PIENEMANN. 1983. *Deutsch als Zweitsprache: der Spracherwerb ausländischer Arbeiter*. Tübingen: Gunter Narr Verlag.

CLARK, H. and E. CLARK. 1977. *Psychology and Language: An Introduction to Psycholinguistics*. New York: Harcourt Brace Jovanovich.

CLARK, H. and R. GERRIG. 1990. 'Quotations as demonstrations.' *Language* 66: 764–805.

CLARK, R., N. FAIRCLOUGH, R. IVANIC, and M. MARTIN-JONES. 1987. 'Critical Language Awareness.' Centre for Language in Social Life. Working Paper 1.

CLEAR, J. 1987. 'Trawling the language: monitor corpora' in M. Snell-Hornby (ed.): *ZuriLEX Proceedings*. Tübingen: Francke.

CLEAR, J. 1993. 'From Firth principles: computational tools for the study of collocation' in Baker *et al.* (eds.): 271–92.

CLYNE, M. G. 1983. 'Linguistics and written discourse in particular languages: contrastive studies: English and German.' *Annual Review of Applied Linguistics* 3: 38–49.

CLYNE, M. G. 1987a. 'Discourse structure and discourse expectations: implications for Anglo-German academic communication' in L. E. Smith (ed.): 1987.

CLYNE, M. G. 1987b. 'Cultural differences in the organization of academic texts.' *The Journal of Pragmatics* 11: 211–47.

COLEMAN, A. 1928. *The Teaching of Modern Foreign Languages in the United States.* New York: Macmillan.

COLLINS, H. 1994. 'Modal profiling in oral presentations.' *DIRECT Working Paper* 13. CEPRIL, Catholic University of São Paulo, and AESLU, University of Liverpool.

COMMISSION ON TRENDS IN EDUCATION OF THE MODERN LANGUAGE ASSOCIATION OF AMERICA. 1944. 'Foreign languages and the army program.' *Hispania* 27: 382–83.

CONNOR, U. 1987. 'Argumentative patterns in student essays: cross-cultural differences' in Connor and Kaplan (eds.).

CONNOR, U. and R. KAPLAN (eds.). 1987. *Writing Across Languages: Analysis of L2 Text.* Reading, MA: Addison-Wesley.

CONNOR, U. and J. LAUER. 1985. 'Understanding persuasive essay writing: linguistic/rhetoric approach.' *Text* 5/4: 309–26.

COOK, G. 1989. *Discourse.* Oxford: Oxford University Press.

COOK, G. 1992. *The Discourse of Advertising.* London and New York: Routledge.

COOK, G. 1994. *Discourse and Literature: The Interplay of Form and Mind.* Oxford: Oxford University Press.

COOK, V. 1985. 'Chomsky's Universal Grammar and second language learning.' *Applied Linguistics* 15: 1–20.

COOK, V. 1988. *Chomsky's Universal Grammar: an Introduction.* Oxford: Basil Blackwell.

COOK, V. 1989. 'Universal Grammar Theory and the classroom.' *System* 17: 169–82.

COOK, V. 1991. *Second Language Learning and Language Teaching.* London: Edward Arnold.

COPPIETERS, R. 1987. 'Competence differences between native and near-native speakers.' *Language* 63: 544–73.

CORDER, S. P. 1973. *Introducing Applied Linguistics.* Harmondsworth: Penguin.

CORDER, S. P. 1981. *Error Analysis and Interlanguage.* Oxford: Oxford University Press.

COUGHLAN, P. and P. A. DUFF. 1994. 'Same task, different activities: analysis of a SLA task from an activity theory perspective' in Lantolf and Appel (eds.).

COULMAS, F. (ed.). 1981. *A Festschrift for Native Speaker.* The Hague: Mouton.

COULMAS, F. (ed.). 1986. *Direct and Indirect Speech.* Berlin: Mouton.

COULTHARD, R. M. 1992. 'Forensic discourse analysis' in R. M. Coulthard (ed.): *Advances in Spoken Discourse Analysis*: 242–57. London: Routledge.

COULTHARD, R. M. 1993. 'Beginning the study of forensic texts: corpus, concordance, collocation' in *Data Description Discourse*: 86–97. London:

HarperCollins.

COULTHARD, R. M. 1994a. 'Powerful evidence for the defence: an exercise in forensic discourse analysis' in J. Gibbons (ed.): *Language and the Law*: 414–42. London: Longman.

COULTHARD, R. M. 1994b. 'On the use of corpora in the analysis of forensic texts.' *Forensic Linguistics* 1/1: 27–43.

COWAN, J. M. and M. GRAVES. 1944. 'A statement on intensive language instruction.' *Hispania* 27: 65–66.

CRIPER, C. and H. G. WIDDOWSON. 1975. 'Sociolinguistics and language teaching' in Allen and Corder (eds.): 1975.

CROOKES, G. 1989. 'Planning and interlanguage variation.' *Studies in Second Language Acquisition* 11: 367–83.

CROOKES, G. 1992. 'Theory format and SLA theory.' *Studies in Second Language Acquisition* 14: 425–49.

CUMMING, A. 1990. 'Metalinguistic and ideational thinking in second language composing.' *Written Communication* 7: 482–511.

DALTON, C. and B. SEIDLHOFER. 1994. *Pronunciation*. Oxford: Oxford University Press.

DAS, S. K. 1989. 'The common reader and translation of poetry.' *International Journal of Translation* 1/1: 33–40.

DATTA, D. M. 1967. 'Epistemological methods in Indian philosophy' in C. Moore (ed.): *The Indian Mind*. Honolulu, HI: The University Press of Hawaii.

DAVIES, A. 1991. *The Native Speaker in Applied Linguistics*. Edinburgh: Edinburgh University Press.

DAVIES, A. and H. G. WIDDOWSON. 1974. 'Reading and writing' in Allen and Corder (eds.): 1974.

DAVIES, A., C. CRIPER, and A. P. R. HOWATT (eds.). 1984. *Interlanguage*. Edinburgh: Edinburgh University Press.

DAVIS, T. (forthcoming) 'Clues and opinions: ways of looking at evidence' to appear in H. Kniffka, R. M. Coulthard, D. Eades, and S. Blackwell (eds.): *Papers from the First International Conference of Forensic Linguists*. July 14-16, 1993, Bonn.

DAY, E. and S. SHAPSON. 1991. 'Integrating formal and functional approaches in language teaching in French immersion: an experimental study.' *Language Learning* 41: 25–58.

DICKERSON, L. 1975. 'The learner's interlanguage as a system of variable rules.' *TESOL Quarterly* 9: 401–07.

DIJK, T. VAN 1977. *Text and Context*. London: Longman.

DISSANAYAKE, W. 1985. 'Towards a decolonized English: South Asian creativity in fiction.' *World Englishes* 4/2: 233–42.

DISSANAYAKE, W. 1989. 'Introduction: literary history, narrative, and culture: perplexities of meaning' in *Literary History, Narrative and Culture*:

selected conference papers. Honolulu: University of Hawaii Press.

DISSANAYAKE, W. 1990. 'Self and modernism in Sri Lankan poetry in English.' *World Englishes* 9/2: 225–36.

DONATO, R. 1994. 'Collective scaffolding in second language learning' in Lantolf and Appel (eds.).

DONATO, R. and J. P. LANTOLF. 1990. 'Dialogic origins of L2 monitoring' in L. F. Bouton and Y. Kachru (eds.): *Pragmatics and Language Learning* (Vol. 1). Urbana-Champaign, IL: Division of English as an International Language.

DUBOIS, B. 1989. 'Pseudoquotation in current English communication: "Hey, she really didn't say it".' *Language in Society* 18: 343–59.

DULANY, D. E., R. A. CARLSON, and G. I. DEWEY. 1984. 'A case of syntactical learning and judgement: how conscious and how abstract?' *Journal of Experimental Psychology: General* 113: 541–55.

DURANTI, A. 1986. 'The audience as co-author: an introduction.' *Text* 6/3: 239–47.

DURANTI, A. and C. GOODWIN (eds.). 1992. *Rethinking Context: Language as an Interactive Phenomenon*. Cambridge: Cambridge University Press.

EAGLETON, T. 1991. *Ideology*. London and New York: Verso.

ECO, U. 1992. 'Between author and text' in S. Collini (ed.): *Interpretation and Overinterpretation*. Cambridge: Cambridge University Press.

EDWARDS, D. and N. MERCER. 1987. *Common Knowledge*. London: Routledge.

EDWARDS, J. A. and M. D. LAMPERT (eds.). 1993. *Talking Data: Transcription and Coding in Discourse Research*. Hillsdale, NJ: Lawrence Erlbaum.

EGGINGTON, W. G. 1987. 'Written academic discourse in Korean: implications for effective communication' in Connor and Kaplan (eds.).

ELDER, C. A. (forthcoming) 'Proficiency' in A. Davies, A. Brown, C. A. Elder, T. Lumley, and T. F. McNamara: *Language Testing Dictionary*. Cambridge: UCLES/Cambridge University Press.

ELIOT, T. S. [1919] 1951. 'Tradition and the individual talent' in *Selected Essays*. 1951. London: Faber and Faber.

ELIOT, T. S. [1920] 1960. 'Euripides and Professor Murray' in *The Sacred Wood*: 91–7. London: Methuen.

ELLIOTT, R. K. 1967. 'Aesthetic theory and the experience of art.' *Proceedings of the Aristotelian Society* 67: 111–26.

ELLIS, G. and B. SINCLAIR. 1989. *Learning How to Learn English*. Cambridge: Cambridge University Press.

ELLIS, R. 1982. 'Informal and formal approaches to communicative language teaching.' *ELT Journal* 36/1: 73–81.

ELLIS, R. 1985. *Understanding Second Language Acquisition*. Oxford:

Oxford University Press.

ELLIS, R. (ed.). 1987a. *Second Language Acquisition in Context*. London: Prentice Hall International.

ELLIS, R. 1987b. 'Interlanguage variability and narrative discourse: style shifting in the use of the past tense.' *Studies in Second Language Acquisition* 9: 12–20.

ELLIS, R. 1988. 'The role of practice in classroom language learning.' *AILA Review* 5: 20–39.

ELLIS, R. 1994. *The Study of Second Language Acquisition*. Oxford: Oxford University Press.

ERICKSON, F. 1992. ' Ethnographic micro-analysis of interaction' in M. D. LeCompte, W. L. Millroy, and J. Preissle (eds.): *The Handbook of Qualitative Research in Education*. New York: Academic Press.

FÆRCH, C. and G. KASPER. 1980. 'Processes and strategies in foreign language learning and communication.' *Interlanguage Studies Bulletin Utrecht* 5: 47–118.

FÆRCH, C. and G. KASPER. 1983. *Strategies in Interlanguage Communication*. London: Longman.

FÆRCH, C. and G. KASPER. 1984. 'Pragmatic knowledge: rules and procedures.' *Applied Linguistics* 5/3: 214–25.

FAIRCLOUGH, N. 1989. *Language and Power*. London: Longman.

FAIRCLOUGH, N. 1992a. *Discourse and Social Change*. Cambridge: Polity Press.

FAIRCLOUGH, N. 1992b. 'Introduction' in N. Fairclough (ed.): *Critical Language Awareness*. 1992. London: Longman.

FELIX, S. 1978. *Linguistische Untersuchungen zum natürlichen Zweitsprachenerwerb*. Munich: Fink.

FELIX, S. 1985. 'More evidence on competing cognitive systems.' *Second Language Research* 1: 47–72.

FERRARA, K. and B. BELL. 1991. 'Variation and innovation in constructed dialogue introducers.' Paper presented at the annual meeting of the Linguistic Society of America, Chicago.

FILLMORE, C. J. 1968. 'The case for case' in E. Bach and R. T. Harms (eds.): *Universals in Linguistic Theory*. New York: Holt, Rinehart.

FILLMORE, L. W. 1979. 'Individual differences in second language acquisition' in C. J. Fillmore, D. Kempler, and W. Wang (eds.): *Individual Differences in Language Ability and Language Behavior*. New York: Academic Press.

FIRTH, J. R. 1935. 'The technique of semantics.' Transactions of the Philological Society.

FIRTH, J. R. [1930/1937] 1964. *Tongues of Speech and Men* (ed. P. Strevens). Oxford: Oxford University Press.

FIRTH, J. R. 1968. *Selected Papers of J. R. Firth 1952–1959* (ed. F. R.

Palmer). London: Longmans.

FISH, S. 1980. *Is There a Text in This Class?* Cambridge, MA: Harvard University Press.

FLYNN, S. 1987. *A Parameter-setting Model of L2 Acquisition.* Dordrecht: Reidel.

FLYNN, S. and W. O'NEIL (eds.). 1990. *Linguistic Theory in Second Language Acquisition.* Dordrecht: Reidel Press.

FORSTER, L. 1970. *The Poet's Tongues: Multilingualism in Literature* (The de Carle Lectures at the University of Otago 1968). Cambridge: Cambridge University Press (in association with University of Otago Press).

FOSTER, M. 1994. 'Language change and Darwinian principles.' Paper presented at the BAAL Annual Meeting, University of Leeds.

FOSTER, P. and P. SKEHAN. 1994. 'The role of planning and task characteristics in task-based performance.' Paper presented at the BAAL Annual Meeting, University of Leeds.

FOUCAULT, M. 1970. *The Order of Things.* New York: Vintage.

FOUCAULT, M. 1980. *Power/Knowledge. Selected Interviews and Other Writings 1972–1977* (ed. C. Gordon). London: Harvester Press.

FOWLER, R. and G. KRESS. 1978. 'Critical linguistics' in R. Fowler, R. I. V. Hodge, G. Kress, and T. Trew: *Language and Control.* London: Routledge and Kegan Paul.

FRANCIS, G. and J. M. SINCLAIR. 1994. '"I bet he drinks Carling Black Label": a riposte to Owen.' *Applied Linguistics* 15/2: 190–200.

FROMKIN, V. A. (ed.). 1980. *Errors in Linguistic Performance: Slips of the Tongue, Ear, Pen, and Hand.* New York: Academic Press.

GARFINKEL, H. and H. SACKS. 1970. 'On formal structures of practical action' in J. C. Mckinney and E. A. Tiryakian (eds.): *Theoretical Sociology.* New York: Appleton Century Crofts.

GARGESH, R. 1989. 'On equivalence: a comparative study of the three translations of a Hindi short story.' *International Journal of Translation* 1/1: 63–73.

GARNES, S. and Z. S. BOND. 1980. 'A slip of the ear: a snip of the ear? a slip of the year?' in Fromkin (ed.): 231–40.

GASS, S. M. 1989. 'Language universals and second language acquisition.' *Language Learning* 39: 497–534.

GASS, S. M. and C. G. MADDEN (eds.). 1985. *Input in Second Language Acquisition.* Rowley, MA: Newbury House.

GASS, S. M. and J. SCHACHTER (eds.). 1989. *Linguistic Perspectives on Second Language Acquisition.* Cambridge: Cambridge University Press.

GASS, S. M. and E. VARONIS. 1989. 'Incorporated repairs in NNS discourse' in M. Eisenstein (ed.): *Variation and Second Language Acquisition.* New York: Plenum.

GEDDES, M. and G. STURTRIDGE. 1979. *Listening links.* London:

Heinemann.

GEDDES, M. and G. STURTRIDGE. 1982. *Reading Links.* London: Heinemann.

GELL-MANN, M. 1992. 'Complexity and complex adaptive systems' in J. A. Hawkins and M. Gell-Mann (eds.): *The Evolution of Human Languages (Proceedings Volume XI), Santa Fe Institute Studies in the Sciences of Complexity.* Redwood City, CA: Addison-Wesley.

GHIGO, F. 1944. 'Standardized tests in the ASTP at the University of North Carolina.' *French Review* 17/6: 358–60.

GLOCK, N. 1986. 'The use of reported speech in Saramaccan discourse' in G. Huttar and K. Gregerson (eds.): *Pragmatics in Non-Western Perspective.* Arlington, TX: SIL Publications.

GOULD, S. J. [1980] 1990. *The Panda's Thumb: More Reflections in Natural History.* Harmondsworth: Penguin.

GOWER, R. 1990. *Past into Present.* London: Longman.

GOWER, R. and M. PEARSON. 1986. *Reading Literature.* London: Longman.

GRABE, W. 1987. 'Contrastive rhetoric and text type research' in Connor and Kaplan (eds.).

GRABE, W. and R. B. KAPLAN. 1991. 'Introduction' in W. Grabe and R. B. Kaplan (eds.): *Introduction to Applied Linguistics.* Redwood City, CA: Addison-Wesley.

GREGG, K. 1984. 'Krashen's Monitor and Occam's Razor.' *Applied Linguistics* 5: 79–100.

GREGG, K. 1989. 'Second language acquisition theory: the case for a generative perspective' in Gass and Schachter (eds.).

GREGG, K. 1990. 'The variable competence model of second language acquisition and why it isn't.' *Applied Linguistics* 11/4: 364–83.

GREGG, K. 1993. 'Taking explanation seriously; or, let a couple of flowers bloom.' *Applied Linguistics* 14/3: 276–94.

GRICE, H. P. 1975. 'Logic and conversation' in P. Cole and J. L. Morgan (eds.): *Syntax and Semantics Vol. 3: Speech Acts.* New York: Academic Press.

GRIFFITHS, R. 1991. 'The paradox of comprehensible input: hesitation phenomena in L2 teacher talk.' *JALT Journal* 13/1: 23–41.

GUMPERZ, J. J. 1972. 'Sociolinguistics and communication in small groups' in Pride and Holmes (eds.).

HAIMAN, J. and S. THOMPSON. 1984. 'Subordination in universal grammar.' *Berkeley Linguistics Society Proceedings* 10: 510–23.

HALLIDAY, M. A. K. 1970. 'Language structure and language function' in J. Lyons (ed.): *New Horizons in Linguistics.* Harmondsworth: Penguin.

HALLIDAY, M. A. K. 1973. *Explorations in the Function of Language.* London: Edward Arnold.

HALLIDAY, M. A. K. 1975. *Learning How to Mean: Explorations in the Development of Language.* London: Edward Arnold.

HALLIDAY, M. A. K. 1978. *Language as Social Semiotic.* London: Edward Arnold.

HALLIDAY, M. A. K. 1985. *An Introduction to Functional Grammar.* London: Edward Arnold.

HALLIDAY, M. A. K. 1989. *Spoken and Written Language* (2nd edn.). Oxford: Oxford University Press.

HALLIDAY, M. A. K. 1990. 'New ways of meaning: a challenge to applied linguistics.' *Journal of Applied Linguistics* 6. Thessaloniki: Greek Applied Linguistics Association.

HALLIDAY, M. A. K. and R. HASAN. 1976. *Cohesion in English.* London: Longman.

HALLIDAY, M. A. K., A. MCINTOSH, and P. STREVENS. 1964. *The Linguistic Sciences and Language Teaching.* London: Longman.

HARLEY, B. 1989. 'Functional grammar in French immersion: a classroom experiment.' *Applied Linguistics* 10: 331–59.

HARLEY, B. and M. SWAIN. 1984. 'The interlanguage of immersion students and its implications for second language teaching' in Davies *et al.* (eds.): 1984.

HARMAN, I. P. 1990. 'Teaching indirect speech: deixis points the way.' *ELT Journal* 44/3.

HARRIS, Z. 1952. 'Discourse analysis.' *Language* 28. (Reprinted in J. A. Fodor and J. Katz (eds.): *The Structure of Language: Readings in the Philosophy of Language.* 1964. New Jersey: Prentice Hall.)

HATCH, E. 1978. 'Discourse analysis and second language acquisition' in E. Hatch (ed.): *Second Language Acquisition: A Book of Readings:* 402–35. Rowley, MA: Newbury House.

HATCH, E. 1992. *Discourse Analysis and Language Education.* Cambridge: Cambridge University Press.

HATCH, E., Y. SHIRAI, and C. FANTUZZI. 1990. 'The need for an integrated theory: connecting modules.' *TESOL Quarterly* 24: 697–716.

HAWKINS, B. 1985a. 'Is an "appropriate" response always so appropriate?' in Gass and Madden (eds.): 1985.

HAWKINS, B. 1985b. 'Learning to complain through experience.' Paper presented at the Second Language Research Forum, February 1985. University of California, Los Angeles.

HAWKINS, E. 1984. *Awareness of Language: An Introduction.* Cambridge: Cambridge University Press.

HEATH, S. B. 1983. *Ways with Words: Language, Life and Work in Communities and Classroom.* Cambridge: Cambridge University Press.

HEYMAN, R. D. 1986. 'Formulating Topic in the Classroom.' *Discourse Processes* 9: 37–55.

HINDS, J. 1980. 'Japanese expository prose.' *Papers in Linguistics: International Journal of Human Communication* 13: 117–58.

HINDS, J. 1983a. 'Linguistics and written discourse in particular languages: contrastive studies: English and Japanese.' *Annual Review of Applied Linguistics* 3: 78–84.

HINDS, J. 1983b. 'Contrastive rhetoric: Japanese and English.' *Text* 3/2: 183–95.

HINDS, J. 1987. 'Reader versus writer responsibility: a new typology' in Connor and Kaplan (eds.).

HOCKETT, C. F. 1958. *A Course in Modern Linguistics.* New York: Macmillan.

HOEY, M. 1983. *On the Surface of Discourse.* London: George Allen and Unwin.

HOPPER, P. J. and E. C. TRAUGOTT. 1993. *Grammaticalization.* Cambridge: Cambridge University Press.

HOWATT, A. 1984. *A History of English Language Teaching.* Oxford: Oxford University Press.

HOWDEN, M. 1984. 'Code and creativity in word formation.' *Forum Linguisticum* 8/3: 213–22.

HUDSON, T. 1993. 'Nothing does not equal zero: problems with applying developmental sequence findings to assessment and pedagogy.' *Studies in Second Language Acquisition* 15/4: 461–94.

HUNFELD, H. 1990. *Literatur als Sprachlehre. Ansätze eines hermeneutisch orientierten Fremdsprachenunterrichts.* Munich: Langenscheidt.

HYMES, D. H. 1972. 'On communicative competence' in Pride and Holmes (eds.).

HYMES, D. H. 1974. *Foundations in Sociolinguistics: An Ethnographic Approach.* Philadelphia: University of Pennsylvania Press.

HYMES, D. H. 1975. 'Breakthrough into performance' in D. Ben-Amos and K. Goldstein (eds.): *Folklore.* Berlin: Mouton.

IWASHITA, N. 1993. 'Comprehensible output in NNS–NNS interaction in Japanese as a foreign language.' M.A. Thesis. Melborne: University of Melborne.

JAMES, C. and P. GARRETT. 1991. *Language Awareness in the Classroom.* London and New York: Longman.

JOHNS, T. 1986. 'Micro-concord: a language learner's research tool.' *System* 14/2: 151–62.

JOHNS, T. 1988. 'Whence and whither classroom concordancing?' in T. Boengaerts, T. van Els, and H. Wekker (eds.): *Computer Applications in Language Learning.* Dordrecht: Foris.

JOHNS, T. 1991. 'Should you be persuaded: two examples of data-driven learning' in Johns and King (eds.).

JOHNS, T. 1994. 'Contexts: the background, development and trialling of a concordance-based CALL program.' Paper presented at TALC '94, Lancaster.

JOHNS, T. and P. KING (eds.). 1991. *Classroom Concordancing (ELR Journal 4)*. Birmingham: English Language Research.

JOHNSON, J. and E. NEWPORT. 1989. 'Critical period effects in second language learning: the influence of maturational state on the acquisition of English as a Second Language.' *Cognitive Psychology* 21: 60–99.

JOHNSON, K. 1982. *Communicative Syllabus Design and Methodology*. Oxford: Pergamon.

JOHNSTONE-KOCH, B. 1983. 'Presentation as proof: the language of Arabic rhetoric.' *Anthropological Linguistics* 25/1: 47–59.

JORDAN, G. 1992. 'Concordancers: research findings and learner processes.' Unpublished MA dissertation. University of London Institute of Education.

JUSSAWALLA, F. and R. W. DASENBROCK. 1992. *Interviews with Writers of the Post-colonial World*. Jackson and London: University Press of Mississippi.

KACHRU, B. B. 1981a. 'Socially realistic linguistics: the Firthian tradition.' *International Journal of the Sociology of Language* 31: 65–89.

KACHRU, B. B. 1981b. *Kashmiri Literature*. Wiesbaden: Otto Harrassowitz.

KACHRU, B. B. 1985. 'Standards, codification and sociolinguistic realism: the English language in the Outer Circle' in Quirk and Widdowson (eds.).

KACHRU, B. B. 1987. 'The bilingual's creativity: discoursal and stylistic strategies in contact literatures' in L. E. Smith (ed.).

KACHRU, B. B. 1992a. 'The second diaspora of English' in T. W. Machan and C. T. Scott (eds.): *English in its Social Contexts: Essays in Historical Linguistics*. 1992. Oxford: Oxford University Press.

KACHRU, B. B. 1992b. 'Cultural contact and literary creativity in a multilingual society' in E. Dimock Jr., B. Kachru, and Bh. Krishnamurti (eds.): *Dimensions of Sociolinguistics in South Asia: Papers in Memory of Gerald Kelley*. 1992. New Delhi: Oxford and IBH Publishing.

KACHRU, B. B. (ed.). 1992c. *The Other Tongue: English Across Cultures* (2nd edn.). Urbana, IL: University of Illinois Press.

KACHRU, B. B. 1992d. 'Meaning in deviation: toward understanding non-native English texts' in B. Kachru (ed.): 1992c.

KACHRU, B. B. 1995. 'The speaking tree: a medium of plural canons' in J. Alatis (ed.): *Georgetown Round Table of Language and Linguistics, GURT*. 1995. Washington, DC: Georgetown University Press.

KACHRU, Y. 1983. 'Linguistics and written discourse in particular languages: contrastive studies: English and Hindi.' *Annual Review of Applied Linguistics* 3: 50–77.

KACHRU, Y. 1987. 'Cross-cultural texts, discourse strategies and discourse interpretation' in L. E. Smith (ed.).

KACHRU, Y. 1988. 'Writers in Hindi and English' in Purves (ed.).

KACHRU, Y. 1991. 'Speech acts in world Englishes: toward a framework for research.' *World Englishes* 10/3: 299–306.

KACHRU, Y. 1992. 'Culture, style and discourse: expanding noetics of English' in B. Kachru (ed.): 1992c.

KACHRU, Y. 1994. 'Monolingual bias in Second Language Acquisition research.' *TESOL Quarterly* 28/4: 795–800.

KACHRU, Y. (forthcoming) 'Language and cultural meaning: expository writing in South Asian English' in R. Baumgardner (ed.): *South Asian English: Structure, Use and Users*. In the series *English in the Global Context*. Urbana, IL: University of Illinois Press.

KAPLAN, R. B. 1966. 'Cultural thought patterns in inter-cultural education.' *Language Learning* 16: 1–20. (Reprinted in K. Croft (ed.): *Readings on English as a Second Language for Teachers and Teacher Trainees*. 1980: 399–418. Cambridge, MA: Winthrop.)

KAPLAN, R. B. 1972. *The Anatomy of Rhetoric: Prolegomena to a Functional Theory of Rhetoric*. Philadelphia: Center for Curriculum Development (distributed by Heinle and Heinle).

KAPLAN, R. B. 1987. 'Cultural thought patterns revisited' in Connor and Kaplan (eds.): 9–20.

KAPLAN, R. B. 1988. 'Contrastive rhetoric and second language learning: notes toward a theory of contrastive rhetoric' in Purves (ed.).

KAPLAN, R. B. and H. G. WIDDOWSON. 1992. 'Applied Linguistics' in W. Bright (ed.): *International Encyclopedia of Linguistics* (Vol. 1): 76–80. New York and Oxford: Oxford University Press.

KATCHEN, J. 1982. 'A structural comparison of American English and Farsi expository writing.' *Papers in Linguistics* 15: 165–80.

KAUL, J. 1945. *Kashmiri Lyrics*. Srinagar: Rinemisary.

KEEFERS, L. E. 1988. *Scholars in Foxholes: The Story of the Army Specialized Training Program in World War II*. Jefferson, NC: McFarland and Company.

KELLERMAN, E. 1991. 'Compensatory strategies in second language research: a critique, a revision, and some (non-)implications for the classroom' in R. Phillipson, E. Kellerman, L. Selinker, M. Sharwood Smith, and M. Swain (eds.): *Foreign/Second Language Pedagogy Research*. Clevedon, Avon: Multilingual Matters.

KELLERMAN, E. and M. SHARWOOD SMITH (eds.). 1986. *Cross-linguistic Influence in Second Language Acquisition*. Oxford: Pergamon.

KENKEL, J. 1991. 'Argumentation pragmatics, text analysis and contrastive rhetoric.' Ph.D. dissertation. Urbana-Champaign: University of Illinois.

KLEIN, W. 1986. *Second Language Acquisition*. Cambridge: Cambridge University Press.

KLEIN, W. 1991. 'Seven trivia of language acquisition' in L. Eubank (ed.): *Point Counterpoint: Universal Grammar in the Second Language*. Amsterdam: John Benjamins.

KOWAL, M. and M. SWAIN. (forthcoming) 'Using collaborative language production tasks to promote students' language awareness.' *Language Awareness.*

KRAMSCH, C. 1993a. 'Foreign languages for a global age.' *ADFL Bulletin* 25/1: 5–12.

KRAMSCH, C. 1993b. *Context and Culture in Language Teaching.* Oxford: Oxford University Press.

KRAMSCH, C. and L. VON HOENE. 1994. 'The dialogic emergence of difference: Feminist explorations in foreign language learning and teaching' in D. Stanton and A. Stewart (eds.): *Rethinking the Disciplines: Feminism in the Academy.* Ann Arbor: University of Michigan Press.

KRASHEN, S. D. 1982. *Principles and Practice in Second Language Acquisition.* Oxford: Pergamon.

KRASHEN, S. D. 1989. 'We acquire vocabulary and spelling by reading: additional evidence for the input hypothesis.' *Modern Language Journal* 73: 440–64.

KRASHEN, S. D. and T. D. TERRELL. 1983. *The Natural Approach: Language Acquisition in the Classroom.* Oxford: Pergamon.

KRESS, G. 1977. 'Tense as modality' in *U.E.A. Papers in Linguistics 5.* Norwich: University of East Anglia.

KRESS, G. 1989. *Linguistic Processes in Sociocultural Practice.* Oxford: Oxford University Press.

KRESS, G. 1991. 'Critical Discourse Analysis.' *Annual Review of Applied Linguistics* 11: 84–100. Cambridge: Cambridge University Press.

KRESS, G. 1993. 'Against arbitrariness: the social production of the sign as a foundational issue in critical discourse analysis.' *Discourse and Society* 4/2: 169–91.

KRUEGER, M. and F. RYAN (eds.). 1993. *Language and Content: Discipline- and Content-based Approaches to Language Study.* Lexington, MA: D. C. Heath.

KRUSCHE, D. 1985. *Literatur und Fremde.* Munich: Iudicium Verlag.

LABOV, W. 1972a. *Sociolinguistic Patterns.* Philadelphia, PA: University of Pennsylvania Press.

LABOV, W. 1972b. *Language in the Inner City.* Philadelphia, PA: University of Pennsylvania Press.

LABOV, W. 1988. 'The judicial testing of linguistic theory' in D. Tannen (ed.): *Linguistics in Context: Connecting Observation and Understanding.* Norwood, NJ: Ablex.

LAKOFF, G. and M. JOHNSON. 1980. *Metaphors We Live By.* Chicago: University of Chicago Press.

LANKSHEAR, C. 1994. 'Critical literacy.' Occasional Paper 3. Australian Curriculum Studies Association.

LANTOLF, J. P. and G. APPEL (eds.). 1994. *Vygotskian Approaches to*

Second Language Research. Norwood, NJ: Ablex.

LAPIERRE, D. 1994. 'Language output in a cooperative learning setting: determining its effects on second language learning.' M.A. Thesis. Toronto: University of Toronto (OISE).

LARSEN-FREEMAN, D. and M. LONG. 1991. *An Introduction to Second Language Acquisition Research.* London: Longman.

LARSON, M. 1978. *The Functions of Reported Speech in Discourse.* Arlington, TX: SIL Publications.

LASS, R. 1990. 'How to do things with junk: exaptation in language evolution.' *Journal of Linguistics* 26.

LAVE, J. and E. WENGER. 1991. *Situated Learning.* Cambridge: Cambridge University Press.

LAVER, J. 1980. *The Phonetic Description of Voice Quality.* Cambridge: Cambridge University Press.

LAW, J. and M. LYNCH. 1990. 'Lists, field guides, and the descriptive organization of seeing: bird-watching as an exemplary observational activity' in M. Lynch and S. Woolgar (eds.): *Representation in Scientific Practice.* Cambridge, MA: MIT Press.

LEECH, G. N. 1969. *A Linguistic Guide to English Poetry.* London: Longmans.

LEECH, G. N. 1983. *Principles of Pragmatics.* London: Longman.

LEECH, G. N. 1989. *An A–Z of English Grammar and Usage.* London: Edward Arnold.

LEECH, G. N. 1991. 'The state of the art in corpus linguistics' in Aijmer and Altenberg (eds.).

LEECH, G. N. 1993. '100 million words of English.' *English Today* 9/1.

LEFEVERE, A. 1990. 'Translation: its genealogy in the West' in S. Bassnett and A. Lefevere (eds.): *Translation, History and Culture*: 14–28. London and New York: Pinter Publishers.

LEKI, I. 1991. 'Twenty-five years of contrastive rhetoric: text analysis and writing pedagogies.' *TESOL Quarterly* 25/1: 123–43.

LI, C. 1986. 'Direct and indirect speech: a functional study' in Coulmas (ed.).

LIGHTBOWN, P. M. 1985. 'Great expectations: second language acquisition research and classroom teaching.' *Applied Linguistics* 6: 173–89.

LIGHTBOWN, P. M. 1994. 'Teachers and researchers in second language learning: both oars in the water.' Plenary address at the AAAL Annual Meeting, Baltimore, Md.

LIGHTBOWN, P. M. and R. H. HALTER. 1993. *Comprehension-Based ESL Program in New Brunswick: Grade 8.* Final report to the Department of the Secretary of State, Ottawa.

LIGHTBOWN, P. M. and N. SPADA. 1990. 'Focus on form and corrective feedback in communicative language teaching: effects on second language learning.' *Studies in Second Language Acquisition* 12: 429–48.

LIGHTBOWN, P. M. and L. WHITE. 1987. 'The influence of linguistic theories on language acquisition research: description and explanation.' *Language Learning* 37: 483–510.

LIND, M. 1948. *Modern Language Learning: the Intensive Course as Sponsored by the United States Army, and Implications for the Undergraduate Course of Study*. Provincetown, MA: The Journal Press.

LIU, G. 1991. 'Interaction and second language acquisition: a case study of a Chinese child's acquisition of English as a Second Language.' Unpublished Ph.D. Thesis, La Trobe University.

LIU, G. 1994. 'Interaction and SLA: a case study.' Unpublished manuscript, Deakin University, Melbourne, Australia.

LOGAN, G. D. 1988. 'Towards an instance theory of automatisation.' *Psychological Review* 95: 492–527.

LONG, M. 1983. 'Native speaker/non-native speaker conversation and the negotiation of comprehensible input.' *Applied Linguistics* 4/2: 126–41.

LONG, M. 1985. 'Input and second language acquisition theory' in Gass and Madden (eds.): 377–93.

LONG, M. 1990a. 'The least a second language acquisition theory needs to explain.' *TESOL Quarterly* 24: 649–66.

LONG, M. 1990b. 'Maturational constraints on language development.' *Studies in Second Language Acquisition* 12/3: 251–85.

LONG, M. 1993. 'Assessment strategies for SLA theories.' *Applied Linguistics* 14: 225–49.

LOUW, B. 1993. 'Irony in the text or insincerity in the writer: the diagnostic potential of semantic prosodies' in Baker *et al.* (eds.): 157–76.

LOVEDAY, L. 1982. *The Sociolinguistics of Learning and Using a Non-Native Language*. Oxford: Pergamon Press.

LYONS, J. 1977. *Semantics* (2 vols.). Cambridge: Cambridge University Press.

LYSTER, R. 1993. 'The effect of functional-analytic teaching on aspects of sociolinguistic competence: an experimental study in French immersion classes at the grade eight level.' Ph.D. Dissertation. Toronto: University of Toronto (OISE).

MACAULEY, R. 1991. *Locating Dialect in Discourse*. Oxford: Oxford University Press.

MALEY, A. 1983. '"I Got Religion!": evangelism in TEFL' in J. A. Clarke and J. Hanscombe (eds.): *On TESOL 82: Pacific perspectives on language learning and teaching*: 77–83. Washington DC: TESOL.

MALEY, A. and A. DUFF. 1989. *The Inward Ear: Poetry in the Language Classroom*. Cambridge: Cambridge University Press.

MARTIN, J. E. 1992. *Towards a Theory of Text for Contrastive Rhetoric: An Introduction to Issues of Text for Students and Practitioners of Contrastive Rhetoric*. New York, NY: Peter Lang.

MARTIN, T. 1982. 'Introspection and the listening process.' Unpublished M.A. Thesis in TESL, University of California, Los Angeles.

MATHIS, T. and G. YULE. 1994. 'Zero quotatives.' *Discourse Processes* 18: 63–76.

MAYES, P. 1990. 'Quotation in spoken English.' *Studies in Language* 14: 325–63.

MAYNARD, S. 1984. 'Functions of *to* and *koto-o* in speech and thought representation in Japanese written discourse.' *Lingua* 64: 1–24.

MCCARTHY, M. J. 1991. *Discourse Analysis for Language Teachers*. Cambridge: Cambridge University Press.

MCCARTHY, M. J. 1992. 'English idioms in use.' *Revista Canaria de Estudios Ingleses* 25: 55–65.

MCCARTHY, M. J. 1993. 'Spoken discourse markers in written text' in J. M. Sinclair, M. Hoey, and G. Fox (eds.): *Techniques of Description*. London: Routledge: 170–82.

MCCARTHY, M. J. 1994. 'Conversation and literature: tense and aspect' in J. Payne (ed.): *Linguistic Approaches to Literature*. Birmingham: English Language Research.

MCCARTHY, M. J. and R. A. CARTER. 1994. *Language as Discourse: Perspectives for Language Teaching*. London: Longman.

MCLAUGHLIN, B. 1987. *Theories of Second Language Learning*. London: Edward Arnold.

MCRAE, J. 1991. *Literature with a Small 'l'*. Basingstoke: Macmillan/ Modern English Publications.

MCRAE, J. and L. PANTALEONI. 1991. *Chapter and Verse*. Oxford: Oxford University Press.

MEHAN, H. 1979. *Learning Lessons*. Cambridge, MA: Harvard University Press.

MILLS, S. 1992. 'Knowing your place: a Marxist feminist stylistic analysis' in M. Toolan (ed.): *Language, Text and Context*. London and New York: Routledge Kegan and Paul.

MINSKY, M. 1975. 'Frame-system theory' in P. Johnson-Laird and P. Wason (eds.) 1977: *Thinking: Readings in Cognitive Science*. Cambridge: Cambridge University Press.

MITCHELL, T. F. 1957. 'The language of buying and selling in Cyrenaica: a situational statèment.' *Hesperis* 44. (Reprinted in T. F. Mitchell (ed.): *Principles of Firthian Linguistics*. 1975. London: Longman.)

MITTWOCH, A. 1985. 'Sentences, utterance boundaries, personal deixis and the E-hypothesis.' *Theoretical Linguistics* 12: 137–52.

MOERAN, B. 1984. 'Advertising sounds as cultural discourse.' *Language and Communication* 4/2: 147–58.

MOITA LOPES, L. P. 1993. 'Interactional patterns in the mother tongue classroom.' Mimeo. Paper presented at the 10th International Congress of

Applied Linguistics, Amsterdam.

MOITA LOPES, L. P. 1995. 'Perceptions of language in L1 and L2 teacher–pupil interaction: the construction of readers' social identities' in C. Schaffner and A. Wenden (eds.): *Language and Peace*. Aldershot: Dartmouth Publishing Company.

MOODY, H. L. B. 1983. 'Approaches to the study of literature: a practitioner's view' in Brumfit (ed.).

MORLEY, J. 1991. 'Listening comprehension in second/foreign language instruction' in Celce-Murcia (ed.). 1991b: 81–106.

MURATA, K. 1994. *A Cross-cultural Approach to the Analysis of Conversation and its Implications for Language Teaching*. Tokyo: Liber Press.

MURISON-BOWIE, S. 1993. *MicroConcord: Manual*. Oxford: Oxford University Press.

MURPHY, R. 1989. *English Grammar in Use*. Cambridge: Cambridge University Press.

MURRAY, G. 1910. *Medea*. London: George Allen and Unwin.

MYRON, H. B. 1944. 'Teaching French in the Army.' *French Review* 17/6: 345–52.

NASH, W. 1986. 'The possibilities of paraphrase in the teaching of literary idiom' in Brumfit and Carter (eds.): 70–89.

NATIONAL CONGRESS ON LANGUAGES IN EDUCATION. 1985. 'Report on Language Awareness.' London: Centre for Information on Language Teaching and Research.

NATTINGER, J. R. and J. S. DECARRICO. 1992. *Lexical Phrases and Language Teaching*. Oxford: Oxford University Press.

NAVALKISHORE, M. A. n.d. *Nibadh Garimaa* [The Importance of Essay]. Jaipur: Jaipur Publishing House.

NELSON, C. 1991. 'New Englishes, new discourses, new speech acts.' *World Englishes* 10/3: 317–23.

NEWMAN, D., P. GRIFFIN, and M. COLE. 1989. *The Construction Zone*. Cambridge: Cambridge University Press.

NICHOLAS, H. 1987. 'A comparative study of the acquisition of German as a first and a second language.' Unpublished Ph.D. Thesis, Monash University.

NIDA, E. 1953. 'Selective listening.' *Language Learning* 4/3–4: 92–101.

NOBUYOSHI, J. and R. ELLIS. 1993. 'Focused communication tasks and second language acquisition.' *ELT Journal* 47: 203–10.

NUNAN, D. 1989. *Designing Tasks for the Communicative Classroom*. Cambridge: Cambridge University Press.

NYSTRAND, M. and J. WIEMELT. 1991. 'When is a text explicit? Formalist and dialogical perspectives.' *Text* 11/1: 25–41.

OAKESHOTT, M. 1959. *Rationalism in Politics and other Essays*. Indianapolis: Liberty Classics.

OCHS, E. 1988. *Culture and Language Development: Language Acquisition and Language Socialization in a Samoan Village.* Cambridge: Cambridge University Press.

OCHS, E., C. TAYLOR, D. RUDOLPH, and R. SMITH. 1992. 'Storytelling as theory-building activity.' *Discourse Processes* 15: 37–72.

OLLER JR., J. W. (ed.). 1993. *Methods that Work: Ideas for Literacy and Language Teachers* (2nd edn.). Boston, MA: Heinle and Heinle.

OMAGGIO, A. 1986. *Teaching Language in Context. A Proficiency-oriented Approach.* Boston, MA: Heinle and Heinle.

O'MALLEY, J. and A. CHAMOT. 1989. *Learning Strategies in Second Language Acquisition.* Cambridge: Cambridge University Press.

OSTLER, S. K. 1987. 'English in parallels: a comparison of English and Arabic Prose' in Connor and Kaplan (eds.).

OXFORD, R. 1990. *Language Learning Strategies. What Every Teacher Should Know.* New York: Newbury House.

PAIKEDAY, T. M. 1985. *The Native Speaker is Dead!* Toronto: Paikeday Publishing Inc.

PANDHARIPANDE, R. 1983. 'Linguistics and written discourse in particular languages: contrastive studies: English and Marathi.' *Annual Review of Applied Linguistics* 3: 118–36.

PARANJAPE, M. 1993. *Indian Poetry in English.* Madras: Macmillan.

PARKER, W. R. 1954. *The National Interest and Foreign Languages.* Washington DC: US Government Printing Office.

PARTEE, B. 1973. 'The syntax and semantics of quotation' in S. Anderson and P. Kiparsky (eds.): *A Festschrift for Morris Halle.* New York: Holt.

PAWLEY, A. and F. H. SYDER. 1983. 'Two puzzles for linguistic theory: nativelike selection and nativelike fluency' in J. Richards and R. Schmidt (eds.): *Language and Communication.* London: Longman.

PENNYCOOK, A. 1990. 'Towards a critical applied linguistics for the 1990s.' *Issues in Applied Linguistics* 1/1: 8–28.

PENNYCOOK, A. 1994. 'Incommensurable discourses?' *Applied Linguistics* 15/2: 115–38.

PETERS, A. 1983. *The Units of Language Acquisition.* Cambridge: Cambridge University Press.

PETERS, A. 1985. 'Language segmentation: operating principles for the perception and analysis of language' in D. Slobin (ed.): *The Crosslinguistic Study of Language Acquisition: Theoretical Issues.* London: Lawrence Erlbaum.

PETERSON, P. W. 1991. 'A synthesis of methods for interactive listening' in Celce-Murcia (ed.). 1991b: 106–22.

PHILLIPSON, R. 1992. *Linguistic Imperialism.* Oxford: Oxford University Press.

PICA, T. and C. DOUGHTY. 1985. 'Input and interaction in the communicative language classroom: a comparison of teacher-fronted and group activities' in Gass and Madden (eds.): 115–32.

PICA, T., L. HOLLIDAY, N. LEWIS, and L. MORGENTHALER. 1989. 'Comprehensible output as an outcome of linguistic demands on the learner.' *Studies in Second Language Acquisition* 11: 63–90.

PIENEMANN, M. and M. JOHNSTON. 1987. 'Factors influencing the development of language proficiency' in D. Nunan (ed.): *Applying Second Language Acquisition Research*: 45–141. Adelaide, Australia: National Curriculum Resource Centre.

PINE, J. M. and E. V. M. LIEVEN. 1993. 'Reanalysing rote-learned phrases: individual differences in the transition to multi-word speech.' *Journal of Child Language* 20/3: 551–72.

PINKER, S. 1994. *The Language Instinct: The New Science of Language and Mind*. London: Allen Lane.

POTTLE, F. A., N. S. BUCK, W. C. DEVANE, and H. M. HUBBELL. 1944. 'Yale University: report of the president's committee on the teaching of modern foreign languages.' *Hispania* 27: 386–93.

POYATOS, F. 1991. 'Paralinguistic qualifiers: our many voices.' *Language and Communication* 11: 181–95.

PRABHU, N. S. 1987. *Second Language Pedagogy*. Oxford: Oxford University Press.

PRESTON, D. 1989. *Sociolinguistics and Second Language Acquisition*. Oxford: Blackwell.

PRIDE, J. B. and J. HOLMES (eds.). 1972. *Sociolinguistics*. Harmondsworth: Penguin.

PSATHAS, G. (ed.). 1979. *Everyday Language: Studies in Ethnomethodology*. New York: Irvington Publishers.

PURVES, A. (ed.). 1988. *Writing across Languages and Cultures: Issues in Contrastive Rhetoric*. Newbury Park, CA: Sage.

QUINE, W. 1960. *Word and Object*. Cambridge, MA: MIT Press.

QUINN, N. and D. HOLLAND. 1987. 'Culture and cognition' in D. Holland and N. Quinn (eds.): *Cultural Models in Language and Thought*. Cambridge: Cambridge University Press.

QUIRK, R. and S. GREENBAUM. 1973. *A University Grammar of English*. London: Longman.

QUIRK, R. and H. G. WIDDOWSON (eds.). 1985. *English in the World: Teaching and Learning the Language and Literatures*. Cambridge: Cambridge University Press, for the British Council.

RAO, R. 1938. *Kanthapura*. London: Allen and Unwin.

RAO, R. 1960. *The Serpent and the Rope*. London: Murray.

REBER, A. 1989. 'Implicit learning and tacit knowledge.' *Journal of Experimental Psychology: General* 118: 219–35.

REYNOLDS. D. W. 1993. 'Illocutionary acts across languages: editorializing in Egyptian English.' *World Englishes* 12/1: 35–46.

RIBEIRO, B. 1994. *Coherence in Psychotic Discourse.* New York: Oxford University Press.

RIDDLE, E. 1986. 'The meaning and discourse function of the past tense in English.' *TESOL Quarterly* 20/2.

RIVERS, W. 1981. *Teaching Foreign Language Skills* (2nd edn.). Chicago: University of Chicago Press.

RODGER, A. 1983. 'Language for literature' in Brumfit (ed.).

ROGOFF, B. 1990. *Apprenticeship in Thinking.* New York: Cambridge University Press.

ROMAINE, S. and D. LANGE. 1991. 'The use of *like* as a marker of reported speech and thought: A case of grammaticalization in progress.' *American Speech* 66: 227–79.

ROSCOE, A. 1971. *Mother is Gold.* Cambridge: Cambridge University Press.

RULON, P. J. 1943. 'Report on contract test constructed for the ASTD, ASF Contract No W-19-073 AST(Sc-1)-26: Report on scales for measuring ability to speak German and Russian, Term 5.' Harvard University.

RULON, P. J. 1944a. 'Report on contract test constructed for the ASTD, ASF Contract No W-19-073 AST(Sc-1)-26: comprehension of spoken German, Term 6.' Harvard University.

RULON, P. J. 1944b. 'Report on contract test constructed for the ASTD, ASF Contract No W-19-073 AST(Sc-1)-26: comprehension of spoken Russian, items proposed for use in War Department tests.' Harvard University.

RULON, P. J. 1944c. 'Report on contract test constructed for the ASTD, ASF Contract No W-19-073 AST(Sc-1)-26: comprehension of spoken Russian, Term 6.' Harvard University.

RUMELHART, D. 1977. 'Toward an interactive model of reading' in S. Dornic (ed.): *Attention and Performance VI.* Hillsdale, NJ: Lawrence Erlbaum.

RUMELHART, D. 1980. 'Schemata: the building blocks of cognition' in R. J. Spiro, B. C. Bruce, and W. F. Brewer (eds.): *Theoretical Issues in Reading Comprehension. Perspectives from Cognitive Psychology, Linguistics, Artificial Intelligence and Education.* Hillsdale, NJ: Lawrence Erlbaum.

RUSHDIE, S. 1993. *Midnight's Children.* Delhi: Rupa and Co.

RUTHERFORD, W. E. 1984. *Language Universals and Second Language Acquisition.* Amsterdam: John Benjamins.

RUTHERFORD, W. E. 1987. *Second Language Grammar: Learning and Teaching.* London: Longman.

SACKS, H. 1972. 'On the analysability of stories by children' in J. J. Gumperz and D. Hymes (eds.): *Directions in Sociolinguistics.* New York: Holt Rinehart.

SACKS, H., E. SCHEGLOFF, and G. JEFFERSON. 1974. 'A simplest systematics for the organization of turn-taking for conversation.' *Language*

50/4: 696–735.

SAID, E. W. 1994. *Representations of the Intellectual*. New York: Pantheon.

SATO, C. 1990. *The Syntax of Conversation in Second Language Development*. Tübingen: Gunter Narr Verlag.

SAUSSURE, F. DE [1915] 1974. *Course in General Linguistics* (trans. Wade Baskin). London: Fontana.

SAVIGNON, S. 1983. *Communicative Competence: Theory and Classroom Practice*. Reading, MA: Addison-Wesley.

SCHACHTER, J. 1988. 'Second language acquisition and its relationship to Universal Grammar.' *Applied Linguistics* 9: 219–35.

SCHAEFER, F. 1982. 'An analysis of the discourse and syntax of oral complaints in English.' Unpublished M.A. Thesis in TESL, University of California, Los Angeles.

SCHANK, R. C. 1980. 'Language and memory.' *Cognitive Science* 4/3: 243–284.

SCHANK, R. C. and R. P. ABELSON. 1977. *Scripts, Plans, Goals, and Understanding: An Inquiry Into Human Knowledge*. Hillsdale, NJ: Lawrence Erlbaum.

SCHIFFRIN, D. 1987a. *Discourse Markers*. Cambridge: Cambridge University Press.

SCHIFFRIN, D. 1987b. 'Sociolinguistic approaches to discourse: towards a synthesis and expansion.' Mimeo. Keynote address at New Ways of Analysing Variation, University of Texas.

SCHMIDT, R. W. 1990. 'The role of consciousness in second language learning.' *Applied Linguistics* 11/2: 129–58.

SCHMIDT, R. W. 1992. 'Psychological mechanisms underlying second language fluency.' *Studies in Second Language Acquisition* 14: 357–85.

SCHMIDT, R. W. and S. N. FROTA. 1986. 'Developing basic conversational ability in a second language: a case study of an adult learner of Portuguese' in R. R. Day (ed.): *Talking to Learn: Conversation in Second Language Acquisition*: 237–326. Rowley, MA: Newbury House.

SCHOURUP, L. 1982. *Common Discourse Particles in English Conversation*. Working Papers in Linguistics 28. Columbus, OH: The Ohio State University.

SCHOUTEN, M. 1979. 'The missing data in second language learning research.' *Interlanguage Studies Bulletin* 4: 3–14.

SCHULTZ, J., S. FLORIO, and F. ERICKSON. 1982. 'Where's the floor? Aspects of the cultural organization of social relationships in communication at home and in school' in P. Gilmore and A. Glatthorn (eds.): *Ethnography and Education: Children in and out of School*. Washington DC: Center for Applied Linguistics.

SCHUMANN, J. 1978. *The Pidginization Process: A Model for Second Language Acquisition*. Rowley, MA: Newbury House.

SCHUMANN, J. 1983. 'Art and science in second language acquisition research.' *Language Learning* Special Issue 33: 49–75.

SCHUMANN, J. 1993. 'Some problems with falsification: an illustration from SLA research.' *Applied Linguistics* 14: 295–306.

SCOTT, M. and T. JOHNS. 1993. *MicroConcord*. Oxford: Oxford University Press.

SCRIBNER, S. and M. COLE. 1981. *The Psychology of Literacy*. Cambridge, MA: Harvard University Press.

SEIDENBERG, M. S. 1994. 'Language and connectionism: the developing interface.' *Cognition* 50/1–3: 385–401.

SEIDLHOFER, B. 1994. 'Sum and substance: some aspects of doing applied linguistics.' *Vienna English Working papers* 3/1: 34–44.

SEIDLHOFER, B. and H. G. WIDDOWSON. 1994. 'The metalanguage of summary statement.' Paper presented at the AAAL Annual Meeting, Baltimore, Md.

SELINKER, L. 1972. 'Interlanguage.' *International Review of Applied Linguistics* 10: 209–31.

SELINKER, L. and D. DOUGLAS. 1985. 'Wrestling with "context" in interlanguage theory.' *Applied Linguistics* 6: 190–204.

SETH, V. 1993. *A Suitable Boy*. New York: HarperCollins.

SHARWOOD SMITH, M. 1986. 'Comprehension vs. acquisition: two ways of processing input.' *Applied Linguistics* 7: 118–32.

SHERZER, J. 1983. *Kuna Ways of Speaking*. Austin, TX: University of Texas Press.

SHILLS, E. 1988. 'Citizen of the world: Nirad C. Chaudhuri.' *The American Scholar*. Autumn 1988: 549–73.

SHKLOVSKY, V. B. [1940] 1974. *Mayakovsky and His Circle*. London: Pluto.

SINCLAIR, J. M. (ed.). 1987a. *Looking Up: An Account of the COBUILD Project in Lexical Computing*. London: Collins ELT.

SINCLAIR, J. M. 1987b. 'Grammar in the dictionary' in Sinclair (ed.). 1987a.

SINCLAIR, J. M. 1987c. 'The nature of the evidence' in Sinclair (ed.). 1987a.

SINCLAIR, J. M. 1987d. 'Collocation: a progress report' in R. Steele and T. Threadgold (eds.): *Language Topics: Essays in Honour of Michael Halliday*. Amsterdam: John Benjamins.

SINCLAIR, J. M. 1991a. *Corpus, Concordance, Collocation*. Oxford: Oxford University Press.

SINCLAIR, J. M. 1991b. 'Shared knowledge' in Alatis (ed.): 1991.

SINCLAIR, J. M. and R. M. COULTHARD. 1975. *Towards an Analysis of Discourse*. Oxford: Oxford University Press.

SINCLAIR, J. M., G. FOX, *et al.* 1990. *Collins Cobuild English Grammar*. London: Collins.

SINCLAIR, J. M., P. HANKS, *et al.* 1987. *Collins Cobuild English Language Dictionary.* London: HarperCollins.

SINCLAIR, J. M. and A. RENOUF. 1988. 'A lexical syllabus for language learning' in R. Carter and M. McCarthy (eds.): *Vocabulary and Language Teaching.* London: Longman.

SKEHAN, P. 1986. 'Cluster analysis and the identification of learner types' in V. J. Cook (ed.): *Experimental Approaches to Second Language Acquisition.* Oxford: Pergamon.

SKEHAN, P. 1992. 'Second language acquisition strategies and task-based learning.' *Thames Valley University Working Papers in English Language Teaching* 1: 178–208. (Reprinted in V. De Scarpis, L. Innocenti, F. Marucci, and A. Pajalich (eds.): *Intrecci e Contaminazioni.* 1993. Venice: Supernova.)

SKEHAN, P. 1994. 'Foreign language learning ability: cognitive or linguistic?' *Thames Valley University Working Papers in English Language Teaching* 2: 151–91.

SMITH, L. E. (ed.). 1987. *Discourse across Cultures: Strategies in World Englishes.* London: Prentice Hall International.

SMITH, L. E. 1992. 'Spread of Englishes and issues of intelligibility' in B. Kachru (ed.): 1992c.

SMITH, L. E. and C. L. NELSON. 1985. 'International intelligibility of English: directions and resources.' *World Englishes* 4/3: 333–42.

SMITH, W. F. and D. LIEDLICH. 1980. *Rhetoric for Today.* New York: Harcourt Brace Jovanovich.

SOYINKA, W. [1978] 1993. 'Language as boundary' in *Art, Dialogue and Outrage*: 82–94. New York: Pantheon Books.

SPADA, N. and P. M. LIGHTBOWN. 1993. 'Instruction and the development of questions in L2 classrooms.' *Studies in Second Language Acquisition* 15: 205–24.

SPERBER, D. and D. WILSON. 1981. 'Irony and the use-mention distinction' in P. Cole (ed.): *Radical Pragmatics.* New York: Academic Press.

SPERBERG-MCQUEEN, M. and L. BURNARD. 1994. *Guidelines for the Encoding and Interchange of Machine-readable Texts.* Chicago and Oxford: ACL-ACH-ALLC.

SPIRO, J. 1991. 'Writing the literature test' in C. J. Brumfit (ed.): *Assessment in Literature Teaching*: 67–84. Review of ELT 1/3. Basingstoke: Modern English Publications/The British Council/Macmillan.

SPOLSKY, B. 1968. 'Linguistics and language pedagogy – applications or implications?' in J. Alatis (ed.): *Twentieth Annual Round Table on Languages and Linguistics*: 143–55. Washington DC: Georgetown University Press.

SPOLSKY, B. 1990. 'Introduction to a colloquium: the scope and form of a theory of second language learning.' *TESOL Quarterly* 24: 609–16.

SPOLSKY, B. 1995. *Measured Words: the Development of Objective*

Language Testing. Oxford: Oxford University Press.

SRIDHAR, K. K. and S. N. SRIDHAR. [1986] 1992. 'Bridging the paradigm gap: second language acquisition theory and indigenized varieties of English' in B. Kachru (ed.). 1992c: 91–107.

STERLING, R. and W. SCOTT. 1985. *Plato: The Republic.* New York: Norton.

STERN, H. H. 1983. *Fundamental Concepts of Language Teaching.* Oxford: Oxford University Press.

STERNBERG, M. 1982. 'Proteus in quotation-land: Mimesis and the forms of reported discourse.' *Poetics Today* 3: 107–56.

STREVENS, P. 1980. *Teaching English as an International Language.* Oxford: Pergamon Press.

STUBBS, M. 1983. *Discourse Analysis.* Oxford: Blackwell.

STUBBS, M. 1990. *Knowledge about Language: Grammar, Ignorance and Society.* London: University of London Institute of Education.

STUBBS, M. 1994. 'Grammar, text, and ideology: computer-assisted methods in the linguistics of representation.' *Applied Linguistics* 15/2: 201–23.

STUBBS, M. 1995. 'Collocations and semantic profiles: on the cause of the trouble with quantitative studies.' *Functions of Language* 2/1.

STUBBS, M. (forthcoming) 'Keywords: collocations and corpora, coding and culture' in *Text and Corpus Analysis.* Oxford: Blackwell.

SVARTVIK, J. 1968. *The Evans Statements: A Case for Forensic Linguistics.* Göteborg: University of Gothenburg Press.

SWAIN, M. 1985. 'Communicative competence: some roles of comprehensible input and comprehensible output in its development' in Gass and Madden (eds.): 235–53.

SWAIN, M. 1988. 'Manipulating and complementing content teaching to maximize second language learning.' *TESL Canada Journal* 6: 68–83.

SWAIN, M. 1993. 'The output hypothesis: just speaking and writing aren't enough.' *Canadian Modern Language Review* 50: 158–64.

SWAIN, M. and S. LAPKIN. 1994. 'Problems in output and the cognitive processes they generate: A step towards second language learning.' Manuscript. Toronto: Modern Language Centre, OISE.

TANAKA, K. 1992. 'The pun in advertising: a pragmatic approach.' *Lingua* 87/1–2: 91–102.

TANNEN, D. 1981. 'New York Jewish conversational style.' *International Journal of the Sociology of Language* 30: 133–49.

TANNEN, D. 1984. *Conversational Style: Analyzing Talk among Friends.* Norwood, NJ: Ablex.

TANNEN, D. 1986. 'Introducing constructed dialogue in Greek and American conversational and literary narrative' in Coulmas (ed.): 1986.

TANNEN, D. 1989. *Talking Voices: Repetition, Dialogue and Imagery in Conversational Discourse.* Cambridge: Cambridge University Press.

TARONE, E. 1977. 'Conscious communication strategies in interlanguage' in H. D. Brown, C. A. Yorio, and R. C. Crymes (eds.): *On TESOL '77*. Washington, DC: TESOL.

TARONE, E. 1979. 'Interlanguage as chameleon.' *Language Learning* 29/1: 181–91.

TARONE, E. 1983. 'On the variability of interlanguage systems.' *Applied Linguistics* 4/2: 143–63.

TARONE, E. 1988. *Variation in Interlanguage*. London: Edward Arnold.

TARONE, E. 1990. 'On variation in interlanguage: a response to Gregg.' *Applied Linguistics* 11/4: 392–400.

TAY, M. W. J. 1982. 'The uses, users and features of English in Singapore' in J. B. Pride (ed.): *New Englishes*: 51–70. Rowley, MA: Newbury House.

TERRELL, T. 1977. 'A natural approach to second language acquisition and learning.' *Modern Language Journal* 61: 325–36.

THAROOR, S. 1989. *The Great Indian Novel*. New Delhi: Penguin.

THOMAS, J. 1983. 'Cross-cultural pragmatic failure.' *Applied Linguistics* 4/3: 91–112.

THUMBOO, E. 1985. 'Twin perspectives and multi-ecosystems: tradition for a commonwealth writer.' *World Englishes* 4/2: 213–21.

THUMBOO, E. 1990. 'Conversion of the tribes: societal antecedents and the growth of Singapore poetry.' *World Englishes* 9/2: 155–73.

THUMBOO, E. 1992. 'The literary dimension of the spread of English' in B. Kachru (ed.). 1992c: 255–82.

TIKKU, G. L. 1971. *Persian Poetry in Kashmir 1339–1846: An Introduction*. Berkeley: University of California Press.

TRIBBLE, C. and G. JONES. 1990. *Concordances in the Classroom*. London: Longman.

TSAO, F-F. 1983. 'Linguistics and written discourse in particular languages: contrastive studies: English and Mandarin.' *Annual Review of Applied Linguistics* 3: 99–117.

VÄHÄPASSI, A. 1988. 'The problem of selection of writing tasks in cross-cultural study' in Purves (ed.): 51–78.

VALDMAN, A. 1988. 'The assessment of foreign language oral proficiency.' *Studies in Second Language Acquisition* 10/2: 121–28.

VALENTINE, T. 1988. 'Developing discourse types in non-native English: strategies of gender in Hindi and Indian English.' *World Englishes* 7/2: 143–58.

VALENTINE, T. 1991. 'Getting the message across: discourse markers in Indian English.' *World Englishes* 10/3: 325–34.

VAN BUREN, P. and M. SHARWOOD SMITH. 1985. 'The acquisition of preposition stranding by second language learners and parametric variation.' *Second Language Research* 1: 18–26.

VAN PATTEN, B. 1992. 'Second language acquisition research and foreign language teaching.' *ADFL Bulletin* 23/2: 52–56; 23/3: 23–27.

VIZMULLER-ZOCCO, J. 1985. 'Linguistic creativity and word formation.' *Italica* 62/4: 305–10.

VOSS, B. 1979. 'Hesitation phenomena as sources of perceptual errors for non-native speakers.' *Language and Speech* 22: 129–44.

VYGOTSKY, L. S. 1978. *Mind in Society: The Development of Higher Psychological Processes*. Cambridge, MA: Harvard University Press.

VYGOTSKY, L. S. 1986. *Thought and Language*. Cambridge, MA: MIT Press.

WAJNRYB, R. 1990. *Grammar Dictation*. Oxford: Oxford University Press.

WALLACE, C. 1992a. *Reading*. Oxford: Oxford University Press.

WALLACE, C. 1992b. 'Critical Literacy Awareness in the EFL classroom' in N. Fairclough (ed.): *Critical Language Awareness*. 1992. London and New York: Longman.

WATERS, A. 1994. 'ESP – things fall apart' in R. Khoo (ed.): *LSP – Problems and Prospects*. Singapore: Seameo/RELC.

WEAVER, C. 1972. *Human listening: Processes and Behavior*. New York: Bobbs-Merrill.

WERTSCH, J. (ed.). 1985. *Culture, Communication and Cognition: Vygotskian Perspectives*. Cambridge: Cambridge University Press.

WERTSCH, J. 1991. *Voices of the Mind*. Cambridge, MA: Harvard University Press.

WESCHE, M. 1993. 'Discipline-based approaches to language study: Research issues and outcomes' in Krueger and Ryan (eds.).

WHITE, H. 1978. *Tropics of Discourse. Essays in Cultural Criticism*. Baltimore, Md: John Hopkins University Press.

WHITE, L. 1989. *Universal Grammar and Second Language Acquisition*. Amsterdam: John Benjamins.

WIDDOWSON, H. G. 1972a. 'Stylistic analysis and literary appreciation.' *The Use of English* 24/1. (Reprinted in M. K. L. Ching, M. C. Haley, and R. C. Lunsford (eds.): *Linguistic Perspectives on Literature*. 1980. London: Routledge.)

WIDDOWSON, H. G. 1972b. 'On the deviance of literary discourse.' *Style* 6/2.

WIDDOWSON, H. G. 1972c. 'A linguistic approach to written communication.' *The Use of English* 23/3.

WIDDOWSON, H. G. 1972d. 'Directions in the teaching of discourse.' Paper presented at the First Neuchâtel Colloquium in Applied Linguistics, May 1972 (also in Widdowson 1979a).

WIDDOWSON, H. G. 1973. 'An applied linguistic approach to discourse analysis.' Unpublished Ph.D. Thesis, Department of Linguistics, University of Edinburgh.

WIDDOWSON, H. G. 1974a. 'Literary and scientific uses of English.' *ELT*

Journal 28/4.

WIDDOWSON, H. G. 1974b. 'Stylistics' in Allen and Corder (eds.): 1974.

WIDDOWSON, H. G. 1975. *Stylistics and the Teaching of Literature.* London: Longman.

WIDDOWSON, H. G. 1976. 'The authenticity of language data.' Paper presented at the TESOL Convention, New York (also in Widdowson 1979a).

WIDDOWSON, H. G. 1978a. 'Time and Tense in *The Ancient Mariner*.' *Annales de Lyon* 3/1. L'Université de Jean Moulin.

WIDDOWSON, H. G. 1978b. *Teaching Language as Communication.* Oxford: Oxford University Press.

WIDDOWSON, H. G. 1979a. *Explorations in Applied Linguistics.* Oxford: Oxford University Press.

WIDDOWSON, H. G. 1979b. 'Notes on educational and vocational aspects of EFL diploma courses.' *ELT Documents* 104.

WIDDOWSON, H. G. 1979c. 'Discourse and text.' Paper given at Ealing College of Further Education Conference on 'The Reading Skill'.

WIDDOWSON, H. G. 1980a. 'Models and fictions.' *Applied Linguistics* 1/2: 165–70.

WIDDOWSON, H. G. 1980b. 'Conceptual and communicative functions in written discourse.' *Applied Linguistics* 1/3.

WIDDOWSON, H. G. (ed.). 1981–1983. *Reading and Thinking in English* (4 vols.). Oxford: Oxford University Press.

WIDDOWSON, H. G. (ed.). 1981–1985. *Communicative Grammar* (6 vols.). Beirut: ELTA/Oxford University Press.

WIDDOWSON, H. G. 1982a. 'The conditional presence of Mr Bleaney' in Carter (ed.): 1982.

WIDDOWSON, H. G. 1982b. 'Othello in person' in Carter (ed.): 1982.

WIDDOWSON, H. G. 1982c. 'English as an international language: what do we mean by "international language"?' in C. J. Brumfit (ed.): *English for International Communication.* 1982. London: Pergamon.

WIDDOWSON, H. G. 1983a. 'Talking shop: on literature and ELT.' *ELT Journal* 37/1.

WIDDOWSON, H. G. 1983b. *Learning Purpose and Language Use.* Oxford: Oxford University Press.

WIDDOWSON, H. G. 1983c. 'The learner in the language learning process' in S. Holden (ed.): *Focus on the Learner.* 1983. London: Macmillan/Modern English Publications.

WIDDOWSON, H. G. 1984a. *Explorations in Applied Linguistics 2.* Oxford: Oxford University Press.

WIDDOWSON, H. G. 1984b. 'Theoretical implications of interlanguage studies for language teaching' in Davies *et al.* (eds.): 1984.

WIDDOWSON, H. G. 1984c. 'The incentive value of theory in teacher education.' *ELT Journal* 38/2.

WIDDOWSON, H. G. 1984d. 'Educational and pedagogical factors in syllabus design.' *ELT Documents* 118.

WIDDOWSON, H. G. 1984e. 'Reading and communication' in J. C. Alderson and A. H. Urquhart (eds.): *Reading in a Foreign Language*. 1984. London: Longman.

WIDDOWSON, H. G. 1985a. 'Against dogma.' *ELT Journal* 39/3. (Reprinted in R. Rossner and R. Bolitho (eds.): *Currents of Change in English Language Teaching*. 1985. Oxford: Oxford University Press.)

WIDDOWSON, H. G. 1985b. 'The teaching, learning and study of literature' in Quirk and Widdowson (eds.): 1985.

WIDDOWSON, H. G. 1986a. 'Forty years on.' *ELT Journal* 40/4.

WIDDOWSON, H. G. 1986b. 'The untrodden ways' in Brumfit and Carter (eds.): 1986.

WIDDOWSON, H. G. 1986c. 'Design principles in communicative grammar.' *ELT Documents* 124.

WIDDOWSON, H. G. 1987a. 'On the interpretation of poetic writing' in N. Fabb, D. Attridge, A. Durant, and C. MacCabe (eds.): *The Linguistics of Writing: Arguments between Language and Literature*. 1987. Manchester: Manchester University Press.

WIDDOWSON, H. G. 1987b. 'Significance in conventional and literary discourse' in L. E. Smith (ed.): 1987.

WIDDOWSON, H. G. 1987c. 'Aspects of syllabus design' in M. Tickoo (ed.): *Syllabus Design: The State of the Art*. 1987. Singapore: RELC.

WIDDOWSON, H. G. 1988a. 'Poetry and pedagogy' in D. Tannen (ed.): *Linguistics in Context*. 1988. Norwood, NJ: Ablex.

WIDDOWSON, H. G. 1988b. 'Language spread in modes of use' in P. H. Lowenberg (ed.): *Language Spread and Language Policy*. 1988. Washington DC: Georgetown University Press.

WIDDOWSON, H. G. 1989a. 'The significance of poetry' in C. S. Butler, R. A. Cardwell, and J. Channell (eds.): *Language and Literature – Theory and Practice*. 1989. University of Nottingham Monographs in the Humanities.

WIDDOWSON, H. G. 1989b. 'Divergence and convergence in the interpretation of poetry' in D. Cuccurullo, A. Notaro, and A. Tuzzi (eds.): *Il Muro del Linguaggio: Conflitto e Tragedia*. 1989. Istituto Universitario Orientale.

WIDDOWSON, H. G. 1989c. 'Knowledge of language and ability for use.' *Applied Linguistics* 10/2: 128–37.

WIDDOWSON, H. G. 1990a. *Aspects of Language Teaching*. Oxford: Oxford University Press.

WIDDOWSON, H. G. 1990b. 'Discourses of enquiry and conditions of relevance' in J. E. Alatis (ed.): *Linguistics, Language Teaching and Language Acquisition*. 1990. Washington DC: Georgetown University Press.

WIDDOWSON, H. G. 1991a. 'Types of equivalence in translation.' *Triangle* 10. Paris: Diffusion Didier Erudition.

WIDDOWSON, H. G. 1991b. 'The description and prescription of language' in Alatis (ed.): 1991.

WIDDOWSON, H. G. 1992a. *Practical Stylistics: An Approach to Poetry.* Oxford: Oxford University Press.

WIDDOWSON, H. G. 1992b. 'Aspects of the relationship between culture and language' in H. Antor and R. Ahrens (eds.): *Text–Culture–Reception. Cross-Cultural Aspects of English Studies.* 1992. Carl Winter Universitaetsverlag.

WIDDOWSON, H. G. 1992c. 'ELT and EL teachers: matters arising.' *ELT Journal* 46/4.

WIDDOWSON, H. G. 1993a. 'Person to person. Relationships in the poetry of Tony Harrison' in P. Verdonk (ed.): *Twentieth Century Poetry. From Text to Context.* 1993. London: Routledge.

WIDDOWSON, H. G. 1993b. 'Proper words in proper places.' *ELT Journal* 47/4.

WIDDOWSON, H. G. 1993c. 'The relevant conditions of language use and learning' in Krueger and Ryan (eds.): 1993.

WIDDOWSON, H. G. 1993d. 'Communication, community, and the problem of appropriate use' in Alatis (ed.): 1993.

WIDDOWSON, H. G. 1993e. 'Perspectives on communicative language teaching: syllabus and methodology' in Alatis (ed.): 1993.

WIDDOWSON, H. G. 1993f. 'Innovation in teacher development.' *Annual Review of Applied Linguistics* 13.

WIDDOWSON, H. G. 1994a. 'The ownership of English.' *TESOL Quarterly* 28/2.

WIDDOWSON, H. G. 1994b. '"Old song that will not declare itself." On poetry and the imprecision of meaning' in R. Sell and P. Verdonk (eds.): *Literature and the New Interdisciplinarity: Poetics, Linguistics, History.* 1994. Amsterdam: Rodopi.

WIDDOWSON, H. G. 1994c. 'The appropriate language for learning.' *Perspectives* XX/1.

WIDDOWSON, H. G. 1994d. 'Some observations on teacher development' in K. Richards and P. Roe (eds.): *Distance Learning in ELT.* 1994. London: Macmillan Modern English Publications.

WIDDOWSON, H. G. 1994e. 'Discourse analysis: a critical view.' Paper presented at a British Council Applied Linguistics Seminar, University of Lancaster, August 1994.

WIDDOWSON, H. G. 1994f. 'Partial meaning and pragmatic correspondence.' Paper presented at the ESOL Department Research Seminar, University of London Institute of Education, June 1994.

WIDDOWSON, H. G. (ed.). From 1996. *The Oxford Guides to Language Study.* Oxford: Oxford University Press.

WIDDOWSON, H. G. 1996. *Linguistics* in The Oxford Guides to Language

Study. Oxford: Oxford University Press.

WIERZBICKA, A. 1974. 'The semantics of direct and indirect discourse.' *Papers in Linguistics* 7: 267–307.

WILKINS, D. 1994. 'Applied Linguistics' in R. E. Asher (ed.): *The Encyclopedia of Language and Linguistics* (Vol. 1). Oxford: Pergamon Press.

WILLIAMS, R. 1976. *Keywords*. London: Fontana.

WILLIS, J. D. 1990. *The Lexical Syllabus*. London: Collins.

WILLIS, J. D. 1993. 'Syllabus, corpus and data-driven learning.' *IATEFL 1993 Annual Conference Report*: 25–32.

WILLIS, J. D. and J. R. WILLIS. 1987. *Collins Cobuild English Course*. London: Collins.

WINOGRAD, T. 1977. 'A framework for understanding discourse' in M. Just and P. Carpenter (eds.): *Cognitive Processes in Comprehension*. Hillsdale, NJ: Lawrence Erlbaum.

WITTGENSTEIN, L. [1953] 1968. *Philosophical Investigations*. Oxford: Blackwell.

WONG FILLMORE. 1976. 'The second time around: cognitive and social strategies in second language acquisition.' Unpublished Ph.D. dissertation, Stanford University.

WOOD, D. 1994. 'Output unbound: making a case for the role of output in adult learners' acquisition of Japanese as a foreign language.' Master's Research Paper. Toronto: Modern Language Centre, OISE.

WOOD, D., J. S. BRUNER, and G. ROSS. 1976. 'The role of tutoring in problem solving.' *Journal of Child Psychology and Psychiatry* 17: 89–100.

WYLER, S. 1992. *Colour and Language: Colour Terms in English*. Tübingen: Gunter Narr Verlag.

YOUNG, R. 1991. *Variation in Interlanguage Morphology*. New York: Lang.

YULE, G. 1993. 'Vera Hayden's dilemma, or the indirection in direct speech' in M. Eid and G. Iverson (eds.): *Principles and Prediction: The Analysis of Natural Language*. Amsterdam: John Benjamins.

YULE, G. (forthcoming) 'Reported discourse in contemporary English.' *Revista Canaria de Estudios Ingleses* Num. 26.

YULE, G. and T. MATHIS. 1992. 'The role of staging and constructed dialogue in establishing speaker's topic.' *Linguistics* 30: 199–215.

YULE, G., T. MATHIS, and M. F. HOPKINS. 1992. 'On reporting what was said.' *ELT Journal* 46/3: 245–51.

Index

The Index covers Chapters 1 to 24 (not the bibliography). Entries are arranged in letter-by-letter alphabetical order, in which spaces between words are ignored; 'grammaticalization' therefore comes after 'grammatical competence' and before 'grammatical knowledge'. References to chapter notes are indicated by page and note number, e.g. 'attitudinal markers 212n4'.